PERSPECTIVES *on* ORGANIZATIONAL COMMUNICATION

FOURTH EDITION

PERSPECTIVES *on* ORGANIZATIONAL COMMUNICATION

TOM D. DANIELS
OHIO UNIVERSITY, ATHENS

BARRY K. SPIKER
RATH & STRONG, INC.

MICHAEL J. PAPA
OHIO UNIVERSITY, ATHENS

Brown & Benchmark
PUBLISHERS

Madison, WI Dubuque Guilford, CT Chicago Toronto London
Mexico City Caracas Buenos Aires Madrid Bogotá Sydney

Book Team

Executive Publisher *Edgar J. Laube*
Project Editor *Kassi Radomski*
Publishing Services Coordinator *Peggy Selle*
Proofreading Coordinator *Carrie Barker*
Production Manager *Beth Kundert*
Design and New Media Development Manager *Linda Meehan Avenarius*
Production/Costing Manager *Sherry Padden*
Visuals/Design Freelance Specialist *Mary L. Christianson*
Marketing Manager *Amy Halloran*
Copywriter *Jennifer Smith*

Basal Text *10/12 Times Roman*
Display Type *Copperplate*
Typesetting System *Macintosh™ QuarkXPress™*
Paper Stock 45# Restore Cote
Production Services *Shepherd, Inc.*

Brown & Benchmark PUBLISHERS

Executive Vice President and General Manager *Bob McLaughlin*
Vice President, Business Manager *Russ Domeyer*
Vice President of Production and New Media Development *Victoria Putman*
National Sales Manager *Phil Rudder*
National Telesales Director *John Finn*

A Times Mirror Company

Cover design by Kristyn A. Kalnes

Cover illustration by Mary Geving

Copyedited by Sarah Greer Bush; Proofread by Ann M. Kelly

Library of Congress Catalog Card Number: 96–83543

ISBN 0–697–28896–01

Printed in the United States of America by Times Mirror Higher Education Group, Inc.,
2460 Kerper Boulevard, Dubuque, IA 52001

10 9 8 7 6 5 4 3 2 1

CONTENTS

Part
Three
Dynamics of Organizational Culture 201

Chapter 10
Communication and Organizational Culture 202

Chapter 11
Cultural Control, Diversity, and Change 225

Chapter 12
Power 250

Chapter 13
Conflict 268

Part

Four

Communication and Executive Strategy 295

Chapter 14

Strategic Communication 296

PREFACE

In the preface to the first edition of *Perspectives on Organizational Communication,* we admitted that we probably had fallen short of our goal "to present an artful mosaic which would somehow include every subtle nuance of this phenomenon" (1987, p. xii). Even so, we were confident that we had produced a sound survey text for the study of organizational communication. Our confidence was affirmed by wide acceptance of that first edition and the even broader adoption of the two editions that followed it. We are thankful that those who have adopted the book also are constructive critics who have offered us many ideas that we have incorporated as improvements in the subsequent editions.

The first two editions of this text were addressed primarily to the need to adequately survey and understand theoretical pluralism in the field. When we produced the third edition, we began to shift our focus to problems and paradoxes of organizational communication and the changing features of organizational life that have been revealed through the application of pluralistic perspectives. We noted in the third edition that organizations were becoming more racially and culturally diverse, yet African Americans, especially males, generally continue to be left out of the organizational equation. Feminization of organizations was occurring at a quickened pace, focusing attention on issues in organizational life that are of particular importance to women. A virtual revolution in information technologies was reshaping communication practices in ways that we would not have imagined only a few years ago. Finally, American economic organizations were undergoing great change in an effort to respond to global competition. All of these trends are continuing as we approach the turn of the century, so much of the fourth edition of the book provides a substantially expanded treatment of their implications for organizational communication.

This new edition includes a great deal of new material. We have added to our coverage of many topics, including theories of organization, communication structure, technology, diversity and cultural change, power, conflict, leadership, and strategic communication. In order to accommodate all of the new material, quite a bit of older material has been deleted, most notably chapters 2, 11, 12, and 13 from the third edition.

Two very obvious changes will provide you with some clues to many of the other changes that we have incorporated in the fourth edition. First, Michael Papa of Ohio University has joined us as an author on the work. The changes that you will see in the chapters on organizational culture, diversity and change, power, and conflict reflect the new thinking that Professor Papa has brought to the project. He also is responsible for the content of the chapter on new millennium thinking in organization theory. Second, you will see from the table of contents that we have gone to a fourteen-chapter volume. Some chapters are entirely new. Others are the product of expanded treatment of topics that were combined and addressed with more brevity in previous editions. Since we essentially have eliminated four older chapters, the net effect is that much of the fourth edition is new material. All of the third edition chapters that have been carried over to the new edition are updated with new ideas, research, examples, and editorial improvements.

It is difficult to summarize simply all of the substantive changes that have occurred, but the most important ones are reflected in the addition of new chapters. In previous editions, a single chapter was devoted to theories of organization and organizational effectiveness. The fourth edition includes three. Classical, scientific, human relations, and human resource development theories are covered in a chapter on prescriptions for control. Systems theory has been combined with equivocality reduction theory and the new theory of evolutionary psychology in a chapter on theories that are literally or metaphorically grounded in biology. And new ideas and research on workplace democratization, self-managed teams, and worker-owned cooperatives are presented in a chapter on new millennium thinking—an appropriate subject as we approach the turn of the century.

We deleted an old chapter on the concept and basic theories of communication, but material on information and meaning from that chapter is combined with our original material on communication functions. Material on communication structure has been expanded into a chapter of its own, primarily through additional coverage of network perspectives on structure.

The old chapter on dyadic communication that featured an extensive and tedious review of research in superior-subordinate communication has been fundamentally revised into a chapter on leadership and leader-member relations, with more attention to leader-member exchange theory and the addition of motivation theory (brought back by popular demand from users who were troubled by the absence of motivational theory in the third edition).

Computer-based technologies for mediating communication seem to change more quickly than we can keep up with them on the revision schedule for this book, but we have added current research on the uses and effects of these technologies and a new section on organizational uses of the Internet and World Wide Web.

Significant expansions also have occurred with the third edition chapter on culture and diversity and the chapter on power and conflict to the point that each has been divided into two, so there are four chapters in the fourth edition where only two appeared in the third. The coverage of organizational culture was broadened to include the critical perspective along with traditional and interpretive perspectives and a discussion of narrativity as an approach to the study of organizational culture. Implications of diversity for communication and culture now occupy an entire chapter because of new material on affirmative action issues and feminizing of organizations. The new chapter on power was required because of additional material on critiques and reconceptualizations of power drawn from feminist and critical theories. The coverage of conflict in a new chapter now includes additional techniques of conflict resolution and discussion of a competence-based theory of interpersonal conflict.

Finally, we have refurbished the old chapter on public communication into a chapter on strategic communication. In one sense this change gives some old material a refreshingly new look, but it also provides a point of view for understanding the forces that shape these communicative efforts, especially in the case of crisis communication, which gets expanded coverage in this edition.

As in the third edition, we have included several case studies, but we have made one major change in their presentation. In the past, each chapter was accompanied by a case. In this edition, cases are located at the end of each of the book's four major parts. We have done this because the cases for each part cut across many different topics presented within the part, so a given case might be applicatible to two or more chapters in a part. The questions included with each case suggest the concepts to which we think the case is best applied. Most of the cases in the text, that is, those with no bylines, were written by Tom Daniels or by some of Barry Spiker's former colleagues at Anderson Consulting Company in Chicago. The remaining cases were written by Michael Smilowitz of the University of North Carolina–Charlotte, and by Hylton Villett, a talented graduate student from Namibia in Southern Africa. As always, our cases are based on actual incidents or an amalgam of two or more real incidents, but the cases have been written with fictitious names, settings, and other elements in order to protect the identities of the persons and the organizations involved in these incidents.

We also have added one more learning tool to this edition. In addition to the reference list for each chapter, each chapter is accompanied by a list of relevant additional materials to which we do not refer in the chapter. In the spirit of the times, some of the additional materials for each chapter are to be found at homepage addresses on the World Wide Web. At the time of manuscript submittal, all listed Web sites were functional. Given the rather protean nature of the Web, some addresses may be obsolete by the time that you are using this book. We are simply trying to acquaint students with the tremendous potential of the Internet and World Wide Web as information resources.

Organization of the Text

The fourth edition of the book is, like its predecessors, organized in four parts, but the parts, like much of the book, have changed. The old scheme of Foundations, Themes, Contexts, and Applications has been replaced by Foundations; Communication, Relationships, and Media; Dynamics of Organizational Culture; and Communication and Executive Strategy. Part 1, which includes the first four chapters, provides some basic *foundations* for understanding the ideas and forces that have shaped the field of organizational communication. In chapter 1, we define organizational communication and discuss some of the history as well as the present status of the field. We give special attention to several different perspectives that influence the study of organizational communication, namely, traditionalism, interpretivism, critical theory, and feminist theory. In chapter 2, we review theories of organization and organizational effectiveness that developed from the early twentieth century through the 1970s, namely classical, scientific, human relations, transitional theories, human resource development, and variations on human resource development. Generally we classify these theories as prescriptions for organizational control. They are followed by the third chapter on organization theories that are rooted literally or metaphorically on principles of biology. These theories include systems theory, equivocality reduction theory, and the emerging theory of evolutionary psychology. Chapter 4 has some of the most current thinking that is occurring in organization theory as we approach the turn of the century, so we have labeled it New Millennium Thinking. It includes discussions of workplace democratization, self-managed work teams, worker owned cooperatives, feminist organizational concepts, and other new ideas.

Part 2 includes five chapters on the concept of communication, organizational communication relationships, and media. In chapter 5, we discuss organizational communication concepts and functions, primarily from the traditional perspective. Chapter 6 is devoted to the subject of organizational communication structure, including formal and informal systems and network characteristics. Chapter 7 covers communication in group relationships with attention to groups as organizational units and group decision-making, problem-solving, and task performance. Chapter 8, on leader-member relations, includes theories of leadership and leader behavior, leader-member exchange, motivation, and other important topics in superior-subordinate communication. The final chapter in the unit focuses on computer-mediated communication and information technology in organizations.

The third part of the book consists of chapters on organizational culture and the important factors in the dynamics of organizational culture. Chapter 10 presents the cultural perspective of organizational communication themes, with special attention to interpretive and critical-interpretive uses of this perspective. In chapter 11, we address the challenges and opportunities of cultural diversity and their implications for cultural change and cultural control. Chapter 12 covers the concept of power in organizations, with particular attention to critical and feminist perspectives on power. This part is completed with chapter 13 on the subject of conflict and its management.

The final part consists of one chapter on communication and executive strategy. This chapter is concerned with strategic communication addressed to major audiences or constituencies at a macro level.

Special Features

The book includes topic outlines and summaries for each chapter. Key terms are displayed in bold face type at or near points where they are first defined or used in a meaningful way. Activities, discussion questions, and complete references are included at the end of each chapter.

Instructor's Manual

The instructor's manual, prepared by Michael Smilowitz of the University of North Carolina–Charlotte in collaboration with Tom Daniels and Michael Papa, is a very useful tool for both experienced and new instructors. It includes a statement of learning objectives, a very detailed full-content outline, and multiple-choice test items for each chapter in the book.

Acknowledgements

We especially wish to thank scholars who provided very careful reviews of the revision plan for this edition. These individuals are Brenda Allen, University of Colorado; Deborah Brunson, University of North Carolina at Wilmington; Renee Meyers, University of Wisconsin–Milwaukee; Vernon Miller, Michigan State University; R. Glenn Ray, Marietta College; and J. Andrew Roob, Communication Decisions.

The Authors

Tom D. Daniels (Ph.D., Ohio University, 1979) is Professor of Interpersonal Communication and Assistant to the Provost at Ohio University. He also served as an assistant professor of communication at the University of Wisconsin–Green Bay and at the University of New Mexico. He has held line management positions in both private and public-sector organizations and is an experienced trainer and consultant. He has authored and coauthored articles and book chapters on various topics in organizational communication, communication theory, philosophy of social science, and research methods. Daniels is past secretary of the organizational communication division in the Speech Communication Association, past chair of the organizational communication division in the Central States Communication Association, a member of the organizational communication division of the International Communication Association, and has served as an editorial board member for *The Quarterly Journal of Speech, Communication Education*, and *Communication Quarterly.* When Tom is not writing, teaching, or administering, he vacations with his children or paddles his kayak on West Virginia whitewater.

Barry K. Spiker (Ph.D., Ohio University, 1979) is vice president for business development with Rath and Strong. Before assuming this position, he held positions with Price-Waterhouse, Mercer Management, Andersen Consulting Co., and Honeywell, Inc. He also was an assistant professor in the Department of Communication at the University of New Mexico and corporate chief of staff for a privately held, midwestern manufacturing corporation. He has authored and coauthored articles and book chapters on topics in organizational communication, technological advancement and integration, and social science research methods. He is a member of the organizational communication divisions of the International Communication Association and the Academy of Management, a member of the American Society for Training and Development, a member of the Organization Development Network, and an associate editor for *Management Communication Quarterly.* When Barry is not traveling for Rath and Strong, he travels for himself, often to exotic locations. Barry flies airplanes and cooks gourmet meals.

Michael J. Papa (Ph.D., Temple University, 1986) is Associate Professor of Interpersonal Communication at Ohio University. Prior to joining Ohio University, he served on the faculty at University of North Carolina–Greensboro where he also directed the Institute for Communication Research. He has published numerous research studies on problems in organizational communication, especially in the areas of conflict management, technology, and economic development programs. He serves on the editorial board of *Communication Education* and as a reviewer for several other professional journals. He is an experienced consultant to educational and industrial organizations and is a member of the organizational communication division of the International Commmunication Association. Michael's hobbies include hiking and skiing.

Tom and Barry have worked together on research studies and consulting projects in organizational communication since 1976. Tom and Michael have been colleagues since 1989. Among the three of them, they have over fifty years of management, consulting, and teaching experience. They have tried to incorporate as much of that experience as possible in this text.

Tom D. Daniels, Athens, Ohio
Barry K. Spiker, Santa Fe, New Mexico
Michael J. Papa, Athens, Ohio

PART ONE
FOUNDATIONS

CHAPTER 1

AN ORIENTATION TO ORGANIZATIONAL COMMUNICATION

Outline

Organizational life is a major feature of human experience. We are not only social creatures but also organizational creatures. We work in, play in, cope with, and depend on many types of organizations. They include business, industrial, governmental, educational, professional, religious, social, and political organizations.

If you stop to think about it for a moment, you probably will realize that you have been involved with organizations in one form or another for most of your life. As a child, you may have been in youth organizations such as the Boy Scouts or Girl Scouts. As an adult, you may belong to service or social organizations, and you almost certainly will earn your living within some kind of work organization. Even as a student, you participate in the complex organizational dynamics of your college or university. You must deal with your institution's policies, procedures, expectations, customs, and habits. You may even be caught up in its internal conflicts, territorial rivalries, and power struggles.

Basically, human beings **organize** in order to get things done. When we organize, we define and arrange positions or roles in complex relationships. We engage in concerted action with one another by coordinating these roles in order to accomplish some purpose. Organizations, then, are elaborate and complicated forms of human endeavor.

We often talk about organizations as if they are separate from the people who comprise them. A young engineer speaks of "going to work for IBM," or a news report advises us that "Chrysler has announced a recall," as if IBM and Chrysler are actual places or beings. This is not especially surprising because many organizations do seem to exist apart from individual members. People come and go, but the organization remains. Even so, the image of the organization as an independent object is misleading. It implies that the organization is like the shell of the notorious little jumping bean—a container in which some mysterious activity (in this case, human behavior) is occurring. We need to remember that an organization is not merely a container for behavior. Rather, an organization literally *is* human behavior.

An organization is constituted by interaction among the people who comprise it. In other words, an organization really is defined by its members' joint actions. Since the basis for joint action is communication, the process of human communication is the central feature of an organization. As Daniel Katz and Robert Kahn, two prominent organizational psychologists, observed, "Communication . . . is the very essence of a social system or organization" (1978, p. 428).

This book is about the communication processes that characterize human organizations, processes referred to collectively as **organizational communication.** We have tried to present our discussion of organizational communication from a comprehensive, contemporary point of view that will provide you with a sound foundation of concepts for understanding and discussing this subject. No one book or course is going to cover everything that you could or should learn about organizational communication. This book is no exception. It is intended only as an introduction to the field of study.

We think that this book will be more useful to you if you understand something about the background for the book and for the course in which it is being used. In order to provide that background, we need to answer three basic questions:

1. Why is the study of organizational communication useful to you?
2. How did this field of study develop?
3. What is the status of the field today?

The answers to these three questions provide background for this book and for the course in which it is being used. A good understanding of the field depends on some familiarity with this background.

Studying Organizational Communication

You may have wondered from time to time just why you should enroll in a particular course or of what relevance and importance the course is going to be to you. In the case of organizational communication, we see at least three reasons for studying this topic:

1. You can improve your understanding of organizations and of your own experiences as an organization member.
2. You can develop awareness of the kinds of communication skills that are important in organizations.
3. The course may start you down the path to a career as a communication professional in an organization or as an academic scholar in the field.

Understanding Organizations

"I've seen all of this before, but I never had a way to make sense of it until I took this course." This is a common remark that we hear from students who have just completed their first course in organizational communication. Because communication is such a central feature of life in organizations, the study of organizational communication provides a basis for understanding virtually every *human* process that occurs in organizations. Conflict, cooperation, decision making, the use of power and authority, compliance gaining, resistance, morale and cohesion, and the creation and maintenance of relationships are all reflected in human interaction.

Of course, organizational communication does not provide insights about *every* aspect of human organizations. It is not a study of the technology for creating a product or service or of the methods for producing and marketing these things. It is not a study of cost control and financing or of laws and regulations governing business and employment practices. Such topics, however, often are relevant to organizational communication. Some people in the field spend a lot of time discussing them, but organizational communication is concerned primarily with the content and structure of human interaction in organizations' day-to-day activities. Unless you plan to be a hermit, you are almost certain to participate in and cope with organizational communication throughout most of your life.

Awareness of Skills

There is general agreement that well-developed communication skills are essential to personal effectiveness in organizations or, at least, in managerial, professional, and leadership positions (Huse & Bowditch, 1977). Review any survey of skills that organizations expect of new college graduates upon entry into the job market, and you probably will find communication skills placed somewhere on the list (Di Salvo, 1980).

The kinds of communication skills that new college graduates should possess in order to meet organizational expectations can be developed through courses in public speaking, interviewing, group discussion, listening, and writing. Sometimes, a number of these skills are taught in one course with a title such as Business and Professional Communication. The introductory course in organizational communication usually is not concerned with providing training in specific individual communication skills. It does focus attention, however, on many of the functional demands in organizations that require good personal communication skills. These demands and the situations in which they arise are reflected in examples throughout this text.

Career Opportunities

The study of organizational communication also is important because many organizations have developed an intense interest in this subject. Leaders and decision makers in such organizations not only want themselves and others to possess good communication skills, but they also want an understanding of the dynamics of organizational communication. Many apparently are convinced that there is a strong connection between communication effectiveness and organizational effectiveness (Williams, 1978). Although organization leaders often understand "organizational effectiveness" only in terms of increased productivity, improved work performance, or higher morale, the belief that effective communication is essential to these conditions has led to a variety of career opportunities in organizational communication.

Today, many organizations employ writers, editors, and media specialists to produce and distribute company magazines, newsletters, films, videos, and even closed-circuit television programs for an audience comprised of the organization membership. People in these occupations usually are trained in journalism or media production. Recently, a flourishing training and development industry also has emerged as organizations have hired staff professionals and outside consultants to help them evaluate and change organizational communication practices. This industry includes people who teach communication concepts and skills to organization members (usually to managers and supervisors); evaluate the effectiveness of organizational communication; and help to improve interpersonal, group, and public communication processes in organizational settings (Eich, 1977). The career path into training and development is not restricted to any one academic field, but people who enter this profession often receive their preparation in organizational communication (Redding, 1979).

The demand for communication professionals in organizations does not mean that a course or even a major related to organizational communication will lead to a job in the field. Although several occupations are concerned in some way with organizational communication, students who think that they will get a job in something called "organizational communication" need to understand that this label refers to a field of academic study and not to any identifiable profession. "Organizational communication" does not appear as a job category anywhere in the U.S. Department of Labor's *Dictionary of Occupational Titles,* and many employers may not even know that the field exists. In 1988, the Bureau of Labor Statistics (BLS) predicted faster-than-average growth throughout the 1990s for occupations related to organizational communication, but it also noted that most of the job openings will occur through turnover. Indeed, the abundant supply of trained college graduates and experienced professionals has produced intense competition for the available jobs. It is very difficult to break into this field. Many of the positions in training and development now require a master's degree and, in some cases, even a doctoral degree (Redding, 1979). If you are thinking of a career related to organizational communication, you must obtain a thorough education and be able to apply what you know. Even then, you may be unable to find the kind of job that you would like to have. Whether or not you pursue such a career, an organizational communication course should be helpful to you in any organizational role that you may assume.

Development of the Field

While scholars in various disciplines have studied communication in organizations for many years, the development of organizational communication as an identifiable field with courses and academic programs in university departments of communication is a relatively recent occurrence. W. Charles Redding traces the origin of the field to a convergence of interest in "business speech" and "industrial communication" that emerged in the wake of World War II (Redding, 1985; Tompkins & Redding, 1988). By the early 1950s, doctoral students in speech departments at Northwestern University, Ohio State University, Purdue University, and the University of Southern California were producing dissertations on industrial communication. In 1952, Purdue's speech department established its Industrial Communication Research Center. Annual conferences that brought together professors of speech and communication with social scientists from other disciplines provided forums for discussion and definition of the emerging field.

Skills-oriented "how to" books on communication for managers began to appear in the late 1950s, but the concerns of the field already were expanding beyond these narrow prescriptive interests to embrace description and explanation of organizational communication processes in general. The nation's first undergraduate major in "organizational communication" was established by Edward Penson and Elizabeth Andersch at Ohio University in 1962 (Boase & Carlson, 1989). According to Redding, general academic acceptance of the field of organizational communication was signaled by several events in 1967 and 1968, which included a NASA-sponsored conference on organizational communication and the creation of the organizational communication division of the International Communication Association. Redding's personal influence on the development of the field is legendary. As Redding's doctoral students graduated from the program at Purdue, they initiated courses in organizational communication at other institutions. Academic programs in organizational communication at many of the nation's colleges and universities today were established by Redding's protégés and colleagues. Even exceptions such as the Ohio University program appear to have been influenced directly by their creators' familiarity with Redding's work at Purdue.

The relatively recent and rapid emergence of organizational communication as an academic field has been accompanied by some healthy, but occasionally troublesome, growing pains. Scholars have found it difficult to create an identity for the field. At first, this difficulty arose from similarities between organizational communication and other fields of study. Later, it involved the development of several different and sometimes competing approaches to the study of organizational communication. While both of these identity problems have been troubling, each in its own way has helped to develop and refine the field. In order to explain the point of view of this book, we must first review some of the history involved in these two identity problems.

Relationship to Other Fields

Communication scholars began to study organizations at a time when other social and behavioral sciences already had a long history of organizational research. The new field of organizational communication borrowed heavily from ideas developed in these more established disciplines. Consequently, it was difficult at times to tell the difference between organizational communication, organizational psychology, organizational sociology, and organizational behavior as fields of study. Sharing ideas among different academic disciplines is both useful and necessary in order to develop a good understanding of our world. Ideas from one field, however, often have to be adapted to fit the needs of another field. Organizational communication sometimes borrowed ideas without making important adaptations.

When psychologists, sociologists, and social psychologists began to study organizations in the twentieth century, they certainly were concerned with many processes related to human communication. They often encouraged organizations to pay attention to communication and interpersonal relationships, but their explanations of organizational behavior did not focus on human communication.

For example, management theorists such as Paul Hersey and Ken Blanchard (1982) often are interested in the problem of motivating employees to be productive. They rely on theories of motivation in which the behavior of individual human beings is explained as a means of meeting physical, psychological, or social needs. If asked about the role of communication in organizational behavior, these theorists might say that communication is one of several types of motivated behavior in organizations or that it is a means of motivating organization members. From this point of view, communication is only one ingredient among many in a recipe for organizational behavior. The central problem is to understand human motivation in organizations and the role of motivation in **organizational effectiveness,** (i.e., in getting people to work more productively). Communication is merely a peripheral concern.

When the field of organizational communication imported concepts from other disciplines, it also imported their peripheral views of human communication in organizations along with a preoccupation with organizational effectiveness. Communication scholars identified dozens of elements in organizational communication, then studied the relationships of these elements to a veritable grab bag of factors in organizational effectiveness. For example, we asked questions about the relationship between organizational communication and productivity, job satisfaction, turnover, and absenteeism. Most researchers studied "economic" organizations engaged in the creation and delivery of products or services. Communication became "one more variable" that figured into organizational effectiveness.

The field's early emphasis on organizational effectiveness is entirely understandable because effectiveness has been (and generally still is) the principal concern of people in charge of economic organizations. Attempts to relate many elements in organizational communication to various indicators of organizational effectiveness, however, quickly produced a large body of disjointed and fragmented research (Dennis, Goldhaber, & Yates, 1978). The field consisted of hundreds of individual facts and bits of knowledge like so many pieces of an unassembled jigsaw puzzle. We needed theories of organizational communication, per se, in order to integrate and organize our work.

The need to define the field of organizational communication more clearly led to several new developments in the late 1970s and early 1980s. While many scholars worked to refine the traditional social science themes that already had developed in the field, others began to study organizational communication in ways that differed substantially from the traditional approach. Consequently, several different points of view or perspectives on the study of organizational communication have developed in recent years. The description of these perspectives in the next section completes the map of the development of organizational communication as a field of study. This will put us in a position to answer the final question for this chapter regarding the status of the field.

Perspectives on Organizational Communication

There are various ways of organizing and describing organizational communication perspectives. Some scholars identify several. Others identify only two. We come down somewhere in the middle by describing three that we call traditional, interpretive, and critical. Our discussion here is essentially a synthesis of previous descriptions presented by Linda Putnam (1982) and Philip Tompkins and Charles Redding (1988).

The Traditional Perspective

The traditional perspective is so called simply because it is the oldest of the three. For many years, scholars accepted almost without question the notion that organizational communication would be studied mainly from this point of view.

Traditionalists regard organizations as *objects* that can be studied with the concepts and methods of traditional social science. Traditionalists believe that organizational communication behavior is an objectively observable activity. It can be measured, labeled, classified, and related to other organizational processes. For example, suppose we want to know whether managers' styles of communication with employees have any effect on employee job satisfaction. We think that employees will be more satisfied when managers adopt an "open" style of communication, but we are not sure. A traditionalist might answer this question through the following actions:

1. Observe and measure managers' communicative behaviors in order to classify each manager as high or low in "communication openness."
2. Measure the levels of job satisfaction among each manager's employees.
3. Statistically analyze the measurements to see whether employee job satisfaction is greater under "high-openness" managers than it is under "low-openness" managers.

Traditionalists in organizational communication often are concerned with the relationship between communication processes and organizational effectiveness. They study factors in organizational communication such as information flow within organizational networks, distortion of messages, breakdowns in channels of communication, strategies of managers and supervisors in communicating with their subordinates, and the dynamics of group problem solving and decision making. If some of these ideas are unfamiliar to you at this point, there is no need to worry. Some of the chapters that follow this one are concerned with defining and elaborating these concepts.

Since traditionalism has changed over the years, it is useful to distinguish between its early and more recent forms. Early traditionalists treated the organization as a *machine*. This machine is an engineered set of interconnected parts that operates by managerial control and depends on well-maintained communication in order to function efficiently and effectively. Managers control the machine through principles and techniques of gaining compliance and cooperation from employees. The various parts of the machine (departments, individuals) are supposed to act in a coordinated manner. Both control and coordination depend on effective communication. Communication is understood primarily as a process of sending and receiving messages. **Communication effectiveness** involves two conditions: (1) the processes of message sending and receiving are accurate and reliable; (2) the message receiver understands and responds to the message in the way that the message sender intends.

This emphasis on communication effectiveness for managerial control also suggests a distinct political position in early traditionalism. There is no getting around the fact that organizations are political entities. Organizations are political because they have systems for allocating and using power and resources and because they have ways of protecting and maintaining these systems. Organizational politics is about who has power; who gets resources, privileges, and rewards; which groups or individuals control the fates of others; and how the goals of the organization are to be defined and accomplished. By working to produce communication effectiveness, early traditionalists implicitly privileged the political interests of managers and leaders over those of other organizational groups.

While some traditionalists continue to embrace the early view of organizations, most have refined their perspective with more contemporary ideas that differ substantially from the early version. The early concept of the organization as a machine that managers design, engineer, and control has been replaced by the idea that the organization is a *living system* (Monge, Farace, Eisenberg, Miller, & White, 1984). Organizations are more like living systems than machines in two ways. First, the idea of management control over the organizational machine sounds something like a person's running a lawn mower or driving a car. Organizations, like living systems, are a bit more complicated. They have many systems of *self-regulation* and control. Managerial designs and intentions are important factors, but they are not the only factors that regulate an organizational system. Internally, unions, trade and professional groups, and even informal coalitions may exert substantial control over the organization. Externally, local, state, and federal government agencies, as well as consumer or community groups, also regulate or, at least, influence the system.

Moreover, different organizational subsystems (e.g., departments, work groups, and individuals) do not generally work together in machinelike harmony. Although they cooperate to accomplish a common purpose, they also are in conflict. They often compete for resources, assert different values, and desire different ways of ordering work and organizational life. Even "management" usually is not an undifferentiated monolith that acts with a single-minded purpose. Vice-presidents of different divisions may squabble over territory, or middle managers may disagree with their bosses over the best way to accomplish an organization's mission.

Second, organizations, unlike machines, grow and adapt to change. The people who make up organizations process information and make choices based on interpretations of situations and circumstances. They plan in order to accomplish goals. They make decisions to expand or to cut back, to begin new activities, to redefine or stop old activities, and to restructure the order of the organization or to maintain it.

Traditionalists also have changed their ideas about organizational effectiveness. They are still concerned with the relationship between communication and organizational effectiveness, but they have expanded the idea of organizational effectiveness to include more than managerial objectives such as productivity and morale. Organizational effectiveness also includes the welfare of organization members in general and the overall quality of organizational life (Dessler, 1980; French, Bell, & Zawacki, 1983; Pace, 1983). This shift in emphasis changes the political position of traditionalism as well inasmuch as attention to the welfare of organization members in general means that managerial and leadership interests cannot automatically be privileged over everyone else's.

The Interpretive Perspective

The second important perspective is the interpretive perspective, which regards organizations as *cultures* (Pacanowsky & O'Donnell-Trujillo, 1984). When we think about the idea of a people's culture, most of us probably think about their way of life, including everything from their homes and clothing to their language and customs. A culture certainly includes all of these things, but it also involves a lot more. According to anthropologist W. A. Haviland (1993), "Culture consists of the abstract values, beliefs, and perceptions that lie behind people's behavior" (p. 29). This idea captures the essential difference between the interpretivist and the traditionalist. The traditionalist understands the world of social action by studying and relating observable and tangible behaviors. The interpretivist tries to uncover the culture that, as Haviland says, lies behind these behaviors.

To the interpretivist, the organization is a subjective rather than objective phenomenon. Social action is possible only to the extent that people can share subjective meanings. The culture of an organization is a network of such meanings. Thus, an organization exists in the shared experiences of the people who comprise it. This does not mean that the organization is an unreal figment of someone's imagination. It means, instead, that organizational reality is socially constructed through communication (Putnam, 1982).

Now what exactly is a socially constructed reality? It is a reality that is created and sustained through our interaction with one another. Consider, for example, the "reality" of a five dollar bill. Objectively, it is a piece of paper with ink markings on it and worth no more than the miniscule costs of that paper and ink and the process needed to produce it. Yet you can trade this objectively worthless piece of paper for lunch at your favorite fast-food restaurant, with no questions asked. In fact, you probably will get some change back from the cashier. Why? Because we have a socially constructed agreement about the "worth" of a five dollar bill. There are many objective factors that will influence this social construction (e.g., the availability of goods and services for exchange), but the five dollar bill is what it is only because we make it so and maintain its value in our transactions. Its social reality is sustained in our network of shared meanings.

Interpretive scholars are interested in revealing the socially constructed realities of organizations. They study communication as the process through which this social construction occurs. Consequently, they are interested in the symbols and meanings involved in various forms of organizational behavior. Interpretivists attempt to describe the ways in which organization members understand their experiences through communication and how they enact "the organization" on the basis of shared meanings. In this sense, an organization is a **negotiated order,** that is, a product of our collective discourse and transactions.

In our description of traditionalism, we illustrated how a traditionalist might try to find out about the relationship between management communication style and employee job satisfaction by measuring these two conditions and statistically analyzing the measurements. How would an interpretivist approach the problem of understanding employee experiences of managers' communication styles?

To begin with, the interpretivist probably would neither ask specific questions about concepts like "openness" and "satisfaction" nor attempt to measure these conditions. Instead, the interpretivist is more likely to ask organization members to provide illustrations or stories about their experiences. Then, the interpretivist analyzes and describes the themes that appear in these reports. These themes reveal the ways in which organization members share their experiences and socially construct an understanding of these experiences. If an idea like the importance of openness in managers' communication happens to appear as a theme in the reports, the interpretivist might discuss it as an indication of how organization members use "openness" to understand their relationships with managers. The interpretivist's goal is to reveal those communicative activities that occur in a variety of settings to produce the unique character of an organization (Smilowitz, 1982).

You may be thinking at this point, "When an interpretivist asks someone to tell a story, isn't the act of storytelling an objective behavior that anyone else can observe? And when a traditionalist studies something like satisfaction, isn't that a subjective feeling? So what is the difference between the two?" It is true that interpretivists have to study human behavior in order to get at the culture behind it, but getting at the culture is the whole point of the exercise, and it is done with qualitative analysis. Statistical analysis of measurements—the stock-in-trade of the traditionalist—does not make much sense in the interpretive framework because the interpretivist wants to describe organization members' experiences *from the members' frame of reference* in order to reveal the negotiated order and socially constructed reality of the organization.

It is also true that most traditionalists these days are concerned not only with studying the concrete features of organizational communication but also with the ways in which organization members perceive and subjectively experience organizational communication (Falcione & Werner, 1978). The traditional researcher, however, generally will ask organization members to report their subjective experiences *in terms defined by the researcher.* A traditionalist who wants to know if employees perceive managers to be open communicators probably would identify several characteristics of openness, then ask employees to rate on some type of measuring scale the extent to which they perceive managers to exhibit these characteristics. This kind of procedure will allow a traditionalist to find out how communication variables and other organizational variables are related to each other, but it will not reveal much about the network of shared meanings that constitutes the organizational culture.

The Critical Perspective

Critical scholars differ from traditional and interpretive scholars in various ways, but one difference is especially significant: Critical scholars regard organizations as instruments of oppression. They focus their attention on members of oppressed organizational classes (i.e., workers, women, minorities, or other groups that fit the critical theorists' definition of an oppressed class).

Although the idea may at first seem odd to you, you almost certainly have heard about or possibly even have experienced oppressive aspects of organizational life. Sometimes the sources of organizational oppression seem to be located in systems of language and meaning. For example, some writers say that sexual discrimination and harassment of women in organizations arise from a language that demeans and debases women (Bosmajian, 1983). In other words, common ways of *talking* about women influence ways of *thinking* about and *acting* toward women.

In other cases oppression seems to reside in power differences and inequalities that exist in the design of organizational structure. Discrimination against women, for example, is not merely a problem of language, but it is also a problem of physical segregation and isolation from sources of power and information (Crawford, 1977). If a woman is assigned to a "do-nothing" job, or denied promotion and advancement, or cannot get past the boss's secretary in order to get an appointment, she faces *structural* barriers to her goals.

Not surprisingly, remedies for sex discrimination appeal to changes in both language and structure, for example, eliminating sexist language in order to reconstruct symbolic expressions of male dominance and requiring the male-dominated power structure to integrate women into its ranks. But treating oppression as a language problem or a structure problem with palliatives directed at one or the other may miss the true nature of organizational oppression, and this is the point at which the critical perspective has something important to contribute to our understanding of organizations.

At the risk of oversimplification, we might say that critical scholars are concerned simultaneously with social structure *and* with symbolic processes. Organizational oppression does not reside in structure alone or in symbols alone. It resides in the *relationship* between structure and symbols.

A good example of the linkage between structure and symbols can be found in Dennis Mumby's (1987) comments about interpretivism. Mumby, a critical theorist, agrees that interpretive research "demonstrates that organizational reality is fundamentally symbolic in nature" (p. 120), but he also believes that interpretive research is naive because "it does little to explicate the *deep structure* process through which certain organizational realities come to hold sway over competing world-views" (p. 113). In other words, it does little to explain the role of symbols in dominance and oppression of some classes over others.

Why does Mumby make this argument and what does he mean by *deep structure?* As he explains it, "Domination involves getting people to organize their behavior around a particular rule system" (p. 115). This rule system is the deep structure of the organization. It defines power relationships. Some of the symbolic forms that we find in organizational communication function to "produce, maintain, and reproduce these power structures" (Mumby, p. 113). This occurs through the **systematic distortion** of communication (Deetz, 1982).

Tompkins and Redding (1988) point out that distortion of communication does not mean the same thing to a critical scholar that it might mean to a traditionalist. When traditionalists talk about distortion, they usually are concerned with inaccuracies or errors in information that lead to inefficiency and ineffectiveness in communication. But critical scholars regard distortion as a systematic and deliberate *symbolic* process through which "the owner/manager's interests are falsely joined with those of the worker in ideological communication" (Tompkins and Redding, p. 27). For example, one can find many instances in organizations of stories that are told about company heroes—legendary women and men in the history of the organization. These legendary figures personify values and beliefs that are important to the success of the organization. The stories are presented with great drama so as to inspire organization members to rally around and embrace the values that they promote. But whose interests do these values serve—those of all organization members or only those of an elite group or class?

We will have a lot more to say in chapter 12 about the critical scholars' idea of systematic distortion. For now, however, it is only important to know that critical scholarship, as its label implies, *criticizes* systematic distortion in organizational communication with the goal of consciousness-raising and emancipation for oppressed organizational classes. It does this by examining the way in which systematic distortion occurs through the use of language and symbols.

Feminism

We include **feminism** here as a special case of the critical perspective because feminist theory and scholarship in organizational communication also are concerned with criticism and emancipation, but feminism is focused first and foremost on the oppression of women and on patriarchy (institutionalized male domination) as the instrument of that oppression. Actually, there are several different versions of feminist theory that vary from each other primarily in their strategies for addressing the problem of patriarchy. For example, Tong (1989) and Iannello (1992) distinguish between liberal and radical feminism. Iannello says that liberal feminism aims at advancing women's rights and achieving equality by "eliminating patriarchy from the larger institutions that govern society" (p. 39). In liberal feminism, "socially constructed differences between the sexes are the chief source of female oppression" (Iannello, p. 39).

Radical feminism also asserts that gender roles are socially constructed, but specifically blames "male power" (Iannello, p. 40) for that construction. Thus, according to Tong, "It is not just patriarchy's legal and political structures that must be overturned; its social and cultural institutions (especially the family, the church, and the academy) must also go" (p. 3). Under the radical feminist agenda, there is no room for interpretivist ideas about negotiated order!

Status of the Field

Having considered the major perspectives that have developed in the study of organizational communication, we can now offer an assessment of the field's present status. We think the status is best reflected in the current influence of each perspective as well as in new developments that are shaping the direction of the field as we approach the next century.

Influence of the Perspectives

Although there are other ways of categorizing and describing the major perspectives that guide our study of organizational communication, the ones that we have labeled as traditional, interpretive, and critical seem to be the most influential (*cf.* Tompkins & Redding, 1988). The traditional perspective was for many years the dominant orientation to organizational communication. Although interpretive and critical approaches are relatively new in organizational communication, they have gained adherents very rapidly. The growing acceptance and influence of these perspectives arise from at least two major sources of dissatisfaction with traditionalism.

First, traditionalism was responsible for the disorganized state of the field in the 1960s and 1970s. Although several major textbooks and articles attempted to assemble the jigsaw puzzle of organizational communication in the 1970s, questions remained about our ability to make sense of our own work. As recently as 1984, H. Lloyd Goodall, Jr., concluded from a review of organizational communication research that different studies "read like newspapers from different planets" (p. 135).

Second, some scholars objected that traditionalism is "managerially biased" because it is concerned primarily with work organizations and with the relationships between communication and organizational effectiveness. This bias is compounded because the organizational communication scholar's audience consists mainly of managers, administrators, professionals, and, of course, college students who plan to enter similar roles. Michael Pacanowsky and Nick O'Donnell-Trujillo summed up this criticism when they argued that traditionalists try "to understand organizations better so that organizations can be made to run better. . . . What has come to count as 'better organizational function' are notions with a distinctly managerial flavor" (1982, p. 119).

While attention to managerial perspectives and problems certainly is not wrong, many interpretivists point out that an exclusive preoccupation with these concerns results in a very narrow definition of our field of study. Much of the day-to-day communication in organizations has relatively little to do with managerial definitions of organizational effectiveness. Managerial processes involve only one slice of the organizational communication pie.

Critics of traditionalism began to turn to interpretive and critical concepts as a way of at least escaping, if not correcting, the problems that they saw in the traditionalist perspective. Instead of identifying dozens of communication and organizational variables, then explaining their relationships in piecemeal statistical studies, interpretivists concentrate on the communication process of constructing the meanings and frames of reference from which members experience organizational life. Critical theorists concentrate on criticizing oppression and systematic distortion of organizational communication. Just a few years ago, we asserted in earlier editions of this book that interpretivism and critical theory are minority views of organizational communication in the sense that fewer scholars and practitioners work from these perspectives than from the traditionalist perspective. Today, it does not appear that any one perspective dominates the study of organizational communication. In any case, debates about dominance and validity of perspectives may be pointless. Important contributions to organizational communication scholarship are being made from all three perspectives, and we have tried to reflect these contributions throughout this book.

New Developments and Emerging Perspectives

As we have taken this book through various editions since 1987, we have been amazed at how much we have had to change the text to keep up with developments in the field. Something new always seems to be in the making. To begin with, the traditional, interpretive, and critical perspectives are evolving over time. It also looks as if one or more new perspectives may be on the horizon. We will have more to say about these new directions at various points in the book, especially in chapters 3, 4, 11, and 12, but some forecasting of the discussion is in order now.

We already have suggested some ways in which the traditional perspective has changed. Because the traditional perspective emphasizes improved communication for the sake of organizational effectiveness as managers and leaders generally understand it, many traditional academic scholars historically have worked not only as college professors but also as part-time organizational consultants. Moreover, traditionalists have trained many nonacademic, professional practitioners over the years, especially in training and development (Redding, 1979). The relationship between "scholars" and "practitioners" is close enough that new ideas developed by either group often are picked up in one way or another by the other. In recent years especially, traditionalists have been adapting their concepts and methods to take advantage of rapid changes in American economic organizations. These changes range from downsizing and delayering in many large organizations, shifts to self-managed work teams, and elimination or simplication of job classification systems to adoption of large scale total quality management efforts, organizational re-engineering programs, revolutionary information technologies, and growing diversity in the workforce. Such changes expand the need for effective communication from its old status as a management problem to an issue that affects virtually every organization member in a direct way (Spiker & Lesser, 1995).

Similarly, the movements toward interpretive and critical perspectives not only have produced a new kind of scholarship in the field but also have attempted to reframe the objectives of professional practices. In particular, these two perspectives have led to a strong and growing workplace democracy movement that is dedicated to breaking down the power inequities inherent in hierarchical organizations and empowering ordinary organization members to exercise more self-determination in their organizational lives (Deetz, 1992). One indication of this change is a major effort to study and foster the adoption of forms of organization that are radically different from traditional American systems. Particular attention has been given to collective or cooperative systems where power and control are distributed and held in common by all organization members (Cheney, 1995;

Papa, Singhal, & Auwal, 1995). One good example of this type of system is the employee-owned organization, but there are others.

Another new development in organizational communication studies that is too recent to even be called a trend is interest across all three major perspectives in the effects of internationalization and globalization of organizations. As recently as 1993, Cynthia Stohl, one of the leaders in this area, complained that coverage of international organizing is "markedly absent from organizational communication discourse" (p. 378), but this situation is beginning to change rapidly. For example, the studies cited above by Cheney and by Papa and others as examples of work on alternative organizations were conducted outside the United States of America—one in Spain, the other in Bangladesh. The multinational condition of many large organizations will no doubt reinforce the growing interest in the international study of organizational communication. In the corporate world alone, Stohl noted that there are more than 10,000 such organizations with 90,000 affiliates worldwide (1993, p. 377).

As if evolution of the current perspectives were not enough, we might actually see some new perspectives within the next few years. You might be wondering how anyone could think up another point of view, but we think at least one is worth noting because it challenges an important assumption that may be about the only belief common to the traditional, interpretive, and critical points of view. The present perspectives aim in one way or another to direct human organizations toward some ideal state. Traditionalists, interpretivists, and critical scholars may disagree with each other over the objectives for which they should work and the methods for attaining these objectives, but we all seem to embrace one common assumption: Change is possible because human beings become what they are through learning, socialization, and acculturation. The field of sociobiology and, more recently, the rapidly developing discipline of evolutionary psychology are challenging this assumption in a way that has provoked heated debate. The question posed by the new movement is simply this: To what extent is our human behavior, including our social and organizational behavior, an outcome not only of learning, socialization, and acculturation but also of our biological makeup and evolutionary influences? Present perspectives on the psychosocial application of evolutionary theory in explaining human behavior do not subscribe to the idea of total biological determinism that characterized earlier movements such as Social Darwinism and 1930s German facism. But these perspectives also reject the idea of total environmental determinism that pervades much of modern social science (Tooby & Cosmides, 1989).

Summary

The study of organizational communication can be important to you for at least three reasons. It can improve your understanding of organizational life, provide you with an awareness of important communication skills in organizations, and perhaps start you on a path to a career in the field. In order to appreciate the field, though, you should also know something about its background and the factors that shaped our approach to this book.

Organizational communication is a relatively new field of study. When it began, it borrowed ideas from other social and behavioral sciences in such a way that its focus on communication was unclear. Many critics felt that the new field was fragmented and disorganized. These problems led to at least three different perspectives of organizational communication: traditional, interpretive, and critical. Feminist theory also is included here as a special case of the critical perspective.

These perspectives differ in the ways that they study organizational communication and in the assumptions that they make about the nature of organizations. Traditionalism has evolved from an early form into a different contemporary form. Early traditionalism understands organizations as machines and regards communication as a machinelike process. Recent traditionalism sees organizations as living systems and sees communication as a dynamic, organismic process. Despite these changes in traditionalism, interpretivism and critical theory have developed as serious alternatives to the traditionalist study of organizations. Interpretivists are concerned with the symbolic processes through which organizational reality is socially constructed. Critical theorists are concerned with the relationship between structure and symbolic processes in the efforts to criticize oppression and the systematic distortion of organizational communication.

Most recently, scholars in the field have begun to focus on issues such as organizational change, globalization, and workplace democracy. The field of evolutionary psychology has presented the beginnings of a fourth perspective, one that regards human social and organizational behavior as products of both evolutionary and environmental forces.

Discussion Questions/ Activities

1. What are some common examples of communication in organizations? What do these examples indicate about the importance of communication in organizational life? Try to generate some examples from your own experiences in organizations, then compare them with those of another person.
2. How would you describe the similarities and differences among traditionalist, interpretivist, and critical perspectives of organizational communication?
3. What are some of the reasons that might explain the dominance of traditionalism in the study of organizational communication?
4. According to the text, there are some questions that traditionalism is not equipped to answer. What do you think some of the questions might be? How could they be answered from other perspectives?

Additional Resources

Books

Bantz, C. R. (1993). *Understanding organizations: Interpreting organizational communication cultures.* Columbia, SC: University of South Carolina Press.

Eisenberg, E. M., & Goodall, H. L., Jr. (1993). *Organizational communication: Balancing creativity and constraint.* New York: St. Martin's Press.

Farace, R. V., Monge, P. R., & Russell, H. M. (1977). *Communicating and organizing.* Reading, MA: Addison Wesley.

Miller, K. (1994). *Organizational communication: Approaches and processes.* Belmont, CA: Wadsworth.

Stohl, C. (1995). *Organizational communication: Connectedness in action.* Thousand Oaks, CA: Sage.

Web Sites

http://www.hamline.edu/../depts/commdept/faculty/cbruess.html
  Organizational communication course description by Carol Bruess, Hamline
  University.
http://conted.sjsu.edu/~snguyen/orgcom.html
  Description of organizational communication internship program, San Jose State
  University.
http://sage.cc.purdue.edu/~penkoff/welcome.html
  Many additional resources on organizational communication and computer-
  mediated communication provided by Diane Witmer Penkoff, Purdue University.

References

Boase, P. H., & Carlson, C. V. (1989). *The School of Interpersonal Communication: An historical perspective.* Unpublished manuscript, School of Interpersonal Communication, Ohio State University.

Bosmajian, H. A. (1983). *The language of oppression* (2nd ed.). Lanham, MD: University Press of America.

Bureau of Labor Statistics (1988). *Occupational outlook handbook* (1988–89 ed.). Washington, DC: U.S. Department of Labor. (Bulletin 2300).

Cheney, G. (1995). Democracy in the workplace: Theory and practice from the perspective of communication. *Journal of Applied Communication Research, 23,* 167–200.

Crawford, J. S. (1977). *Women in middle management: Selection, training, advancement, performance.* Ridgewood, NJ: Forkner.

Deetz, S. (1992). *Democracy in an age of corporate colonialization.* Albany, NY: State University of New York Press.

Deetz, S. A. (1982). Critical interpretive research in organizational communication. *Western Journal of Speech Communication, 46,* 131–149.

Dennis, H. S., III, Goldhaber, G. M., & Yates, M. P. (1978). Organizational communication theory and research: An overview of research methods. In B. D. Ruben (Ed.), *Communication yearbook 2* (pp. 243–269). New Brunswick, NJ: Transaction Books.

Dessler, G. (1980). *Organization theory: Integrating structure and behavior.* Englewood Cliffs, NJ: Prentice-Hall.

Di Salvo, V. (1980). A summary of current research identifying communication skills in various organization contexts. *Communication Education, 29,* 283–290.

Eich, R. K. (1977). *Organizational communication consulting: A descriptive study of consulting practices and prescriptions.* Unpublished doctoral dissertation, Michigan State University, East Lansing.

Falcione, R. L., & Werner, E. (1978). *Organizational climate and communication climate: A state of the art.* Paper presented at the annual meeting of the International Communication Association, Chicago.

French, W. L., Bell, C. H., Jr., & Zawacki, R. A. (Eds.). (1983). *Organization development: Theory, practice, and research* (2nd ed.). Plano, TX: Business Publications.

Goodall, H. L., Jr. (1984). The status of communication studies in organizational contexts: One rhetorician's lament after a year-long odyssey. *Communication Quarterly, 32,* 133–147.

Haviland, W. A. (1993). *Cultural anthropology* (7th ed.). Fort Worth, TX: Harcourt Brace Jovanovich.

Hersey, P., & Blanchard, K. (1982). *Management of organizational behavior: Utilizing human resources* (4th ed.). Englewood Cliffs, NJ: Prentice-Hall.

Huse, E. F., & Bowditch, J. L. (1977). *Behavior in organizations: A systems approach to managing* (2nd ed.). Reading, MA: Addison-Wesley.

Iannello, K. P. (1992). *Decisions without hierarchy: Feminist interventions in organization theory and practice.* New York: Routledge.

Katz, D., & Kahn, R. L. (1978). *The social psychology of organizations* (2nd ed.). New York: John Wiley & Sons.

Monge, P. R., Farace, R. V., Eisenberg, E. M., Miller, K. I., and White, L. L. (1984). The process of studying process in organizational communication. *Journal of Communication, 34,* 22–43.

Mumby, D. K. (1987). The political function of narrative in organizations. *Communication Monographs, 54,* 113–127.

Pacanowsky, M. E., & O'Donnell-Trujillo, N. (1982). Communication and organizational cultures. *Western Journal of Speech Communication, 46,* 115–130.

Pacanowsky, M. E., & O'Donnell-Trujillo, N. (1984). Organizational communication as cultural performance. *Communication Monographs, 50,* 126–147.

Pace, R. W. (1983). *Organizational communication: Foundations for human resource development.* Englewood Cliffs, NJ: Prentice-Hall.

Papa, M., Singhal, A., & Auwal, M. (1995). Dialectic of control and emancipation in organizing for social change: A multitheoretic study of the Grameen Bank in Bangladesh. *Communication Theory, 5,* 189–223.

Putnam, L. L. (1982). Paradigms for organizational communication research: An overview and synthesis. *Western Journal of Speech Communication, 46,* 192–206.

Redding, W. C. (1979). Graduate education and the communication consultant: Playing God for a fee. *Communication Education, 28,* 346–352.

Redding, W. C. (1985). Stumbling toward identity: The emergence of organizational communication as a field of study. In R. D. McPhee & P. K. Tompkins (Eds.), *Organizational communication: Traditional themes and new directions* (pp. 15–54). Newbury Park, CA: Sage.

Smilowitz, M. (1982). *Ought as was in organizational reality.* Paper presented at the Second Conference on Interpretive Research in Organizational Communication, Alta, UT.

Spiker, B. K., & Lesser, E. (1995). We have met the enemy. *Journal of Business Strategy, 16,* 17–21.

Stohl, C. (1993). International organizing and organizational communication. *Journal of Applied Communication Research, 21,* 377–384.

Tompkins, P. K., & Redding, W. C. (1988). Organizational communication—past and present tenses. In G. M. Goldhaber & G. A. Barnett (Eds.), *Handbook of organizational communication* (pp. 5–33). Norwood, NJ: Ablex.

Tong, R. (1989). *Feminist thought.* Boulder, CO: Westview.

Tooby, J., & Cosmides, L. (1989). Evolutionary psychology and the generation of culture, Part I. *Ethology and Sociobiology, 10,* 29–49.

Williams, L. C., Jr. (1978). What 50 presidents and CEOs think about employee communications. *Public Relations Quarterly, 23,* 6–11.

CHAPTER 2

ORGANIZATION THEORY: PRESCRIPTIONS FOR CONTROL

Organizational behavior is as old as the human social experience. We know from historical accounts that early civilizations sometimes had elaborate organizational systems for governmental, military, religious, and economic purposes. The ancient peoples who created these organizations had "theories" of organizational behavior—concepts, principles, and prescriptions for organizational structure and function. These theories were fitted to the needs of agricultural societies only a few generations removed from their tribal origins. During the Middle Ages of western civilization, the dominance of institutionalized religion and ordering of society into localized feudal economies produced principles of divine right and social class systems of authority and labor as guidelines for organizing. Feudal serfs (average citizens), as well as their lords, had tradition to tell them what to do in an era when the patterns of life and society were virtually unchanged for centuries (Dessler, 1980).

The Renaissance and, later the Industrial Revolution, effectively removed the basic foundations of feudal life. As a consequence, organizations in the developed nations of today's world function within a complex and sometimes rapidly changing economic, legal, political, and social environment. This environment has evolved from four centuries of commercialization and industrialization, international trade, secularization of social and governmental institutions, and compression of time and distance through technological advances in transportation and communications. In this chapter and the next two, we review theories of organization and organizational effectiveness that have developed during the twentieth century and are continuing to develop in today's world. This chapter covers theories usually associated with traditionalism, namely, scientific and classical management theory, human relations theory, human resource development theory, and two transitional theories that were ahead of their time in the sense that they provided a foundation earlier in the century for some very contemporary ideas.

When the industrialized world entered the twentieth century, it was apparent that new and clearer concepts of organizational behavior would be required to deal with the complexities of modern society (Dessler, 1980). The first modern perspectives on organizational behavior were developed in the early 1900s when several prominent theorists advanced the basic principles of scientific and classical management. Scientific and classical theories envisioned organizations as machinelike objects driven by management plan and control. Individual organization members often were regarded as simple parts in the machine.

Scientific and classical theories were followed quickly by eclectic theories of organization and by the emergence of the human relations movement. The eclectic theories, which cut across several different schools of thought about organizations, were much broader than scientific and classical theories. The human relations movement actually challenged scientific and classical notions by arguing that organizational effectiveness depends more on the social processes of organization than on management design. These principles never really replaced classical and scientific views. Instead, many assumptions about organizational behavior drawn from human relations theory simply were grafted onto classical and scientific management ideas about organizational structure.

Later, new concepts in human motivation, along with influences from earlier eclectic theories and the emergence of system theory, led to human resource development theory. Human resource development theory, based on motivational principles of the human need for self-fulfillment, began to compete with earlier human relations and classical/scientific perspectives of organizational behavior.

These theories are concerned not only with the characteristics of organizations but also with the problems of organizational effectiveness and managerial control. They are *prescriptive* theories that indicate how organizational processes (including communication) should function and what managers are to do in order to achieve organizational effectiveness. Consequently, we have characterized the theories in this chapter as prescriptions for control. Whether or not prescriptions for organizational structure, managerial strategy, and communication always work, the pursuit of reliable methods for attaining organizational effectiveness has been a traditional concern in organizational theory. This concern carries over into the field of organizational communication.

Scientific and Classical Management

Scientific and classical theories of management represented the earliest attempts to cope with the complexities of twentieth-century organizations. Three of the most influential theorists during the early 1900s were Frederick Taylor, an American engineer; Henri Fayol, a French industrialist; and Max Weber, a German university professor. Taylor published his system of "Scientific Management" as early as 1911. Fayol and Weber wrote classical treatises on the principles of organization and management at about the same time, although their works were not available in English translations for an American market until the 1940s. The most recent compilation of Taylor's work also was not published until 1947. These three theorists differed from one another in many of the principles that they advocated, but they shared a common idea that effective organizational performance is determined by efficient design of work and organizational structure.

Taylor's Scientific Management

Frederick Taylor was concerned primarily with the scientific study and design of work processes. Most of his principles addressed problems of work efficiency, but he also offered recommendations regarding organizational structure and processes. Essentially, Taylor (1947) advanced four ideas:

1. There is "one best way" to perform any job. The best way can be determined through scientific analysis. For example, a time and motion study can reveal the fewest number of steps and shortest amount of time required to perform a task efficiently. Experiments can determine the physical working conditions under which productivity will be highest.
2. Personnel should be selected scientifically. One should choose and assign people to tasks according to their skills or potential for developing skills.
3. Workers should be compensated on an incentive plan that pays them in direct proportion to the work that they produce. An hourly wage is inappropriate, not so much because of differences in individual productivity but because economic need is the principal factor that motivates people to work. Workers will produce more if they realize that they will be paid acccordingly.
4. Labor should be divided so that managers plan the work and workers follow the plan. In Taylor's scheme, each aspect of any task is supervised by a different "functional foreman." A given worker takes orders from any one or all of these foremen, depending on the characteristics of the task.

Taylor believed that the central problem in organizational effectiveness involved management's inability to obtain compliance from workers. He argued that if organizations followed his principles, then managers and workers would realize that they can cooperate to increase the organization's wealth and resources "until the surplus becomes so large that it is unnecessary to quarrel over how it shall be divided." In other words, everybody would benefit under scientific management.

Taylor applied his principles at Bethlehem Steel Company in order to improve the work efficiency of coal and iron ore shovelers. According to Taylor's own analysis, in the third year of working under his plan at Bethlehem, the volume of material moved each day jumped by more than 350 percent, the cost of moving the material was cut in half, and the average pay for shovelers increased from $1.15 to $1.88. This was, by the way, $1.88 *per day,* not per hour! The results were fantastic from the standpoint of efficiency, but this particular silver lining surrounded an ominous cloud. The workforce of more than 400 shovelers was reduced to 140. Taylor himself pointed with pride to this outcome, claiming that the most important result of his plan "was the effect on the workmen themselves, . . . [namely,] out of the 140 workmen only two were said to be drinking men" (p. 71). Although Taylor claimed that he did not want workers to be "brutally" discharged, he did not say what became of the hundreds of shovelers who were laid off at Bethlehem Steel.

Fayol's General Management

While Taylor focused on the technical details of production work, Henri Fayol was concerned primarily with the basic principles of organizational structure and management practice. Fayol (1949) offered fourteen fundamental principles; most are prescriptions for organizational structure and design:

1. *Division of work.* Each member has one and only one job to do.
2. *Authority and responsibility.* Authority includes the right to give orders and the power to exact compliance. Official authority depends on one's position. Personal authority depends on ability and experience.
3. *Discipline.* Good discipline depends on good superiors, clear and fair policies, and judiciously applied sanctions.
4. *Unity of command.* An employee receives orders from one and only one superior for any action.
5. *Unity of direction.* A group of activities with the same objective should have "one head with one plan."
6. *Subordination of individual interests.* The interests of the organization must prevail over those of any given group or person.
7. *Remuneration.* Employees should be paid fairly, in a manner that satisfies them and the firm.
8. *Centralization.* Whether decision making is centralized (restricted to higher-level management) or decentralized (allocated to subordinates) depends on the organization's circumstances.
9. *Scalar chain.* The system of authority is structured as a hierarchy with clear lines of command from one level to the next, but the system must allow for departure from the chain of command when necessary.
10. *Order.* There is a place for each employee, and each employee is to be in his or her place.
11. *Equity.* Personnel should be treated with kindness and justice, but this does not exclude forcefulness and sternness.
12. *Stability in tenure.* Assuming that an employee has the ability to do a job, he or she must still have time to learn and to succeed in performing it.
13. *Initiative.* The ability to think out and execute a plan is a valuable organizational resource.
14. *Esprit de corps.* Management should strive to promote a sense of unity, harmony, and cohesion.

Fayol's ideas were based on his experience during a fifty-eight-year career with a large mining company. He spent twelve of those years as a mining engineer, sixteen years as a middle-level manager, and thirty years as the company's managing director. The company was nearly bankrupt when Fayol assumed the directorship in 1888, but it gradually became a profitable model of effective management and organizational practices. The company's success helped Fayol to popularize his management theory after his retirement in 1918.

Weber's Bureaucratic Theory

Max Weber borrowed the French term, **bureaucracy,** as a label for his concept of the ideal modern organization. Weber believed that complex organizations in an industrial age required speed, precision, certainty, and continuity. These conditions could be realized most effectively if organizational designs were as machinelike as possible. According to Weber (1947), the bureaucratic machine should have six basic features:

1. A clear hierarchical system of authority.
2. Division of labor according to specialization.
3. A complete system of rules regarding the rights, responsibilities, and duties of personnel.
4. Exhaustive procedures for work performance.
5. Impersonality in human organizational relationships.
6. Selection and promotion of personnel solely on the basis of technical competence.

Weber intended for bureaucracy to eliminate ambiguity and capriciousness in organizational life. Formalized rules, clear descriptions of authority and responsibility at all organizational levels, and predictability in human relationships should lead to several desirable outcomes. In particular, decision making should be faster, efficiency in task performance should improve, and treatment of personnel should be more equitable (fair and impartial). According to Weber, all actions in a bureaucracy are derived mechanically from rules in a rational system based on military discipline. The individual organization member "is only a single cog in an ever-moving mechanism which prescribes to him an essentially fixed route of march" (1969, p. 34).

The theories that Taylor, Fayol, and Weber developed certainly were not identical. Taylor's concept of functional foremanship in which any worker might receive orders at various points from several different superiors ran counter to the idea of unity of command that Fayol and Weber both advocated. Moreover, Fayol's attitudes toward flexibility in organizational structure, centralizing or decentralizing decision making to fit the organization's circumstances, and encouragement of esprit de corps were quite inconsistent with Weber's prescriptions for fixed, constant rules and impersonal relationships. Yet several clear themes are common to scientific and classical management theory.

First, the organization is driven by management authority. Employees are simply the instruments for carrying out the management plan. This implies that organizational communication is merely a tool for managerial **control** and **coordination** of organizational processes. Communication involving planning and decision making is **centralized** (concentrated) near the top of the organizational hierarchy (although Fayol allowed for some flexibility on this point). Organizational policies and task-oriented messages regarding the execution of orders flow from the top down. Upward communication from subordinates to superiors serves only a reporting function to verify compliance with orders or to indicate any work-related problems.

Second, scientific and classical theorists believed that people behave according to rational, economic models. The primary motivation for work is money. If people are compensated in a fair manner, they will be more productive and more compliant with authority. Social and political motivations in organizational behavior were regarded as irrelevant or detrimental to organizational effectiveness. A rationally specified system of organization structure and functions would reduce the ill effects of group conflicts, personal rivalries, vindictiveness, power struggles, and petty egoism.

Finally, each theorist advanced a machinelike prescription for organizational design. The analogy between the human organization and the well-maintained machine performing at peak efficiency is most obvious in Weber's work, but Taylor's concept of scientific management envisioned exactly the same ideal for work processes. Even Fayol, who argued that his principles of organizational structure and management should be applied flexibly, still insisted that order, discipline, hierarchical authority, and fixed division of labor were the basic elements in a tried and true formula for organizational effectiveness. A summary for easier comparison of the central principles in each theory is presented in table 2.1.

Scientific and classical management theories have been very influential in the design of modern organizations. Time and motion studies of the type that Taylor's followers introduced are used as basic tools to determine the most efficient procedures for task performance in large organizations. Organization charts; detailed job descriptions; and elaborate policy manuals spelling out lines of

Table 2.1 Principles in Scientific and Classical Management.

Summary of Principles in Scientific and Classical Management

Scientific Management	Classical Management	
Theme: Effectiveness Is a Function of Work Design	*Theme: Effectiveness Is a Function of Organizational Design*	
Taylor	*Fayol* (flexible hierarchy)	*Weber* (bureaucracy)
1. Find the "one best way" to perform each job. 2. Scientifically select and train workers. 3. Reward workers in direct proportion to productivity. 4. Use "functional foremanship"; managers plan, workers produce, expert supervisors (potentially several) direct various aspects of a given worker's job.	1. Order based on divison of labor, unity of command and direction, but centralization must "vary according to different cases." 2. Managerial authority is derived from both official and personal bases. 3. Equity through kindness and justice, but does not exclude "forcefulness and sternness." 4. Esprit de corps.	1. Order based on division of labor, clear authority structure, and a complete system of technical rules for conduct and procedure. 2. Authority derived from a rational-legal system where a person is "only a single cog in an ever-moving mechanism." 3. Justice "mechanically derived from a code." 4. Impersonality in interpersonal relations.

authority, work procedures, and individual rights and responsibilities are quite common in American organizations. Such documents often define channels of message flow and appropriate communicative behavior for organization members as well. For example, the U.S. Postal Service makes it clear that all official communication in the organization must conform to Fayol's principles of unity of command, unity of direction, and scalar authority:

Any communication on matters requiring discretion or policy determination shall proceed through each successive level of authority upward and downward without bypassing any. . . . An administrative reporting relationship establishes a clear line of authority between positions or units in the organizational hierarchy. . . . Subordinate positions never report administratively to more than one higher-level supervisor. (1979, sec. 153)

In other organizations, the influence of classical organizational theory is more subtle. The principles are intuitively understood rules for defining relationships among organization members—rules that generally are taken for granted. Consider the case of a large grocery store that we will call Supervalue Market. The owner, who is also the general manager, insists that Supervalue does not have organization charts and policy manuals: "We're all just one big happy family here." But the people who work at Supervalue understand that their organization has a specific structure. The store is arranged in departments. Each department has a supervisor. Every employee has a job title (checker, sacker, stocker, etc.) and a specific assignment in a designated department.

The employees at Supervalue communicate with their department supervisors on all work-related matters. In turn, the supervisors report to designated assistant managers, and the assistant managers report to the general manager. Although managers occasionally carry on casual conversations and light banter with most of the employees, they rarely speak officially with anyone except department supervisors. Supervisors relay any official information from managers to the employees. In general, different supervisors (and employees) stay out of one another's departments unless they are assigned to help out or cover for someone else. Unlike the U.S. Postal Service, Supervalue has no written policies that specify these rules. But when you go to work at Supervalue, you find out quickly from observing and listening to others that "This is the way we do it here." Even though nobody has ever published an organization chart for Supervalue, all of the members understand and use the rules to enact this organizational structure.

If we translate the implicit operating rules of Supervalue Market into an explicit organization chart, it might look something like the diagram in figure 2.1.

Figure 2.1 illustrates a functional **division of labor** with different departments and job classifications for different types of work. The organization chart also specifies a **scalar chain of command** with lines of authority and reporting relationships from the general manager to the assistant managers, from these assistants to department supervisors, and from supervisors to employees. This type of **hierarchical structure** provides the basic framework for many different types of organizations, both private and public, profit and nonprofit.

Despite the influence of scientific and classical principles in contemporary organizations, these theories have been criticized extensively. Most of the critics

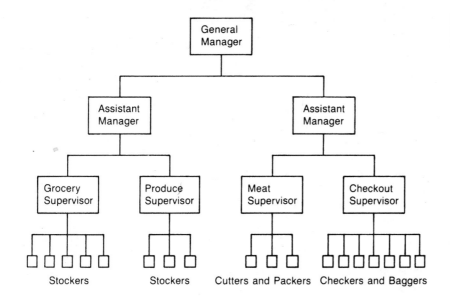

Figure 2.1
Fictitious organization chart for Supervalue Market.

point out that classical and scientific assumptions about human motivation are naive. Human organizational behavior depends on many complex factors besides the desire for economic reward or blind obedience to authority. The theories also are criticized for producing rigid, unadaptive organizational structures. Hierarchies with centralized decision making, many levels of authority, and highly specialized divisions of labor can function reasonably well in a stable environment, but they lack the flexibility to adapt to change. The very fact that "bureaucracy" conjures up images of red tape, inefficiency, and indifference (features quite the opposite of those that Weber extolled) suggests that classical and scientific theorists failed to understand the social and psychological dynamics of organizational behavior and human communication.

During the 1920s and 1930s, two developments in theories of organization and human relationships began to point to shortcomings in scientific and classical theory. One of these developments involved the appearance of two transitional theories of organization. The second development was the emergence of the human relations movement.

Transitional Theories

While scientific and classical theories focused rather narrowly on questions of organizational structure and work design, at least two **transitional theories** addressed broader concerns, including the use of power, the psychology of compliance, variability in the behavior of individual organization members, and the importance of communication in organizational processes. Mary Parker Follett introduced the first in the 1920s. Chester Barnard developed the second in the 1930s. We identify these theories as transitional because they include ideas that returned decades later in areas such as human resource development theory and system theory (to be discussed in chapter 3).

Follett's Administrative Theory

If Mary Parker Follett's theory of administration is not easily classified, neither is Follett herself. After completing an undergraduate degree at Radcliffe and graduate work in Paris, Follett pursued an array of interests ranging from the establishment of a job placement bureau for young people that covered the entire city of Boston to lecturing at the Bureau of Personnel Administration in New York (Fox & Urwick, 1982). But we believe it was her extensive work as a community organizer and activist that most obviously influenced the development of her theory. In effect, she mastered the principles of cooperative effort in community action, then advocated the application of these principles to business organizations.

Fox and Urwick contend that Follett's theory hinges on two basic concepts. The first is the principle of reciprocal response, that is, human interaction always involves mutual and simultaneous influence, "and the total result is one that neither participant could have produced even half of alone" (p. xxiv). The second principle is Follett's universal goal of integration, that is, "a harmonious marriage of differences . . . that produces a new form, a new entity, a new result made out of the old differences and yet different from any of them" (p. xxv). Thus, Follett was concerned primarily with ways of building and sustaining democracy through integration of different, competing interests. In order to achieve integration of interests as Follett understood it, traditional ideas about power and authority had to be redefined. Integration of interests depends on shared power. As Follett explained the issue,

Whereas power usually means power-over, the power of some person or group over some other person or group, it is possible to develop the conception of power-with, a jointly developed power, a co-active, not a coercive power. . . . That should be one of the tests of any plan of employee representation—is it developing joint power? (1982a, p. 72)

Follett did not believe that power was abused only by capitalists. She also chastized organized labor and political activists, saying that management had a right "to resist any effort of the unions to get power-over" (p. 72) and that "reformers, propagandists, many of our 'best' people are willing to coerce others in order to attain an end which *they* think is good" (p. 73). Nor did Follett advocate empowerment of workers just to make employees feel better about themselves. She had learned the value of joint power in integrating different interests to produce successful community actions like her Boston placement bureau; and she understood that successful business required the knowledge and experiences of both management and labor and that pluralistic responsibility based on function, not hierarchy or rank, is essential to organizational effectiveness.

While "power-with" is a necessary condition for integration of interests in Follett's theory, the vehicle for integration is employee representation. She acknowledged that employee representation was in fact used in that era as a way to get employees to consent, comply, and cooperate with management plans and decisions, but Follett herself envisioned employee representation as **participation** in order to achieve pluralistic responsibility. Follett gave her theory an explicit communication basis not only through her concept of reciprocal response, but also by arguing that participation "requires *conference* [emphasis added] as its method" (1982b, p. 139) in joint committees of workers and managers who meet "to get from each other the special knowledge and experience each has" (p. 139). Follett died in 1933, but her idea of participation was destined to become a bedrock concept for management scholars who published human resource development theories in the 1960s.

Barnard's Executive Functions

Mary Parker Follett probably would not have accepted some features of Chester Barnard's theory, but Barnard, who said that Follett "had great insight into the dynamic elements of organization" (1938, p. 122 footnote), was one of the first important American business leaders to be influenced by her work. Barnard, who was president of New Jersey Bell Telephone and at one time chaired the National Science Foundation, apparently felt that classical theories of organization failed to provide adequate explanations of organizational behavior as he had experienced it. In his 1938 book, *The Functions of the Executive,* Barnard attempted to correct these shortcomings in three areas: *individual behavior, compliance,* and *communication.*

In Barnard's view, classical theorists had underestimated both the variability of individual behavior in organizations and the impact of this behavior on organizational effectiveness. Organization members are not simply so many cogs in a machine who behave predictably out of rational, economic interests. Members are individuals who differ from one another in many respects. Barnard believed that the individual is the "basic strategic factor" in all organizations and that organizational effectiveness depends on the individual's willingness to cooperate. This assumption led directly to Barnard's ideas about compliance.

Barnard regarded compliance as willingness to cooperate. Compliance in this sense requires individuals to surrender their personal preferences. An order has authority to the extent that a person is willing to surrender personal preference to carry out the order. Orders must fall within a person's *zone of indifference,* meaning that orders must be perceived in neutral terms so that they are carried out without conscious questioning of their authority. Incentives, inducements, and rewards can be used to expand a person's zone of indifference, but material incentives alone are limited in their power to effect compliance. Inducements such as status, prestige, and personal power also are necessary.

Finally, while Follett explicitly had linked management-employee communication with participation and representation, Barnard made communication an indispensable concept in the analysis of organizational structure. He pointed out that decision-making processes hinge on communication and described the characteristics and importance of communication in the informal organization (i.e., the interaction in a social, political, and unofficial world that is not specified on the formal organization chart). Barnard's strong belief in the centrality of communication for organizational processes is indicated in his argument that "the first function of an executive" is to establish and maintain a system of communication. According to Dessler, Barnard "presented a new theory of organization structure, one that focused on the organization as a communication system" (1980, p. 38).

The Human Relations Movement

The **human relations movement** emerged from various currents of thought during the 1930s. The most important of these was the Harvard-affiliated human relations school of management that emerged in the wake of a complex series of industrial investigations known as the Hawthorne Studies.

The Hawthorne Studies and Elton Mayo

The first seeds of the human relations movement were sown in 1924 with a series of studies at Western Electric Company's Hawthorne Plant in Illinois. The **Hawthorne Studies** were conducted over a period of several years in four phases: the illumination studies, the relay assembly-room studies, the interview program, and the bank-wiring studies (Roethlisberger & Dickson, 1939). The results challenged scientific management principles by suggesting that interpersonal communication, group dynamics, and organization members' attitudes and values are more important than work structure and organizational design in determining organizational effectiveness. These studies provided the foundation for the Harvard-affiliated human relations school of management.

The Illumination Studies

The Hawthorne Studies began because an industrial engineering research group wanted to determine the relationship between lighting (illumination) conditions in a work area and worker productivity. In line with scientific management theory, the researchers believed that productivity would be greatest under some optimum or ideal level of lighting (i.e., neither too little nor too much light). They set out to find this optimum condition by experimenting with the lighting levels, but the results of the study defied explanation. Productivity increased regardless of what the researchers did to the lighting. When the light was increased, productivity went up. When the light was held constant, productivity still went up. Even when the level of light was decreased, productivity continued to increase until workers literally could no longer see what they were doing.

Relay Assembly-Room Studies

The results of the illumination studies were disturbing to engineers schooled in the principles of scientific management. In order to understand why these principles apparently failed in the illumination studies, researchers decided to isolate a small group of telephone relay assembly workers in order to study systematically the relationships between various working conditions and productivity. The studies included changes in compensation, rest periods, work schedules, and work methods. In general, productivity increased during the studies regardless of changes in the work conditions. The researchers finally concluded that the *relationship* between the researchers and the workers accounted for the results. The test-room observer had shown a personal interest in the workers, consulted with and kept them informed about changes that were being made during the experiments, and listened sympathetically to their concerns and opinions. This relationship was quite different from the task-oriented, rule-bound, impersonal manner of supervision that characterized the rest of the plant (Roethlisberger & Dickson, 1939).

The Interview Program

The results of the relay assembly-room studies led researchers to conduct interviews with thousands of employees in order to discover their attitudes toward working conditions, supervisors, and work in general. The interviews soon indicated that *people who worked under similar conditions experienced these conditions in different ways and assigned different meanings to their experiences.* For example, a given style of supervision could be satisfying to some people and dissatisfying to others.

When researchers tried to account for different reactions to similar conditions, they found that personal background and expectations contributed to satisfaction. In particular, "the meaning a person assigns to his position depends on whether or not that position is allowing him to fulfill the social demands he is making of his work" (Roethlisberger & Dickson, 1939). They concluded that *employees' attitudes depend on the social organization of the groups in which they work and their positions in these groups.*

Bank-Wiring Studies

The interview program was followed by another intensive study with a small group of employees who wired circuit banks. The purpose was to observe the effects of the work group's social processes on productivity. The results of the study indicated that work group norms exert substantial influence over performance standards.

Employees in the bank-wiring study shared a clear idea of the "right" amount of output for a day's work. Production from day to day should be constant—neither too much nor too little. Even though they were paid on an incentive plan, group members pressured faster workers to slow down. Production reports were falsified to reflect either more or less output in order to maintain the appearance of a constant rate of production. The group developed an informal system that controlled and regulated the members' behavior and, at the same time, protected them from outside interference (e.g., from higher-level managers). The findings puzzled industrial engineers, but the workers who lost their jobs in the wake of Taylor's studies at Bethlehem Steel easily would have understood the norms in the bank-wiring group against producing "too much."

Implications of the Studies

The Hawthorne Studies occupy such a prominent place in the history of organizational research that questions about the appropriateness of the methods used in these studies and the validity of the conclusions drawn from the results have been debated for many years. For example, Carey (1967) argued that several serious flaws in the research methods prevent any reliable interpretation of results from these studies. More recently, Franke and Kaul (1978) developed a statistically based reinterpretation of the results that led them to conclusions that differed dramatically from those drawn by Roethlisberger & Dickson. According to Franke and Kaul, "It is not release from oppressive supervision but its reassertion that explains higher rates of productivity [in the Hawthorne Studies]" (p. 636).

Whatever the weaknesses that may have afflicted the Hawthorne Studies, these studies were significant because they led to the emergence of the human relations school of management under the leadership of Elton Mayo and his colleagues at the Harvard Business School. Mayo, who intensely disliked conflict and competition, tried to promote a concept of worker-management harmony (Landsberger, 1958). He was involved in the Hawthorne Studies almost from their beginning and interpreted the results as support for a "people-oriented" approach to management.

According to Mayo (1947), managers should be friendly in their relationships with workers, listen to worker concerns, and give workers a sense of participation in decisions in order to meet their *social* needs. In many respects, Mayo's advice was much like Dale Carnegie's (1936) prescription for "winning friends and influencing people." In fact, both Mayo and Carnegie have been criticized for promoting highly manipulative, managerial communication strategies intended only to gain compliance from workers and to promote acceptance of managerial authority (Redding, 1979). Human relations principles *did not change* the classical features of organizations. Instead, human relations ideas simply provided a tool for management relationships with employees under traditional systems of authority and hierarchy.

Although classical and scientific management theories offer prescriptions for organizational structure and communication, they are theories of worker motivation and compliance, not theories of organizational communication. Miles (1965) pointed out that this also is true of human relations. Classical and scientific theorists believed that workers are motivated by economic need. If this need is satisfied and the organization is properly designed, compliance with managerial authority will follow. Human relations advocates stressed the importance of social rather than economic needs and urged managers to adopt communication strategies that give workers a sense of participation. According to Miles, the heart of the human relations model is the idea that participation improves morale and morale leads to greater compliance with managerial authority. Consequently, all of these theories see communication only as a managerial tool for motivating workers and controlling organizational processes.

Human Resource Development

Just as human relations challenged some of the key assumptions in classical and scientific management, the forward-looking work of scholars like Follett and the development of new theories of human motivation led to concepts of **human resource development** that challenged human relations. These new theories pointed out that motivation is not merely economic or social but also tied to one's sense of self-worth or **self-actualization.** Abraham Maslow's need hierarchy is a commonly cited example of this change in ideas about motivation.

Maslow's Need Hierarchy

Maslow (1954) argued that motivational needs can be hierarchically organized. His hierarchy includes five needs:

1. *Physiological needs* for food, oxygen, and other basic requirements to sustain life. These are fundamental needs at the lowest level of the hierarchy.
2. *Safety needs* for security, protection from danger, and freedom from threat.

3. *Social needs* for love, affection, affiliation, and acceptance.
4. *Esteem needs* for a sense of status, recognition, and self-respect.
5. *Self-actualization needs* to realize one's full potential as a human being. Self-actualization is the most abstract and highest-level need in the hierarchy.

Maslow believed that lower-level needs are stronger than higher-level needs. In general, any need at a given level of the hierarchy must be relatively satisfied before the need at the next higher level is activated. Thus, a person who has reliable and stable means of meeting physiological and safety needs will become motivated to fulfill social needs, while a starving, homeless individual is preoccupied only with finding food and shelter.

More importantly, Maslow believed that self-actualization differs fundamentally from the other needs. Physiological, safety, social, and esteem needs are **deficiency needs.** They involve physical or psychological conditions that a person strives to maintain within an acceptable range—a kind of balance in which there is neither "too much" nor "too little." If you are deprived of a need such as food, the need becomes a **drive** (hunger) that causes behavior to satisfy the need (foraging for food). Once the need is fulfilled, the drive (motivation) is reduced and the behavior stops. In contrast, self-actualization is a **growth need.** The process of satisfying this need actually increases rather than decreases motivation.

McGregor's Theory X and Theory Y

As management theorists became familiar with Maslow's work, they soon realized the possibility of connecting higher-level needs to worker motivation. If organizational goals and individual needs could be *integrated* so that people would acquire self-esteem and, ultimately, self-actualization through work, then motivation would be self-sustaining. According to Douglas McGregor (1960), the key to linking self-actualization with work lies in managerial trust of subordinates. McGregor identified two sets of underlying assumptions about human nature that affect managers' trust of subordinates. He called these sets of assumptions Theory X and Theory Y.

Many managers subscribe to Theory X. They believe that employees dislike work and will attempt to avoid it if possible. Employees value security above everything else, dislike responsibility, and want someone else to control and direct them. If organizational goals are to be accomplished, managers must rely on threat and coercion to gain employee compliance. Theory X beliefs lead to mistrust, highly restrictive supervision, and a punitive atmosphere.

Theory Y managers believe that work is as natural as play. Employees want to work. They have the ability for creative problem solving, but their talents are underused in most organizations. Given proper conditions, employees will learn to seek out and accept responsibility and to exercise self-control and self-direction in accomplishing objectives to which they are committed. According to McGregor, Theory Y managers are more likely than Theory X managers to develop the climate of trust with employees that is required for human resource development.

In order for human resource development to occur, managers must communicate openly with subordinates, minimize status distinctions in superior-subordinate relationships, solicit subordinates' ideas and opinions, and create a climate in which subordinates can develop and use their abilities. This climate would include decentralization of decision making, delegation of authority to subordinates, variety in work tasks to make jobs more interesting, and **participative management** in which subordinates have influence in decisions that affect them.

As described by Miles (1965), the human resource development concept is based on a model that differs greatly from human relations. Here, participation leads to better performance, better performance improves morale, and morale feeds even more improvement in performance. The end result of human resource development is not so much compliance with managerial authority as it is a form of self-development through fulfillment of organizational goals. Participation in the process presumably provides even greater motivation to accomplish these goals.

As human resource development concepts emerged, it became clear that these concepts not only involved managerial communication with employees but also included many aspects of organizational communication in general. If an organization is to implement the principles of participative management and decentralized decision making, those who participate must have effective interpersonal and group communication skills, open and flexible channels of communication, and adequate information for a variety of organizational functions. The importance of these conditions for human resource development was stressed in the results of studies by Rensis Likert.

Likert's Four Systems

Likert (1961) argued that there are four basic types of management orientations or systems: **exploitative-authoritative** (system 1); **benevolent-authoritative** (system 2); **consultative** (system 3); and **participative** (system 4). Although Likert and McGregor worked independently, their ideas are quite similar. Likert's system 1 corresponds to McGregor's Theory X, while system 4 is similar to Theory Y. Systems 2 and 3 are located in between the other two positions. Likert's research indicated that organizations with system 4 participative characteristics were more effective than organizations based on other systems. The characteristics of system 4 include the following:

1. Communication between superiors and subordinates is open and extensive. Superiors solicit ideas and opinions, and subordinates feel free to discuss problems with superiors.
2. Decision making is decentralized. Decisions are made at all levels of the organization through group processes. Both superiors and subordinates are able to influence performance goals, work methods, and organizational activities.
3. Information flows freely through flexible channels of communication and in all directions—upward, downward, and laterally. Information is relatively accurate and undistorted.

4. Performance goals are developed through participative management. The goals are high but realistic. Goals are supported by favorable attitudes and motivation of organization members and by organizational commitment to development of human resources.
5. Control processes also are decentralized. Organization members seek and use feedback in order to exercise self-control.

In contrast, the characteristics of system 1 are as follows:

1. Superior-subordinate communication is minimal and characterized by mutual mistrust.
2. Decision making is centralized. Input from lower levels is neither solicited nor desired.
3. Flow of information is restricted to specified channels. Information usually moves downward in the form of orders, policies, procedures, and directions.
4. Employees do not support managerial goals. The organizational climate is characterized by fear, intimidation, and dissatisfaction.
5. Control processes are exercised by management, but an active informal organization usually develops among lower-level personnel in order to resist or oppose managerial control.

We are not overstating the case when we say that much of the scholarship and practice in organizational communication from the 1960s through the 1980s rested on the belief that Likert's participative system 4 represents the ideal climate for which organizations should strive. Characteristics such as those in system 4 have been advocated extensively as prescriptions for effective organizational communication. The **structure of communication** (channels and networks), **communication functions** (purposes, content, and adequacy), and the **quality of communication at interpersonal and group levels** (e.g., superior-subordinate communication, the dynamics of group decision making, and social processes) are regarded as indicators of **organizational communication climate.** Scholars and practitioners (e.g., Goldhaber, 1993; Pace & Faules, 1989) generally have equated the following characteristics of organizational communication climate with organizational effectiveness:

1. Flexible networks with open channels of communication and multidirectional message flow (upward, downward, and lateral).
2. Availability of accurate, adequate information on matters such as work procedures, evaluation of job performance, organizational policies, decisions, and problems.
3. Mutual trust, openness, and supportiveness in superior-subordinate communication.
4. Participation and cohesiveness in group decision making, problem solving, and other task-related processes under "team-oriented" or democratic leadership.

Despite the influence of human resource development concepts in the field of organizational communication, the theory is essentially a managerial approach to employee motivation. It happens to have clear implications for organizational communication, but its primary concern does not differ from earlier scientific, classical, and human relations theories: *the promotion of organizational effectiveness through prescriptions for organizational structure and/or managerial practice.* A complete comparison of traditional, human relations, and human resource development assumptions is presented in table 2.2.

Like the theories that preceded it, human resource development has been criticized for placing too much faith in the power of its prescriptions for virtually any organizational setting. One of the earliest critics was Abraham Maslow himself,

Table 2.2 Comparison of Traditional, Human Relations, and Human Resource Development Assumptions about People. From "Leadership Attitudes Among Public Health Officers," by R. E. Miles, L. W. Porter, and J. A. Craft, 1966, *American Journal of Public Health,* 56, pp. 1990–2005.

Traditional Model	Human Relations Model	Human Resources Model
Assumptions	*Assumptions*	*Assumptions*
1. Work is inherently distasteful to most people.	1. People want to feel useful and important.	1. Work is not inherently distasteful. People want to contribute to meaningful goals which they have helped establish.
2. What they do is less important than what they earn for doing it.	2. People desire to belong and to be recognized as individuals.	2. Most people can exercise far more creative, responsible self-direction and self-control than their present jobs demand.
3. Few want or can handle work which requires creativity, self-direction, or self-control.	3. These needs are more important than money in motivating people to work.	
Policies	*Policies*	*Policies*
1. The manager's basic task is to closely supervise and control his subordinates.	1. The manager's basic task is to make each worker feel useful and important.	1. The manager's basic task is to make use of his "untapped" human resources.
2. He must break tasks down into simple, repetitive, easily learned operations.	2. He should keep his subordinates informed and listen to their objections to his plans.	2. He must create an environment in which all members may contribute to the limits of their ability.
3. He must establish detailed work routines and procedures, and enforce these firmly but fairly.	3. The manager should allow his subordinates to exercise some self-direction and self-control on routine matters.	3. He must encourage full participation on important matters, continually broadening subordinate self-direction and control.
Expectations	*Expectations*	*Expectations*
1. People can tolerate work if the pay is decent and the boss is fair.	1. Sharing information with subordinates and involving them in routine decisions will satisfy their basic needs to belong and to feel important.	1. Expanding subordinate influence, self-direction, and self-control will lead to direct improvement in operating efficiency.
2. If tasks are simple enough and people are closely controlled, they will produce up to standard.	2. Satisfying these needs will improve morale and reduce resistance to formal authority: subordinates will "willingly cooperate."	2. Work satisfaction may improve as a "by-product" of subordinates making full use of their resources.

who expressed concerns that his need hierarchy could not be applied to organizational behavior in the way that McGregor wanted to use it. Maslow confessed, "I'm a little worried about this stuff which I consider tentative being swallowed whole by all sorts of enthusiastic people" (1965, p. 55).

Other critics such as Lawrence and Lorsch (1969) pointed out that no one formula for organizational effectiveness will work in all situations. The conditions of effective organizational performance vary from one situation to another. This position is known as contingency theory. Those who embrace it argue that we should be less concerned with "searching for the panacea of the one best way to organize" and focus more attention on "situational factors that influence organizational performance" (Lawrence & Lorsch, p. 1).

Are such criticisms fair? On the one hand, research and case studies in management and in organizational communication support McGregor and Likert's positions. Many studies of organizational communication have shown that conditions such as participation, openness, supportiveness, and information adequacy are related not only to members' satisfaction (Gibb, 1961; Spiker & Daniels, 1981) but also to member commitment to the organization (Trombetta & Rogers, 1988; Guzley, 1992). One good case example is American Steel and Wire Company as described by Oswald, Scott, and Woerner (1991). AS&W began operating in 1986 in an industry where foreign competition has all but eliminated American firms, yet the company competes effectively and is highly profitable. Oswald, Scott, and Woerner attribute AS&W's success directly to "the philosophy that people are their number-one resource and that quality and customer advantage come from the efforts of hard-working, dedicated 'entrepreneurial' employees" (p. 77). Thus, at AS&W, employees own 18 percent of the company, hire their own coworkers, participate in and chair "customer value teams" to solve work problems or improve performance, and receive the same benefits as managers. Employees as well as managers are salaried, and families are included in many AS&W activities.

There are other success stories in addition to AS&W's. Consider Saturn Corporation's revolution in the American approach to automobile manufacturing, the highly decentralized and distributed management at Johnson and Johnson, and other major efforts at participative management. Despite these successes, the adoption of HRD has been resisted by many American companies, and highly respected scholars remain skeptical of any prescriptive model that promises an effective organization.

Some studies suggest that the skeptics' reservations may be well founded. Investigations conducted in Europe indicate that employee dissatisfaction may result from a highly open communication climate as a consequence of information overload and unrealistic expectations for the results of participative decision making (Wiio, 1978). One study of data from eighteen American organizations found that some organization members who were very well informed were also dissatisfied with their immediate superiors (Daniels & Spiker, 1983). Finally, Pettegrew (1982) presented what he has termed "The S.O.B. Theory of Management" based on a study of a large medical facility where differences in administrators' styles of communication had no apparent impact on their subordinates. Whether the administrators were authoritative or participative, subordinates generally regarded them as S.O.B.s. Pettegrew thought that this might occur because the administrators had to make win-lose decisions in which one group would be helped while another would be hurt. Even though the relationship between adequate or open communication and satisfaction generally is positive, there apparently are important exceptions to this rule.

The Transition to Theory Z

Although many American organizations resisted adoption of human resource development principles during the 1960s and 1970s, these principles caught on very quickly in a country that rose from the ruins of World War II to become an economic giant in the second half of this century. That country is, of course, Japan.

The Japanese industrial establishment became an avid and committed consumer of human resource development ideas that fit very neatly with key values in Japanese culture. These ideas were returned to the United States during the 1980s under the label Japanese Management. According to Matejka and Dunsing (1991), "Japanese Management" is based on a conglomeration of ideas that includes many American principles, beginning with Douglas MacArthur's post-World War II reconstruction plans for Japanese industry and statistical quality control techniques developed by W. E. Deming—techniques initially rejected by American industry, but widely adopted in Japan. Moreover, say Matejka and Dunsing;

A stream of Japanese students have [sic] come to America's best graduate schools over the last few decades to learn about American Management. These students took their best ideas from our best writers and actually put them to use . . . something we still have not done. (p. 55)

It is important to note that the collectivistic Japanese culture with its emphasis on group loyalty provided a more compatible and fertile ground than the individualistic culture of American organizations for the application of human resource development theory, but the fact remains that Japanese industry actually has been more effective than American industry in putting these principles into practice. Matejka and Dunsing point out two key reasons for their success. First, the Japanese have a willingness and capacity "to think long-term and devise strategies and contingency plans to minimize . . . losses" (pp. 55–56). Second, since the Japanese manage by groups, "the rising star in Japanese Management is the one who can consistently, day after day, make decisions that do the most to benefit the entire operation. Whereas selfishness fuels the American star, self-lessness drives the Japanese star" (p. 57).

The Japanese also derive some advantage from the fact that theirs is a highly homogeneous culture, but this should not be taken to mean that cultural diversity is a handicap to American industry. Matejka and Dunsing contend that our great diversity ensures a continuous flow of new ideas and creates great potential for small- to medium-sized companies to respond to the challenge of reinventing our economy. Lest anyone decide, however, that unquestioning acceptance of human resource development will ensure a future burdened by a

$5 trillion national debt, we are obliged to note that the Japanese are not having an easy time of it economically either. Robert Rehder (1981) noted fifteen years ago that pressures common to both Japanese and American organizations were beginning to force both groups to adopt each others' best features, resulting in a new form of organization that Ouchi has called the "Type Z" organization (Ouchi & Jaeger, 1978).

As described by Rehder, traditional American organizations depend on a highly structured hierarchical bureuacracy of the sort envisioned by classical management theorists, that is, a system characterized by fixed positions, rigid lines of authority, centralized decision making, formalized manager-employee relationships, written orders and job descriptions, and individualized performance standards. Although traditional Japanese organizations assuredly are hierarchical, too, the hierarchy is fuzzy. Job descriptions are informal, and decision making is highly decentralized, with heavy reliance on group motivation and performance. Companies take a paternalistic interest in employees and their families. The hybrid or mixed American/Japanese system—Ouchi's Theory Z organization that Rehder regards as the future for both countries—falls somewhere between the two traditional types. Job specialization in the hybrid organization is moderate, but many functions are accomplished through project teams and task forces that may be transient and temporary. Decision making is less centralized and depends on informal consensus seeking. There is a concerted effort to integrate employee and organizational goals, but "written communications and individual responsibility continue to predominate" (Rehder, p. 67).

Recent events have pressed the Japanese to move even more quickly in the direction of Americanization. Powell (1992) noted that the Japanese economy is projected to show little or no growth, an alarming condition that "could trigger profound changes in the way Japan does business" and take Japan "down the slippery slope toward the kind of short-term, run-and-gun capitalism that defined American business" (p. 53) at a time when Japanese workers and managers are openly questioning whether work and organizational commitment should be allowed to dominate their lives.

Summary

When the industrialized world entered the twentieth century, it was apparent that new and clearer concepts of organizational behavior would be required to deal with the complexities of modern society. The first modern perspectives on organizational behavior were developed in the early 1900s when theorists such as Taylor, Fayol, and Weber advanced the basic principles of scientific and classical management. Although the theories of Taylor, Fayol, and Weber differed from one another in some important ways, they generally envisioned organizations as machinelike objects driven by management plan and control. They assumed that individual organization members behave on the basis of rational, economic motivation.

Scientific and classical theories were followed quickly by eclectic theories, such as those developed by Follett and Barnard and by the human relations movement. Follett redefined traditional ideas about the exercise of power in order to achieve integration of different interests. She also emphasized a transactional concept of communication and active "conferencing" between management and employees to achieve pluralistic responsibility. Barnard pointed out oversights in scientific and classical theory regarding the variability of individual behavior in organizations. He argued that compliance depends on individual willingness to cooperate—cooperation that must be induced through incentives such as status and prestige as well as economic motives. His theory of organization structure treated the organization as a communication system.

The human relations movement evolved from various sources of influence, but the basic ideas are typified in the work of Dale Carnegie and Elton Mayo. Both encouraged managers to adopt a "people-oriented" approach to influence and gain compliance. Mayo's theory was based primarily on results of the controversial Hawthorne Studies, which challenged scientific and classical notions by concluding that organizational effectiveness depends more on the social processes of organizations than on management design.

Later, the development of system theory and new concepts in human motivation led to further refinements in organizational theory. Human resource development theory, based on motivational principles of the human need for self-fulfillment, began to compete with earlier human relations and classical/scientific perspectives of organizational behavior. McGregor distinguished between Theory X and Theory Y managerial assumptions, arguing that the Theory Y orientation would lead to effectiveness through development of human resources. Similarly, Likert argued that organizational effectiveness is linked to system 4 participative management. System 4 emphasizes flexible, open communication, relatively accurate, undistorted information, and use of group decision making. Much of the scholarship and practice in the field of organizational communication assumes that system 4 represents the ideal climate for which organizations should strive. The prescriptions of human resource development theory have been criticized in the United States, but the Japanese industrial establishment has actively used HRD principles. Today, economic and competitive pressures are forcing Japanese and American organizations to adopt the best of each others' features.

Discussion Questions/ Activities

1. Observe some samples of organizational communication. On the basis of these observations, would you say that the characteristics of the organization are closer to Likert's system 4 or system 1? Do these characteristics seem to have any relationship to organizational effectiveness?

2. Barnard argued that organization structure should be understood as a communication system. How does this argument differ from earlier classical management ideas about organizational structure?

3. A bureaucratic theorist assumes that an organization is like a machine. A system theorist assumes that an organization is like a living organism. If these two theorists observe the same organization and then report on what they saw, in what ways would the two reports most likely differ?

4. Compare and contrast human relations theory with human resource development theory. Which of these theories do you think is most consistent with the actual behavior of contemporary managers?

Books

Donlon, J. P. (Ed.). (1993). *The best of chief executive*. Homewood, IL: Business One Irwin.

Harris, D. M., & DeSimone, R. L. (1994). *Human resource development*. Ft. Worth, TX: Dryden Press.

Kennedy, C. (1991). *Instant management: The best ideas from people who have made a difference in how we manage*. New York: Morrow.

Vickstaff, S. (Ed.). (1992). *Human resource management in Europe*. London: Chapman & Hall.

Web Sites

http://www.alaska.net/~hrmd/
   Blankinship & Associates human resource development consulting firm in Anchorage Alaska.

http://ottawa.microworks.ca/hrd/home.htm
   Target Communication Management's showcase of human resource development products and services.

http://www-ts.cs.oberlin.edu/cs339/metz/metz.html
   A resource list for human resource management and human resource development fields.

Additional Resources

Barnard, C. (1938). *The functions of the executive*. Cambridge, MA: Harvard University Press.

Carey, A. (1967). The Hawthorne Studies: A radical criticism. *American Sociological Review, 30,* 403–416.

Carnegie, D. (1936). *How to win friends and influence people*. New York: Simon & Schuster.

Daniels, T. D., & Spiker, B. K. (1983). Social exchange and the relationship between information adequacy and relational satisfaction. *Western Journal of Speech Communication, 47,* 118–137.

Dessler, G. (1980). *Organization theory: Integrating structure and behavior.* Englewood Cliffs, NJ: Prentice-Hall.

Fayol, H. (1949). *General and industrial management* (Constance Storrs, Trans.). London: Sir Isaac Putnam.

Follett, M. P. (1982a). Power. In E. M. Fox & L. Urwick (Eds.), *Dynamic administration: The collected papers of Mary Parker Follett*. New York: Hippocrene Books.

Follett, M. P. (1982b). The influence of employee representation in a remoulding of the accepted type of business manager. In E. M. Fox & L. Urwick (Eds.), *Dynamic administration: The collected papers of Mary Parker Follett*. New York: Hippocrene Books.

Fox, E. M., & Urwick, L. (Eds.). (1982). *Dynamic administration: The collected papers of Mary Parker Follett*. New York: Hippocrene Books.

Franke, R. H., & Kaul, J. D. (1978). The Hawthorne experiments: First statistical reinterpretation. *American Sociological Review, 43,* 623–643.

Gibb, J. (1961). Defensive communication. *Journal of Communication, 11,* 141–148.

Goldhaber, G. M. (1993). *Organizational communication* (6th ed.). Dubuque, IA: Brown & Benchmark.

Guzley, R. M. (1992). Organizational climate and communication climate: Predictors of commitment to the organization. *Management Communication Quarterly, 5,* 379–402.

Landsberger, H. (1958). *Hawthorne revisited*. Ithaca, NY: Cornell University Press.

Lawrence, P., & Lorsch, J. (1969). *Organization and environment: Managing differentiation and integration*. Homewood, IL: Irwin.

References

Likert, R. (1961). *New patterns of management.* New York: McGraw-Hill.

Maslow, A. H. (1954). *Motivation and personality.* New York: Harper & Row.

Maslow, A. H. (1965). *Eupsychian management.* Homewood, IL: Richard D. Irwin.

Matejka, K., & Dunsing, D. (1991). Japanese/American management myths. *Business Horizons, 34,* 54–57.

Mayo, E. (1947). *The human problems of an industrial civilization.* Boston: Harvard Business School.

McGregor, D. (1960). *The human side of enterprise.* New York: McGraw-Hill.

Miles, R. (1965). Keeping informed: Human relations or human resources. *Harvard Business Review, 43,* 148–163.

Miles, R. E., Porter, L. W., & Craft, J. A. (1966). Leadership attitudes among public health officers. *American Journal of Public Health, 56,* pp. 1990–2005.

Oswald, S., Scott, C., & Woerner, W. (1991). Strategic management of human resources: The American Steel and Wire Company. *Business Horizons, 34,* 77–92.

Ouchi, W., & Jaeger, A. (1978, April). Type Z: Organizational stability in the midst of mobility. *Academy of Management Review,* 305–314.

Pace, R. W., & Faules, D. F. (1989). *Organizational communication* (2nd ed.). Englewood Cliffs, NJ: Prentice-Hall.

Pettegrew, L. S. (1982). Organizational communication and the S.O.B. theory of management. *Western Journal of Speech Communication, 46,* 179–191.

Powell, B. And after the fall? *Newsweek,* April 20, 1992, 53–55.

Redding, W. C. (1979). Organizational communication theory and ideology: An overview. In D. Nimmo (Ed.), *Communication yearbook 3.* New Brunswick, NJ: Transaction Books.

Rehder, R. R. (1981). What American and Japanese managers are learning from each other. *Business Horizons, 24,* 63–70.

Roethlisberger, F. L., & Dickson, W. (1939). *Management and the worker.* New York: John Wiley & Sons.

Spiker, B. K., & Daniels, T. D. (1981). Information adequacy and communication relationships: An empirical examination of 18 organizations. *Western Journal of Speech Communication, 45,* 342–354.

Taylor, F. W. (1947). *Principles of scientific management.* New York: Harper & Brothers.

Trombetta, J. J., & Rogers, D. P. (1988). Communication climate, job satisfaction, and organizational commitment. *Management Communication Quarterly, 1,* 494–514.

United States Postal Service (1979). *Organization structures manual.* Chapter 1, part 130, sec. 153.21.

Weber, M. (1947). *The theory of social and economic organizations* (A. M. Henderson & T. Parsons, Trans.; T. Parsons, Ed.). New York: Oxford University Press.

Weber, M. (1969). Bureaucracy (H. H. Gerth & C. W. Mills, Trans.). In J. A. Litterer (Ed.), *Organizations: Structure and behavior.* New York: John Wiley & Sons.

Wiio, O. A. (1978). *Contingencies of organizational communication: Studies in organization and organizational communication* (Research Rep. No. 1A771218). Helsinki: Institute for Human Communication.

CHAPTER 3

ORGANIZATION THEORY:
METAPHORS OF BIOLOGY

Outline

In chapter 2 we saw how answers to the managerial problem of motivating organization members to perform developed from the mechanistic accounts of economic exchange in scientific and classical theories to satisfaction of social needs in human relations theory and self-actualization and participation in human resource development. All of these theories are at some level theories of motivation, that is, the causes of action, and they offer prescriptions for organizational effectiveness and the conduct of management. At the same time that these theories were maturing, other theories were in development that embraced a different set of concerns by looking to the field of biology for organizational metaphors. These theories are not concerned with the managerial problem of member motivation in and of itself, but with the broader problem of understanding the structure, function, and development of human systems and the people who constitute these systems. The basic metaphor in these theories is the organization as an **adaptive organism** rather than a machine operated solely by management control. We will consider three such theories in this chapter.

The first of these theories, **system theory,** attempts to understand organizations with the same principles that are used to understand living organisms. The second, **equivocality reduction theory,** uses and enhances system theory, but also metaphorically incorporates evolutionary theory to explain organizing and organizational communication. The third area is the psychosocial application of evolutionary theory in the emerging field of **evolutionary psychology,** where the use of evolutionary theory is no longer merely metaphorical, but quite literal.

A System Theory

System theory is the product of work begun in the field of philosophy during the nineteenth century and expanded by many scholars in various fields during the twentieth century. Much of the formal elaboration of system theory was presented in Ludwig von Bertalanffy's *General System Theory* (1968), first published in the 1950s. Bertalanffy, a Canadian biologist, wanted to develop a set of concepts and principles that would apply generally to any type of system (hence, the label general system theory).

The perspective that Bertalanffy and other early system theorists developed soon was adapted to the study of organizations in works by March and Simon (1958), Katz and Kahn (1966), and Huse and Bowditch (1973). The influence of system theory in the study of organizational communication also has been substantial. For example, Farace, Monge, and Russell (1977) developed a structural-functional model of organizational communication that is drawn directly from systems principles. Karl Weick's (1979) equivocality reduction theory that we will discuss in the next section also came out of systems theory.

Gary Kreps (1990) has adapted Weick's work along with other systems principles to provide the foundation for an entire text on organizational communication. Even before publication of Bertalanffy's major works, Chester Barnard had presented some systems principles in his theory of organizational structure (Dessler, 1980; Littlejohn, 1992). As Monge pointed out, "Organizational communication has predominantly been studied from the viewpoint of system theory" (1982, p. 245).

System theory provided a new analogy for the study of organizations and organizational communication—the living organism. While scientific and classical scholars regarded the organization as a machinelike object operated by management control, system theorists stressed the point that organizations are more like living creatures than machines. Organizations experience birth, development, and death. They are dynamic entities that act in purposeful ways. System theory relies on several important concepts in order to explain the organismic characteristics of organizations. These concepts include wholeness, hierarchy, openness, and feedback.

Wholeness

A system is a set of elements bound together in interdependent relationships. Elements in a system are interdependent in the sense that they affect one another. If the relationships are highly interdependent, a change in one part of the system can lead to changes throughout the entire system. This interdependence among parts or elements results in an integrated whole.

Wholeness means that the effect of elements working in relationship to one another differs from the effect of their isolated, individual actions taken collectively. This effect is sometimes referred to as synergy—a condition in which the whole is greater than the sum of its parts. Perhaps you have experienced synergy as a participant in group problem solving. For example, a group of advertising professionals might "brainstorm" in order to generate a novel, creative idea for promoting a product. As they interact, they build on and modify one anothers' ideas until they arrive at a workable concept. Suppose that we ask these same professionals to generate ideas by working in isolation from one another, then we collect and list the ideas that they produce. We might see many of the same ideas that would appear in a group brainstorming session, but the list would not include ideas that emerged as a result of interaction within the group, and it probably would provide barely a hint of the final solution that the group developed. The individuals working as an integrated group (system) produced something greater than they would have produced in a simple collection of isolated, individual efforts. We cannot simply "add up" their individual actions in order to understand how they function as a system.

Hierarchy

The relationships among elements in a system are specified by rules. One of the more important rules is the principle of **hierarchy.** Elements are organized into subsystems. Subsystems are related to one another to form the system. The system itself operates within a larger environment. In an organization, we might think of the elements as individual human beings; subsystems as work groups, departments, or divisions; and the system as the entire organization.

As we already have seen in this chapter, the principle of hierarchy applies readily to most western organizations. Even organizations that depart from traditional ideas about division of labor, unity of command, and unity of direction can still be characterized by a basic system hierarchy—elements, subsystems, system, and environment. This type of hierarchy occurs in new contemporary structures such as matrixed organizations. Matrix structures are intended to give organizations great flexibility in responding to specialized, temporary needs. Consider the case of Universal Products Company (UPC) as described by Mee (1964). UPC has four product divisions (automotive, electrical, chemical, and aerospace). Each division consists of five basic departments (production, engineering, materials, personnel, and accounting). In this form, UPC is a traditionally structured organization, but a major departure from this concept occurs in the aerospace division, as illustrated in figure 3.1.

Aerospace has three major, but temporary, projects underway (Venus, Mars, and Saturn). Each of the three projects is directed by a manager who has full authority and responsibility for its completion. Each project manager has been assigned personnel from the five departments in the aerospace division. Until completion of the project, the manager decides on tasks, work schedules, promotions, and salary increases for those personnel who are assigned to the project. A purchasing agent who normally would report to the manager of the materials department now reports to a project manager as well. Sometimes, the project manager has total control over personnel assigned to a project, but a project manager's control in many matrixed organizations is shared with functional department heads in the regular line organization. In this case, any individual organization

Figure 3.1
Matrix organization.
(From "Matrix organizations,"
by J. Mee, 1964, *Business
Horizons, 7,* pp. 92–95.
Adapted by permission.)

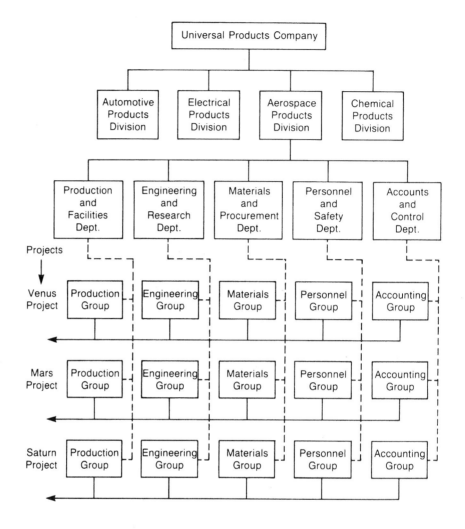

member literally participates in two subsystems at once, fulfilling functions as a regular department member and as a project team member, while reporting to two different superiors. The use of such matrix structures handily illustrates the power of organizational systems to adapt to changing circumstances.

Openness

Systems may be regarded as relatively open or closed. **Open systems** are characterized by active exchange with their outside environment. Organizations are open systems. They take in energy and materials (input), transform this input in some way (throughput), then return products and by-products of throughput to the environment (output).

When the environment is stable, it is tempting to ignore the fact that organizations are open systems. Given a stable environment, an organization is able to operate in a steady, machinelike state. Its performance is regular and routine because nothing in the environment demands anything else. Under such conditions, the organization seems to be a closed, static system that is unaffected by its environment. This view is deceptively simple and can be hazardous when the environment changes in some dramatic way.

During the 1960s, executives in the automobile industry seemed to see their corporations in much the same way as their cars—well-engineered machines continually getting bigger and better through managerial design. The rise of foreign competition and the energy crisis of the 1970s quickly taught auto companies that they are, indeed, open systems faced with a demand to adapt to a changing and sometimes turbulent environment. General Motors and Ford made fundamental changes to respond to unanticipated consumer demand for smaller, more efficient cars. Chrysler was saved from bankruptcy only by government-backed loans. American Motors barely clung to life by creating linkages with Jeep and Renault. When the corporations recovered, they were smaller and leaner. Thousands of workers were laid off with no hope of ever recovering their old jobs, and many auto dealers went out of business.

Feedback

Open systems are characterized by two basic processes: maintenance and adaptation. **Maintenance processes** are regulatory. They are intended to keep certain system conditions within acceptable ranges. **Adaptive processes** bring about change and growth. Both of these processes depend on **feedback** responses to system actions that provide information for use in adjusting system conditions.

Feedback may be negative or positive. **Negative feedback** indicates deviations from desired conditions. The system adjusts by correcting the deviation. Maintenance processes depend on negative feedback. These processes involve the same principle of dynamic balance associated with deficiency needs in motivation. Suppose that a small manufacturing company wants to maintain a product inventory of 175 to 225 finished units at all times, with an ideal inventory of 200 units. If the inventory rises above 225 because sales slow down, someone sends negative feedback to the production department to ease back on production until the inventory is reduced. If the inventory falls below 175, production receives negative feedback to speed up until the shortage is corrected.

In contrast to negative feedback, **positive feedback** reinforces deviations rather than signaling for a correction. Positive feedback is used to create new system conditions rather than to maintain old ones. This form of feedback is the basis for change and adaptation. For example, government willingness to guarantee loans for Chrysler only if the corporation would adapt to its environment provided an incentive that led to many fundamental changes in the corporate structure, leadership, and products. If Chrysler people wanted to survive as a corporation, they were going to have to act in entirely new ways. As the changes were initiated, public acceptance provided positive reinforcement for Chrysler to continue the adaptation process.

Of course, feedback in living, open systems is not simply a mechanical process of automatic response to deviation-correcting or reinforcing messages. Roger D'Aprix (1982) tells a story about an employee-communications department in a large corporation that decided to publish an article in the corporate magazine about the company's employee-compensation system. When the article was submitted to the personnel department for review, the employee-compensation manager, who feared that the story revealed too much, rejected it. The personnel department proposed a "revision" in the article that would have made it unintelligible to most readers. The employee-communications department appeared to have two options: run the revised version or drop the story. The department manager chose a third path—convincing the compensation manager that most of the personnel department's fears were unfounded. The article that finally appeared in print was based on a compromise between the two managers.

D'Aprix's story is an excellent illustration of informal negotiations in management ranks, the politics of organizational decision making, and even Eisenberg's (1984) principles of strategic ambiguity. It also demonstrates several important points about feedback in episodes of communication that are acted out every day in thousands of organizations. First, deviations from desired conditions often are defined by human values instead of by physical circumstances. The compensation manager's desire to conceal information about compensation decisions provided the standard for judging the acceptability of the article. Second, the recipient of feedback may choose to act on it in various ways or even ignore it. The communications manager did not simply make the changes that the compensation manager wanted but chose another action instead. Finally, organizational subsystems and individuals influence each other through *reciprocal* feedback and may employ different standards for evaluating and responding to feedback. The personnel and employee-communications departments differed in their assessments of the article's acceptability. The personnel department's rejection was negative feedback. The communications department's response to rejection also was, in effect, a form of feedback. The solution to the conflict emerged from an interaction between the two departments, not from one unit's mechanical acquiescence to feedback from another.

Taken collectively, the basic concepts of system theory—wholeness, hierarchy, openness, and feedback—provide a dynamic view of organizations in action. System theory has been influential in the study of organizational communication because it places the organizing role of communication in a new light (Littlejohn, 1992). Communication is not merely an activity that occurs "within" an organization, nor is communication merely a tool for managerial control. Rather, all of the human processes that define an organization arise from communication. Relationships among individual organization members are defined through communication. The linkages and interactions among subsystems depend on communication and information flow. All feedback processes involve communication.

A good example of the influence of system theory on management and organizational theory is in the development of the contingency theory that we mentioned earlier in criticisms of human resource development theory. Lawrence and Lorsch (1969) and Joan Woodward (1958) used a system perspective in large studies of industrial companies that led them to doubt the universal effectiveness of any one approach to management and organization. Instead, Lawrence and Lorsch concluded that effectiveness depends upon the "fit" between organizational attributes and the environment, while Woodward found that the most successful organizations were those in which management practices were consistent with the technical processes of production, and these processes varied across industries.

Despite the influence of system theory on management theory and the popularity of system theory in the field of organizational communication, its impact on organizational communication research actually has been very limited. What does one do after declaring the newfound revelation that organizations are open systems? So far, this question has received only partial and incomplete answers (Monge, Farace, Eisenberg, Miller, & White, 1984). We have been much more successful in talking about organizational communication with the vocabulary of system theory than we have been in using system theory as a basis for our research. At the very least, however, system theory has provided us with a different and potentially powerful set of ideas and assumptions to frame our thinking about organizational communication, and there are more studies these days that do depend clearly upon a systems theory foundation (e.g., Lee & Jablin, 1995).

Equivocality Reduction Theory

One of the more important products of system theory in the study of organizational communication is Karl Weick's theory that organizing and communicating activities are directed toward the reduction of equivocality in information. Most writers refer to this theory as Weick's theory of organizing because equivocality reduction is only one part of it. We call it the equivocality reduction theory because we think it happens to be the most important part of Weick's theory. Here is how it works.

Basic Concepts

First, we begin with the systems principle that organizations function in an environment and are influenced by the environment along with Weick's observation that late twentieth century organizational environments generally are complicated and often turbulent. Change and uncertainty abound. The information that an organization must process about its environment in order to function effectively also can be very complicated and equivocal. Information is **equivocal** when it can be given different interpretations because it is ambiguous, conflicted, obscure, or introduces an element of uncertainty into a situation.

In order to understand the connection between equivocality reduction and organizational communication, compare the way we handle routine, run-of-the-mill situations with the way in which we respond to unexpected events or a crisis. Situations that we understand to be "routine" are routine precisely because they have predictable regularities. In a routine situation, a stable set of **rules** defines the situation and tells us how to act in that situation. Consider, for example, the rules that define placing and getting a food order at a McDonald's. It makes no difference whether the McDonald's is in Kalamazoo, Michigan or half way around the world in Singapore; you know what to expect when you walk into one. In spite of the cultural differences between the United States and Singapore, the rules that define the McDonald's experience are essentially the same in both places. You know where to place your order, where to look for the menu, how your order will be transacted with the counter person, about how long it will take to get it, and even how your Big Mac, fries, and a Coke will taste. There is little if any equivocality in the situation. And because there is little equivocality, there is little need for communication to reduce it. The execution of your transaction at McDonald's is communicatively simple and neatly sterile, whether it occurs in Michigan or Singapore.

Now suppose that you went to a table service restaurant instead of a fast-food place. You and your date have just finished a meal, and the server has delivered your check on a small tray. You have had two different kinds of past experiences with this procedure. Sometimes the check-on-a-tray means that the server is coming back in a few minutes to retrieve the check along with your credit card in order to handle the payment transaction for you. And sometimes it means that you are supposed to take the check to the cashier yourself. Which is it this time? Resolving this kind of uncertainty requires a bit more communicative effort. For example, you say to your date, "I wonder if the server is coming back for this." Your date replies, "Oh yes. They always do that here." You thank your date for this information, although it may have introduced another element of uncertainty, that is, with whom did your date last dine at this restaurant?

The check-on-the-tray is an example of simple uncertainty. What happens in highly novel or equivocal situations? Crisis situations certainly are not the only circumstances in which organizations confront high levels of uncertainty and equivocality, but they lend themselves readily to our purposes here because the very idea of a crises means that something out of the ordinary has happened. Consider what may happen in a community that has been hit by some natural disaster such as a flood or tornado. You may have heard stories in such situations that the disaster actually "brought the community closer together" in some way. Why? Because the rules for managing routine situations are useless in the crisis. People are compelled to interact and communicate in order to figure out what do to, that is, in order to manage and reduce the equivocality in the situation. Someone who is trained to respond to the specific kind of crisis (e.g., a Red Cross worker or an emergency medical technician) does not experience the same equivocality in the situation, but training is, in a sense, communicating in advance to manage the equivocality of an emergency before it actually happens. Communication still has to occur in order to figure out what will be done, even if this occurs before the crisis.

Fundamental Propositions

These somewhat simplified examples get us to three fundamental propositions in Weick's theory. First, where environmental inputs (information) have little equivocality, organizations can rely heavily on rules to guide their responses, just as most of us probably have done at one time or another in managing our way through a transaction at McDonald's. As equivocality increases, organizations are less able to rely on rules. Second, as equivocality increases, more communicative effort is required to respond to it. This is what we often see in crisis situations, and even in an episode as simple as the check-on-the-tray. Weick has a special term for communication in this case. It is called an **interlocked behavior cycle**, which consists of a **double-interact**. Person A says something to B, B replies to A, and A provides an adjustment message (e.g., a confirmation, request for clarification, etc.) to B. For example, "I wonder if the server is coming back for this." "Oh yes. They always do that here." "Thanks. Now I know what to expect." Strictly speaking, Weick does not talk about the relationship between equivocality and communication, but the relationship between equivocality and interlocked behavior cycles. As equivocality increases, the use of interlocked behavior cycles (i.e., communication) increases in an effort to reduce the equivocality. This leads us to the third point. All of this happens because equivocality makes rules less useful. As equivocality increases, we are less able to rely on rules to handle the situation.

The Evolutionary Metaphor

We mentioned earlier that Weick not only relies on system theory but also uses the analogy of evolutionary processes in his theory. In the Darwinian version of evolutionary theory, known as natural selection, the members of a species exhibit **variations** in their makeup. These variations are, of course, genetic, although Darwin certainly did not know this in 1859. The connection to genetics did not occur until well into the twentieth century. Some genetic variations will turn out to be more adaptive than others, that is, they will help the organism to survive in a given environment. The fittest organisms, namely, those whose variations are the most adaptive, get to pass on their traits through reproduction. Thus, the adaptive traits are **selected** for continuation and eventually **retained** as characteristics of the species. Natural selection explains how whales evolved from a land mammal, how humans and apes sprang from a common ancestor millions of years ago, and why bacteria are able to develop resistance to antibiotic drugs.

The idea of using Darwin's theory of the evolution of biological organisms as an analogy to explain sociocultural adaptation has been around for more than thirty years (e.g., Campbell, 1965). This approach uses the same concepts of variation, selection, and adaptation. Here the variations are behavioral, and they occur in the face of environmental stresses. Gary Kreps (1990) explained most succinctly the premise of this theory and the way that Weick uses it:

The most advantageous variations are selected by the cultural group for use and retained as functional attributes of the cultural group. Weick borrows this three-stage model of adaptation [variation, selection, and retention of behaviors], modifying it to the three phases of organizing: enactment, selection, and retention. (p. 113)

The idea of **enactment** in Weick's theory means that human beings do not just passively respond to conditions in an environment. We attend actively to the environment and selectively interpret it, recognizing the level of equivocality in the information that we have. The selection phase begins when we make decisions about the rules and interlocked (communication) cycles that we will use to manage the equivocality. Remember that routine rules are of little use in the highly equivocal situation, so we depend on creating communication cycles. To the extent that the cycles created in this process are successful in reducing equivocality, they are retained for future use. In effect, they become new rules that may guide the organization's actions in future situations.

Retrospective Sense-Making

Our reading of Weick's theory is fairly similar to the reading provided by Gary Kreps, but to emphasize the point that we just made about selective interpretation, all communication scholars do not read Weick in the same way, and one important variation is found in Eisenberg and Goodall's (1993) emphasis on selection and retention of *interpretions* rather than selection and retention of interlocked behavior cycles. In their reading,

Once an environment is enacted, organizing requires that participants select from a number of possible alternative explanations of what the environment means. Selection is collective sense-making and is accomplished through communication. Finally, those interpretations that are believed to work, or make sense, are retained for future use. (p. 109)

There clearly is some merit in looking at Weick's theory in the way that Eisenberg and Goodall do because another important idea that Weick has about organizational communication is the concept of **retrospective sense-making**. Most modern management and organization theories, beginning with scientific management and classical organization theory, assume that organizational behavior is (or at least should be) rational in character, that is, planned, calculated, and directed toward goals. Weick contends that organizational behavior is not so much rational as it is *rationalized*. What if intentions and motives do not really exist prior to action? What if they are only accounts that we construct to explain our behavior *after* we have already done it? In a simple sense, retrospective sense-making means that we construct interpretations of organizational experiences and actions by reflecting upon them.

The concept of retrospective sense-making has something in common with the concept of socially constructed reality in the interpretive perspective on organizational communication. Both depend on the idea that human beings figure out what things mean through constitutive interpretation. We puzzle and mull over, fret and stew over, and generally select, manipulate, and transform meanings to come up with an interpretation of a situation. In this sense, we construct reality. Interpretive theory adds to this the idea that much of this interpretive process is carried out through interaction with our fellow members of the organization. Hence, the result is a *socially* constructed reality.

Weick may have carried this idea a little too far by implying that human beings do not plan when most of us clearly think that we do, but consider as an example a situation that unfolded as we were finishing this edition in December of 1995. President Clinton had decided to send American soldiers to Bosnia in order to support a peace agreement. Russia agreed to join in this effort, combining its forces with the Americans under American command. At the same time, highly sophisticated, intelligence-gathering Russian submarines were detected near the coasts of California and Georgia, obviously spying on U. S. military operations at both locations. How does one make sense of such a contradiction? The rationalist would say that we have to get all of the facts, then work through them systematically for an explanation that fits the facts. The interpretivist would say that facts as well as explanations get constituted in interpretation. Interpretations do not correspond to objective truths; they are instead intersubjective agreements.

Aside from the prospect that Weick's theory might provide a good account of the scramble by officials in the U. S. State Department to figure out what was going on, how could we ever know for sure why the Russian military was allying with us in Bosnia and spying on us in California? The State Department's final interpretation might not depend as much upon the cold rationality of logic as it depends upon the warm comfort of affect. Put another way, will the interpretation feel good because it fits the facts, or will it fit the facts because it feels good?

The concepts of equivocality reduction through interlocked behavior cycles, the evolutionary analogy of the process, and retrospective sense-making are some of Weick's more important contributions to the study of organizational communication, but there are more Weickean notions that we will discuss in later chapters.

Evolutionary Psychology and Sociobiology

As we noted in chapter 1, traditional, interpretive, and critical perspectives on organizational communication do not agree on very much, but they do seem to embrace one common idea: human beings become what they are through learning, socialization, and acculturation. Generally, whether we are talking about human cooperation or human conflict, learning is the mechanism that is invoked to explain why human beings think, feel, and act as they do. We can call this the presumption of **environmental determinism**, namely, the idea that who we are and what we do is a product of environmental influences, including the physical, social, and cultural environment. The most extreme version of environmental determinism is found in theories where humans are described as little more than passive reactors to environmental stimuli (e.g., the behaviorist school of psychology represented by B. F. Skinner). Even those theories that regard human beings as active, choice-making agents situate that choice making within cultural constraints and implicitly privilege culture as the enabler of human action (Anderson, 1987).

Because environmental determinism is so thoroughly ingrained as a bedrock premise of modern social science, any suggestion that biology, genetics, and evolution might have something to do not just with the physical characteristics of human beings but also with our psychological and, therefore, behavioral and social characteristics is met with scalding attacks, even attacks by some prominent evolutionists such as Stephen Jay Gould (1978). But this is precisely the suggestion with which the fields of **evolutionary psychology** and its more controversial cousin, **sociobiology**, confront us.

Nature vs. Nurture: A False Dichotomy?

The debate over this question often is presented as the "nature vs. nuture" controversy, that is, is behavior biologically determined (nature) or socially acquired (nuture)? Early in this century, the nature side of the question received a great deal of attention, especially in European scholarship. Misuses of the scholarship, however, most notably in Nazi Germany, and plain factual errors in Social Darwinism led to widespread rejection of biological or genetic explanations of human action. American scholars, who favored nurture theories anyway, essentially dismissed any role for biology at all in understanding human society. But looking at the problem only in terms of these two alternatives (nature vs. nuture) misrepresents the issue (Barlow, 1991). While some theorists absolutely insist that human behavior is entirely a socio-cultural product that has no genetic, biological basis (e.g., Lewontin, 1977), others suggest that both biology and culture shape what we are (e.g., Bouchard & McGue, 1990; Nielsen, 1994; Udry, 1995). If the advocates of environmental-biological interaction are correct, the nature vs. nuture dichotomy is a false one. This is essentially the position that is taken by evolutionary psychologists and sociobiologists.

The Theory of Evolutionary Psychology

One of the major premises in evolutionary psychology is that human behavior and, by extension, culture are influenced by **innate psychological mechanisms** in human beings that did not develop under modern conditions but evolved into their present form during the Pleistocene Epoch, which ended over 10,000 years ago (Tooby & Cosmides, 1989). Although cultural change began to move faster than biological evolution in the Neolithic (Stone Age) period, modern behavior is nonetheless evolutionarily patterned. Identifying Pleistocene mechanisms that might continue to reverberate in modern behavior actually is one of the tasks that evolutionary pyschologists have set for their field, so we are a long way from seeing anything like a taxonomy of such mechanisms, but here are a few examples:

- factors predisposing males to compete aggressively for sexual opportunities and predisposing females to be more concerned with relationships than with sexual opportunities per se (Studd & Gattiker, 1991);

- factors predisposing young children and elderly adults to aggregate in large, protective groups (Burgess, 1989);

- factors predisposing interaction patterns among unrelated individuals (Kofoed, 1989).

Attributing to Pleistocene psychological mechanisms a predisposing influence on modern behavior does not mean that our behavior is biologically determined, nor does it deny the significance of cultural dynamics in human experience. Even our primate cousins, the Pan troglodytes (known also as chimpanzees), seem to exhibit primitive forms of social learning that are at least analogous to cultural transmission in human society, for example, tool use and food-gathering techniques (McGrew, 1994). On the other hand, biological accounts of human behavior take on intuitive appeal when we see that our primate cousins share some characteristics with us ranging from empathy and conflict mediation to dominance seeking and even murder of their own kind (Liska, 1990; Miller, 1995), especially when there is no basis for concluding that the Pan troglodytes "learned" how to do these things.

The point of evolutionary psychology is that human behavior arises from an interaction of the present environment with the evolutionary heritage of a past epoch, that is, the evolved and innate psychological mechanisms of the Pleistocene with which modern human beings come into the world fully equipped. As explained by John Tooby and Leda Cosmides, "By directly regulating individual behavior and learning, these mechanisms directly govern cultural dynamics" (1989, p. 30). This statement should not be misunderstood as an argument for biological determinism. It is instead a recognition that human beings construct the conditions of their cultures and a claim that constructing behavior is influenced by an essentially Pleistocene psyche.

Tooby and Cosmides have developed one of the foundational discussions of the theory of evolutionary psychology and the generation of human culture. To begin with, there appears to be no modern connection between evolutionary adaptation and cultural dynamics. Such an admission would make environmental determinists happy, but it is coupled with the observation that much so-called culturally constructed human behavior clearly is *not* adaptive or fitness-promoting under modern conditions. On the other hand, such behaviors might be predicted quite well from a knowledge of underlying psychological mechanisms evolved at a time when they would have been adaptive. How does evolutionary psychology go about doing this? Here is a simplied version of the method described by Tooby and Cosmides:

1. Identify the adaptive problems that Pleistocene humans had to solve;
2. Determine as nearly as possible how these adaptive problems might have presented themselves under Pleistocene conditions;
3. Specify the information-processing conditions that must be met to solve the adaptive problem;
4. Devise models of the cognitive structures that could have evolved to solve the problem;
5. Determine which is the best model;
6. Compare the model to behavior produced under modern conditions. If the model works, it should predict behaviors that are produced by information inputs in the modern environment.

The quality of studies employing the discipline of evolutionary psychology is, to put it charitably, highly variable. Tooby and Cosmides themselves caution that one cannot simply skip steps 2 through 5 by moving directly from step 1 to step 6, and some studies appear to shortcut the method in exactly this way. Well-constructed studies, however, have shown good predictions of behavior in modern environments with hypotheses drawn from evolutionary assumptions.

Organizational Applications

Studies in evolutionary psychology have involved many sociopsychological phenomena, but the only ones of relevance to us are those conducted in organizational environments or addressing processes that occur in organizational environments. We will consider one example here, namely, a study of sexual harassment in the workplace (Studd & Gattiker, 1990). This study is a useful example to consider because it not only concerns the organizational environment but also provides a biological account of aspects of human interaction.

Studd and Gattiker began their project with the general purpose of determining whether the theory of evolutionary psychology can explain human behavior in "the most artificial and 'unnatural' of all social environments, the modern organizational workplace" (p. 250). Because sociosexual behavior is one area where the operation of domain-specific psychological mechanisms for the reproductive strategy of each sex has been demonstrated, they elected to explore this area in general and sexual harassment in particular. For their purposes, sexual harassment was defined to include only cases of uninvited sexual attention, for example, sexual advances, coercion, bribery, and imposition.

Using evolutionary premises about sex-specific reproductive strategies, Studd and Gattiker devised a model from which they derived nine specific predictions about patterns of sexual harassment in the workplace. The basic evolutionary premises are essentially that human males in an environment of evolutionary adaptedness would try to maximize reproductive success aggressively by competing for and seeking out opportunities for sex with females of high reproductive value. In contrast, females, because of the demands of pregnancy and parental investment, would want to limit their sexual accessibility to long-term exchange for economic resources and/or parental investment with carefully chosen partners.

We will not detail all nine predictions, but you probably can guess some of them without much effort, for example, that women are far more likely than men to be harassed or that women of reproductive age, especially those younger and single, are most likely to experience harassment. Other predictions may not be quite so obvious, for example, that females who initiate sexual harassment of males are also more likely to be young and single. The important point is that each prediction is grounded on evolved psychological mechanisms.

Studd and Gattiker relied on data from dozens of other studies to test their predictions. They found generally that patterns of sexual harassment in modern organizations conform to the predictions derived from an evolutionary model, although two predictions regarding specific motives of both male and female harassers could not be examined with the available data. Recognizing that one serious limitation of this kind of theory testing is the potential for competing theories to explain the same results, Studd and Gattiker also considered other theories of workplace sexual harassment (e.g., the hypotheses that sexual harassment is a function of power exercise, sex-role spill-over, or sex-segregation). They showed how sex-role spill-over and segregation theories could be enhanced by and subsumed under the evolutionary explanation and that significant predictions from the power hypothesis are not supported in studies. Thus, they conclude that "evolutionary psychology provides the most coherent theory to date for the gender differences . . . and behavioral variation in initiation of, and reaction to, sexual advances in the workplace" (p. 285).

Sociobiology and the Politics of Science

Although evolutionary psychologists have worked to refine both their theory and their method, the premises with which they begin are quite provocative and continue to draw criticism. Sociobiology, an even more controversial field of study introduced by Harvard biologist E. O. Wilson in 1975, has been the subject of especially acrimonious debate. The basic premise of sociobiology is very straightforward: Human social behavior is influenced by functions of kinship that are genetic, not cultural. The treatise was attacked by scientists from a wide range of disciplines almost immediately as a claim of genetic determinism that would legitimize everything from racism to economic inequities (Kitcher, 1985; Wade, 1976). Although more perceptive critics such as Gould have focused on theoretic problems with importation of evolutionary theory into the social sphere with criticisms that might actually improve the theory, most of the criticism clearly has its basis in political and moral concerns.

Much of the concern appears to flow from an anxiety that is not altogether unwarranted: If behavior can be attributed to evolutionary origins, then it must be natural and perhaps even inevitable. Those who would abuse such attributions can then claim that there is no point in trying to alter culturally even the most outrageous injustices and immoralities. This condition certainly occurred in Nazi Germany, and you may recall that Richard Herrnstein and Charles Murray's inflammatory book, *The Bell Curve* (1994), claimed hereditary intelligence differences between groups as a basis for arguing against the usefulness of government social programs for the disadvantaged.

Clearly, the work of evolutionary psychology and sociobiology can be abused, and responsible evolutionary psychologists and sociobiologists go to great lengths to point out that biological influence is not the same thing as biological determinism, and even where evolutionary and biological influences are demonstrated, the demonstration is not a warrant for tolerating a socially repugnant behavior (Wilson, 1976; Studd and Gattiker, 1991).

Behavioral Genetics and Work Values

Aside from the need to guard evolutionary psychology and sociobiology from abuse, the more direct question is the degree to which psychological mechanisms are evolved and therefore tied to genetics. These fields can answer the question only in the most indirect way by modeling conditions that might have existed many thousands of years in the past and by testing predictions from those models in the modern environment. One group of U.S. researchers associated with Thomas Bouchard, Jr. at the University of Minnesota's Institute for Human Genetics has found a somewhat more direct way to get at the problem. This group began by studying factors such as intelligence but has now moved into the study of how individuals approach and respond to their work environments, so we are including a discussion of this research here.

Bouchard and his colleagues conduct studies in which they look for the **heritability** of characteristics such as intelligence and personality traits by studying monozygotic and dizygotic twins who have been reared apart. Monozygotic twins are also called identical twins because they come from the same ovum (egg) and share 100 percent of their genes. Dizygotic twins, sometimes called fraternal twins, come from different ova. Although they are born at the same time, they have no more genetic similarity than any two siblings produced by the same parents. Roughly speaking, heritability of a characteristic is indicated by greater similarity between identical twins than between fraternal twins on that characteristic.

Bouchard's group probably is most famous for studies of intelligence, which have shown that genetic influence appears to account for about 70 percent of this characteristic (Bouchard, 1993). The clear demonstration of genetic influence on individual intelligence does not, by the way, support Herrnstein and Murray's claim that heredity produces intelligence differences between groups.

More recently, the Bouchard group has taken up the study of factors relevant to organizations and organizational communication, in particular, job satisfaction and work values. The results of these studies have shown that about 30 percent of a person's experience of job satisfaction is attributable to genetic influence (Bouchard, Arvey, Keller, & Segal, 1992) and about 40 percent of a person's orientation to work values is due to genetics (Keller, Bouchard, Arvey, & Segal, 1992). The rest is a result of environmental factors and measurement error.

As Keller and the others point out, these findings do not mean that a person is simply born to be satisfied or dissatisfied or to have a particular orientation toward work. The results do mean that "genetic factors are significantly associated with the learning or acquiring of work values" (p. 85). Put another way, environment is still the major influence on job satisfaction and work values, but our genetic makeup will shape the way that we adapt and respond to that environment. The implication for organizational communication is that social processes ranging from group decision making and leader-member interaction to the content and patterns of organization gossip may be influenced by traits and characteristics that individuals bring to the situation, and these individual traits and characteristics are to some extent genetically predisposed (Keller et al., 1992).

Once again, the indication that genes affect our traits and behavior is not a justification to simply let nature take its course. Even though studies by the Bouchard group indicate that many psychological traits in addition to intelligence are at least partially inherited, Bouchard and his colleagues note the effect of heritability depends upon the environment in which it occurs, so that "strong heritability of most psychological traits . . . does not detract from the value or importance of parenting, education, and other . . . interventions" (1990, p. 223).

Summary

Several theories with the potential for application to organizational communication embrace metaphors drawn from biology or use biological principles literally in their explanations of behavior. These theories are not concerned with the managerial problem of member motivation in and of itself, but with the broader problem of understanding the structure, function, and development of human systems and the people who constitute these systems.

System theories, which view organizations as adaptive organisms rather than machines, gained wide acceptance during the 1960s in the wake of Bertalanffy's general system theory. System theories attempt to describe and explain how organizations function from the standpoint of some very general principles that are presumed to apply to all systems. These general principles include wholeness, hierarchy, openness, and feedback.

Following system theory, Weick theorizes that organizing and communicating activities are directed toward the reduction of equivocality in information. Where information has little equivocality, organizations can rely heavily on rules to guide their responses. As equivocality increases, organizations are less able to rely on rules. As equivocality increases, more communicative effort is required to respond to it. Weick discussed communication as an interlocked behavior cycle, which consists of a double-interact. As equivocality increases, we are less able to rely on rules to handle the situation and must rely on more cycles.

Weick uses an evolutionary metaphor with the concepts of enactment, selection, and retention. We attend actively to the environment, recognizing the level of equivocality in the information. The selection phase begins when we make decisions about the rules and interlocked (communication) cycles that we will use to manage the equivocality. Cycles that reduce equivocality are retained for future use.

Evolutionary psychology starts with the premise that human behavior and, by extension, culture are influenced by innate psychological mechanisms in human beings that did not develop under modern conditions, but evolved into their present form during the Pleistocene Epoch. Studies in evolutionary psychology attempt to identify Pleistocene mechanisms that might continue to reverberate in modern behavior, for example, in areas such as workplace sexual harassment and human grouping behaviors. Sociobiology, a related field, has been even more controversial. The basic premise of sociobiology is that human social behavior is influenced by functions of kinship that are genetic, not cultural.

Genetic psychology looks for the heritability of characteristics such as intelligence and personality traits by studying twins who have been reared apart. Researchers have begun to study heritability of factors in responses to organizational environments, including job satisfaction and work values. The results of these studies show that job satisfaction and work values are attributable in part to genetic influences.

None of these movements in the sociopsychological application of evolutionary theory and genetics accepts the idea of biological determinism.

Discussion Questions/ Activities

1. Observe the work of a task group at work on some sort of project, for example, for a student organization. Is the group more like a machine or more like an organism? How well do the principles of system theory characterize the group and its processes?
2. In the same group observation above, how much of the communicative effort is directed toward managing or reducing equivocality? What kinds of conditions create equivocality for the group, and how well does Weick's theory explain the group's effort to manage equivocality?
3. The subjects of sociobiology and evolutionary psychology are rather controversial. Have a class or group discussion on this topic. From what you have read in this chapter, what are the arguments for and against biological accounts of human behavior, including organizational behavior? The Studd and Gattiker study of sexual harassment may provide a good object for discussion.

Additional Resources

Books

Bailey, K. (1994). *Sociology and the new systems theory: Toward a theoretical synthesis.* Albany, NY: State University of New York Press.
Baldwin, J. D., & Baldwin, J. I. (1981). *Beyond sociobiology.* New York: Elsevier.

Barkow, J. H., Cosmides, L., & Tooby, J. (Eds.). (1992). *The adapted mind: Evolutionary psychology and the generation of culture*. New York: Oxford University Press.

Rapoport, A. (1986). *General systems theory: Essential concepts and applications*. Cambridge, MA: Abacus Press.

Web Sites

http://www.psych.ucsb.edu/research/cep/
   The Center for Evolutionary Psychology, University of California, Santa Barbara.
http://www.bga.org
   The Institute for Behavioral Genetics, University of Colorado.
http://lenti.med.umn.edu/~ihg/behav.gen.html
   The behavioral genetics group of the University of Minnesota Institute for Human Genetics.

References

Anderson, J. A. (1987). *Communication research: Issues and methods*. New York: McGraw-Hill.

Barlow, G. W. (1991). Nature-Nurture and the debates surrounding ethology and sociobiology. *American Zoologist, 31*, 286–296.

Barnard, C. (1938). *The functions of the executive.* Cambridge, MA: Harvard University Press.

Bertalanffy, L. V. (1956). General system theory. *General Systems, 1,* 1.

Bertalanffy, L. V. (1968). *General system theory.* New York: George Braziller.

Bouchard, T. J., Jr. (1993). The genetic architecture of human intelligence. In P. E. Vernon (Ed.), *Biological approaches in the study of human intelligence*. New York: Plenum.

Bouchard, T. J., Jr., Arvey, R. D., Keller, L. M., & Segal, N. L. (1992). Genetic influences on job satisfaction: A reply to Cropanzano and James. *Journal of Applied Pyschology, 77*, 89–93.

Bouchard, T. J., Jr., Lykken, D. T., McGue, M., Segal, N. L. & Tellegen, A. (1990). Sources of human psychological differences: The Minnesota study of twins reared apart. *Science, 250*, 223–238.

Bouchard, T. J., Jr., & McGue, M. (1990). Genetic and rearing environmental influences on adult personality: An analysis of adopted twins reared apart. *Journal of Personality, 58*, 263–292.

Burgess, J. W. (1989). The social biology of human populations: Spontaneous group formation conforms to evolutionary predictions of adaptive aggregation patterns. *Ethology and Sociobiology, 10*, 343–359.

Campbell, D. T. (1965). Variations and selective retention in socio-cultural evolution. In H. R. Barringer et al. (Eds.), *Social change in developing areas: A reinterpretation of evolutionary theory*. Cambridge, MA: Schenkman.

D'Aprix, R. (1982). *Communicating for productivity.* New York: Harper & Row.

Dessler, G. (1980). *Organization theory: Integrating structure and behavior.* Englewood Cliffs, NJ: Prentice-Hall.

Eisenberg, E. M. (1984). Ambiguity as a strategy in organizational communication. *Communication Monographs, 51,* 227–242.

Eisenberg, E. M., & Goodall, H. L., Jr. (1993). *Organizational communication: Balancing creativity and constraint*. New York: St. Martin's Press.

Farace, R. V., Monge, P. R., & Russell, H. M. (1977). *Communicating and organizing.* Reading, MA: Addison-Wesley.

Gould, S. J. (1978). Review of *On human nature* by E. O. Wilson. *Human Nature, 1*, 20–28.

Herrnstein, R. J., & Murray, C. (1994). *The bell curve: Intelligence and class structure in American life*. New York: Free Press.

Huse, E. F., & Bowditch, J. L. (1973). *Behavior in organizations: A systems approach to managing.* Reading, MA: Addison-Wesley.

Katz, D., & Kahn, R. (1966). *The social psychology of organizations.* New York: John Wiley & Sons.

Keller, L. M., Bouchard, T. J., Jr., Arvey, R. D., Segal, N. L., & Dawis, R. V. (1992). Work values: Genetic and environmental influences. *Journal of Applied Psychology, 77,* 79–88.

Kitcher, P. (1985). *Vaulting ambition: Sociobiology and the quest for human nature.* Cambridge, MA: MIT Press.

Kofoed, L. (1989). Darwinian evolution of social behavior: Implications for group psychotherapy. *Psychiatry, 52,* 475–481.

Kreps, G. L. (1990). *Organizational communication: Theory and practice* (2nd ed.). New York: Longman.

Lawrence, P., & Lorsch, J. (1969). *Organization and environment: Managing differentiation and integration.* Homewood, IL: Irwin.

Lee, J., & Jablin, F. M. (1995). Maintenance communication in superior-subordinate work relationships. *Human Communication Research, 22,* 220–257.

Lewontin, R. (1977). Biological determinism as an ideological weapon. *Science for People, 9,* 36–38.

Liska, J. (1990). Dominance-seeking strategies in primates: An evolutionary perspective. *Human Evolution, 5,* 75–90.

Littlejohn, S. W. (1992). *Theories of human communication* (4th ed.). Belmont, CA: Wadsworth.

March, J., & Simon, H. (1958). *Organizations.* New York: John Wiley & Sons.

McGrew, W. C. (1994). Tools compared: The material of culture. In R. W. Wrangham, W. C. McGrew, F. B. M. de Waal, & P. G. Heltne (Eds.), *Chimpanzee culture* (pp. 25–40). Cambridge, MA: Harvard University Press.

Mee, J. (1964). Matrix organizations. *Business Horizons, 7,* 70–72.

Miller, P. (Dec. 1995). Crusading for chimps and humans . . . Jane Goodall. *National Geographic, 188,* 102–128.

Monge, P. R. (1982). System theory and research in the study of organizational communication: The correspondence problem. *Human communication Research, 8,* 245–261.

Monge, P. R., Farace, R. L., Eisenberg, E. M., Miller, K. I., & White, L. L. (1984). The process of studying process in organizational communication. *Journal of Communication, 34,* 22–43.

Nielsen, F. (1994). Sociobiology and sociology. *Annual Review of Sociology, 20,* 267–303.

Studd, M. V., & Gattiker, U. E. (1991). The evolutionary psychology of sexual harassment in organizations. *Ethology and Sociobiology, 12,* 249–290.

Tooby, J., & Cosmides, L. (1989). Evolutionary psychology and the generation of culture, Part I: Theoretical considerations. *Ethology and Sociobiology, 10,* 29–49.

Udry, J. R. (1995). Sociology and biology: What biology do sociologists need to know? *Social Forces, 37,* 1267–1278.

Wade, N. (1976). Sociobiology: Troubled birth for new discipline. *Science, 191,* 1151–1155.

Weick, K. (1979). *The social psychology of organizing* (2nd ed.). Reading, MA: Addison-Wesley.

Wilson, E. O. (1975). *Sociobiology: The new synthesis.* Cambridge, MA: Belknap.

Wilson, E. O. (1976). Academic vigilantism and the political significance of sociobiology. *Biological Science, 26,* 183, 187–190.

Woodward, J. (1958). *Management and technology.* London: Her Majesty's Stationery Office.

CHAPTER 4

ORGANIZATION THEORY:
NEW MILLENNIUM THOUGHT

Outline

As we approach the new millennium, that is, the beginning in 2000 A.D. of the next thousand years of human civilization, a number of important questions are being raised by organizational stakeholders and researchers. Among these questions are (a) What forms of organizing make the best use of human resources; (b) What constitutes a humane working environment; (c) How can organizations operate effectively in a globally competitive environment; (d) What are the benefits and challenges of sustaining a diverse workforce; (e) How do organizational operations need to change in order to protect the environment; and (f) How can workers be empowered in ways that allow them to accomplish individual and organizational goals. In this chapter, we will address these questions by focusing on recent theoretical developments in organizational studies. First, we will examine the recent emergence of self-managed work teams as an alternative to bureaucracy. Second, we will consider the possibility of sustaining democratic workplace systems. Third, we will describe how organizational theory is changing due to the contributions of feminist researchers. Finally, we will discuss the idea of employee emancipation.

Self-Managed Work Teams and Concertive Control

One of the most interesting and popular alternatives to bureaucratic structure is to shift from multilayered organizational hierarchies to a flat collection of **self-managed work teams.** For example, over the last several years Xerox, General Motors, and Coors Brewing have initiated this sort of change (Barker, 1993). One reason for the shift to self-managed teams is that bureaucratic constraints stifle worker creativity and innovation. Also, when worker-run teams are responsible for completing work assignments, the organization can eliminate unneeded supervisors and other bureaucratic staff (Barker, 1993).

As more organizations shift to various forms of self-management, there will be significant changes in the daily experiences of employees. Barker (1993) explains thus:

Instead of being told what to do by a supervisor, self-managing workers must gather and synthesize information, act on it, and take collective responsibility for those actions. Self-managing workers generally are organized into teams of 10 to 15 people who take on the responsibilities of their former supervisors. Top management often provides a value-based corporate vision that team members use to infer parameters and premises (norms and rules) that guide their day-to-day actions. Guided by the company's vision, the self-managing team members direct their own work and coordinate with other areas of the company. (p. 413)

Organizations that utilize self-managed teams require team members to complete specific, clearly defined tasks. Often, team members are cross-trained so that any member can perform all of the tasks needed to complete a given job. Also, team members are given "the authority and responsibility to make the essential decisions necessary to complete the function" (Barker, 1993, p. 413). In addition to performing specific tasks assigned to the team, self-managed workers establish their own work schedules, order needed materials, and coordinate their actions with other work groups. Importantly, researchers have found that systems of self-management increase employee motivation, productivity, and commitment (Mumby & Stohl, 1991; Osbourne, Moran, Musselwhite, & Zenger, 1990; Wellins, Byham, & Wilson, 1991).

On the surface it would seem that self-managed teams give workers the sort of flexibility and empowerment that is not possible within bureaucracies. Workers establish their own work rules and norms, emphasis is placed on working collaboratively with others to reach co-determined goals, and worker creativity and innovation are encouraged. Recent examinations of work teams in different organizations, however, show that there is a negative side to the control mechanisms workers establish for themselves. In order to clarify how and why this occurs, we need to describe the different forms of organizational control.

Edwards (1981) originally identified three strategies of control in organizations: **simple, technological,** and **bureaucratic.** Simple control is the direct, personal control of work by supervisors who oversee the performance of subordinates. Technological control emerges from the physical technology used in an organization. Computer systems that monitor worker performance would exemplify this form of control. Bureaucratic control emanates from hierarchically based social relations within an organization. This form of control is based on rational-legal rules that reward compliance and punish noncompliance.

Self-managed teams often enact a form of control referred to as **concertive control** (Tompkins & Cheney, 1985). Concertive control is built upon the three traditional control strategies described above. Specifically, concertive control systems require a shift in control from management to workers who collaborate with one another to create rules and norms that govern their behavior. So, in these systems, control emanates from the concertive, value-based actions of an organization's members. Top management stimulates this collaborative process by providing a value-based corporate vision "that team members use to infer parameters and premises (norms and rules) that guide their day-to-day actions" (Barker, 1993, p. 413). Using the corporate vision statement as their guide, workers collaborate with one another to create social rules that "constitute meaning and sanction modes of social conduct" (Barker, 1993, p. 412).

Identification

For concertive control systems to be effective in regulating worker behavior, the workers must **identify** with a set of value and factual premises that guide their decision making and work activities (Barker & Tompkins, 1994). These decision premises are accepted in exchange for incentives offered by the organization such as wages, salary, and continued employment. As explained above, concertive control systems emerge when top management produces a value-based corporate vision that is intended to serve as a guide for member behavior and decision making. Workers then exhibit their **identification** with this vision when, in making a decision, they perceive the organization's values or interests as relevant in evaluating the alternatives of choice (Tompkins & Cheney, 1983). Through identification the decision maker's range of "vision" is narrowed "by selecting particular values, particular items of empirical knowledge, and particular behavior alternatives for consideration, to the exclusion of other values, other knowledge, other possibilities" (Simon, 1976, p. 210). Indeed, the organizational member "sees" that with which he or she identifies. When considering decision options, a member is limited to alternatives linked to his or her identifications; "other options will simply not come into view, and therefore will not be considered" (Tompkins & Cheney, 1985, p. 194).

Disciplinary Techniques

The concept of identification is clearly linked to concertive control systems. Also important to consider within these systems are **disciplinary techniques.** More specifically, worker-designed systems of control include microtechniques of discipline to regulate and normalize individual and collective action in organizations. When members internalize these disciplinary techniques (because of their identification with the organizational value system), they become part of "standard operating procedure." Of course, organizations cannot operate without some form of discipline. As Barnard (1938/1968) argued over a half-century ago, the master paradox of organizational life is that "to accomplish our individual goals, we must frequently relinquish some autonomy to the organizational system" (p. 17). Barker and Cheney (1994) extend this line of reasoning by observing that disciplines are "enabling because they allow us to create reality in concert with others and, simultaneously constraining because the disciplines shape our behavior in directions that are functional for the organization" (p. 30).

Discursive Formations

A particularly rich description of microtechniques of discipline is provided by Foucault (1972, 1977). According to Foucault (1972), disciplines are **discursive formations.** Defined as such, discipline functions as a social force in the organization, "demarcating good behavior from bad, providing a context for organizational interaction, and, in general, shaping day-to-day organizational activity" (Barker & Cheney, 1994, p. 26). Thus, Foucault presents us with an embracing notion of disciplinary discourse. Such discourse emerges in those social relations that serve to control, govern, and normalize individual and collective behavior. Disciplinary discourse leads to the construction of "apparatuses of knowledge and a multiplicity of new domains of understanding" (Foucault, 1980, p. 106). Eventually, social production of the apparatuses of knowledge and domains of understanding lead organizational actors to the conclusion: "That's the way we do things around here."

Let's take a moment to clarify Foucault's notion of discipline as a discursive process. Foucault believes that disciplinary systems emerge through conversations among organizational members. In these conversations workers develop rules and norms to govern their behavior as they attempt to reach individual, group, and organizational goals. Importantly, as explained earlier, employees are motivated to develop rules and norms that are consistent with the values communicated by management in its vision statement (e.g., We at ACE Manufacturing are committed to producing high-quality merchandise at a reasonable price), because they identify strongly with this statement and the organization. The techniques of discipline the workers then produce allow them to accomplish work-related goals.

Microtechniques of discipline both punish and reward. Foucault (1977) refers to "micropenalties" as the practice of "making the slightest departures from correct behavior subject to punishment, and of giving punitive function to the apparently indifferent elements of the disciplinary apparatus" (p. 178). Within this disciplinary apparatus, "everything might serve to punish the slightest thing; each subject finds himself caught in a punishable, punishing universality (Foucault, 1977, p. 178). Conversely, disciplinary systems also reward by means of awards. Subjects are judged against a norm or average in a way that continually creates ranks. Those judged to be significantly better than the norm are rewarded by the fact of the judgment itself.

When workers within a concertive control system identify strongly with an organization, disciplinary systems are created that allow members to reach work-related goals. Although these control systems can empower workers in ways that elude them in traditional bureaucracies, these systems can also limit behavioral options open to employees. As Barker (1993) recently explained, the irony of this shift from management-designed control systems to worker-designed systems is that workers may create forms of control that are more powerful, less apparent, and more difficult to resist than those of the former bureaucracy. In order to clarify how and why this occurs, let's consider a couple of examples.

Barker and Cheney (1994) conducted an investigation of disciplinary techniques in a manufacturing organization that relied upon a system of concertive control. To protect the confidentiality of the respondents, the organization was called "Tech USA." During the course of conducting the study, one of the work teams faced a problem. On a Thursday afternoon, the workers began to recognize that they were in jeopardy of missing a deadline to ship a customer's order by Friday. The only way they could meet the deadline was to work overtime. One of the team leaders (Teri) called everyone together and addressed the team. The scenario unfolded in the following manner:

"You know we all said that we were going to have these boards ready to go by tomorrow. It ain't gonna happen unless we stay late. Who's gonna help out here?" [Teri] After some exchanging of conspicuous looks at each other, Johnny, another one of the team's leaders stood up and exclaimed: "We all agreed and committed ourselves to get this out on time. We have a responsibility here. I'm gonna stay here, who else will?"

The other team members began to raise their hands, except for Vicki, whom the team viewed as someone who tended to 'shirk' her fair share of overtime. All eyes turned toward her as she said: "Look, I've got to pick up my kids at 3:00 P.M. [long pause] Let me do that and I'll come in at 5:30 tomorrow [one and a half hours early] and start packing [for shipment] what you get finished tonight."

The team members expressed satisfaction with this "deal." Vicki complied with her commitment and the team did complete this order on time. (Barker & Cheney, 1994, pp. 33–34)

The preceding vignette shows how powerful concertive control systems can be. These workers were not being paid to work overtime, but they were motivated to do so because they had collectively made a commitment to fulfill a customer order by the next day. So, there was pressure to acquiesce to Teri's request and she reminded the team members of their commitment. A manager is not needed to demand the overtime because these workers operate under peer pressure to abide by their agreement to meet the customer's deadline. This peer pressure is the form of discipline workers enact to gain compliance from resistant members. Although Vicki had planned to pick up her children at 3:00 P.M. (after her shift had ended), she felt compelled to offer the team something to make up for leaving before the order was finished. Of course, arriving at work by 5:30 A.M. the next day may also have caused inconveniences for her and her children. Also, note that Vicki was perceived as an employee who shirked her *fair share* of overtime. What this means is that workers are establishing (with some regularity) deadlines that are difficult to meet in a normal forty-hour work week. This raises issues of fairness, particularly since workers are pressured to sacrifice their personal lives and time with their families to meet team goals. Barker

(1993) commented on this peer pressure when he observed: "If [workers] want to resist their team's control, they must be willing to risk their human dignity, being made to feel unworthy as a 'teammate.'" (p. 436)

Papa, Auwal, and Singhal (1996) also conducted a study that focused on concertive control systems. The organization selected for their study was the Grameen Bank in Bangladesh. This financial institution is dedicated to helping the poorest of the poor by offering them social services, economic programs, and loans for small business development. The bank has been incredibly successful over the past twenty years. Over two million borrowers have received loans and the bank sustains a remarkable 99 percent loan recovery rate. One of the main reasons for the success of this institution is the exceptional dedication of the bank field workers who administer the loan programs. Working under a system of concertive control in which they establish their own norms and rules, the workers exhibit an almost fanatical devotion to upholding the humanitarian mission of the bank. For example, Atiquar Rahman is a bank field worker who regularly works twelve-hour days and often works for months at a time without a single day off. When asked why he works so diligently, he responded: "How can I let down the other field workers and the poor people we serve? We work together as a team, and in working together we help the poor to improve their lives" (Papa, Auwal, & Singhal, 1996, p. 15). Furthermore, if a field worker experiences problems with loan recovery in a given branch office, he or she will be criticized by fellow field workers and pressured to do whatever is necessary to recover the loan (including working extra hours to help a loan recipient with his or her small business). Papa and colleagues conclude thus:

The field workers so strongly identify with the Grameen's goal of uplifting the poor that they socially construct standards that place extraordinary pressure on everyone to succeed. Not surprisingly, the depth of their organizational commitment clouds their ability to assess objectively the micro-techniques of discipline that are part of the bank's concertive control system. (p. 18)

Are there systems of concertive control within organizations that do not result in an oppressive environment for workers? Certainly, it seems possible that humane concertive control systems can be designed by workers. The key to designing more humane control systems, however, is linked to the emergence of competing value systems to guide member behavior. If workers are concerned only with responding to management's vision statement, then they may design a control system that pressures them to place organizational goals over individual needs. Designing a more humane workplace may require managers and workers to consider more democratic forms of decision making and governance. So, let's now turn to a discussion of workplace democracy.

Workplace Democracy

Although democracy as a form of political governance has a long and rich history, the application of democratic principles to the workplace, or **workplace democracy,** is a relatively recent phenomenon. Indeed, Cheney (1995) observed: "Surely one of the great ironies of the modern world is that democracy, imperfect as it is in the political realm, seldom extends to the workplace" (p. 167). Why has this been the case? Well, corporate owners and top management personnel have long viewed it as their job to direct, manage, and coordinate the efforts of those people who work for them to ensure the continued attainment of organizational goals. McGregor's Theory X provides us with a clear example of this perspective in that threat and coercion are considered the primary ways to assure employee compliance with managerial directives.

Since so many organizations have experienced success with nondemocratic forms of management, why is the issue of workplace democracy important for us to consider now? Well, over the last thirty years a number of organizations have benefitted from involving employees more directly in various forms of decision making. Remember the examples we cited of AS & W Steel, Saturn, and Johnson and Johnson in the last chapter. Furthermore, on a theoretical level, McGregor's Theory Y and Likert's System IV both emphasize the value of employee participation in workplace decisions. Just because employees participate in decision making, however, does not mean that a democratic form of workplace governance exists. So, let's turn to a definition of workplace democracy that was advanced by Cheney (1995):

[W]orkplace democracy is broadly defined as a system of governance which truly values individual goals and feelings (e.g., equitable remuneration, the pursuit of enriching work and the right to express oneself) as well as typically organizational problems (e.g., effectiveness and efficiency, reflectively conceived), which actively fosters the connection between those two sets of concerns by encouraging individual contributions to important organizational choices, and which allows for the ongoing modification of the organization's activities and policies by the group. (pp. 4–5)

What are the key components of the preceding definition? Clearly, the goals and feelings of individual employees are valued in democratic workplace systems. Individual goals and feelings, however, cannot be considered independent of organizational problems. What Cheney is arguing here is that organizational survival depends on a certain level of effectiveness and efficiency in attaining important organizational goals (e.g., sales, profits, providing services, etc.). So in a democratic workplace, the employees play an active role in determining how individual and organizational goals can be accomplished simultaneously. Importantly, in their conversations with one another workers play a role in deciding what the organization's goals should be and how they should be reached. Finally, employees are also expected to evaluate and, if necessary, modify the organization's activities and policies to accomplish new goals.

Worker Cooperatives

Although workplace democracy is not widely practiced, various forms of democracy do exist in different types of organizations. Most examples of workplace democracy are found in varying forms of **worker cooperatives** and in certain types of employee-owned organizations (Clarke, 1984; Gherardi & Masiero, 1987; Harrison, 1994; Mellor, Hannah, & Stirling, 1988). These organizations tend to be employee owned in a collective sense. What this means is that members typically "equalize share ownership (or membership) and voting rights between individuals, usually through a one person-one vote formula" (Harrison, 1994, p. 261). Such worker-owned cooperatives can be found in the U.S. and in other countries around the world. One very interesting description of a worker-owned cooperative is provided by Cheney (1995), who spent time researching the Mondragon worker cooperatives in the Basque region of Spain. The first of these cooperatives opened for business in 1956, making it one of the oldest worker-owned cooperatives in the world. As of 1995, there were more than 150 of these cooperatives employing over 23,000 people in a wide array of businesses (e.g., a supermarket chain, a bank, machine tool manufacturers, an electronics firm, etc.).

Employee Stock Ownership

Certain larger organizations with **employee stock ownership plans** (ESOPs) also practice forms of workplace democracy. In democratically run ESOPs, ownership is linked to owning shares of the firm. These shares can be distributed on the basis of seniority, pay scale, or some other formula. The basis for participation is linked to one's status as a share holder, and organizations differ in terms of how they allocate voting power. For example, in some organizations owners may possess votes equal to the number of shares they own. Other organizations follow a one person-one vote rule. Finally, some organizations vary the formula for participation depending on the issue (Blasi, 1987).

Participatory vs. Representative Democracy

Workplace democracy is often enacted differently depending on the size of the organization (an issue we will return to later). The most basic difference is practicing a participatory versus a representative form of democracy. **Participatory** forms are more common in smaller organizations where a one person-one vote formula is used. In larger organizations, for the purposes of efficiency in decision making, representative forms of democracy are more common. In a **representative** form of democracy, workers elect representatives to present their interests to the main decision-making body of the organization. In order to clarify the differences between these two forms of democratic participation, let's consider a couple of examples.

In small organizations where democracy is practiced, group meetings are the only routinized form of interaction. Other interaction among members occurs when and as it is needed (Harrison, 1994). Relying on a one person-one vote decision-making formula, these organizations "are committed to achieving consensus and strive to make decisions that are satisfactory to all" (Harrison, 1994, p. 264). Of course the interaction that occurs in these meetings can be long and fraught with conflict as members assert their individual needs and interests. For example, Hafen (1993) conducted a study of a small worker-owned restaurant in Athens, Ohio. There are thirty-three worker-owners in this restaurant who all participate in decisions concerning organizational operations (e.g., shift assignments, menu development, ordering food, marketing, etc.). Interestingly, the workers have different perceptions of this participative system. One worker-owner stated: "We're just too big to make decisions by 100% consensus. We're going to have to make more decisions among small groups of people. . . . Our lives are indebted to consensus ruling, and its [*sic*] time consuming and inefficient and expensive" (p. 19). Another worker-owner also recognized the challenges associated with consensus decision making, but ultimately felt it was worth it:

If there's one person who says, "I think what you're doing is a big mistake, I cannot in any conscience let you go through with that decision," that one person can block that decision. And that's happened in the past, and its been very cumbersome and very difficult–but we have always reached a better decision because of it. (Hafen, 1993, pp. 19–20)

In larger organizations it is simply not practical to include every member in every decision that needs to be made. So in larger organizations, "opportunities for participatory and representative decision-making are woven together in an effort to maximize individual autonomy within a large group" (Harrison, 1994, p. 264). One example of a larger organization that practices democratic decision making is Hoedads (a reforestation cooperative that is composed of approximately 300 members). The members of this organization plant trees, thin forests, construct forest trails, and fight fires. This work is performed by teams or crews that work for weeks at a time in locations that are distant from the central office (see Gunn, 1984). Harrison (1994) offered the following description of Hoedad's decision-making system:

Decisions are distributed into three tiers of responsibility: individual crews act as autonomous work groups in the conduct of day-to-day activities; a council, composed of members elected from each of the crews, considers issues that affect the cooperative as a whole; and, task forces, whose membership may be open to the crews or elected, are created to research problems that require specific information or particular expertise. General meetings, which can last for several days, take place a couple of times a year to consider task force issues as well as any other issues that are known by the council as likely to be controversial. (p. 264)

Principles and Practices of Workplace Democracy

Now that we have covered some of the decision-making strategies in democratic organizations, let's consider some of the broader principles and practices that are linked to workplace democracy. Cheney (1995) provides an overview of five major principles and practices of workplace democracy: (a) interaction with external systems; (b) size, structure, and patterns of interaction; (c) maintaining integrity; (d) self-reflection and self-regeneration; and (e) consistency between goals and process. These five principles and practices provide the basis for our subsequent discussion.

Interaction with External Systems

Since most organizations are not structured by democratic principles, Cheney contends that democratic organizations must be buffered from outside pressures to alter their core values and practices. This can be accomplished in one of two ways. First, the democratic organization can imbed itself in a network of relationships with organizations that also practice forms of democracy. This, of course, is contingent upon finding a sufficient number of organizations in reasonable proximity that practice democracy. If relationships can be formed with suppliers and other allied partners, the democratic organization buffers itself from outside pressures to operate in a more bureaucratic manner. Alternatively, the democratic organization can "try to sustain a special identity while also doing business with other types of organizations" (Cheney, 1995, p. 7). For example, Cheney recommends that democratic organizations establish and maintain certain "sacred" values, principles, practices, and rituals "that help to remind members of where their organization 'stands' with respect to the rest of the organizational world" (p. 7).

Size, Structure, and Patterns of Interaction

Regarding size, structure, and patterns of interaction, Cheney focuses on the challenges of sustaining democracy in large organizations. Indeed, he makes the observation that the "intense face-to-face interaction required by real democratic participation cannot be maintained in something larger than what we call a small group" (Cheney, 1995, p. 8). As an alternative, large organizations (as noted earlier) need to enact a representational form of democracy. Cheney raises another important issue, however: namely, what can be done when the majority enacts decisions that become a source of oppression for the minority of employees who adopt dissenting views? Here Cheney recommends an *adversarial* model of democracy in which competing interests are institutionalized and have proportional representation and influence. Of course, such an adversarial form of democracy is likely to engender more frequent conflict, but a larger percentage of workers are likely to feel supported within this system.

Maintaining Integrity

Maintaining integrity, the third of Cheney's democratic principles and practices, refers to sustaining workplace democracy despite the pressures to become more bureaucratic. This position can be linked to Weber's (1978) inevitable "march of rationalization." According to Weber, most organizations exhibit a tendency to move toward bureaucratic order. What can be done to resist this? Cheney recommends that democratic organizations can occasionally restructure themselves in order to preserve spontaneous aspects. For example, new types of groups can be formed within the larger organization to prevent any established group from becoming too dominant and creating a hierarchical system of control.

Self-Reflection and Self-Regeneration

Self-reflection and self-regeneration constitute the most challenging aspects of sustaining democracy in organizations. The starting point for self-reflection is to define the deep value consensus that unifies organizational members. For example, an organization may be held together by values such as democratic participation and equality. For democratic organizations to sustain themselves over time, however, members must be willing to discuss critically the benefits of sustaining their particular value consensus. Indeed, a given democratic form of governance should not be accepted blindly as the only form of democracy that is possible. Democratic structures and processes should be viewed as evolutionary. What this means is that the particular form of democracy that an organization adopts needs to change as the beliefs and values of the members change. As Cheney (1995) observes, "the values of the organization and their pursuit must be available to both members and outside observers for review and critique. In particular, sacred notions of democracy and participation must themselves be open to criticism" (p. 12).

The processes of self-reflection and self-regeneration were observed by Cheney in his association with the Rocky Mountain Peace Center of Boulder, Colorado. One of the most interesting facets of this organization is that members periodically reexamine what peace, nonviolence and sustainable development mean for different people at different times. This ongoing process of reflection and discussion makes individual members aware of the different viewpoints that exist within the organization. "As a result, both the structure and some of the practices of the organization are distinctly different now from what they were ten years ago: Today, for instance, the organization has a radial design with work groups that involve numerous citizens that elect representatives to a core group" (pp. 12–13).

Obviously, there are challenges associated with sustaining an environment where employees challenge one another's ideas, values, and actions. Sustaining such an environment, however, is at the core of what democracy really is. So, if a diversity of opinions exists within the organization, how can these diverse views be given recognition and value? One way is to advocate what Cheney referred to earlier as an adversarial form of democracy. Another way is to promote dialogue among members who hold differing viewpoints. Eisenberg (1994) suggests following three guidelines to promote dialogue in organizations. First, every person has the right to be heard, and each is given the opportunity to present his or her views. Second, members must exhibit empathy for different perspectives, ideas, and opinions. Third, members must be encouraged to speak from personal experience. By following these guidelines, members who hold diverse views may find a superordinate goal that links them together, or they may discover that their interests dovetail on certain critical issues. Perhaps the strongest rationale for sustaining dialogue in the workplace is provided by Evered and Tannenbaum (1992):

[Dialogue] is one of the richest activities that human beings can engage in. It is the thing that gives meaning to life, it's the sharing of humanity, it's creating something. And there is this magical thing in an organization, or in a team, or in a group, where you get unrestricted interaction, unrestricted dialogue, and this synergy happening that results in more productivity, and satisfaction, and seemingly magical levels of output from a team. (p. 8)

Consistency between Goals and Process

The final principle of workplace democracy advocated by Cheney is to insure consistency between goals and process. What this means is that the goal of a democratic workplace can exist only if democratic, participative processes are sustained within the system. Monge and Miller (1988) contend that three factors should be considered in evaluating an organization's commitment to employee participation. First, employee input must cover a wide range of issues. Second, employees must be able to exhibit influence over matters that are important to them (e.g., wages, policies, etc.). Third, participation must be exhibited at all levels of the organization and employees must be empowered to deal with higher-level issues.

Organizational survival in the twenty-first century will be linked to the creativity and innovation exhibited by employees. One way of harnessing worker creativity is to create a democratic workplace where employees are encouraged to challenge one another's ideas, actions, and values. Now let's consider another recent theoretical development in organizational studies that also promotes equality and participation. Specifically, feminist theorists have offered provocative and insightful insights into the nature of communicating and organizing within the workplace.

Feminist Theories and Organizational Communication

Before describing the major feminist perspectives, let's consider a comment by Kathy Ferguson in her 1984 book *The Feminist Case Against Bureaucracy*:

Real social change comes about when people think and live differently. Feminist discourse and feminist practice offer the linguistic and structural space in which it is possible to think, live, work, and love differently, in opposition to the discursive and institutional practices of bureaucratic capitalism. At least it is a start. (p. 212)

The reason we selected the preceding passage is that it gets to the heart of what feminist perspectives offer to all of us. Too many management systems disqualify or minimize the contributions of certain groups or participants, especially women and minorities (Bullis, 1993; Deetz, 1992). As a result, the organizational benefits of including their diverse perspectives are not realized (Maruyama, 1994). In an era of global competition, worker creativity and innovation are central to organizational survival and success. One way to promote creativity and innovation is to bring people together who have different ways of viewing the world. The perspectives of women and minority group members are often unique because of different socialization experiences that shape their world views. So to increase the pool of creative and innovative ideas within organizations, managers must empower members whose views have typically been silenced and include their diverse perspectives in all important forms of decision making. Now that we have presented our rationale for focusing on feminist perspectives, let's take a moment to consider what is meant by the term "feminist ideology."

At a general level, feminist ideology views women as a "sex-class," and acknowledges that women are oppressed and disadvantaged as a group (Martin, 1990). This oppression is rooted in social arrangements (e.g., in the home, at work, in government, etc.) in which the values and interests of men are privileged over those of women. So in order for women to be empowered, social, political, and economic changes are needed in society (Eisenstein, 1981). At the core of all of these changes is recognizing that women's experiences and meanings need to be honored and valued (Natalle, Papa, & Graham, 1993).

It is important to note that there is no single feminist perspective. Rather, there are many diverse perspectives that are unified by the themes of cooperation, caring for others, integrative thinking, connectedness, and openness to the environment (Marshall, 1989). Buzzanell (1994) identified eight major feminist approaches: Liberal, Marxist, Radical, Psychoanalytic, Contemporary Socialist, Existentialist, Postmodern, and Revisionist. Each of these approaches takes a somewhat different stance toward the sort of individual and societal changes that are necessary for women to be empowered. Let's briefly consider the sorts of changes advocated by each feminist perspective.

Liberal feminists believe that legal remedies can balance the power between men and women by ensuring that women are not systematically disadvantaged in their competition with men for scarce resources. For the liberal feminist, empowerment means that women obtain their fair share of control of institutions formerly dominated by men.

Marxist feminists draw attention to a societal class structure that devalues women's contributions and excludes them from owning the means of production. This group of feminists argues for equality in the satisfaction of material (e.g., economic) needs and for an educational system that emphasizes the pursuit of common rather than individual goals. From the Marxist perspective, women's empowerment must also include ownership of the means of production in an economy.

Radical feminists argue that patriarchal (male-controlled) institutions must be torn down so new ones can be built based on feminist principles.

Psychoanalytic feminists posit that the experience of sexuality must be socially constructed rather than defined solely from the male perspective.

Contemporary socialist feminists point to systemic power relations that oppress women. For example, domestic labor is devalued in comparison with earning wages. Changes advocated by this group include valuing and mainstreaming women's perspectives. Also, contemporary socialists contend that women's values and activities must be considered an essential part of the survival and success of any system (e.g., family, organizational, political, etc.).

Existential feminists claim that women have historically been marginalized and treated as "the other" in society. So the key to women's empowerment is a form of self-development where women recognize and internalize a belief in their value to society and its various institutions.

Postmodern feminists believe in the value of societal and institutional diversity (as reflected in women's views and the views of other marginalized groups such as racial and ethnic minorities). They also argue that dominant (male-oriented) value systems and activities must be deconstructed so women's perspectives can be integrated into all of society's institutions.

Finally, **revisionist** feminists observe that women are oppressed by a dominant male value system and by stereotypes that minimize their contributions to society. This oppression can be eliminated only by a re-valuing of women's values and activities (see Buzzanell, 1994, for a more complete description of these eight feminist perspectives; also see Adamson, Briskin, & McPhail, 1988; Donovan, 1985; Jaggar, 1983; Langston, 1988; Nye, 1988; Tong, 1989).

Traditional vs. Feminist Views of Organizations

From the perspective of organizational communication theorizing, how do the various feminist perspectives alter traditional (male-oriented) views of organizational operations? Buzzanell (1994) offered some valuable theoretical insights into this very question. She observed that traditional views of organizations are associated with three primary themes: competitive individualism, cause-effect linear thinking, and separation and autonomy. Conversely, feminist perspectives emphasize the cooperative enactment of organization, integrative thinking, and connectedness. In order to understand the differences that underlie these contrasting themes, let's examine each one in detail.

Competitive Individualism vs. Cooperative Enactment

The ethic of **competitive individualism** separates people and organizations into winners and losers. An employee is viewed as a winner if his or her performance exceeds all other co-workers (who consequently become losers). Of course, organizations also battle one another (frequently over market share). Organizations that survive are the winners, while those that must close their doors are the losers. Importantly, an emphasis on winning within organizations brings with it some serious negative consequences such as "distrust, lower self-esteem, neglected family and friendships, and health problems" (Buzzanell, 1994, p. 345).

Feminist organizational communication theory can provide us with insight into the ways women emphasize a **cooperative** ethic in their talk and behavior. For example, when a group of workers is encouraged to work cooperatively on a project, their success is linked to how much they help one another. Consider for a moment a group of sales representatives who are required to work cooperatively with one another to increase the number of cars that are sold in a given geographic area. Would this emphasis on cooperation result in lower sales than a system that encourages the sales representatives to compete against one another? Of course, both models (competitive and cooperative) can yield positive results. But how do workers perceive each system? The competitive system produces winners and losers, whereas the cooperative system allows all workers to excel. Cooperation does not mean accepting substandard or inferior performance. Rather workers can labor together in pursuit of common goals (Lugones & Spelman, 1987).

When decisions are made by consensus and the voices of all members are heard, a cooperative environment is enacted. When success is equated more with value fulfillment (e.g., producing environmentally safe products) than personal advancement within a hierarchy, workers realize that cooperation produces its own rewards. Of course, for a cooperative workplace environment to flourish, workers need to understand how they are interconnected and interdependent. In addition, they need to engage in dialogue so they can figure out how to coordinate their efforts in the pursuit of common goals. Only through such cooperation can the unique talents of each worker be tapped for the attainment of personal and organizational goals (Wachtel, 1983).

Tapping the unique talents of workers, particularly those whose views have traditionally been excluded from mainstream decision making, can provide enormous benefits to organizations. Maruyama (1994) observed that a diverse workforce is a valuable organizational asset, waiting to be discovered. Indeed, genuine creativity is made possible by the interaction of ideas among many people. So through fostering cooperation among diverse workers and empowering those workers, organizations can fully realize the benefits of diversity.

Cause-Effect Linear Thinking vs. Integrative Thinking

The second traditional (male-oriented) theme identified by Buzzanell (1994) is **cause-effective linear thinking.** This form of thinking is preferred in most organizations because it is viewed as rational, direct, and solution oriented. Linear thinking assumes that there is one best way to accomplish organizational activities, so the goal of employee interaction is to discover this best approach and then to enact it.

Cause-effect linear thinking also privileges traditional social science research over interpretive or critical approaches. Working from the traditional social science model, "issues can be dissected and examined linearly; situations can be analyzed to uncover true and solitary symptoms and solutions; and deviations can be controlled" (Buzzanell, 1994, p. 360). Results stemming from social science research can then be applied to the bottom-line interests of organizational owners and management (e.g., effectiveness, efficiency, profitability, etc.).

In contrast to cause-effect linear thinking, feminist theorists emphasize holistic or **integrative thinking.** For example, feminists argue that women tend to engage in more contextual thinking. What this means is considering how any given action or decision will influence workers' lives, contribute to power imbalances, or impact on the environment. So instead of considering only how a decision will improve productivity, women are more likely to be concerned with the broader implications of implementing that decision. As Buzzanell (1994) notes, employees often lapse into forgetting that there are alternatives to addressing any issue or situation.

In taking a holistic perspective on decision making, many feminists focus on how organizational decisions impact environmental issues. In order to protect the environment, feminists advocate alternative approaches to solving organizational problems. Maruyama (1994) provides an excellent example that shows the organizational benefits of sustaining a concern for the environment by promoting alternative thinking:

When the environmentalist movement was mounted in the USA, most firms opposed stricter regulations, but one firm made use of the movement: a fish-farming firm devised a system to remove toxic elements from water beyond the current requirement, and pressed the government to establish a new requirement that the firm could meet but its competitors could not. (p. 12)

Although women engage in interaction that contributes to the bottom-line interests of management, they also interact to enhance the socio-emotional climate, to nurture others, and to share power. Integrative thinkers recognize that there is more going on in organizations than pursuing goals, sustaining profits, and engaging in strategic decision making. Workers form relationships with one another, they express their emotions, they pursue dreams and endure failure. Furthermore, leading a full life requires balancing family, leisure, work, and community activities (Buzzanell, 1994). These are issues that feminists believe should be central to workplace conversations.

Let's refer back to Barker's (1993) example of the self-managed team that needed to work overtime to fulfill a customer's order. What issues were considered when the workers accepted the customer's deadline? Was the only concern making money from that particular contract? Feminists would be more likely to raise questions such as (a) What is a fair work load? or (b) How often should we be required to work overtime? Balancing family and leisure time with work means that work cannot always dominate one's life. By drawing attention to such questions, feminists can make important contributions to creating a more humane workplace.

From a research perspective, feminists encourage researchers to focus more directly on the lived experiences of workers within organizations. Organizational communication research should not be confined to the examination of issues or problems that are linked to bottom-line results such as efficiency or productivity. Researchers can also point us toward the examination of communication processes that "encourage community, value diversity and integration, promote alternatives, and demonstrate caring and cooperative ethics" (Buzzanell, 1994, p. 365). Such research can be executed from a traditional social science perspective or from an interpretive or critical perspective.

Separation and Autonomy vs. Connectedness

The third traditional (male-oriented) theme identified by Buzzanell (1994) is **separation** and **autonomy.** She explains that socialization practices "urge men to distinguish themselves as individuals through action, work, and status; men learn to separate truth and fairness from emotionality" (Buzzanell, 1994, pp. 365–366). From this perspective, qualities such as nurturance and cooperation are considered weak. So within organizations, women must often denounce their values of cooperation, relationships, interdependence, continuity, and collective success (Buzzanell, 1994).

Women contrast the values of separateness and autonomy with a concern for connectedness. **Connectedness** refers to attempts to integrate the mind, body, and emotions in making sense of the world around us. Humans are holistic beings, not limited to displays of rationality; rather, there is an emotional side to all of us. As Buzzanell (1994) observes, "Until we embrace and integrate human emotion into standard organizational communication theory and research, we cannot truly value difference, accept the hidden fears in all humans, and change the motif of organizational life to promote diversity and connectedness" (p. 369).

If we turn to the issue of sexual harassment in the workplace, we can contrast the perspectives of separateness and autonomy with connectedness. One way of addressing sexual harassment is to listen to the accusations of the person making the complaint, focus on the behaviors committed by the violator, evaluate those behaviors in terms of corporate policy, and engage in corrective action if it is deemed necessary. Of course, if a man who sexually harasses women is fired from his job, a more humane workplace is created for the remaining men and women. However, who is attending to the emotional experiences of the women who were harassed? Do those emotional feelings end upon the termination of the violator's job contract? The harassed women are living, feeling human beings and their emotions cannot be forgotten because one harasser is no longer around to humiliate them. For an excellent treatment of this very subject, you may wish to turn to a special issue of the *Journal of Applied Communication Research* (Eadie, 1992). In this issue academic men and women describe their emotional experiences with sexual harassment in powerful detail.

Praxis and Consciousness-Raising

In terms of organizational communication theorizing, the feminist concern for connectedness is clearly relevant. For example, Marxist feminists are committed to the concept of **praxis.** Praxis refers to the linkage between theory and action. More specifically, praxis links theory and action so the members of an oppressed group come to understand fully the nature of their oppression. This is referred to as **consciousness-raising.** Once workers recognize how and why they are oppressed, they can search for ways to change their circumstances through empowerment and emancipation.

The feminist's concern for empowerment and emancipation provides us with a link to the next section of this chapter. Organizational researchers who work from the perspective of critical theory focus on how to raise the consciousness of oppressed workers so they can enact changes that lead to their empowerment and emancipation. How can this sort of change be promoted? Let's consider some of the arguments raised by critical researchers.

The Concept of Emancipation in Organizational Studies

When organizational researchers refer to the term "emancipation" they are describing the process "through which individuals and groups become free from repressive social and ideological conditions, in particular those that place socially unnecessary restrictions on the development and articulation of human consciousness" (Alvesson & Willmott, 1992, p. 432). The purpose of critical organizational theory is to facilitate this process through raising the consciousness of oppressed members so they can gain a clear understanding of the nature of the oppression they face. Once employee consciousness is raised, employees can consider alternative means of organizing and communicating that offer opportunities for empowerment and emancipation.

Some researchers, as well as practicing managers and corporate owners, scoff at the idea of employee emancipation because it minimizes the interests of those organizational stakeholders who want to control the actions of employees for their own ends (e.g., organizational survival, profitability, etc.). This does not mean, however, that employee emancipation always threatens organizational survival and effectiveness. Human relations approaches, quality of life programs, and calls for workplace democracy can promote the realization of higher-order human needs (e.g., self-actualization) while simultaneously improving job satisfaction and increasing productivity (Alvesson & Willmott, 1992). The key is to discover ways in which employee desires for emancipation dovetail with improved organizational performance.

Self-Reflection and Self-Transformation

Fostering an environment where worker emancipation is possible is not simple and it is not without drawbacks. Employees must engage in a painful process of resistance so they can overcome socially unnecessary restrictions such as the fear of failure and sexual and racial discrimination. Alvesson and Willmott (1992) observed thus:

[A]ny substantial and lasting form of emancipatory change must involve a process of critical self-reflection and associated self-transformation. From this perspective, emancipation is not to be equated with, or reduced to, piecemeal social engineering directed by a somewhat benevolent management. Rather, its conception of the emancipatory project encompasses a much broader set of issues that includes the transformation of gender relations, environmental husbandry, the development of workplace democracy, and so forth. (p. 434)

Central to critical theory is the belief that human reason possesses emancipatory potential. Through critical reflection people can come to understand how the reality of the social world and the construction of the self are socially produced. In other words, the social and structural arrangements that exist in organizations are produced by members who interact with one another. Furthermore, a person's self-perceptions emerge through interacting with other people (e.g., in talking with others we receive feedback concerning our actions in different social situations). Importantly, actions that are socially produced are open to transformation. This point is made most clearly by Giddens (1979) who observed that every social actor within a system has the capacity to exercise power and control through resisting and challenging dominant meaning systems.

Microemancipation

One argument that critical theorists face when addressing the issue of worker emancipation is that their claims are too grandiose. For example, if workers free themselves from the controls of management, will they be able to produce products or provide services at a level that sustains organizational competitiveness and ensures survival? This has led some theorists to call for "microemancipation." Alvesson and Willmott (1992) explain that **microemancipation** focuses attention on "concrete activities, forms, and techniques that offer themselves not only as means of control, but also as objects and facilitators of resistance and, thus, as vehicles for liberation" (p. 446).

A microemancipatory practice could involve redefining a verbal symbol advanced by management for a particular purpose. For example, managers sometimes try to promote a family metaphor to encourage employees to work together in the pursuit of organizational (family) goals. Just as families pull together in tough times, workers would be expected to pitch in by working overtime or increasing the pace of their activities so the organization can continue to survive. Employees could recognize how they are being manipulated by this metaphor, however, and redefine it in ways that are empowering for them. Families, for instance, encourage self-development for their children. This means that children can be expected to resist rules put forth by parents as a sign of their independence. Family members also engage in heated conflicts when any member attempts to enforce a rule that limits the options available to other members. These conflicts can result in certain members not talking or listening to one another for prolonged periods of time. So workers who feel oppressed by the family metaphor can redefine it in ways that are empowering. Indeed, workers can say to their managers that families argue, challenge unfair rules, and encourage individuality and separateness as well as closeness. If this redefinition is accompanied by resistant action to the more confining family metaphor advocated by management, a form of microemancipation surfaces for employees.

Questioning, Utopian, and Incremental Emancipation

In addition to their description of microemancipation, Alvesson and Willmott (1992) propose three other types of emancipatory projects. The first type, **questioning,** involves workers who challenge and critique dominant forms of thinking within the organization. The aim here is to contest the taken-for-granted by resisting authority. For example, workers could resist a management directive to perform a certain task because it is both inefficient and potentially dangerous. The challenge to managerial authority, however, occurs without proposing an alternative action.

The second type of emancipation is called **utopian.** This form of emancipation surfaces when employees present management "with a new form of ideal which aims at opening up consciousness for engagement with a broader repertoire of alternatives" (Alvesson & Willmott, 1992, p. 450). Defined as such, utopian emancipation represents an invitation to consider alternative ways of thinking rather than a suggestion for a ready-made course of action. The feminist call for holistic or integrative thinking versus cause-effect linear thinking as a guide for decision making would be representative of utopian emancipation.

Between these two types of emancipation is a third type called **incremental.** This type of emancipation is concerned with liberation from certain specific forms of oppression. A demand for a higher level of employee participation in organizational decision making would be an example of this type of emancipation.

If we refer back to our descriptions of workplace democracy and the various perspectives posed by feminist theorists, other paths to emancipation can also be identified. A democratic workplace empowers and emancipates employees as their voices become a central part of organizational decision making. An organization that is structured and influenced by feminist principles empowers women and other groups who are marginalized by the dominant themes that pervade most modern organizations (e.g., competitive individualism, cause-effect linear thinking, separation and autonomy, etc.). So although worker emancipation can not occur without attention to such organizational realities as the need to sustain productivity, various types and levels of emancipation are clearly possible. Perhaps the most interesting potential outcome linked to worker emancipation is the possibility that it may increase the productive capacity of workers by giving them more control over their actions and decisions.

Summary

In this chapter we looked at some of the most recent theoretical developments in organizational communication. First, we described the shift from bureaucratic forms of control to self-managed work teams. Although self-managed work teams offer opportunities for worker participation and self-governance, workers are not always pleased with their experiences in these work groups. Of particular concern has been the emergence of concertive control systems in which workers display more intense levels of control and discipline than exist in many bureaucracies. Democratic workplace systems were also examined in this chapter as a form of governance that can offer clear opportunities for worker participation and empowerment.

Particularly interesting are those organizations that empower employees to reconsider the very nature of organizational goals in order to sustain a vibrant, evolutionary form of democracy. Feminist theorists have highlighted paths to employee empowerment, especially by focusing on such themes as cooperation, integrative thinking, and connectedness. The enactment of these themes in the workplace maximizes the contributions of diverse members (e.g., women and racial/ethnic minorities) who are typically silenced in more traditional management systems.

Finally, the concept of emancipation in organizational studies was considered. Although worker emancipation cannot occur without attention to organizational concerns (e.g., profits, survival, etc.), workers can be freed from many of the restrictions placed upon them in bureaucracies. Giving workers a greater say in how to accomplish individual and organizational goals enables them to realize higher-order human needs such as self-actualization while simultaneously increasing productivity. Through carefully examining those organizations that encourage employee emancipation, we will learn more about alternative forms of communicating and organizing in the workplace.

Discussion Questions/Activities

1. How can the members of self-managed work teams sustain a balance between the attainment of individual and organizational goals? What needs to be done by these employees to prevent the sorts of problems reflected in the Barker and Cheney (1994) study?
2. What are the key advantages and disadvantages of enacting various forms of workplace democracy? How would worker experiences differ under participatory versus representative forms of democracy?
3. What are the key challenges to implementing feminist themes (e.g., cooperation, integrative thinking, connectedness) into the workplace? What are the major individual and organizational benefits of valuing these themes?
4. Is the concept of employee emancipation a utopian dream? What actions do workers need to take to experience some form of emancipation from repressive workplace rules?

Additional Resources

Books

Bachrach, P., & Botwinick, A. (1992). *Power and empowerment: A radical theory of participatory democracy.* Philadelphia: Temple University Press.

Ellerman, D. (1990). *The democratic worker-owned firm: A new model for East and West.* Boston: Unwin Hyman.

Greenberg, E. (1986). *Workplace democracy: The political effects of participation.* Ithaca, NY: Cornell University Press.

Levering, R., & Moskowitz, M. (1993). *The 100 best companies to work for in America* (rev. ed.). New York: Doubleday-Bantam-Dell.

Weisbord, M. (1991). *Productive workplaces: Organizing and managing for dignity, meaning and community.* San Francisco: Jossey-Bass.

Web Sites

http://ccme-mac4.bsd.uchicago.edu/DSALit/sf/sum95
    Democratic socialists discussion bulletin board.
http://www.osler.com/Resources/Labour_0.html
    Workplace democracy promotion in Ontario.

References

Adamson, N., Briskin, L., & McPhail, M. (1988). Entering the world of the women's movement. In N. Adamson, L. Briskin, & M. McPhail (Eds.), *Feminist organizing for change: The contemporary women's movement in Canada* (pp. 3–26). Toronto: Oxford University Press.

Alvesson, M., & Willmott, H. (1992). On the idea of emancipation in management and organization studies. *Academy of Management Review, 17,* 432–464.

Barker, J. R. (1993). Tightening the iron cage: Concertive control in self-managing teams. *Administrative Science Quarterly, 38,* 408–437.

Barker, J. R., & Cheney, G. (1994). The concept and practices of discipline in contemporary organizational life. *Communication Monographs, 61,* 19–43.

Barker, J. R., & Tompkins, P. K. (1994). Identification in the self-managing organization: Characteristics of target and tenure. *Human Communication Research, 21,* 223–240.

Barnard, C. (1938/1968). *The functions of the executive.* Cambridge, MA: Harvard University Press. (Originally published in 1938).

Blasi, J. R. (1987). *Employee ownership through ESOPs: Implications for the public corporation.* New York: Pergamon.

Bullis, C. (1993). At least it is a start. In S. A. Deetz (Ed.), *Communication Yearbook 16* (pp. 144–154). Newbury Park, CA: Sage.

Buzzanell, P. (1994). Gaining a voice: Feminist organizational communication theorizing. *Management Communication Quarterly, 7,* 339–383.

Cheney, G. (1995). Democracy in the workplace: Theory and practice from the perspective of communication. *Journal of Applied Communication Research, 23,* 167–200.

Clarke, T. (1984). Alternative modes of co-operative production. *Economic and Industrial Democracy, 5,* 97–129.

Deetz, S. A. (1992). *Democracy in an age of corporate colonization: Developments in communication and the politics of everyday life.* Albany: State University of New York Press.

Donovan, J. (1985). *Feminist theory: The intellectual traditions of American feminism.* New York: Frederick Unger.

Eadie, W. F. (Ed.). (1992). Sexual harassment issue. *Journal of Applied Communication Research, 20*(4).

Edwards, R. C. (1981). The social relations of production at the point of production. In M. Zey-Ferrell & M. Aiken (Eds.), *Complex organizations: Critical perspectives* (pp. 156–182). Glenview, IL: Scott, Foresman.

Eisenberg, E. M. (1994). Dialogue as democratic discourse: Affirming Harrison. In S.A. Deetz (Ed.), *Communication Yearbook 17* (pp. 275–284). Thousand Oaks, CA: Sage.

Eisenstein, Z. (1981). *The radical future of liberal feminism.* New York: Longman.

Evered, R., & Tannenbaum, R. (1992). A dialogue on dialogue. *Journal of Management Inquiry, 1,* 43–55.

Ferguson, K. (1984). *The feminist case against bureaucracy.* Philadelphia: Temple University Press.

Foucault, M. (1972). *The archaeology of knowledge* (A. Sheridan, Trans.). New York: Vintage.

Foucault, M. (1977). *Discipline and punish* (A. Sheridan, Trans.). New York: Vintage.

Foucault, M. (1980). *Power/knowledge* (G. Gordon, L. Marshal, J. Mepham, & K. Soper, Trans.; L. Gordon, Ed.). New York: Pantheon.

Gherardi, S., & Masiero, A. (1987). The impact of organizational culture in life-cycle and decision-making processes in newborn cooperatives. *Economic and Industrial Democracy, 8,* 323–347.

Giddens, A. (1979). *Central problems in social theory.* Berkeley: University of California Press.

Gunn, C. (1984). Hoedads co-op: Democracy and cooperation at work. In R. Jackall & H. Levin (Eds.), *Worker cooperatives in America* (pp. 141–170). Berkeley, CA: University of California Press.

Hafen, S. (1993, October). *Worker-owners and the experience of myness: A phenomenological study at Restaurant Casa Nueva.* Paper presented at the second annual Kentucky conference on narrative. Lexington, KY.

Harrison, T. M. (1994). Communication and interdependence in democratic organizations. In S.A. Deetz (Ed.), *Communication Yearbook 17* (pp. 247–274). Thousand Oaks, CA: Sage.

Jaggar, A. (1983). Political philosophies of women's liberation. In L. Richardson & V. Taylor (Eds.), *Feminist frontiers: Rethinking sex, gender, and society* (pp. 332–329). New York: Random House.

Langston, D. (1988). Feminist theories and the politics of difference. In J. W. Cochran, D. Langston & C. Woodard (Eds.), *Changing our power.* (pp. 10–21). Dubuque, IA: Kendall/Hunt.

Lugones, M. C., & Spelman, E. V. (1987). Competition, compassion, and community: Models for a female ethos. In V. Miner & H. E. Longino (Eds.), *Competition: A feminist taboo?* (pp. 234–247). New York: Feminist Press, The City University of New York.

Marshall, J. (1989). Re-visioning career concepts: A feminist invitation. In M. B. Arthur, D. T. Hall & B. S. Lawrence (Eds.), *Handbook of career theory* (pp. 275–291). Cambridge: Cambridge University Press.

Martin, P. Y. (1990). Rethinking feminist organizations. *Gender & Society, 4,* 182–206.

Maruyama, A. (1994). *Mindscapes in management: Use of individual differences in diversity management.* Hanover, NH: Dartmouth Publishing.

Mellor, M., Hannah, J., & Stirling, J. (1988). *Worker cooperatives in theory and practice.* Milton, Keynes, England: Open University Press.

Monge, P. R., & Miller, K. I. (1988). Participative processes in organizations. In G. M. Goldhaber & G. A. Barnett (Eds.), *Handbook of organizational communication* (pp. 213–229). Norwood, NJ: Ablex.

Mumby, D. K., & Stohl, C. (1991). Power and discourse in organizational studies: Absence and the dialectic of control. *Discourse & Society, 2,* 313–332.

Natalle, E. J., Papa, M. J., & Graham, E. E. (1993). Feminist philosophy and the transformation of organizational communication. In B. Kovacic (Ed.), *New approaches to organizational communication* (pp. 245–270). Albany, NY: State University of New York Press.

Nye, A. (1988). *Feminist theories and the philosophies of man.* London: Croon Helm.

Osbourne, J. D., Moran, L., Musselwhite, E., & Zenger, J. H. (1990). *Self-directed work teams: The new American challenge.* Homewood, IL: Irwin.

Papa, M. J., Auwal, M. A., & Singhal, A. (1996, April). *Organizing for social change within concertive control systems: Member identification, discursive empowerment, and the masking of discipline.* Paper presented at the annual meeting of the Eastern Communication Association. New York, NY.

Simon, H. (1976). *Administrative behavior.* New York: Free Press.

Tompkins, P. K., & Cheney, G. (1983). Account analysis of organizations: Decision-making and identification. In L. L. Putnam & M. E. Pacanowsky (Eds.), *Communication and organizations: An interpretive approach* (pp. 123–146). Beverly Hills, CA: Sage.

Tompkins, P. K., & Cheney, G. (1985). Communication and unobtrusive control in contemporary organizations. In R. D. McPhee & P. K. Tompkins (Eds.), *Organizational communication: Traditional themes and new directions* (pp. 179–210). Newbury Park, CA: Sage.

Tong, R. (1989). *Feminist thought: A comprehensive introduction.* Boulder, CO: Westview.

Wachtel, P. L. (1983). *The poverty of affluence: A psychological portrait of the American way of life*. New York: Free Press.

Weber, M. (1978). *Economy and society*. 2 vols. (G. Roth & C. Wittich, Trans.). Berkeley, CA: University of California Press.

Wellins, R. S., Byham, W. C., & Wilson, J. M. (1991). *Empowered teams: Creating self-directed work groups that improve quality, productivity, and participation*. San Francisco: Jossey-Bass.

Part One
Case Studies

This part concludes with two case studies that can be used to illustrate concepts of organization theories and perspectives on organizational communication. Questions with the case studies focus on these uses.

Prophecy Fulfilled

Mary Ann Stevens had worked at Jones, Smith & Co., a major accounting and consulting firm, for three years before she was promoted to senior auditor. She loved her job, but Jones, Smith's active acquisition of new clients had made her workload burdensome. She was elated when her manager told her that two young staff accountants were being assigned to work under her supervision on an audit of a new client, Acme Biscuit Company. The relief, however, was short-lived.

The next day Mary Ann had lunch with Tom Alvarez, also a senior auditor at Jones, Smith & Co. When Mary Ann told Tom her good news, he said, "Actually, that is both good news and bad news. One of your new assistants, Mike, worked for me on the Capco Manufacturing engagement. I don't think I'd be interested in having him on another assignment. When Mary Ann pressed Tom for more details, he replied, "Every time the client's Controller walked by, Mike was on the phone. He was always late for meetings, and when he did show up, it looked like he had slept in his suit. The worst of it is that the guy never met the deadline for any assignment that I asked him to do. There is, however, some good news. Your other assistant, Jeanine, looks like a real star. Very smart, hard worker, and clients love her."

That night, Mary Ann worried over what to do. The Acme engagement had a short time frame so she needed two staff people. On the other hand, she did not have the time to "babysit" a staff person who could not do his job. She was also concerned because of Acme's status as a new client. She was under a lot of pressure to keep clients and to obtain follow-up work whenever possible. One bad encounter could ruin her chances of a successful selling engagement, let alone additional work. The next morning, Mary Ann thought she had a solution. She decided to break down the work steps involved in the completion of the engagement. When she assigned work steps to her staff people, she gave Mike the tasks that were easy and required no interaction with the client. Since she knew from Tom that Jeanine was a good performer, she assumed that Jeanine would have no problem completing the higher-visibility, more difficult tasks. When she called Mike and Jeanine to announce their engagement planning meeting, she felt relieved and satisfied with her decision.

Mary Ann, Mike, and Jeanine met the next morning to discuss Acme Co. and review the work schedule and assignments. Mary Ann laid out the time table for the project, described the plan of work, and gave each assistant a list of assignments for the project. At the conclusion of her presentation, Mary Ann asked Mike and Jeanine if they had any questions. They said, "No." Both had expressions on their faces, however, that Mary Ann could not interpret. She thought for a moment about asking what was bothering them, but didn't. The Jones, Smith way of conducting business is for seniors to direct assignments and for juniors to carry out instructions. If anything goes wrong, it is the senior's responsibility. She had been very clear in her instructions, her assistants had no questions, and she did not want to appear indecisive by continuing the discussion.

Jeanine and Mike walked back to their work area in silence. Both were thinking about the meeting and the Acme engagement.

"Once again," Mike thought, "someone else gets all the challenging stuff, and I get the gofer work. This is the same thing that Alvarez did to me when my mom was sick, and I was spending a lot of time at the hospital. I can't believe that I have to live through another three months of this garbage."

"Why did she have to play favorites?" Jeanine thought. "Why was she so obvious about the assignments? Mike and I have both been here a year. They aren't even giving him a chance. Why doesn't he tell them why he had problems with the Capco engagement? Should I say something to Mary Ann?"

The project went off basically as Mary Ann had planned it, and she generally was pleased with the results. Acme Biscuit committed to bringing Jones, Smith & Co. back for the next year's audit. When it came time to complete Jeanine's and Mike's performance evaluations, Mary Ann retrieved her files and reviewed the following facts:

Mike:

Date	Comment
10/1	Complained about working overtime.
10/4	Directed questions from the Controller to Jeanine or me.
10/13	Completed compilation of assets data two days late.
10/15	Chose not to attend client picnic with Jeanine and me.
11/14	Missed lunch with the engagement partner.
12/1	Controller made comment about Mike not being a team player.

Jeanine:

Date	Comment
10/5	Completed inventory review two days ahead of schedule.
10/7	Controller made comment about being pleased with Jeanine's work. Also said he would like to have her back next year.
10/29	Jeanine impressed the Partner with her understanding of Acme and the manufacturing industry.
11/15	Jeanine came to me to ask what additional tasks she could complete.
11/22	Wrote an engagement status memo to Beth Williams without being asked.

After reviewing her files, Mary Ann determined that Jeanine was an outstanding performer and that Mike was a marginal performer. Then she thought back to her conversations with Tom Alvarez and said, "Tom's assessment of Mike was right on target."

1. Does Mary Ann seem to operate from any particular "theory" of management? If so, what is it?
2. What would a human relations theorist say about Mary Ann's approach to this situation? What would a human resource development theorist say?
3. Consider this case from traditional, interpretive, critical, and feminist points of view. What would representatives of each perspective have to say about what happened here?
4. What if anything should Mary Ann have done differently?

Chain of Command

Michael Smilowitz

Paul Ward had wanted to work in advertising since high school. When he was promoted to assistant director of O'Toole Oil and Tool's advertising department, he was a very happy man. The pay was great, and his boss encouraged Paul to be creative. It was the sort of job that suited Paul very well. He was amiable, outgoing, and soon made new friends all over the company, particularly with a group of employees who got together every Thursday night to play poker.

Paul's interests went beyond advertising and poker. He particularly enjoyed working with personal computers. Although he had never taken any computer classes in college, he found working with computers to be fun and easy. At work, he had implemented a number of programs to keep track of the department's budget and advertising plans, as well as had implemented a thorough system to file information about the various media in which O'Toole bought advertising space.

At home, Paul also enjoyed working with the computer he had bought for his personal use. One night, he got the idea that he could write a program that could help the warehousing department keep better control of the ordering of supplies. His friend, Harry Liu, a warehouse supervisor, had been complaining at the regular Thursday night poker game about his problems in monitoring orders. He said that he had repeatedly reported the problems to his boss, but hadn't received any response. So each night for a week, Paul finished dinner and then went to work writing the program. He even skipped that week's poker game in order to finish the program. When the program was ready, he took it to Harry. He showed Harry how to use it, and Harry seemed to think that the program would work very effectively! Paul was pleased with himself and left the program with Harry.

Two weeks later, the director of advertising, Jane Bales, called Paul into her office. Jane asked Paul to sit down, and then sat down on a chair next to him.

"You know Paul, I'm not mad about this at all. I think you're a bright person and a real asset to the company. But you have ruffled a lot of feathers over in manufacturing. You're going to get a real chewing out, and I don't think there's much I can do to prevent it."

"What's up Jane? What are you talking about?" asked Paul.

"It's that computer program you conjured up," Jane replied. "Ralph Ames, the vice president of manufacturing, is real upset that you skipped him over when you gave the program directly to your friend in warehousing. Ames thinks that nothing new should happen unless he personally approves it. He runs a tight ship over there and he doesn't like any interference."

"I wasn't interfering," Paul said, "I was just playing with my computer and thought I could make the jobs in warehousing a little easier."

Jane waited for Paul to calm down. She really wasn't upset with Paul, but she knew that Ames wasn't going to let the matter drop without making sure that Paul had been reprimanded for his actions. Jane didn't want to hurt Paul's feelings, but Ames was, after all, a vice-president. Jane began Paul's lesson.

"Paul, you have to realize that you work in advertising, not in manufacturing. What goes on in Ames' division is none of our business. We don't tell Ames how to make tools, and he doesn't tell us how to sell them. I know you solved a problem for them, but they should be able to solve that problem for themselves.

"Ames is an 'old school' sort of guy. For one thing, he was in the military. He believes in giving and taking orders. Mostly he just believes that a formal structure is the only way to do things. You know, one boss and one job for every person; that things need tight rein if quality is to stay up and costs to stay down. You skipped him when you went to warehousing, and Ames doesn't like to be skipped on any matter, let alone matters that he feels are his to control."

"I wonder why Harry took the program without saying anything about how Ames might react?"

Jane responded, "You mean the warehouse supervisor? Well, that's how Ames found out. When Harry went to him for approval to install the program, but Ames hadn't ordered anyone–least of all someone from advertising–to develop any such program."

"Well, I'm sorry. It's just that I thought it was a good idea, and I really wanted to let Harry evaluate the program for me by putting it to a real test."

"I know, Paul, and I'm not blaming you. But Ames is upset, and he'll stay upset till you go over and apologize for what you've done."

"You want me to see Ames?" asked Paul.

"Yes, Paul, he's waiting for you now. Go on over and take your medicine. I'll buy your lunch today when you get back."

1. What can you infer from this case about the management philosophy of this company and the theory of organization that probably best characterizes it?
2. Why do Paul and Ames have very different understandings of the rules of communication in this company?
3. If you had a free hand to change the way that this company does things, what would you do, and what ideas from the first part of this book would inform your actions?

PART TWO
COMMUNICATION,
RELATIONSHIPS,
AND MEDIA

COMMUNICATION AND ITS FUNCTIONS

The next two chapters in this book are concerned with ideas that truly provide the foundation of the traditional perspective on organizational communication. Traditionalists generally have understood the organization either as a machine or as an organism. One of the most useful and convenient ways of describing either machines or organisms is to characterize them according to their functions and structure. **Functions** are activities of a system that serve some purpose or objective. **Structure** is reflected in the linkages or relationships between elements in a system–linkages used to carry out functional activity. When these ideas are applied to organizational communication, *function* refers generally to the content, goals, and effects of communication. *Structure* refers to channels of communication or, literally, the patterns of interaction among organization members (Farace, Monge, & Russell, 1977). We will discuss the concept of communication function in this chapter, then follow with a discussion of structure in chapter 6.

Two Precautions

Before we begin our description of organizational communication functions and structure, we need to discuss two precautions that you should keep in mind: (1) communication functions and structure are highly interrelated; (2) any notion that the welfare of the organization as a whole is directly linked to efficiency and effectiveness in communication structure and function is misleading because different groups within an organization may pursue conflicting political objectives.

Function and Structure Relationship

We will talk about function and structure as *separate* ideas in two different chapters of this book for the sake of simplicity, but these two concepts are, in fact, highly related. In particular, the communication structure of an organization is developed and elaborated in ways that serve particular purposes. For example, a traditional distinction between formal and informal communication that we will develop later in this chapter implies that the two structures often involve different communication functions. As Farace and colleagues (1977) pointed out, "Both function and structure are intimately linked together, and major breakdowns in either can render the communication system of an organization inoperative" (p. 59).

Impact of Organizational Politics

The comment of Farace and colleagues about the relationship between "breakdowns" in function and structure and organizational communication effectiveness reflects a familiar theme in traditionalism–treatment of communication as a tool for managerial control of a rationally ordered system. Traditionalists often assume that an obvious connection exists between the welfare of the organization as a whole and effectiveness in communication structure and function. This assumption presumes that organizational goals are clearly established. In fact, organizations often pursue "multiple, possibly conflicting, and ambiguous goals" (Stevenson, Pearce, & Porter, 1985, p. 257). Consequently, traditionalist discussions of organizational communication may leave the reader with a troubled feeling that something has been left out, that some pieces of the traditionalist puzzle are missing. Abraham Zaleznik (1970) provided a clue about the location of these missing pieces when he reminded us:

Whatever else organizations may be (problem-solving instruments, sociotechnical systems, reward systems, and so on), they are political structures that provide platforms for the expression of individual interests and motives. (p. 48)

We pointed out in chapter 1 that organizations are political in the sense that they have systems for allocating and using power and resources as well as ways of maintaining and protecting these systems. The processes of organizational politics are concerned not only with the distribution of material resources, prerequisites, and positions but also with the power to define the mission, climate, and culture of an organization. Political battles over resources and power often emerge when different groups or coalitions (people who act temporarily as a group to advance a common interest) pursue conflicting objectives within the same organization (Cyert & March, 1963). Many functions and corresponding structures of organizational communication are intended to serve the special interests of particular groups and coalitions. While the various groups that comprise an organization are bound together by some kind of common purpose, their specific interests often are in conflict.

Aside from some of the more obvious examples of different organizational groups that can come into political conflict (management versus labor, headquarters versus field offices, staff managers versus line managers, or even one work group versus another), serious political conflicts may arise from various sources of cultural diversity in organizations, for example, gender, race, age, and ethnicity. Consider a hypothetical clash between two temporary coalitions. The first coalition arises when organization members who have small children band together to pressure top management for a company-supported day-care center. Suppose that management decides to get the money for a day-care center by reducing the amount that the company pays for employee health insurance. This decision gives rise to a second coalition that resists reduction of health benefits (e.g., older organization members who are more likely to suffer costly catastrophic illnesses). The two coalitions not only argue with management (which is now a victim of Pettegrew's S.O.B. theory), but they also actively oppose each other.

An even more compelling area of diversity-related political conflict involves the widespread occurrence of sexual harassment in the workplace. We will address this subject in more detail in chapter 11, but we want to refer to it here because sexual harassment is political in the sense that it can be a means for intimidating and controlling the targets of harassment–usually women. The Equal Employment Opportunity Commission has recognized that sexual harassment includes not only the overt coercion of sexual favors but also the existence of a hostile work environment. Because a hostile work environment is defined as anything that would offend a reasonable woman, it can include everything from sexual taunting to jokes or displays of sexually oriented material; that is, it may be created by spoken, written, or graphic communication (Wagner, 1992).

The subjects of politics, power, conflict, and diversity will receive a more fully developed treatment later in the text, especially in Chapters 9 through 12. The point of their introduction here is to make it clear that what is "functional" to one group may be "dysfunctional" to another. The communication structure evolved by one coalition to serve its interests may be resisted or countered by another coalition. The problem of understanding organizational communication structure and function is not as neat and simple as our models may appear to make it.

Communication, Information, and Meaning

The accomplishment of communication functions depends on the use of information and the meanings that are invested in that information. From the traditional point of view, information may be regarded as the basic "raw material" of communication. This raw material takes form when meaning is invested in it. Before we try to describe the basic functions of organizational communication, we need to sort out what is involved in communication, information, and meaning.

Each of us has an intuitive understanding of what is involved in human communication. After all, we communicate with others virtually every day of our lives. Yet, it is not easy to develop a precise definition and description of the communication process. The term *communication* has become such a buzzword in modern society that one can use it to mean just about anything. We regard communication as *shared meaning created among two or more people through verbal and nonverbal transaction*. The basic raw material of communication is verbal and nonverbal information. When two or more human beings engage in verbal and nonverbal transaction, they are involved in generating, perceiving, and interpreting such information. To the extent that shared meaning or a *common* interpretation among two or more people results from this process, communication has occurred.

This definition of communication is not unusual. Others have offered similar definitions (Goyer, 1970; Tubbs & Moss, 1980), but not everyone agrees with this approach (Eisenberg & Goodall, 1993). The idea of "shared meaning" is only one way to define communication, but we will elaborate on this definition because the key terms, at least, are common in many definitions of communication.

Information and Meaning

In a simple sense, information includes any kind of pattern that a person can observe or sense in the environment. The significance or meaning attached to the pattern may range from negligible to very substantial. **Meaning** occurs when information is placed within a context. The context may be as simple as pattern recognition or as complex as reflective interpretation, in which one piece of information is related to and understood with reference to many others. For example, consider the following markings:

Although a very small child may perceive little more than the contrast between the color of the page and the color of the markings, a normal adult will see patterns or definite characteristics such as linear and curvilinear features. Beyond these features, the English-speaking reader may assign very little meaning to these markings. If you know something about the structure of languages, you may realize that the markings represent letters or even a word in some language. If you understand Russian, you will recognize the markings as the last three letters of the Russian alphabet. In addition to this denotative meaning, the connection between the markings and "Russian" may also evoke other feelings for you. The level of significance or meaning in each case is different, depending on the frame of reference that your experience has given you. Information provides the basis for communication. Although any perceivable aspect of one's environment is potentially informative, we are concerned with information in the forms of human verbal and nonverbal behavior.

Verbal Behavior

Verbal behavior includes speaking and writing in the code of a language system. The words in a vocabulary and the grammatical rules for arranging them in expressions are the basic features of a language system. Grammar does not necessarily mean an eighth grade English teacher's *prescriptive* rules for how one is supposed to use language. It also includes all of the regularities that occur in the verbal behavior of a group of language users. Any mode of expression that occurs as a common usage within a particular language community represents a rule for that community. A lawyer representing a client who intends to sue you as well as some other people may say, "To protect my client's interests, I have concluded that it will be necessary to join you as a party defendant in the above styled action, to wit steps to effect this joinder have been undertaken." You may find the rules of this language to be odd and even ungrammatical from a prescriptive stand-point, but the phrase will make perfect sense to another lawyer who uses this same language. All of the words in a language are **symbols**. All symbols have three basic characteristics. They are representational, freely created, and cultur-ally transmitted (Pollio, 1974).

A symbol is **representational** because it stands for something other than itself. Word symbols provide labels for objects, actions, and experiences. They also permit us to talk about and share conceptions of the things that they label. A word symbol is a substitute that represents an object by providing a link to the idea or concept of this object (Langer, 1942).

Symbols also are **freely created**. The relationship between a symbol and its referent (the thing the symbol represents) is arbitrary because the users of a par-ticular language make up and choose the symbols. The founders of International Business Machines could just as easily have named the company Acme Typewriters. The referent would have been the same (although "IBM" admittedly has more flare). Human beings are continually inventing new symbols to refer to new conditions. Today, we talk about storing files on "floppy disks," "microwav-ing" our food, and "keyboarding" on "word processors," with meanings for these terms that were virtually nonexistent a decade ago.

Finally, symbols are **culturally transmitted.** This means that symbols are taught and learned, carried on from one generation to another within a language system. Although symbols are freely created and languages do change over time, much of the basic form and content of a language remains stable through cultural transmission. Others created most of our symbols and the rules for using them a long time before we arrived in the world. We are born into a system of symbols and language rules that imposes a particular order on our world. As we acquire the language, we acquire the order that comes along with it.

Language scholars have no problem with the idea that symbols are culturally transmitted, but the fact that language does bring with it a way of ordering the world leads many scholars to regard representation and free creation as inade-quate characterizations of symbols. Symbols are more than just representative and arbitrary because language exerts a very powerful influence on the way we experience the world (Blumer, 1969; Deetz, 1973). For example, Benjamin Whorf (1957) found that Hopi Indian and English languages handle time in very different ways. The Hopi has no means for marking time that corresponds to the English use of past, present, and future tense. Whorf reasoned that the Hopi expe-rience of time must be quite different from the experience of someone whose lan-guage affords convenient ways of carving up time according to verb tense. If Whorf is right, language is much more than a mere tool for expressing thought. Thought itself depends on language, and our notions about "reality" are products of that language. It is even possible that something that is "thinkable" in one language may be "unthinkable" in another. Avis Rent-A-Car encountered this problem some years ago when the company attempted to translate its famous "We Try Harder" slogan into the languages of other countries where Avis did business. The closest approximation in German translates roughly as "We give of ourselves more effort." Somehow, the essence of "We Try Harder" seems to be lost in the German equivalent (Pollio, 1974).

Is language an important factor in structuring our experience of organizational life? Interpretivists and critical theorists certainly seem to think so. In part, this is the point that they are making when they argue that organizational reality is socially constructed. Studies by Koch and Deetz and by Wood and Conrad provide some evidence for this point of view. Koch and Deetz (1981) reported that language systems in organizations revealed "root metaphors" that members use to order and to make sense of their experiences. For example, members might talk about and understand their organization as an efficient, well-oiled machine (mechanical metaphor), a winning team (sports metaphor), a combat group (military metaphor), or even "a big, happy family."

Wood and Conrad (1983) found that organizational languages often contain paradoxes that create double binds for members. A double bind arises from inconsistent messages that result in a "hanged if you do, hanged if you do not" outcome. Consider the manner in which members of a male-dominated management group sometimes solicit ideas from female colleagues:

The invitation often takes the form of soliciting "a woman's perspective" or the "female viewpoint," a form which both subordinates professional expertise and peer status to gender and emphasizes the woman's difference from other members of the group. The woman confronted with such a request is caught in a paradox. If she protests the focus on gender, she runs the risk of being labeled overly sensitive. . . . If she accepts the focus on gender, she collaborates in diminishing her image as a professional. Of course, her colleagues are caught within the same paradox of recognizing her uniqueness, yet being enjoined not to recognize it and to regard her as no different from anyone . . . of equivalent rank in the institution. (pp. 309–310)

Language and symbol systems have two other characteristics that also are important in the study of organizational communication. First, language is ambiguous in the sense that most words and expressions can have more than one meaning. Several scholars state that much of the communication in organizations occurs in an effort to reduce uncertainty associated with ambiguity (Goldhaber, 1993; Weick, 1979). Second, organizational communication often involves the use of group-restricted codes (Baird & Weinberg, 1981). A group-restricted code involves a specialized usage of a language. The vocabulary and rules are unique to a particular group.

Ambiguity

Ambiguity occurs as a consequence of abstract terminology, lack of sufficient detail in messages, and inappropriate or confusing use of modifiers and qualifying phrases (Johnson, 1977). Sometimes, ambiguity is accidental and unintentional, as reflected in the case of a publishing company executive who became angry when someone failed to notify the printing department about a major change in an order. The executive complained to a group of middle managers, "We've got to have better communications around here," then promptly left for a two-week vacation, thinking that the middle managers would lay down the law with employees on the importance of relaying information about any change in a project. When he returned, the middle managers could hardly wait to show him the marketing brochure describing the state-of-the-art office communications system that they had ordered (at a cost of several thousand dollars) during his absence. It was obvious that the middle managers' concept of "better communications" was quite a bit different from the idea that the executive had in mind.

Ambiguity is a common, day-to-day problem in organizational communication, and many organizations expend a great deal of energy in attempting to cope with it. Experts on oral and written expression are quick to advise people that simple, concrete language is the key to reducing ambiguity. But ambiguity in organizational communication involves more than accidental misuse of language or failure to be clear. Ambiguity occurs simply because a symbol or expression has different meanings for different people. There is no guarantee that two people will share the same meaning for a term or expression, even when it is simple and concrete. As Eric Eisenberg (1984) pointed out, ambiguity and clarity are not really embedded in messages but in the *relationship* among source, message, and receiver. Clarity exists only to the extent that "a source has narrowed the possible interpretations of a message and succeeded in achieving a correspondence between his or her intentions and the interpretation of the receiver" (p. 23).

Eisenberg also makes a convincing case that much of the ambiguity in organizational communication is quite deliberate rather than accidental. **Strategic ambiguity,** according to Eisenberg, is not necessarily bad. In fact, it is often very useful and even essential to the organization. Strategic ambiguity helps to promote cohesion by highlighting organization members' agreement on abstract, general ideas and by obscuring their disagreements over specific details. For example, the faculty at University X is "strongly committed to excellence in teaching, research, and service." The university president likes to mention this in public speeches but never attempts to define "excellence" in these areas because different groups of faculty disagree over the specific standards.

Strategic ambiguity in organizational policies and procedures also allows organizations to adapt more readily to change. In 1979–80, Chrysler Corporation used this form of ambiguity to cope with the public perception that the company produced low-quality automobiles. Foss (1984) noted that Chrysler quickly associated itself with Japanese products (generally regarded as high-quality) by marketing the Japanese-made Dodge Colt. The little Colt was advertised as "The Most Technologically Advanced Japanese Import You Can Buy." At the *same* time, according to Foss, Chrysler *denied* its linkage to Japan in an advertising campaign for its U.S.-built K cars: "K cars are proof . . . you don't have to be Japanese to build quality cars." The strategy allowed Chrysler to capitalize on its Japanese connection as a short-term response to its quality problem until a time came when the corporation "no longer had to rely on its Japanese imports for an image of quality and desirability" (p. 82). In effect, Chrysler used strategic ambiguity to play both ends against the middle.

Finally, Eisenberg argues that strategic ambiguity is an important means for supporting status distinctions and maintaining interpersonal relationships in organizations. Consider, for example, the relationship between physicians and nurses in hospital settings. Suppose that a physician gives a nurse an erroneous or inappropriate order for a patient's treatment. If the nurse knows that the order is inappropriate, he or she is legally obligated to confront the situation. But such a confrontation challenges the physician's supreme authority over patient care and nursing actions. The nurse's only way out of this bind "is to use the doctor-nurse game and communicate . . . without appearing to" (Stein, 1967, p. 703). In other words, the nurse uses an *indirect* rather than direct means of communicating with the physician about the problem. Instead of making an unambiguous statement that the order is inappropriate or that it should be changed (statements that would challenge or threaten the physician's authority), the nurse might say, "Doctor, I'm concerned about this order. Could you explain it to me?" This is a face-saving strategy that allows the physician to discover the problem and correct it. Cunningham and Wilcox (1984) noted that nurses will take stronger, less ambiguous actions, however, if the risk to the patient is serious and if indirect strategies are ineffective in getting the physician to change the order.

The idea of anyone being obliged to engage in these kinds of interpersonal gymnastics merely to avoid embarrassment to an authority figure is unpalatable and typical of the kind of paradox that Wood and Conrad describe. But the politics of organizational life are filled with such paradoxes. Ambiguity, as Eisenberg suggests, can be a very effective tool for managing one's way through a paradox.

Group-Restricted Codes

Whether or not ambiguity in organizational communication is accidental or strategically deliberate, it can be reduced only to the extent that people share the same meaning for a code. Groups and organizations often try to ensure that shared meaning will occur by adopting a **group-restricted code** that is highly specialized (Baird & Weinberg, 1981). Many professions and technical occupations use such codes in the form of "jargon"—terms and modes of expression that are known primarily to members of these groups. One's success as a member of such a group depends in part on the ability to master the group's restricted code. We know of one high-technology corporation (Intel) in which the restricted code has become so elaborate that the company issues a comprehensive dictionary of terms and expressions to new employees.

Group-restricted codes are paradoxical. They help to minimize ambiguity and promote a common identity among group members, yet they can be quite confusing to nonmembers. For example, the lawyer's jargon that we used earlier in this chapter may seem like a maze of abstractions to an outsider, but group members (other attorneys) share relatively precise meanings for the code. Even restricted codes that seem to be simple and precise to a nonmember may have "hidden" meanings that are known only within the group itself.

The influence of a restricted code in professional situations is illustrated well by the compelling case of William Borham, who became chief administrator of a large mental hospital in Wisconsin. Borham had no formal education in mental health. In fact, William Borham was not even William Borham. He was really Raymond Metzgar, a former inmate in a psychiatric institution. Metzgar's familiarity with mental hospitals and his ability to speak the language of the mental health profession enabled him to deceive his employer into believing that he was

William Borham, a trained clinical psychologist. The fact that Metzgar, alias Borham, became a prominent advocate for mental health programs in Wisconsin brought great embarrassment to state officials when his deception was uncovered by Chicago police after they arrested him for child molestation.

The influence of language on our interpretations of experience, on the nature of ambiguity in organizational communication, and on the characteristics of group-restricted codes should make it clear that verbal behavior and symbolic processes in organizational communication are quite complicated. This complexity increases when we consider nonverbal behavior as the second source of information in human communication.

Nonverbal Behavior

Much of the information involved in human communication is **nonverbal behavior** that occurs in forms other than the word symbols of a language. Harrison (1970) estimated that 65 percent of the information in day-to-day interaction is nonverbal, but the role of nonverbal behavior in communication is not as clear as the role of verbal behavior. Ekman and Friesen (1972) regarded nonverbal behavior as "communicative" only when the person who exhibits the behavior intends it as a message for someone else. In contrast, Watzlawick, Beavin, and Jackson (1967) argued that any behavior, whether intentional or unintentional, is communicative if another person perceives and interprets it.

We do not want to get into a distracting debate over when nonverbal behavior is communicative and when it is not, but defining communication as the creation of shared meaning does at least require *both* parties in the act to be aware of the behavior, attach some meaning to it, and achieve some commonality in this meaning. The perplexing and intriguing problem with a lot of nonverbal behavior is that even when we are unaware of our own behaviors in the presence of others, they may be interpreting these behaviors and acting toward us on the basis of the interpretation. The behavior itself may not always be "communicative," but it can certainly influence the communication process. With this realization in mind, we will describe three forms of nonverbal behavior that are important in organizational communication: paralanguage, body movement, and the use of space.

Paralanguage

Paralanguage consists of nonverbal speech sounds. Tone, pitch, volume, inflection, rhythm, and rate are elements of paralanguage. Paralanguage is important because the meaning of spoken expression often depends on the paralanguage cues that accompany verbal sounds. We know, for example, that feelings and emotions in spoken expression are indicated primarily by paralanguage cues (Davitz, 1964). Although there is little research on the association between specific paralanguage cues and emotions, it is intuitively obvious that we infer others' attitudes and feelings from paralanguage cues in their speech. The phrase "What a day," spoken quickly, in a bright tone, and with emphasis, may lead us to infer that the speaker is in a jovial mood. The same phrase in a grumbling, colorless drawl suggests that the speaker is miserable.

Paralanguage also provides cues to meaning in less obvious ways. For example, distinctions between statement types often are provided in paralanguage cues. The difference between a declarative statement and a question often is indicated by the sentence structure, but sometimes can be detected only through paralanguage. Suppose that you take a work-related problem to your boss. The boss listens, then replies, "You know what to do. . . ." A downward inflection from beginning to end may suggest a declarative statement. The boss has heard the problem and is *telling* you that you know how to handle it. An upward inflection at the end could be a question. The boss is *asking* whether you know how to proceed. Some authorities believe women often use paralanguage cues in ways that undermine their authority as managers and professionals, for example, by making declarative statements sound like questions suggesting that the speaker is tentative or uncertain (Lakoff, 1975).

Paralanguage also regulates spoken expression. A pause can indicate the end of a thought or provide a cue that another party can take a turn at speaking. In this sense, paralanguage cues are like punctuation marks in written expression. Written expression also has other characteristics that correspond to paralanguage in speech. Italics and boldface type may be used for emphasis. Readers use clarity, crispness, and overall appearance of writing in making inferences about writers in much the same way that listeners use paralanguage to make inferences about speakers. The potential cues in writing may be much more limited than those available in speech because many of the devices that one might use are regarded as inappropriate in formal writing (Perrin, 1965), although anyone who has used electronic mail, computer bulletin board services, or electronic newsgroups either in a local area or on the global internet can tell you that people have adapted many typographical characters such as the almost universally recognized smiley face, :), to add style to their messages.

One of the most important functions of paralanguage in both written and spoken expression in organizational communication may be its role in influencing person perception. Several studies show that employment interviewers' hiring decisions and judgments of an applicant's suitability for a particular type of job are influenced by accent and dialect. De La Zerda and Hopper (1979) found that Hispanic Americans who speak "standard," unaccented English are more likely to be regarded as appropriate candidates for supervisory or managerial jobs than those who speak accented English. Schenck-Hamlin (1978) also found that perceptions of a person's competence, coherence, and character appeal are influenced by dialect, but the effect depends on the content of the message. Midwesterners judged "midwestern" and "southern" dialect speakers about equally on neutral topics, but a topic that evoked midwestern stereotypes of southerners led to much lower ratings for the southern dialect speaker. A "midwesterner" opposing racial desegregation was perceived as more competent, coherent, and appealing than a "southerner" presenting the same message.

Body Movement

Much of the information available in face-to-face communication is provided through **body movement.** Ray Birdwhistell (1952), a leading theorist in this area, claimed that all body movement is meaningful within the context in which it occurs. Birdwhistell believed that body movement can be subjected to systematic analysis and that the characteristics of body movement correspond to the characteristics of language. He based his concepts for the study of body movement, which he called **kinesics,** on the same ideas used in linguistics, the study of language. The idea that body movement is a kind of language has been popularized through work in kinesics, but some scholars have questioned this notion (Littlejohn, 1992).

Is body movement like a language in the sense that it has a vocabulary, grammar, and syntax? Not really, but there is no doubt that body movement has some important functions in human communication. One very useful description of these functions is a system of categories devised by Paul Ekman and Wallace Friesen (1972). Their categories include emblems, illustrators, regulators, affect displays, and adaptors.

Emblems are kinesic substitutes for verbal behavior. An emblem usually is intended to transmit a particular message, but the meaning may depend on the group that uses it and the context in which it occurs. The two-fingered "V" traditionally is an emblem for victory. During the 1960s, college students and other young people also adopted it as an emblem for peace.

Illustrators are kinesic cues that directly support speech behavior. These cues are not substitutes for the spoken word, but they help to emphasize what is being said. Illustrators include behaviors to point out, outline a form, or depict motion. In one sense, an illustrator is a kind of kinesic "visual aid." People who use many illustrators when speaking are likely to be perceived as more animated and energetic than those who use few or no illustrators (Norton, 1978).

Regulators help to control and coordinate face-to-face interaction. These behaviors include eye movements, head positions, and postures that signal taking turns in conversations. Eye contact in particular is important as a signal for seeking feedback, initiating interaction, or terminating conversations (McCroskey, Larson, & Knapp, 1971).

Affect displays are cues to feelings and emotional states. These behaviors may include facial movements such as smiles, frowns, and sneers, as well as certain postures. Facial expression seems to be a good indicator of at least six emotions: happiness, anger, sadness, surprise, disgust, and fear (Knapp, 1978).

Adaptors involve release of physical tension. These behaviors may be either the means for or the results of tension release. For instance, scratching your head may be an instrumental behavior to relieve an itch. In contrast, moment-to-moment wiggles and jiggles of various body parts may result merely from random nervous system activity.

Space

The use of **space** is a subtle but powerful factor in human social and organizational behavior that appears to vary greatly across different cultures. In general, humans seem to be territorial creatures who define and defend the boundaries of our space. We also arrange objects in space to either suit ourselves or to accomplish various purposes. Finally, we use space to define appropriate distance between people in interpersonal settings.

The formal study of the use of space is called **proxemics.** Edward Hall (1959), who developed the field of proxemics along the lines of Birdwhistell's kinesics, identified three basic types of space: fixed-feature, semifixed-feature, and informal.

Fixed-feature space involves either concrete or imaginary but stable boundaries that define territory. Goldhaber (1993) points out that there often is a close relationship between status and territory in organizations. He has identified three principles in this relationship that have the potential to influence organizational communication:

1. The higher up you are in the organization, the more and better space you have.
2. The higher up you are in the organization, the better protected your territory is.
3. The higher up you are in the organization, the easier it is to invade the territory of lower-status personnel. (pp. 193–196)

Whether or not the amount of space in one's territory, the ability to protect it, or the ability to invade someone else's territory are directly communicative, these conditions certainly can influence organizational communication. The allocation of space itself signifies status, and status gives one more control over initiating, structuring, and terminating interaction with others.

Offices and work areas in organizations contain many objects and fixtures that must somehow be positioned in space—desks, chairs, files, equipment, decorations. The arrangement of these objects involves the use of **semifixed-feature space**. Such arrangements may or may not be intended to transmit a particular message, but the idea of communication through placement of objects has become so popular that *any* arrangement is almost certain to provoke an interpretation.

If you can penetrate the well-protected territory of a high-level executive, you may find that this person's space is furnished more like a living room than an office. Presumably, such an arrangement "communicates" an atmosphere of openness and accessibility. The lower-level manager with a cast-off military surplus desk, stacked with volumes of reports and positioned as a barrier behind a door to a cramped office, may be telling visitors, "Go away. I really don't have time for you." Such interpretations may be perfectly valid, but one should exercise them with caution because they presume that the person who occupies the space has a specific intent and purpose for the arrangement of objects within it. In fact, the use of semifixed-feature space may be more dependent on organizational customs and allocation of resources than on any conscious personal choice that the office occupant makes.

The final category, **informal space,** refers to the physical proximity of one person to another in interpersonal settings. Hall (1959) identified four distinct informal zones in American culture: intimate (one to eighteen inches), personal (eighteen inches to four feet), social (four to twelve feet), public (over twelve feet). Most interpersonal conversations occur in the personal zone of informal space, but cultures vary in the use of this space. The Chinese seem to require more personal distance for interaction than Americans require. In turn, Americans require more than Arabs require. Most interaction in American business organizations occurs in the social zone of informal space. A Chinese visitor might find this practice to be appropriate and tasteful. An Arabic visitor might be most uncomfortable under similar conditions.

While paralanguage, body movement, and use of space are three important forms of nonverbal behavior in human communication, researchers have identified other behaviors and characteristics of human demeanor that may also be relevant to our discussion. These include use of time, touch, clothing, and overall physical appearance (body type). Whether these behaviors and personal characteristics are communicative in the sense that we have defined communication will depend on many factors in any given situation. In any case, such behaviors certainly will influence the day-to-day process of communication.

Functions of Communication

Verbal and nonverbal behavior provide the means for accomplishing specific communication functions. These functions in organizational communication may be described in various ways, but most descriptions are tied to three basic processes that occur in an open system: transformation of energy and materials via input, throughput, and output; regulation of system processes; and system growth or adaptation. Farace, Monge, and Russell (1977) describe three communication functions that are traditionally associated with these processes: production, maintenance, and innovation.

Traditional Function Categories

The **production function** includes any communication that controls and coordinates the activities required to produce system outputs. This means communication involved in activities that yield an organization's products or services. Such communication is "work-connected." It includes instructions for the amount and type of output to be produced, job procedures, information about work group organization, and reports on work group activity or problems in the work itself.

The **maintenance function** includes communication that regulates system processes. Regulation implies that system conditions are maintained within certain desirable or acceptable limits. Maintenance communication is concerned with keeping the organization intact and in a steady state of operation. Organizational policies or rules and various forms of deviation-correcting negative feedback serve the maintenance function, but Farace and colleagues suggested that there is more to maintenance communication than policies, rules, and negative feedback:

Maintenance communication is that which (a) affects the member's feelings of personal worth and significance, (b) changes the "value" placed on interaction with coworkers, supervisors, and subordinates, and (c) alters the perceived importance of continuing to meet the organization's production and innovation needs. (p. 59)

Given such a broad definition, maintenance communication could include events ranging from the employee-of-the-month column in a company newsletter to many of the informal, day-to-day conversations that affect human relationships in the organization. In fact, some writers such as Goldhaber (1993) prefer to include any communication affecting members' feelings of self-worth and quality of organizational relationships in a fourth functional category called **human.** This approach restricts the maintenance function only to regulatory processes.

The **innovation function** includes communication concerned with change in the organization. Communication in this category may involve the development of new ideas and practices as well as the means for implementing and securing acceptance of change. The changes may involve organizational mission, philosophy, structure, and functions. Generally, change implies some alteration in organizational values as well as in organizational behavior. Suggestions from organization members for changes in products, services, or work procedures; recommendations from studies of organizational needs; and long-range planning activities all involve the innovation function.

Uncertainty and Information Adequacy

Several authorities argue that the various functions of organizational communication are all related to a single, more general purpose—the reduction of **uncertainty** (e.g., Weick, 1979). Rosabeth Moss Kanter (1977) claimed that organizations, especially large, bureaucratically structured ones, thrive on predictability. Uncertainty, or the absence of predictability, is an unnerving experience to be avoided whenever possible. Hence, communication is used to reduce or at least cope with uncertainty.

Despite frequent claims that communication serves an uncertainty reduction function, we should not simply assume that this always is true. As we pointed out earlier in this chapter, Eric Eisenberg (1984) makes a convincing case that many of the messages in day-to-day organizational communication are deliberately and strategically ambiguous because *creating* uncertainty serves the purposes of particular individuals, groups, or even the entire organization. We need only recall some of the earlier examples to realize that organizational communication sometimes is more concerned with creating uncertainty than with reducing it. For example, consider the university president's speeches about commitments to excellence, Chrysler's advertising strategy to promote an image of quality, the doctor-nurse game, and the compensation manager who wanted to revise the communication department's magazine story on employee wage structure so that employees would not understand it.

Even though different individuals and groups within an organization may try to create uncertainty for one another or even may try to use strategic ambiguity in ways that benefit the organization as a whole, it is probably safe to say that any given individual or group desires certainty for itself. Since information is the key to reduction of uncertainty, organization members usually are concerned with the **adequacy** of this information. Is there enough, too much, or too little information to serve organizational purposes? As Farace and colleagues (1977) contended, "*What* is known in an organization and *who* knows it are obviously very important in determining the overall functioning of the organization" (p. 27).

Although the importance of information adequacy in organizational communication has been recognized for many years, and the subject received rather intensive study in the 1970s and 1980s, problems with information adequacy continue to plague organizations of the 1990s. As Spiker and Lesser (1995) note, many executives "fall into the trap of providing information on a need-to-know basis," that is, they tell subordinates only what they think their subordinates need to know.

Farace and colleagues explained problems associated with information adequacy by employing Brillouin's (1962) distinction between **absolute** and **distributed information.** Absolute information refers to the total body of information that exists within an organization at any time. This information is distributed to the extent that it is **diffused** (spread) throughout the organization. Information adequacy problems may arise because a piece of information simply does not exist in the organization's pool of absolute information or because existing information is not properly distributed.

Although researchers in organizational communication have been interested in the problem of information adequacy for many years, they have made little effort to study adequacy by systematically matching an organization's information needs against *both* absolute and distributed information in order to identify the sources of adequacy problems. Many like Farace and colleagues simply assume that inadequate information usually results from distribution problems. Hence, most studies of information adequacy focus on *individual* organization members as *receivers* of distributed information.

Some researchers have evaluated information adequacy by measuring individual members' knowledge about the organization and its functions (Level, 1959; Tompkins, 1962). More commonly, researchers examine the difference between the amount of information that individual members think they *need* and the amount that they think they *actually receive* (Daly, Falcione, & Damhorst, 1979; Daniels & Spiker, 1983; Goldhaber, Yates, Porter, & Lesniak, 1978; Spiker & Daniels, 1981). In these studies, "adequacy" is defined by organization members' *perceptions* of the difference between what is received and what is desired.

Since most research on information adequacy studies the perceptions of individual organization members, it is not surprising that the kinds of information topics examined in these studies involve individual information needs rather than the information needs of the organization as a whole. Several studies have measured information adequacy with a scale developed by the International Communication Association (ICA). This scale asks organization members to report the extent to which they are adequately informed on the following topics:

1. How well I am doing my job.
2. My job duties.
3. Organizational policies.
4. Pay and benefits.
5. How technological changes affect my job.
6. Mistakes and failures of the organization.
7. How I am being judged.
8. How job-related problems are being handled.
9. How organization decisions are made that affect my job.
10. Promotion and advancement opportunities in my organization.

11. Important new product, service, or program developments in my organization.
12. How my job relates to the total organization.
13. Specific problems faced by management.

While studies of these topics may yield valuable knowledge about the extent to which organization members as individuals feel adequately informed, this scale covers only three basic individual needs for information: task and performance issues, compensation and benefits, and problems and progress of the organization (Daniels & Spiker, 1983). Even studies of information adequacy that do not use this particular scale are still based on information topics very much like those in the ICA scale. They also adopt the same focus on organization members as individuals (e.g., Penley, 1982).

Despite the limitations of the focus on individual rather than organizational information needs, studies of information adequacy do indicate that surprisingly large percentages of organization members consider themselves to be inadequately informed on many important topics that directly concern them. The ICA-sponsored studies of eighteen large organizations found that nearly half of the members generally received less information than they wanted (Spiker & Daniels, 1981). Penley (1982), who classified all of the information topics in his study as task- or performance-related, found that 48 percent of the participants in his study were inadequately informed on performance topics and 8 percent were inadequately informed in both task and performance areas.

Penley also found that information adequacy is closely related to the members' sense of identification with and commitment to the organization. This finding was repeated in a study by Smith and DeWine (1987). Spiker and Daniels' (1981) analysis of data from the eighteen ICA studies revealed that information adequacy is related to members' feelings of personal influence in the organization, satisfaction with their immediate superiors, satisfaction with top management, and, to a lesser extent, satisfaction with co-workers.

Even though organization members who consider themselves to be adequately informed generally are more committed, more satisfied, and identify more closely with the organization than those who see themselves as inadequately informed, information adequacy does not always produce such positive outcomes. In a later study, Daniels and Spiker (1983) found that information adequacy on sensitive topics such as management problems, organizational failures, and organizational decision-making processes is *negatively* related to satisfaction with superiors for some organization members. That is, the more some people know about sensitive organizational issues, the less they like their bosses. Daniels and Spiker argued that this may occur because people who develop their own sources of such information become less dependent on their superiors and eventually see themselves as more knowledgeable and competent than those superiors.

While studies of information adequacy generally have been concerned with the potential impact of adequacy on variables such as satisfaction, the most recent work has attempted to identify the conditions under which organization members perceive themselves to be adequately informed. Alexander, Helms, and Curran (1987) found that levels of communication with supervisors, administrative sources, and peers are greater for members who perceive themselves to be adequately informed than for those who perceive themselves to be inadequately informed. Inadequately informed members also were younger than more adequately informed members, and they had been employed with the organization for less time. These results may not be especially surprising, but they do suggest that information adequacy does not occur in a haphazard and unpredictable manner.

Unanswered Questions about Communication Functions

Our present state of knowledge about organizational communication functions and adequacy of information that supports these functions is somewhat limited. While production, maintenance, innovation, and human functions certainly are important in organizational communication and the information needs of individual organization members are now well understood, the purposes and outcomes of organizational communication are more complicated than current models of functions and information adequacy suggest.

Some forms of organizational communication are difficult to assign to conventional categories of functions. A few simple examples illustrate the point.

A manufacturing division of a large corporation discovers that a new product has potential safety hazards. The division falsifies safety test reports to its own corporate headquarters and to government agencies in order to obtain approval to market the product.

A publicly egotistical, but privately insecure, middle manager spends several hours each week trying to impress subordinates by recounting "heroic" stories of his career accomplishments (e.g., the time that he "single-handedly" saved the company from bankruptcy). The stories are greatly exaggerated, but he has told them so many times that he actually believes them. The subordinates know better. They like to say behind his back, "He's a legend in his own mind."

Another middle manager verbally abuses subordinates whenever the opportunity presents itself. During a recent meeting of all company employees, she publicly chastised a salesclerk for leaving work too early and failing to put enough merchandise on a display table. At the next employee meeting, she chewed out the same clerk for putting too much on a display table and causing unauthorized overtime by leaving work too late. This manager seems to obtain a perverse form of personal gratification from publicly humiliating subordinates.

Top managers in a genetic engineering company instruct their research and development group to begin a highly controversial gene-splicing project that may produce some very dangerous bacteria. The research group also is told to write ambiguous reports to top management about its work. The company president tells the research and development director, "We want to know what's going on, but we don't want to know what's going on—if you get my meaning."

The point of these examples is simple. Every day, human communication in organizations occurs for many purposes, including building empires, self-aggrandizement, acting out sadomasochistic rituals, initiating romantic relationships, accomplishing the political objectives of coalitions, and simply keeping one another entertained. Although such acts may have some connection with production, maintenance, human, or innovation communication functions, they also seem to involve several functions simultaneously and to include functions that do not fit into the traditional categories.

The abusing middle manager who attacked the salesclerk did so over a work problem (production) as well as a policy violation (maintenance), and she did so in a way that degraded the employee (a negative form of the human function). If asked to explain her actions, the manager might say that she was enforcing policy, protecting work standards, and sending a message to other employees by making a public example of this errant clerk. She also may have acted out a sadistic ritual, however, that fulfilled her own need to derive pleasure from hurting others. Sadism seems to lie beyond our traditional ideas about communication functions.

Some of the research methods and concepts associated with the interpretivist perspective may help us to develop a better understanding of communication functions because interpretivists do not assume that any observed episode of communication should fit somewhere in a predetermined set of functional categories. Rather, communicative acts are observed in a specific situation, and the functions served in that situation are derived from these acts.

For example, Harris and Sutton (1986) studied the functions of communication in the parting rituals of eight dying organizations (going out of business, closing down). Since there was nothing to produce, no organizational conditions to maintain (except the status of certain employee benefits and friendships formed during the life of the organization), and certainly no new innovations to discuss (except the demise of the organization), there was no reason to presume that communication would fit into production, maintenance, and innovation categories. Yet, Harris and Sutton's interpretive investigation suggested that several functions are served by such rituals, including motivation of members to move on, information about benefits and personnel dispositions, gaining external stakeholders' acceptance of the loss, managing impressions about the situation, and assuaging guilt over the organization's failure.

Generally, traditionalism itself might benefit from more research on communication functions and from reformulation of the models used to classify functions. It would also be useful to extend the study of information adequacy beyond the needs of individuals as information receivers. We need to know more about the ways in which system and subsystem information needs are defined and how these needs are fulfilled through organizational communication.

Summary

The concepts of communication structure and function are central ideas in the traditional perspective of organizational communication. Functions are activities of a system that serve some purpose or objective. Structure is reflected in the linkages or relationships between elements in a system. Function and structure are closely related concepts in organizational communication. Although traditionalists usually assume a direct connection between effective organizational performance and effective communication functions and structure, functions and structures of different groups and political coalitions within the same organization may clash when they pursue multiple and conflicting goals.

The term *communication* is something of a buzzword in modern society. People use the word to refer to many different human activities and conditions. Even academic scholars who specialize in the study of human communication define this concept in various ways.

We define communication as *shared meaning created among two or more people through verbal and nonverbal transaction*. The basic raw material of communication is information, which includes any aspect of the environment in which one can discern a pattern. Meaning occurs when information is placed within a context. Human communication is concerned with the meaning of verbal and nonverbal information.

Verbal information occurs in the spoken and written forms of a language code. This code involves a system of symbols as well as rules for how symbols are used. Symbols are representative, freely created, and culturally transmitted. Some experts regard symbols as tools for expressing thought. Others argue that thought as we understand it depends on symbols, that our knowledge and sense of reality are products of our language system. The influence of language in organizational communication is suggested by the use of root metaphors to make sense of organizational experiences, certain types of language paradoxes in organizational behavior, strategic use of ambiguity, and the prevalence of group-restricted codes.

Nonverbal information also is important in organizational communication, but the concept of nonverbal communication is troublesome because many nonverbal behaviors may be ambiguous and unreliable signs of emotional states or even random activities that occur without awareness or intent on the part of a source. Although an observer is likely to interpret such behaviors, they lead to no shared meaning. Popular notions that nonverbal behaviors are consistent indicators of specific messages and conditions that can be interpreted reliably if one knows the rules are misleading. One should exercise caution when attaching interpretations to nonverbal behavior.

Three important forms of nonverbal information are paralanguage, body movement (kinesics), and space (proxemics). Paralanguage cues such as volume, rate, rhythm, inflection, tone, and pitch help us to interpret verbal behavior. These cues also influence our perceptions of a speaker. Kinesic behaviors can be organized in five functional categories: emblems, illustrators, regulators, affect displays, and adaptors. Proxemics involves fixed-feature space, semifixed-feature space, and informal space. Fixed-feature space is essentially a territory. Territory and status are highly connected in many organizations. Arrangement of objects in semifixed-feature space can be used to convey a variety of messages. Informal space, the area in which interaction occurs, has four basic zones—intimate, personal, social, and public—that appear to vary widely across cultures.

Communication functions often are classified as production, maintenance, and innovation, although some scholars like to add a fourth category, the human function. This classification scheme is useful, but many instances of organizational communication do not fit easily into these categories.

Discussion Questions/ Activities

1. Try over a period of a few days to construct some good notes on the dialogue that occurs among members of a student organization. Analyze the dialogue to identify the communication functions that are accomplished.
2. Is language merely representational or does it shape the way in which we experience the world? What kinds of examples can you think of in your own experience that would support either position?

3. Try to identify some instances of ambiguous communication. How do people in these situations try to cope with ambiguity? What is the final result of these coping efforts? Is ambiguity used strategically in any of these situations?

4. Observe the nonverbal behaviors of others in public settings. What information can you reliably infer from these behaviors? Under what circumstances would you consider the behaviors to be communicative?

5. Try to observe a group that uses a restricted code, then describe this code in as much detail as you can. What functions does the code seem to serve for this group?

Additional Resources

Books

Bonvillain, N. (1993). *Language, culture, and communication: The meaning of messages*. Englewood Cliffs, NJ: Prentice-Hall.

Burleson, B. R., Albrecht, T. L., & Sarason, I. G. (Eds.). (1994). *Communication of social support: Messages, interactions, relationships, and community*. Thousand Oaks, CA: Sage.

Karp, D. A., and Yoels, W. C. (1979). *Symbols, selves, and society: Understanding interaction*. New York: Lippincott.

Manning, P. K. (1992). *Organizational communication*. New York: A. de Gruyter.

Perinbanayagam, R. S. (1985). *Signifying acts: Structure and meaning in everyday life*. Carbondale: SIU Press.

Vernon, G. M. (1978). *Symbolic aspects of interaction*. Washington, DC: University Press of America.

Web Sites

http://www.bmgt.umd.edu/Business/AcademicDepts/IS/Learning/orglrn.html
    Information on organizational learning and information systems.
http://haas.berkeley.edu/~seidel/ad.html
    The Organizational Issues Clearinghouse

References

Alexander, E. R., III, Helms, M. M., & Curran, K. E. (1987). An information processing analysis of organization information adequacy/abundance. *Management Communication Quarterly, 1*, 150–172.

Baird, J. E., Jr., & Weinberg, S. B. (1981). *Group communication: The essence of synergy* (2nd ed.). Dubuque, IA: Wm. C. Brown Company Publishers.

Birdwhistell, R. (1952). *Introduction to kinesics*. Louisville, KY: University of Louisville Press.

Blumer, H. (1969). *Symbolic interactionism: Perspective and method*. Englewood Cliffs, NJ: Prentice-Hall.

Brillouin, L. (1962). *Science and information theory*. New York: Academic Press.

Cunningham, M. A., & Wilcox, J. R. (1984). *Modifying a bind: The effects of patient harm and physician interpersonal risk on nurse communication in the inappropriate-order situation*. Paper presented at the annual meeting of the International Communication Association. San Francisco.

Cyert, R. M., & March, J. G. (1963). *A behavioral theory of the firm*. Englewood Cliffs, NJ: Prentice-Hall.

Daly, J. A., Falcione, R. L., & Damhorst, M. L. (1979). *Communication correlates of relational and organizational satisfaction*. Paper presented at the annual meeting of the International Communication Association. Philadelphia.

Daniels, T. D., & Spiker, B. K. (1983). Social exchange and the relationship between information adequacy and relational satisfaction. *Western Journal of Speech Communication, 47*, 118–137.

Davitz, J. R. (1964). *The communication of emotional meaning.* New York: McGraw-Hill.

Deetz, S. A. (1973). Words without things: Toward a social phenomenology of language. *Quarterly Journal of Speech, 59,* 40–51.

De La Zerda, N., & Hopper, R. (1979). Employment interviewers' reactions to Mexican American speech. *Communication Monographs, 46,* 126–134.

Eisenberg, E. M. (1984). Ambiguity as a strategy in organizational communication. *Communication Monographs, 51,* 227–242.

Eisenberg, E. M., & Goodall, H. L., Jr. (1993). *Organizational Communication: Balancing creativity and constraint.* New York: St. Martin's Press.

Ekman, P., & Friesen, W. V. (1972). Hand movements. *Journal of Communication, 22,* 353–374.

Farace, R. V., Monge, P. R., & Russell, H. M. (1977). *Communicating and organizing.* Reading, MA: Addison-Wesley.

Foss, S. K. (1984). Retooling and image: Chrysler Corporation's rhetoric of redemption. *Western Journal of Speech Communication, 48,* 75–91.

Goldhaber, G. M. (1993). *Organizational communication* (6th ed.). Dubuque, IA: Brown & Benchmark Publishers.

Goldhaber, G. M., Yates, M. P., Porter, D. T., & Lesniak, R. (1978). Organizational communication: 1978. *Human Communication Research, 5,* 76–96.

Goyer, R. S. (1970). Communication, communication process, meaning: Toward a unified theory. *Journal of Communication, 20,* 6–7.

Hall, E. (1959). *Silent language.* Greenwich, CT: Fawcett.

Harris, S. G., & Sutton, R. I. (1986). Functions of parting ceremonies in dying organizations. *Academy of Management Journal, 29,* 5–37.

Harrison, R. (1970). Nonverbal communication: Explorations into time, space, action, and object. In J. Campbell & H. Helper (Eds.), *Dimensions in communication.* Belmont, CA: Wadsworth.

Johnson, B. M. (1977). *Communication: The process of organizing.* Boston: Allyn and Bacon.

Kanter, R. M. (1977). *Men and women of the corporation.* New York: Basic Books.

Knapp, M. (1978). *Nonverbal communication in human interaction* (2nd ed.). New York: Holt, Rinehart, & Winston.

Koch, S., & Deetz, S. A. (1981). Metaphor analysis of social reality in organizations. *Journal of Applied Communication Research, 9,* 1–15.

Lakoff, R. (1975). *Language and woman's place.* New York: Harper & Row.

Langer, S. (1942). *Philosophy in a new key.* Cambridge, MA: Harvard University Press.

Level, D. A. (1959). *A case study of human communication in an urban bank.* Unpublished doctoral dissertation, Purdue University, West Lafayette, IN.

Littlejohn, S. W. (1992). *Theories of human communication* (4th ed.). Belmont, CA: Wadsworth.

McCroskey, J. C., Larson, C., & Knapp M. (1971). *An introduction to interpersonal communication.* Englewood Cliffs, NJ: Prentice-Hall.

Norton, R. (1978). Foundation of a communicator style construct. *Human Communication Research, 4,* 99–112.

Penley, L. E. (1982). An investigation of the information processing framework of organizational communication. *Human Communication Research, 8,* 348–365.

Perrin, P. G. (1965). *Writer's guide and index to English* (4th ed.). Glenview, IL: Scott, Foresman.

Pettegrew, L. S. (1982). Organizational communication and the S. O. B. theory of management. *Western Journal of Speech Communication, 46,* 179–191.

Pollio, H. R. (1974). *The psychology of symbolic activity.* Reading, MA: Addison-Wesley.

Schenck-Hamlin, W. J. (1978). The effects of dialectical similarity, stereotyping, and message agreement on interpersonal perception. *Human Communication Research, 5,* 15–26.

Smith, G. L., & DeWine, S. (1987). *An investigation of the relationship between organizational commitment and information overload/underload.* Paper presented at the annual meeting of the Central States Speech Association. St. Louis.

Spiker, B. K., & Daniels, T. D. (1981). Information adequacy and communication relationships: An empirical examination of 18 organizations. *Western Journal of Speech Communication, 45,* 342–354.

Spiker, B. K., & Lesser, E. (1995). We have met the enemy. *Journal of Business Strategy, 16,* 17–21.

Stein, L. I. (1967). The doctor-nurse game. *Archives of General Psychiatry, 16,* 699–703.

Stevenson, W. B., Pearce, J. L., & Porter, L. W. (1985). The concept of "coalition" in organization theory and research. *Academy of Management Review, 10,* 256–268.

Tompkins, P. H. (1962). *An analysis of communication between headquarters and selected units of a national union.* Unpublished doctoral dissertation, Purdue University, West Lafayette, IN.

Tubbs, S. L., & Moss, S. (1980). *Human Communication* (3rd ed.). New York: Random House.

Wagner, E. J. (1992). *Sexual harassment in the workplace.* New York: AMACOM-American Management Association.

Watzlawick, P., Beavin, J., & Jackson, D. (1967). *Pragmatics of human communication: A study of interactional patterns, pathologies, and paradoxes.* New York: Norton.

Weick, K. (1979). *The social psychology of organizing* (2nd ed.). Reading, MA: Addison-Wesley.

Whorf, B. L. (1957). *Language, thought, and reality.* New York: John Wiley & Sons.

Wood, J. T., and Conrad, C. (1983). Paradox in the experiences of professional women. *Western Journal of Speech Communication, 47,* 305–322.

Zaleznik, A. (1970). Power and politics in organizational life. *Harvard Business Review, 48,* 47–60.

ORGANIZATIONAL COMMUNICATION STRUCTURE

The concept of communication structure is one of the most important ideas in the study of organizational communication. It is also one of the most complicated because the way we understand structure depends very much on the perspective from which we study it. There are several different ways to think about the structure of organizational communication, but three of them in particular will give you a fairly representative review of the concept and a good idea of just how complex the concept of structure can be.

One way of thinking about structure is to define it as a system of pathways through which messages flow—the so-called lines of communication in an organization (Goldhaber, 1993; Koehler, Anatol, & Applbaum, 1981). This is the *channels* perspective, and it is the traditional definition of communication structure. If you think about this definition for a moment, it is easy to see just what it implies. Messages are regarded as concrete objects that are passed back and forth through literal channels of communication. Many scholars, even traditionalists, are uneasy about this idea because it misrepresents the dynamics of interpersonal communication. Although messages do exist in a tangible way through the written and spoken word (i.e, what Cynthia Stohl (1995) refers to as *ostensive* messages), in another sense, "the message" exists only in the transaction between two or more persons.

The second approach defines communication structure as the patterns of interaction among people who comprise the organization. In this sense, structure depends on who communicates with whom. We will call this the *observable network* perspective where a network "consists of *interconnected* individuals who are linked by *patterned* flows of information, influence, and affect" (Stohl, 1995, p. 18). Since these patterned flows can be observed, the second definition also is consistent with the traditional focus on objective features of organizational communication. Of course, interpretivists are quick to argue that structure is not really an objective property of communication but an idea that is shared by organization members (Trujillo, 1985).

This leads us to a third idea about structure, which really is a second version of the network idea, the *perceived network* perspective. When researchers study networks, they sometimes figure out the network structure from organization members' own reports of their linkages with others, that is, with whom they communicate and how often. But many researchers have noted that these reports by organization members often are inconsistent with observations of the same organization made by trained researchers. So what is it that organization members are reporting if it is not the actual network? Stephen Corman and Craig Scott, two network theorists, describe it this way:

The network is a structure of perceived communication relationships. It is a kind of latent knowledge that guides members' manifest communication behavior. We believe that members' reports of communication reflect this knowledge, not their recollections of specific communication episodes. (1994, p. 174)

Is structure an objective property or a subjective idea? Curiously, it seems to be both. On the one hand, when organization members interact, they are engaging in behavior with objective features. These features include discernible patterns that someone else can observe. On the other hand, it is also true that you generally cannot go into an organization and point to *the* network of communication in the same way that you can point to *the* network of telephones because the networks defined by interaction can be highly changeable, and any given organization member may be in many different networks within the same organization. When outside observers look at *the* communication network, it is a bit like taking a photograph of one particular set of interactions as it exists at a fixed point in time. When organization members talk about *the* communication network, they are talking about "an abstract structure of perceived communication relationships that functions as a set of rules and resources actors draw upon in accomplishing communication behavior" (Corman & Scott, p. 181). We will have more to say later in the chapter about this problem and how the ideas of observable and perceived networks can be reconciled.

The channels perspective, the idea that communication structure is a system of pathways or channels of message flow, goes hand in hand with a common distinction between formal and informal systems of organizational communication. This distinction is very useful, but it has some limitations. Some of these limitations can be overcome by viewing communication structure as a network that arises from the patterns of interaction among organization members. Since each of these ideas provides a particular way of understanding communication structure, we will review both in some detail.

Formal Communication

Formal communication refers to communication through officially designated channels of message flow between organizational positions. In many organizations, the formal system of communication is specified in policy manuals and organization charts. In other organizations, the formal system is implicit, yet organization members understand it well. The examples of the United States Postal Service (USPS) and Supervalue Market in chapter 3 illustrate this point. The USPS has explicit, written policies that define the channels of formal communication, while Supervalue has a system of conventions and rules learned through day-to-day experience.

The USPS and Supervalue examples also involved hierarchical structures based on functional divisions of labor and scalar authority chains. The concept of hierarchy is so ingrained in organizational life that formal communication usually is described in terms of the three directions of message flow within a hierarchical system: downward, upward, and horizontal.

Downward Communication

Downward communication involves the transmission of messages from upper levels to lower levels of the organization hierarchy (i.e., from manager to employee, superior to subordinate). Smith, Richetto, and Zima (1972) claimed that downward communication has been the most frequently studied aspect of formal communication. Twenty years ago, there also was a great deal of evidence that most of the message flow in formal systems was downward (Tompkins, 1967).

Classical and scientific approaches to organizations considered communication primarily as a tool for managerial control and coordination. Consequently, these approaches focused on downward communication of orders and regulations from superiors to subordinates—messages concerned with production and maintenance functions.

Classical theorists assumed that subordinates would accept and comply with downward communication on the basis of superiors' legitimate authority. As the Hawthorne Studies illustrated, compliance with managerial authority is not such a simple matter. The human relations movement stressed the use of downward-communication strategies that would promote morale in the belief that satisfaction would lead to compliance with authority (Miles, 1965). Much of the research that followed human relations assumptions has attempted to determine the conditions under which subordinates comply with messages received from superiors (Smith, Richetto, & Zima, 1972).

More recently, contemporary theorists have argued that organization members have a "need to know" for their own purposes. Satisfaction of this need is important to the successful assimilation of members into an organization. As Koehler and colleagues argued, "The best integrated employees are those who are told what goals and objectives are, how their jobs fit into the total picture, and the progress they are making on the job" (1981, p. 10). This idea is the basis for some of the more recent studies on information adequacy that we described earlier. For example, Penley's (1982) work focused on the role of information adequacy in bringing about members' involvement in and identification with organization goals rather than on downward-communication strategies for producing compli- ance with authority.

Katz and Kahn (1978) identified five types of messages that usually are reflected in downward communication:

1. *Job instructions* involving the work to be done and directions for doing that work.
2. *Job rationales* explaining the purpose of a job or task and its relationship to other organizational activities or objectives.
3. *Procedures and practices information* pertaining to organizational policies, rules, and benefits.
4. *Feedback* providing subordinates with appraisals of their performance.
5. *Indoctrination* of organizational ideology that attempts to foster member commitment to the organization's values, goals, and objectives.

Effective Downward Communication

Despite the attention that downward communication has received in management and communication research, this dimension of formal communication is ineffective in many organizations (Chase, 1970). Problems with downward communication include inadequacy of information, inappropriate means of diffusing information, filtering of information, and a general pervasive climate of dominance and submission.

Adequacy of information obtained from downward messages presents a puzzling paradox. On the one hand, downward-directed messages frequently create overload in organizations (Davis, 1972). Advances in information technology (the mechanical and electronic ability not only to manipulate information more efficiently but also to send more messages to more people) and, ironically, the importance attached to the idea of effective organizational communication have led to floods of memorandums, bulletins, newsletters, technical reports, and data in reams of computer printouts. FedEx, a company specializing in overnight delivery of letters and packages, has gleefully referred to this condition as "The Paper Blob" in its advertising. On the other hand, organization members consistently report in studies of information adequacy that they do not receive sufficient information on topics that are important to them (Goldhaber, 1993; Penley, 1982; Spiker & Daniels, 1981).

The apparent paradox is difficult to explain. One possible conclusion is that organization members receive too much of the wrong information. This does not mean that the information itself is in error. It means that much of the information that members receive may not be relevant to their personal job and organizational concerns. Farace and colleagues argued that problems in information-diffusion policies most commonly *"are due to failures by managers to identify which groups of personnel need to know certain things, or to establish where these groups are supposed to be able to obtain the information they need"* (1977, p. 28). Of course, this claim, along with the argument of Koehler and colleagues (1981) that the best integrated employees are those who are "told" about goals, the big picture, and their progress, presumes that managers are the ones who should define everybody's information needs. This assumption poses another problem: How much input should employees or subordinates have in deciding what they need and how they will obtain it? Reserving for management the exclusive right to decide who gets what information is an idea that may be unacceptable to many members of modern organizations.

The methods of information diffusion that are used for downward communication also can create problems. According to Goldhaber (1993), organizations often rely too heavily on mediated (written, mechanical, and electronic) methods of transmitting messages rather than on personal, face-to-face contact. Goldhaber, Yates, Porter, and Lesniak (1978) concluded from a review of sixteen ICA-sponsored studies that organization members generally desire more face-to-face interaction. This finding also poses another paradox. How do we cope with the human need for direct, interpersonal contact when today's pressure to get more information to more people more rapidly requires us to rely on the most efficient means of communication available (i.e., paper and electronic media)?

Downward communication also is subjected to filtering. As messages are relayed from superior to subordinate through levels of the organizational hierarchy, they may be changed in various ways. Information may be left out, added, combined, or otherwise modified as it passes through a chain of serial reproduction (Pace & Boren, 1973). **Serial reproduction** is the same effect that occurs in the children's game Telephone when messages are passed from one person to the next. Distortions occur as each person in the transmission series attempts to reproduce the message received for relay to the next person. While oral messages are most easily subjected to such distortions, written messages are not immune if they are in any way relayed from level to level of the organization.

In part, distortions occur because different people have different interpretations of the same information (i.e., as a result of ambiguity) or because human beings simply have a limited capacity to process information. When attempting to reproduce a message in serial transmission, people may simply forget some of the information or "chunk" certain details together in order to handle the information more efficiently.

Downward messages also may be filtered deliberately. Information power is a valuable commodity in many organizations. Culbert and Eden (1970) pointed out that managers often "base their power on withholding, rather than sharing, information" (p. 140), because ability to control situations and outcomes may depend on having knowledge that others do not possess. When managers do choose to share information, their subordinates may prevent it from being relayed to lower levels of the organization. Mellinger (1956) found that subordinates who do not trust a superior often choose to block that superior's messages from others.

In general, the greater the number of steps or linkages in a serial reproduction chain and the greater the perceptual differences among participants in that chain, the more likely it is that some form of message distortion or filtering will occur. The type of information also has a bearing even on the extent to which it will be distributed. In a case study of one large organization, Davis (1968) found that important information was more likely than insignificant information to be relayed by superiors to subordinates, but even the important information often was not relayed by superiors to subordinates despite the fact that the superiors had explicit instructions to pass on this information.

Upward Communication

Upward communication involves transmission of messages from lower to higher levels of the organization namely, communication initiated by subordinates with their superiors. The role of upward communication in classical theories of organization was limited primarily to basic reporting functions concerning task-related matters. The human relations movement expanded the role of upward communication by emphasizing "two-way" communication between superiors and subordinates as a means of promoting morale. Later, human resource development theories emphasized the necessity of upward communication for integration of organization members and improved decision-making processes. Upward communication is a prerequisite for employee involvement in decision making, problem solving, and development of policies and procedures (Smith, Richetto, & Zima, 1972).

Katz and Kahn (1978) point out that upward communication can provide superiors with information in the following areas:

1. Performance on the job and job-related problems.
2. Fellow employees and their problems.
3. Subordinates' perceptions of organizational policies and practices.
4. Tasks and procedures for accomplishing them.

In addition to those uses noted by Katz and Kahn, Planty and Machaver (1952) stated that upward communication can (1) provide valuable ideas from subordinates; (2) facilitate acceptance of downward messages; and (3) generally facilitate decision making by fostering subordinates' participation and by providing a better picture of performance, perceptions, and possible problems at all levels of the organization.

Effective Upward Communication

Although contemporary managers and executives praise the virtues of upward communication, actual use of upward communication appears to be limited in many organizations (Goldhaber, 1993; Tompkins, 1967). Management often does not establish effective means for upward communication. Moreover, when upward communication does occur, it may be subject to the same filtering problems that affect downward communication.

While upward communication can be encouraged through means such as suggestion systems, systematic reporting methods, grievance procedures, attitude surveys, and employee meetings, the presence of such systems may be only a token gesture in many organizations. A story that a student told us about her first encounter with a suggestion box during a summer job at a factory is not unusual. The little wooden box hung from a supervisor's office door. When the student asked a co-worker (a veteran of several years in the factory) about the box, she was told, "Don't pay any attention to that, kid. They never open it, and we never put anything in it."

Suggestion systems can be very effective when managers actively encourage their use and employees take them seriously, but our example of the "suggestion box syndrome" typifies two common research findings about upward communication.

First, most organization members would rather receive information than provide information to others (Goldhaber, 1993). Second, even when subordinates make attempts at upward communication, their superiors may not be receptive to these attempts. Koehler and Huber (1974) found that managers tend to be more receptive to upward communication when the information is positive (good news rather than bad news), is in line with current policy (criticism and boat rocking are unwelcome), and has intuitive appeal (fits the managers' own biases).

Subordinates are likely to become quite dissatisfied in organizations in which superiors endorse the idea of upward communication but, in practice, actually ignore it. When subordinates develop the impression that superiors only want to hear good news and support for their own ideas, it should not be surprising that upward communication with those superiors is filtered extensively. Krivonos (1976) reported that subordinates tend to tell their superiors what they think the superiors want to hear or only what they want their superiors to hear. Information is distorted so that it will please superiors and reflect positively on subordinates.

While several factors seem to affect accuracy of upward communication, the most important ingredient may be trust. Studies by Read (1962), Maier, Hoffman, and Read (1963), and Roberts and O'Reilly (1974) indicated that accuracy of upward communication is greater when subordinates trust their superiors. The studies by Read and by Maier, Hoffman, and Read also found that subordinates' upward mobility aspirations are negatively related to accuracy. As subordinates' mobility aspirations increase, accuracy in upward communication decreases. This finding is somewhat suspect because the method that Read used to index accuracy was rather crude. Even so, Read's research reminds us that some people who want to move up may distort information to make themselves look good or to protect their chances of promotion.

Horizontal Communication

Horizontal communication refers to the flow of messages *across* functional areas at a given level of an organization. Although classical approaches to organizing made little provision for horizontal communication, Fayol recognized that emergencies and unforeseen day-to-day contingencies require flexibility in formal channels. Strict adherence to the chain of command would be too time consuming in emergencies, so some provision has to be made for horizontal bridges that permit people at the same level to communicate directly without going through several levels of organization. Fayol's concept (1949) is illustrated in figure 6.1.

Horizontal communication introduces flexibility in organizational structure. It facilitates problem solving, information sharing across different work groups, and task coordination between departments or project teams. It may also enhance morale and afford a means for resolving conflicts (Koehler, Anatol, & Applbaum, 1981). Human resource development theorists regard horizontal communication as an essential feature of participative decision making and organizational adaptiveness (French, Bell, & Zawacki, 1983).

Reliance on horizontal communication for decision making and problem solving does not mean that the process is more *efficient* than simple downward communication of decisions made at top levels of the organization, but horizontal

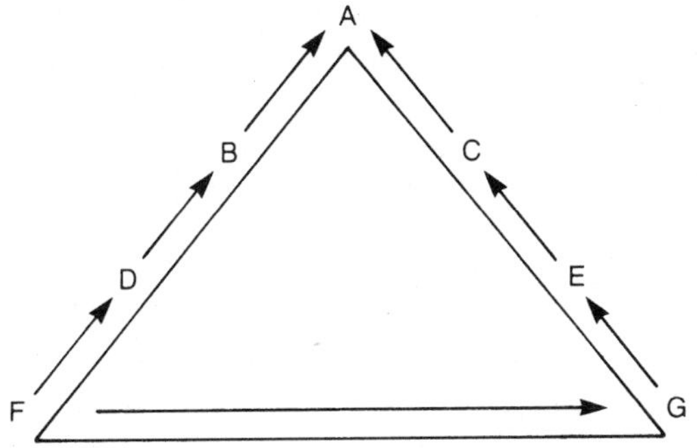

Figure 6.1
Fayol's bridge where F
communicates with G.

communication may be more *effective*. As we noted in chapter 3, this idea is emphasized in human resource development theory and applied broadly in Japanese organizations where decision making and problem solving usually occur through horizontal communication at lower levels. The results of this process are transmitted to top management for review and approval. Ryutard Nomura (1981), chairman of the board of Japan's Triyo Industries, observed that decision making under this system can be a lengthy and difficult process, but once a decision has been made, its implementation is swift and certain. Organization members are committed to the decision because difficulties have been resolved and opposing points of view reconciled through horizontal communication before plans are presented to top management.

In the conventional western organization, decisions are made at the top, then orders for compliance and implementation flow downward. According to Nomura, western-style decision making is fast because it is centralized near the top of the organization. Acceptance and implementation of top management decisions at lower levels, however, is slow to develop. Lack of commitment to decisions and conflicts over implementation arise at lower levels where members have been excluded from the decision-making process.

Effective Horizontal Communication

American organizations generally are unaccustomed to high levels of horizontal communication. Albaum (1964) found that any given department in an organization typically will not relay information directly to another, even when it is understood that the information is vitally important to the other department. Although Albaum's research occurred many years ago, there is little reason to suspect that conditions today are much different.

Horizontal-communication problems occur because of territoriality, rivalry, specialization, and simple lack of motivation. Organizations that traditionally have functioned under rigid authority structures with fixed lines of communication may find that the values and expectations that members have acquired under such systems inhibit attempts at horizontal communication.

One inhibiting value is territoriality. Organization members who control task-related activity within a defined and fixed jurisdictional area often regard others' involvement in that area as territorial encroachment. Departments value their turf and strive to protect it. This problem may be compounded through interdepartmental rivalries that arise from win/lose competition for rewards and resources.

Some years ago, corporate executives in a national department store chain encountered territorial rivalry when they discovered that local stores within each of the company's major sales districts refused to cooperate with one another on sales promotions. For example, if Store X ran out of a sale item, it might call Store Y in the same district to obtain more. Even though Store Y would have an ample supply of the item, it would claim to be out. The explanation was simple. Local managers were rewarded only for the sales performance of their individual stores. Consequently, stores within the same sales region literally were in competition with one another as well as with other department store chains. When the company decided to provide managers with bonuses based on districtwide sales, stores within any given district suddenly began to cooperate with one another on all sorts of projects and promotions.

Specialization also may hamper horizontal communication. During the 1960s, for example, a team of experts from various fields was assembled to work on a NASA-sponsored project. The team hardly had begun its work before its members realized that they were having great difficulty in communicating. The main reason seemed to be that different specialties used the same terms in different ways. The problem was so persistent that the group finally appointed a "vocabulary committee" to develop standard definitions for all of the troublesome terms.

Horizontal communication often fails simply because organization members are unwilling to expend the additional effort that it requires. When we engage in upward or downward communication, those with whom we communicate are easy to reach because of proximity or clearly designated channels. Immediate superiors and immediate subordinates may be just across the office. We know them by name and we have well-established rules for initiating and conducting interaction with them. In contrast, horizontal communication may require contact with people in units that are well removed from our own. The channels and rules of interaction may be unclear. We do not really know these people. The need to communicate with them makes us uneasy or takes too much time, so we avoid or ignore it.

Informal Communication

The *informal system* involves episodes of interaction that do not reflect officially designated channels of communication. As defined by Tompkins (1967), the informal system is "not rationally specified." Classical and scientific theorists made no attempt to account for the role of informal communication in organizational functions and its influence on organizational life. Many classical and scientific principles of management were turned upside down when Barnard's work (1983) and the Hawthorne Studies suggested that a great deal of organizational communication is informal communication. In fact, one of the most important findings in the Hawthorne Studies concerned the influence of informal communication in developing and reinforcing performance standards, member expectations, and values at the work group level.

Some scholars have argued that informal communication is a substitute for an inadequate formal system. Walton (1961) concluded that informal communication systems arise when information transmitted through the formal system is either insufficient or ambiguous. Other scholars claim that the informal system is much more than a simple substitute for an ineffective formal system. Barnard (1938) and Davis (1953) argued that informal communication is an inherent and even necessary aspect of organizational life. Generally, organizational communication theorists agree that at least some informal communication is inevitable in any organization. Management efforts to stamp it out are misguided at best, although some experts urge managers to control the informal system (Hellweg, 1987).

Much of the research on informal communication is concerned with the study of **grapevine** communication. The terms *informal system* and *grapevine* often are used interchangeably as if they refer to the same thing (Davis, 1953; Hellweg, 1987). The use of the word *grapevine* as a metaphor for a communication system began during the American Civil War in the 1860s as a description for telegraph lines that were strung through trees in such a way that they looked like grapevines. The system was not very reliable, so the term was soon applied to any form of unofficial communication (Davis, 1953).

Nearly a century later, organizational communication research indicated that patterns of grapevine communication even look something like a cluster of grapes. Consider the pattern of message flow in figure 6.2. Person A initiates and transmits a message to B and C. B relays the message to D, while C relays it to E and F. The clustering continues as the message is diffused throughout the organization. Some participants in the grapevine act only as receivers. They do not relay information to anyone else. Others relay it to several different people.

Grapevine communication has many other important features. Susan Hellweg (1987) summarized these features in a list of thirty-three general conclusions that she based on a review of nineteen research studies. The conclusions are somewhat cumbersome because the studies themselves are very difficult to relate to one another. Even so, Hellweg presented a comprehensive analysis of what we know about the grapevine. For simplicity, we have reorganized her conclusions under five topic areas.

1. Function and Extent of Grapevine Communication
   The grapevine emerges from the social and personal interests of employees rather than from formal requirements of the organization. It is the system in which most organizational communication actually occurs, emphasizing "people-oriented" information and "news" events.

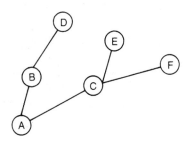

Figure 6.2
A grapevine communication cluster.

2. Participants in Grapevine Communication
   Secretaries and liaisons play key roles in grapevine communication,
   although relatively few people are grapevine liaisons, and many people
   who receive grapevine information do not transmit it to others. Use of the
   grapevine is just as prevalent among managers as it is among other groups
   of employees.
3. Patterns and Media of Grapevine Communication
   Grapevine communication usually is oral and generally occurs in cluster
   transmission patterns. It may begin, flow, and end anywhere in an organization.
4. Volume, Speed, and Reliability of Information
   Although grapevine communication usually is incomplete, information in
   the grapevine tends to be more accurate than inaccurate, and diffusion of
   information through the grapevine is fast.
5. Role in Rumor Transmission
   Three types of rumors are diffused (spread) through the grapevine: anxiety
   rumors, wish-fulfillment rumors, and wedge-driving rumors. Rumors are
   distorted through sharpening, leveling, and assimilation. Once a rumor is
   assigned credibility, other events in the organization are altered to fit in
   with and support the rumor.

In general, Hellweg's review of research on grapevine communication suggests that a great deal of organizational communication occurs through the
grapevine. Communication in this system is fast and more often accurate than
inaccurate, though much of the information is incomplete. Grapevine communication usually is concerned with people-oriented social information, although
other forms of information are diffused through the grapevine. The grapevine
serves as a rumor mill, but rumors comprise only a small proportion of grapevine
communication. Participants in grapevine communication include managers as
well as employees and men as well as women.

Limitations of the Traditional View

The traditional distinction between formal and informal communication is useful
in describing and understanding many aspects of organizational communication,
but it is subject to at least three major limitations. First, the concept of organizational structure itself may be regarded as a socially constructed reality. Second,
there is no universal agreement on the distinction between formal and informal
communication. Finally, it may be easier to understand some features of organizational communication by distinguishing between "tightly coupled" and "loosely
coupled" systems rather than between formal and informal communication.

Structure as a Social Construction

The concepts of formal "hierarchy" and informal "grapevine" are good examples
of interpretivist notions about the social construction of reality. We often speak of
formal messages "flowing upward and downward" and of rumors being "transmitted by the grapevine" as if hierarchy and grapevines are tangible things with
a physical, concrete existence. Interpretivists point out that these concepts are

metaphors that we use to make sense of organizational communication. After all, messages do not literally flow "up" or "down" and organizations and grapevines do not spring to life in order to "transmit" rumors.

We do not mean to suggest here that concepts such as hierarchy are just a figment of organization members' imaginations. For example, scholars working from the critical perspective obviously do not deny the existence of hierarchy, but they do claim that we have reified the idea of hierarchy, that is, we have made it appear to be a natural state of affairs only because hierarchy serves the interests of elite groups (Deetz, 1992). From another point of view, however, the predisposition to create hierarchy may very well be a "natural state of affairs" if it is an adaptation reflected in the evolved psychological mechanisms of human beings (*cf.* Studd & Gattiker, 1991). This possibility gains some additional credence from primatologists' observations of fundamental hierarchical arrangements in other primate species (e.g., chimpanzees) and our presumed evolutionary linkages with these species (Boehm, 1994). As we suggested in chapter 3, biological predispositions do not render behavior immutable, but they may very well influence our actions. Whether hierarchy exists as a reified social construction or as a "natural" order nudged into being through evolutionary adaptation, it is so pervasive that "it may be impossible to move beyond it in formally organized contexts" (Stohl, 1995, p. 115).

Concepts such as hierarchy and grapevine are rich in implications about power, authority, motives, intentions, and patterns of organizational communication. These terms also are embedded in the language that members of most organizations use to understand their own experiences. Our point here is that these concepts are not the only ones available for describing and explaining organizational communication.

Muddled Distinctions

The distinction between formal and informal communication also is somewhat muddled. Most scholars make formal communication synonymous with the organization chart, and informal communication synonymous with the grapevine. As Hellweg (1987) pointed out, grapevine communication usually occurs in cluster-transmission patterns. Since many daily episodes of organizational communication ranging from ritual greetings to coffee-break socializing do not fit this pattern, some scholars prefer a broader definition of informal communication that includes such episodes (Koontz & O'Donnel, 1955). Still others define the formal system as *expected* communication patterns and the informal system as *actual* patterns (Jacoby, 1968). Some even argue that formal communication is written, centralized (vertical), and planned, while informal communication is oral, decentralized (horizontal), and unplanned (Stech, 1983). None of these approaches has proven to be especially workable, so there is no one means of distinguishing between formal and informal communication that scholars uniformly accept.

Loose vs. Tight Coupling

Finally, it may make more sense to distinguish between **tightly coupled** and **loosely coupled systems.** As Glassman (1973) explained, two loosely coupled systems either have few common ties or the ties that join them are very weak. In system theory terms, highly interdependent organizational subsystems are tightly coupled. Subsystems that are related but less interdependent are loosely coupled. When an organization is based on tightly coupled subsystems, changes in one subsystem quickly ripple through others. In loosely coupled subsystems, the ripple effect of change is limited, dampened, or gradual. Any given organization might be described generally as either loosely or tightly coupled, but loose and tight coupling are two sides of the same coin. According to Karl Weick (1976), if tight coupling occurs in some areas of an organization, loose coupling must occur in others.

The distinction between tight and loose coupling is important because an organization that appears to be rigidly structured and formal may contain many loosely coupled subsystems, while one that appears to be informal may be tightly coupled. Weick (1976) demonstrated that educational institutions, usually regarded as bureaucracies, are very durable, loosely coupled systems. *Coupling does not depend so much on the degree of formalization in organizational structure as it does on the level of interdependence that actually exists among subsystems.*

Weick believes that the durability of successful organizations is attributable to loose coupling. Loose coupling allows for localized adaptation. When a new situation or problem arises, one area of the organization can respond without requiring organization-wide adaptation every time a change occurs in the environment. The effects of errors and failures are restricted primarily to the subsystems in which they occur.

Loosely coupled systems and the individuals within them have more autonomy and discretion than those in tightly coupled organizations. From an organizational communication standpoint, however, some of the characteristics of loosely coupled systems may surprise you. According to Weick (1976), such organizations are relatively uncoordinated. No single member of the organization knows exactly what is happening throughout the organization as a whole, yet things get done and the organization more or less accomplishes its mission.

Loose coupling does have some potential disadvantages. It reduces benefits of standardization. It promotes diversity rather than selectivity in organizational values and practices. In other words, different groups may be doing things in very different ways. This condition may help to promote adaptation and innovation, but it also allows isolated subsystems to preserve archaic, outmoded traditions. At the same time, "loosely coupled systems should be conspicuous for their cultural lags," yet they also are "vulnerable to producing faddish responses" because so many independent subsystems have the ability to make ad hoc, isolated changes (Weick, 1976, p. 8).

If the concept of coupling is as important as Glassman and Weick suggest, the study of organizational communication *should be less concerned with traditional distinctions between formal and informal communication and more concerned about identifying and understanding the coupling characteristics of organizational communication networks.* These characteristics may be richer and more complex than the traditional distinction between formal and informal communication leads us to believe. We begin to get a better sense of this richness when we change our definition of communication structure from a "system of channels" to "patterns of interaction" in a network of relationships.

Communication Structure as a Network

While the problems in the traditional concepts of formal and informal communication have not been resolved, they can be avoided or at least reframed to some extent by focusing on the patterns of interaction that occur among organization members, or the **communication network.** Figure 6.3 shows a diagram of a communication network. According to Noel Tichy (1981), such networks can be understood by examining four properties: member roles, characteristics of links, structural characteristics, and content.

Beginning with roles, consider the circles in figure 6.3 as people. The lines connecting the circles are links that show who communicates with whom. The *link* is the fundamental unit of any network (Stohl, 1995). This particular diagram shows several distinct **network roles** that members of this organization assume. Assuming that the diagram represents a small organization, the communication network is comprised of three groups. Basically, a **group** is defined by members who interact more frequently with one another than with members of other groups. Most of the people in this network are **group members.** Person A is a **liaison.** A liaison links different groups but is not a member of any of the groups in that link. Individuals B and C form a **bridge link** between two groups. Unlike liaisons, people in a bridge link are group members. Person D is an **isolate** who is not linked to anyone else in the network. This does not mean that D never communicates with

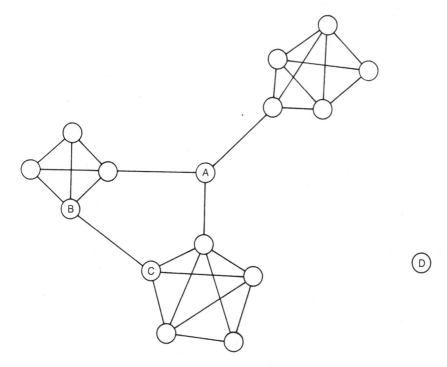

Figure 6.3
A communication network.

anyone else in the organization. It does mean that D has relatively little contact with others (i.e., the amount of interaction that D has with others is negligible in comparison with the amount that occurs among other organization members).

The links that occur between network members may be examined for reciprocity, intensity, and multiplexity. Reciprocity refers to two-way as opposed to one-way flow of messages in the link. Intensity involves commitment of linked members. For example, to what degree will a participant disregard personal costs in order to fulfill obligations (Tichy, 1981)? Multiplexity refers to the number of ways that participants in a link are related.

The structural characteristics of networks include factors such as size of the network, network density (i.e., the proportion of organization members in the network), clustering or the occurrence of dense regions in the network, stability of the network, conditions of membership in the network, and connectedness or the proportion of all possible organizational relationships that actually occur in the network.

Transactional content, according to Tichy (1981), includes four media of exchange: expressions of affect, influence, information, or goods and services. Different types of networks have different transactional content, linkages, and structure. For example, Tichy points out that coalitions tend to deal with information and influence as content, have high reciprocity, moderate density and clustering, but low intensity, little multiplexity, and low stability. In contrast, cliques deal with affect, have moderate intensity, greater multiplexity, low density and clustering, and high stability.

Advantages of a Network Perspective

Given the importance of structure as a concept in organizational communication, the idea that organizations can be understood as networks of communication has a powerful intuitive appeal. Cynthia Stohl (1995) has expanded this idea into a complete textbook on organizational communication. But how does a network perspective of organizational communication solve or at least help us to get around some of the problems with the traditional channels conceptions?

To begin with, it is immediately obvious that analysis of networks will allow us to tap into coupling characteristics that just are not easy to see from a channels frame of reference. Being able to specify some set of formal channels and to compare that set with some sort of alternative informal system will not necessarily tell us anything about issues such as autonomy and discretion, but characteristics of networks such as density, clustering, intensity, multiplexity, and reciprocity within and between systems certainly can.

Second, a network perspective can help us to resolve the ambiguity in distinguishing between formal and informal communication. For example, Tichy (1981) and Stohl (1995) note that the problem is not so much a question of understanding the difference between formal and informal communication as it is a matter of recognizing that a formal system provides a very rough template through which enacted networks emerge. A formal system can guide and constrain emergent networks, but the emergent networks are more complex, elaborate, and varied.

Finally, a network perspective can help us to understand a little better the social construction aspect of organizational communication structure, especially when we try to reconcile the difference between the observable network and the perceived network points of view. We already have suggested that networks are paradoxically objective and subjective phenomena. A network is objective in the sense that an observer almost certainly could come into an organization and describe a set of linkages that can be called *a* network. Describing *the* communication network of the organization is another matter altogether because *the* network of communication just does not exist in the same static sense that *the* network of telephones exists. Networks enacted by organization members are dynamic and take on many different forms. When we try to talk about *the* communication network, we are left with Corman's and Scott's (1994) observation that this is an abstract idea providing rules and reference points for members' interactions, and it may not correspond completely with any observable structure that emerges from these interactions. This is something like Tichy's (1981) idea of the relationship between prescribed and emergent networks, but the so-called prescribed or formal network is probably only one part of an organization member's abstract idea of *the* network. Corman and Scott talk about the network in terms of the individual member's perceived communication relationships, but they also say, "It is a kind of latent knowledge that guides members' manifest communication behaviors" (p. 174). To the extent that this "latent knowledge" is shared among members, the network also exists as a social construction.

Uses of Network Analysis

The basic purpose of network analysis is to provide a picture of the patterns of interaction that define organizational communication structure. Terrance Albrecht and Vickie Ropp (1982) described several ways in which this picture can be developed:

1. Ask organization members to report the interactions that they have with one another (self-report surveys).
2. Make direct, firsthand observations of interaction patterns (naturalistic observation).
3. Unobtrusively "capture" interaction episodes on audiotape or videotape or from other records in the organization (constitutive ethnography).
4. Conduct nondirective interviews with members to obtain information that may help to explain and interpret interaction patterns.

Albrecht and Ropp (1982) argued for the use of various methods in any given network analysis because each method has specific advantages and disadvantages. Self-report surveys and interviews allow the researcher to obtain data from the organization members' perspective and to examine network structure of dyadic, group, and organization-wide levels, but analyses of member reports, as we already have noted, may yield a perceived network that corresponds only loosely with an observable network. Naturalistic observation and constitutive ethnography rely on records of current actual interaction rather than members' potentially faulty reconstructions of past events, but the scope of the analysis is restricted to dyadic and small group levels. Unless you have an army of observers and recording devices, you just cannot be everywhere at once. The various methods also differ in the degree of structure that they impose on the situation and the kind of data that they provide for analysis.

Why go through complex procedures just to obtain a diagram of network structure? What is the utility of this information? At least three different uses of network analysis have been demonstrated in organizational communication research.

First, a network analysis makes it possible to determine the degree to which emergent networks correspond with prescribed or expected channels of communication, group structures, and member roles. Second, network analysis can identify individuals in specific network roles (e.g., liaisons and bridge links that seldom appear on formal organization charts). The presence of these linkages reveals patterns of horizontal communication between different groups and organizational units. Network analysis may also identify isolates. This may help to determine how well members are integrated into the organization.

Identification of network roles can have other important theoretical and practical implications. For example, Albrecht (1984) has reported several important differences between persons in bridge or liaison roles (linkers) and ordinary group members or isolates (nonlinkers). Her research indicates that linkers identify more closely with the organization, have a stronger connection between their jobs and self-concepts, think of their jobs in terms of teamwork and effectiveness, see a closer connection between their jobs and their salaries, and are less frustrated than nonlinkers. Albrecht also reported, however, "They (linkers) also saw their jobs more in terms of problems and pressures than did nonlinkers" (p. 545).

In addition to Albrecht's findings, other studies suggest that isolates do not contribute to organizational functions, tend to withhold information from others, and are relatively dissatisfied (Goldhaber, 1993). An organization committed to a philosophy of participation very likely would want to integrate isolates into the communication network, although there may be situations in which the presence of isolates is welcome news to an organization. For example, some universities and research institutes actively encourage a certain amount of isolation for professors and scientists in order for them to pursue research and scholarly writing.

Network analysis may also be used to reveal correlations between network characteristics and other organizational variables such as performance and satisfaction. For example, Marshall & Stohl (1993) studied the relationship of network and individual indicators of employee participation to employee performance and satisfaction. The network indicators included factors such as the size of a member's personal network (i.e., number of linkages with others) and empowerment (the number of a member's links with managers). Individual indicators of participation included the members' own perceptions of their involvement and empowerment. Interestingly, the best predictor of employee performance was the network indicator of empowerment, that is, the number of linkages with managers, but the best predictor of satisfaction was the individual indicators, that is, the employees' own perceptions of their participation.

A final use of network analysis lies in the study of new or "hidden" network structures in organizations. As Tichy (1981) noted, "All organizations consist of multiple networks. . . . These networks may overlap considerably or be quite separate" (p. 227). Some of these multiple networks may involve interest groups or political coalitions that are in no way identified in the rationally ordered world of the organization chart. An information network might differ greatly from an influence network and any given member's network role may change from one type of network to another.

A study by Albrecht and Hall (1991) provides a good example of this last use of network analysis. They wanted to describe the characteristics of innovation networks (i.e., networks concerned with the development and dissemination of new ideas) in three educational organizations. They found that personal relationships are central to the development of innovations. In particular, each of the three networks had a "central group of relatively dense, interactive elites and either a peripheral, isolated, or less dominant group of outsiders" (p. 553). In effect, each network was anchored by a core group, not by any particular individual, and individuals did not emerge as linkers or liaisons between elites and outsiders. In this way, elites were able to monopolize "the collective talk about new ideas . . . ultimately reinforcing their own relational positions of privilege, power, and influence" (p. 557).

Similarly, McPhee and Corman (1995) found that networks develop around a hierarchy of member activities. Although the traditional idea of a network analysis yields a two-dimensional diagram of groups, bridge links, liaisons, and isolates, McPhee's and Corman's study of one organization revealed four different strata or levels in the network that clearly were tied to the demands of organizational activities. The highest level was a very dense network defined by members who were engaged in the most intensive activities. The lowest was a weakly linked network of members engaged in the least intensive activities.

Although traditionalists have not been completely oblivious to such shadowy networks as coalitions, Stevenson, Pearce, and Porter (1985) pointed out that early organizational theorists ignored these structures by assuming that all organizations have simple and well-defined goals. March and Simon (1958) were the first to call attention to conflict over organizational goals. Cyert and March (1963) extended this idea by discussing competition between conflicting coalitions that might arise in an organization, but traditionalist scholars never really explored the political implications of such coalitions. Given their traditional objectives of explaining organizational effectiveness and goal-setting, traditionalists found it more convenient to simply treat management as a "normally dominant" coalition in order to focus on managerial control and coordination of organizational processes (Stevenson, Pearce, & Porter).

In addition to coalitions, other interest groups may provide the basis for special types of organizational networks. For example, John Van Maanen and Stephen Barley (1984) have shown that "occupational communities" can exert substantial influence over organizational dynamics. An occupational community is a group of people defined by membership in a particular profession or craft (e.g., lawyers, physicians, engineers, police, nurses). These groups develop their own networks—networks that cut across work group, hierarchical, and even organizational lines. Occupational communities develop and reinforce powerful values, vocabularies, and identities among their members. Since individuals' loyalties may be tied much more strongly to their membership in an occupational community than to membership in the work organization, such communities "possess a potentially useful resource to both support and oppose specific organizational policies" (Van Maanen & Barley, p. 334).

Limitations of Network Analysis

Despite the apparent utility of network analysis, Weick (1976) warned researchers to exercise caution when using such techniques. He believes that any technique based on interaction data (who talks to whom) is best suited for revealing tight couplings—"the most visible and obvious couplings . . . the least crucial to understanding what is going on in an organization" (p. 9). In fact, the risks of network analysis may not be as great as Weick claims because the technique allows one to define linkages based on strength and importance as well as frequency of interaction. When these criteria are used, networks that include few liaisons or bridge links or that reveal isolated groups may indicate the loose coupling characteristic with which Weick is concerned. Use of nondirective interviews with methods designed to produce graphic displays of networks also may help in deciding which areas of a network are tightly or loosely coupled.

In addition to the concerns voiced by Weick, there is a second practical, but often overlooked, limitation in network analysis. Because network data are very difficult to obtain and to analyze, network analysis frequently is conducted with a "snap-shot" approach that provides a picture of the organization at a fixed point in time. A study conducted by Stork (1988) on a new research division in a large corporation provides evidence, however, that network structures change over time. It is important to remember that a network is defined by the patterns of interaction that occur among organization members. While some of these patterns may be relatively stable, others are not. It could be very misleading to assume that the results of a network analysis in the present will accurately reflect the structure of the network in the future.

Finally, as we noted earlier, network analysis often depends on memory-based reports of organization members' interaction with one another. Aside from the fact that these reports may be of the abstract, perceived network rather than members' recollections of actual interactions, a network analysis is also limited by the need for most if not all of the members in the network to respond to the survey. If an analysis is based on data that do not include reports from many of the members in the network, it may provide an inadequate picture of the communication network.

Summary The concept of communication structure can be defined in at least two different ways. The traditional way treats structure as a system of pathways or channels through which messages flow. This point of view is associated with a basic distinction between formal and informal systems of communication. Formal communication usually is associated with the use of officially designated channels. Since these channels generally are specified by a hierarchical system of authority, formal communication is described according to the directions of message flow in a hierarchy (i.e., downward, upward, and horizontal).

Informal communication usually is associated with the grapevine. Grapevine communication involves a great deal of information (only a portion of which consists of rumors), usually occurs in cluster transmission patterns, is fast, and is more often accurate than inaccurate.

Although the concepts of formal and informal communication are very useful, there is no uniformly accepted distinction between the two systems. Communication structure can be understood in other ways. In particular, structure can be defined as the actual patterns of interaction that occur among members within a network of relationships. These patterns can be studied with a technique known as network analysis, which reveals the linkages between organization members, including group structures, bridge links, liaisons, isolates, and other network roles. Network analysis can indicate the correspondence between expected and actual networks, identify patterns of horizontal communication, provide clues about the extent to which members are integrated in the organization, and reveal multiple or hidden network structures. The technique may also be useful for inferring tight and loose coupling characteristics in an organization.

Discussion Questions/ Activities

1. Observe some episodes of communication in an organization and attempt to classify them according to production, maintenance, innovation, and human functions. How well does the classification system work?
2. Does it really make any difference whether we define communication structure as a system of channels for messages or as patterns of interaction? Why or why not?
3. Consider the theories presented in chapter 3. How would each of these theories view communication functions and structure?
4. Suppose that we have asked each member of a five-person "organization" to estimate the number of times that he or she interacts with each of the other members during a specified time frame. We have entered each person's report in the matrix below by finding the row with that person's name, then recording the estimates of interaction frequency under the columns associated with the other four. For simplicity, the reports of each pair in our example are identical or very similar. For example, Doaks reports eighteen contacts with Marley, and Marley reports twenty with Doaks.

	Doaks	Monte	Smith	Ching	Marley
1 Doaks		5	10	5	18
2 Monte	5		10	20	5
3 Smith	10	10		10	10
4 Ching	5	18	10		5
5 Marley	20	5	10	3	

Draw a diagram that places those who interact more frequently close together and those who interact less frequently further apart from each other. Connect the individuals with lines to represent linkages. Compare your diagram to those of others in the class.

Additional Resources

Books

Connor, P. E. (1976). *Organizational structure: An administrative tool.* Corvallis, OR: Oregon State University Press.

Olmstead, J. A. (1973). *Organizational structure and climate: Implications for agencies.* Washington, DC: Social and Rehabilitation Services.

Wikstrom, S., & Norman, R. (1994). *Knowledge and value: A new perspective on corporate transformation.* London: Routledge.

Web Sites

http://www.npr.gov/NPR/Reports/tos06.html
   Vice President Gore's National Performance Review report on transformation of organizational structure.

http://www.vanderbilt,edu/owen/froeb/mgt722/topics/organization/organization.htr
   Organizational structure and a case study of Eastman Kodak.

References

Albaum, G. (1964). Horizontal information flow: An exploratory study. *Academy of Management Journal, 7,* 21–33.

Albrecht, T. L. (1984). Managerial communication and work perception. In R. N. Bostrom (Ed.), *Communication yearbook 8* (pp. 538–557). Beverly Hills, CA: Sage.

Albrecht, T. L., & Hall, B. (1991). Relational and content differences between elites and outsiders in innovation networks. *Human Communication Research, 17,* 535–561.

Albrecht, T. L., & Ropp, V. A. (1982). The study of network structuring in organizations through use of method triangulation. *Western Journal of Speech Communication, 46,* 162–178.

Barnard, C. (1938). *The functions of the executive.* Cambridge, MA: Harvard University Press.

Boehm, C. (1994). Pacifying interventions at Arnhem Zoo and Gombe. In R. W. Wrangham, W. C. McGrew, F. B. M. de Waal, & P. G. Heltne (Eds.), *Chimpanzee cultures* (pp. 211–226). Cambridge, MA: Harvard University Press.

Chase, A. B. (1970). How to make downward communication work. *Personnel Journal, 49,* 478–483.

Corman, S. R., & Scott, C. R. (1994). Perceived networks, activity foci, and observable communication in social collectives. *Communication Theory, 4,* 171–190.

Culbert, S. A., & Eden, J. M. (1970). An anatomy of activism for executives. *Harvard Business Review, 48,* 140.

Cyert, R. M., & March, J. G. (1963). *A behavioral theory of the firm.* Englewood Cliffs, NJ: Prentice-Hall.

Davis, K. (1953). Management communication and the grapevine. *Harvard Business Review, 31,* 43–49.

Davis, K. (1968). Success of chain-of-command oral communication in a manufacturing management group. *Academy of Management Journal, 11,* 379–387.

Davis, K. (1972). *Human behavior at work.* New York: McGraw-Hill.

Deetz, S. (1992). *Democracy in an age of corporate colonialization: Developments in communication and the politics of everyday life.* Albany, NY: State University of New York.

Farace, R. V., Monge, P. R., & Russell, H. M. (1977). *Communicating and organizing.* Reading, MA: Addison-Wesley.

Fayol, H. (1949). *General and industrial management* (Constance Storrs, Trans.). London: Sir Isaac Putnam.

French, W. L., Bell, C. H., Jr., & Zawacki, R. A. (1983). *Organization development: Theory, practice, and research* (2nd ed.). Plano, TX: Business Publications.

Glassman, R. B. (1973). Persistence and loose coupling in living systems. *Behavioral Science, 18,* 83–98.

Goldhaber, G. M. (1993). *Organizational communication* (6th ed.). Dubuque, IA: Brown & Benchmark.

Goldhaber, G. M., Yates, M. P., Porter, D. T., & Lesniak, R. (1978). Organizational communication: 1978. *Human Communication Research, 5,* 76–96.

Hellweg, S. (1987). Organizational grapevines: A state of the art review. In B. Dervin & M. Voight (Eds.), *Progress in the Communication Sciences.* Vol. 8. Norwood, NJ: Ablex.

Jacoby, J. (1968). Examining the other organization. *Personnel Administration, 31,* 36–42.

Katz, D., & Kahn, R. L. (1978). *The social psychology of organizations* (2nd ed.). New York: John Wiley & Sons.

Koehler, J. W., Anatol, K. W. E., & Applbaum, R. L. (1981). *Organizational communication: Behavioral perspectives* (2nd ed.). Holt, Rinehart & Winston.

Koehler, J. W., & Huber, G. (1974). *Effects of upward communication on managerial decision making.* Paper presented at the annual meeting of the International Communication Association. New Orleans.

Koontz, H., & O'Donnel, C. (1955). *Principles of management.* New York: McGraw-Hill.

Krivonos, P. (1976). *Distortion of subordinate to superior communication.* Paper presented at the annual meeting of the International Communication Association. Portland.

Maier, N., Hoffman, L., & Read, W. (1963). Superior-subordinate communication: The relative effectiveness of managers who held their subordinates' positions. *Personnel Psychology, 26,* 1–11.

March, J. G., & Simon, H. A. (1958). *Organizations.* New York: Wiley.

Marshall, A. A., & Stohl, C. (1993). Participating as participation: A network approach. *Communication Monographs, 60,* 137–157.

McPhee, R. D., & Corman, S. R. (1995). An activity-based theory of communication networks in organizations, applied to the case of a local church. *Communication Monographs, 62,* 132–151.

Mellinger, G. D. (1956). Interpersonal trust as a factor in communication. *Journal of Abnormal and Social psychology, 52,* 304–309.

Miles, R. (1965). Keeping informed: Human relations or human resources? *Harvard Business Review 43,* 148–163.

Nomura, R. (1981). West learns Japanese ways: Executives wear work clothes. *Neihon Keizai Shimbum.* Translation Service Center, The Asia Foundation.

Pace, R. W., & Boren, R. (1973). *The human transaction.* Glenview, IL: Scott, Foresman.

Penley, L. E. (1982). An investigation of the information processing framework of organizational communication. *Human Communication Research, 8,* 348–365.

Planty, E., & Machaver, W. (1952). Upward communication: A project in executive development. *Personnel, 28,* 304–318.

Read, W. H. (1962). Upward communication in industrial hierarchies. *Human Relations, 15,* 3–15.

Roberts, K. H., & O'Reilly, C. A., III. (1974). Failure in upward communication: Three possible culprits. *Academy of Management Journal, 17,* 205–215.

Smith, R. L., Richetto, G. M., & Zima, J. P. (1972). Organizational behavior: An approach to human communication. In R. Budd & B. Ruben (Eds.), *Approaches to human communication.* Rochelle Park, NJ: Hayden Books.

Spiker, B. K., & Daniels, T. D. (1981). Information adequacy and communication relationships: An empirical examination of 18 organizations. *Western Journal of Speech Communication, 45,* 342–354.

Stech, E. L. (1983). *An empirically derived model of formal and informal communication in work units.* Paper presented at the annual meeting of the International Communication Association. Dallas.

Stevenson, W. B., Pearce, J. L., & Porter, L. W. (1985). The concept of "coalition" in organization theory and research. *Academy of Management Review, 10,* 256–268.

Stohl, C. (1995). *Organizational communication: Connectedness in action.* Thousand Oaks, CA: Sage.

Stork, D. (1988). *Work and social communication networks: Their development in a young organization.* Paper presented at the annual meeting of the International Communication Association. New Orleans.

Studd, M. V., & Gattiker, U. E. (1991). The evolutionary psychology of sexual harassment in organizations. *Ethology and Sociobiology, 12,* 249–290.

Tichy, N. M. (1981). Networks in organizations. In P. C. Nystrom & W. H. Starbuck (Eds.), *Handbook of organizational design.* Vol. 2. London: Oxford University Press.

Tompkins, P. H. (1967). Organizational communication: A state of the art review. In G. Richetto (Ed.), *Conference on organizational communication.* Huntsville, AL: NASA, George C. Marshall Space Flight Center.

Trujillo, N. (1985). Organizational communication as cultural performance: Some managerial considerations. *Southern Journal of Speech Communication, 50,* 201–224.

Van Maanen, J. W., & Barley, S. R. (1984). Occupational communities: Culture and control in organizations. In B. M. Staw & L. L. Cummings (Eds.), *Research in organizational behavior.* Vol. 6. Greenwich, CT: Jai Press.

Walton, E. (1961). How efficient is the grapevine? *Personnel, 28,* 45–49.

Weick, K. E. (1976). Educational organizations as loosely coupled systems. *Administrative Science Quarterly, 21,* 1–16.

GROUP RELATIONSHIPS

Outline

As we take you through the subject matter of this book, we will be talking about organizational culture, diversity, power, conflict, and technology as important subjects in organizational communication, but communication always occurs within and, at the same time, creates a relational context. As Goldhaber, Dennis, Richetto, and Wiio pointed out, "the relationship level is where most of the work of the organization is accomplished, where most of the communication difficulties are primarily encountered, and where the survival potential of the organization is qualitatively judged" (1979, p. 104).

Our approach to understanding organizational communication within relational contexts focuses on group processes and leader-member or superior-subordinate relationships. In this chapter, we will review the functions of norms, conformity, sense-making, decision making, and member roles within groups. One of the more prominent group roles is reflected in leadership behavior. There are too many important ideas about leadership and leader-member relations for us to put everything in this chapter. The topics of leadership and leader-member relations are covered in the next chapter.

Some scholars, such as Herbert Simon (1957), literally regard an organization as a group of groups. Organizations are comprised of many types of groups: special project teams, management teams, committees, functional work groups and departments, social groups, groups derived from occupational and professional communities, and coalitions of special interests that arise from organizational politics. Much of the problem solving, decision making, day-to-day work, and social activity of organizations occurs in groups. Consequently, communication processes within and between groups exert substantial influence on organizational performance and the quality of organization life.

Most of the research on group communication in organizations seems to focus on group decision-making and problem-solving processes, including models of effective decision making, the phases or steps that characterize group decision making, and factors that distinguish effective from ineffective decision-making groups (Littlejohn, 1992). But groups are more than mere decision-making mechanisms. Group membership often is a critical factor in the individual members' sense of identity and self-concept. Groups exercise power in order to gain and control resources. Groups provide values, justifications, and frames of reference from which individual members make sense of their organizational experiences.

Groups as Organizational Subsystems

When Simon (1957) argued that an organization is a group of groups, he seemed to be saying that groups are the most obvious subsystems of an organization. Groups affect and are affected by the organizational system. Homans (1950) noted that certain types of activities, member interactions, and "sentiments" (members' feelings) are required for group survival. These required conditions, according to Homans, are imposed on the group by the larger organizational system. He referred to these imposed conditions as the **external system.** Other activities, interactions, and sentiments arise within the group that are different from and even at odds with the requirements of the external system. Homans called this emergent set of group behaviors the **internal system.** He argued that the emergent internal system is influenced by and, in turn, influences the external system. In particular, the internal system shapes the actions of individual group members and protects the group from outside interference.

Suppose that a special project team is assembled to reposition a company product that has leveled off in sales. The members are Ted, Sally, Juan, Bob, and Jessie, and they are from different departments. They all know one another, but they have never really worked together before. The group's objective is imposed by the larger system. In order to reposition the product, the group has to determine why its sales have declined, then figure out how to recover the old market or find a new market. In order to solve these problems, the group members are required to interact in certain ways. Moreover, the external system demands some feeling of commitment to the project.

The conditions of the external system seem clear, but as the group develops, "it elaborates itself, complicates itself, beyond the demands of the original situation" (Homans, 1950). Ted believes that the product has outlived its usefulness to the company and should simply be discontinued. He resents top management's insistence that it be repositioned in the market. Sally, a "radical feminist," and Bob, a "male chauvinist," quickly develop a severe interpersonal conflict. Juan, an accountant with no marketing background, can contribute little to the task. Jessie, the team leader, is a rigid authoritarian who wants unilateral control over all group decisions.

As the group members approach their task, they not only cope with demands of the external system, but they also adapt to individual idiosyncrasies. The internal system that emerges from this coping and adaptation could have several features. For example, members do not ridicule Juan's inability to contribute to the task because it turns out that he is very adept at mediating conflicts and relieving tension in the group—a critical skill in light of Ted's opinion about the product, Sally's and Bob's dislike for each other, and Jessie's aggressiveness. Jessie's need for control has to be reconciled with the other members' desire for a democratic approach to leadership. The group discards Ted's concerns about the product, establishing a shared expectation that some sort of solution will be developed. Yet, Ted's continued objections serve a purpose by stimulating the group to develop justifications for the project. The gender-related conflict between Bob and Sally creates many uneasy moments and occasional male versus female coalitions in the group, but Juan defuses these situations with humor. The group develops a pattern of conflict followed by humorous tension relief, although it never really resolves the conflict between Sally and Bob.

Any given organization may be composed of a number of identifiable groups. In open systems, these subsystems interact for a variety of purposes. In some cases, the interaction and interdependence may be minimal. In other cases, interdependence of groups is essential to the organization's mission and functions.

The environment of contemporary organizations often is turbulent. Despite the optimism of the 1990s, the past few decades have taught us that we cannot count on stability in markets, technology, government regulations, energy costs, tax revenues, societal needs, and a host of other factors that affect organizations. A turbulent environment seems to promote or even require high levels of intergroup dependence and cooperation (Lippitt, 1982). But which types of organizations are the most adaptive and flexible in the face of environmental change? Those characterized by high levels of coordination and interdependence among subsystems or by relatively awkward and uncoordinated loosely coupled systems? Weick (1976) argued that loosely coupled systems are more flexible and have a better chance of long-term survival. Lippitt (1982) also suggests that high levels of interdependence among organizational subsystems reduce adaptiveness. Yet, interdependence, coordination, and integration of subsystems is precisely what many scholars call for as a response to turbulent environments.

As we saw in the discussion of horizontal communication in chapter 6, many organizations, unaccustomed to the flexibility of communication required for cooperative effort, are finding it difficult to develop effective intergroup relationships. Even in organizations in which group subsystems are relatively independent and loosely coupled, these subsystems still may affect one another. As Beckhard pointed out, "By the very nature of organizations, there are bound to be conditions where, if one department achieves its goals, it frustrates the achievement of some other group's goals" (1969, p. 33). When subsystems are coupled (loosely or otherwise), cooperation and conflict within and between groups is a daily part of organizational life. Consequently, an understanding of intragroup and intergroup communication is essential to an understanding of organizations.

Several concepts are important in developing an understanding of communication processes at the group level of organizations. Groups are characterized by **norms** that regulate the behavior of individual members. Members can generate pressure on one another to **conform** to these norms. Groups function as **sense-making** systems for members and also as vehicles for **decision making** and **problem solving**. All of this is accomplished through group members' enactment of **roles**. Finally, even though group action is more or less a cooperative venture, interaction within and between groups often is characterized by conflict as well as cooperation and by differences between members and between groups in their potential to exercise **power**. The concepts of conflict and power, like leadership, are so important that they get their own chapters in this book. Although we will not discuss leadership, power, and conflict in this chapter, you should keep in mind that they are especially important in understanding group processes.

Each of these elements in group dynamics affects and is affected by communication processes, but the significance of communication in group dynamics runs a bit deeper than most treatments of group dynamics suggest. Social psychologists traditionally have regarded factors such as norms, roles, and power relationships as the causative or "driving" forces in group behavior. People behave as they do in groups because of normative expectations, role requirements, or compliance in the face of power. There is no doubt that groups do develop normative expectations, role requirements, and differences in power. Explaining group dynamics in these terms, however, reduces communication to the status of just one more variable among many in group dynamics—a position that does not coincide with the beliefs of communication theorists.

Blumer (1969) argued that a group cannot be understood without the concept of joint action among members. Joint action does not necessarily depend on mutual agreement in interpretation, but it does depend on some level of mutual understanding of one another's interpretations. This mutual understanding arises only through communication. Hence, all group dynamics, whether they take the form of cooperation, games, sense-making, and even conflict, hinge on communication.

Norms and Conformity

Many scholars and professionals have suggested that organizations do not like uncertainty. Indeed, we depend on some degree of regularity and predictability to structure our interactions with others. In group communication, many of these regularities are derived from norms. As defined by Secord and Backman (1964), "A norm is a standard of behavioral expectations shared by group members against which the validity of perceptions is judged and the appropriateness of feelings and behavior is evaluated" (p. 323).

Norms—shared expectations for behavior, thought, and feeling—may be developed within the group or imported (brought in) from the larger system of which the group is a part (e.g., standards prevailing in the larger organization or mutual expectations acquired through prior experience in other groups). Importation is apparently what occurs in the orientation phase of Fisher's (1970) decision-development model. The internal development of norms occurs as the group negotiates and tests certain rules for interaction. Some of the characteristics in Homans' (1950) concept of internal systems are developed through such negotiation and testing.

Norms also may be explicitly stated or implicitly understood. Explicit normative standards could include policies, written rules, and verbally communicated procedures and standards. Implicit norms and other rules are not explicitly articulated, but the individual group member can observe and learn about their functions. Sometimes, new members of groups discover implicit norms only when they inadvertently violate such norms. This type of violation is illustrated in an example that one of the authors encountered several years ago at a luncheon meeting of an industrial project group.

The group often met over lunch in order to discuss problems associated with its project. On this particular day, however, the initial topic of conversation involved a recent string of losses by the local professional football team. Later, there was some specific discussion of work-related matters but nothing directly relevant to the project itself. Finally, during a lull in the conversation, a new member, who had been with the group for less than one week, made a remark about the unusually brutal November temperatures, then said, "I sure hope it clears up some. I hate for my kids to walk home in this kind of weather."

The comment seemed perfectly harmless, but there was no reply from the other members—only downcast eyes and sullen expressions. The new member was quite embarrassed by this response. When the author later asked some of the other members about their reaction to the comment, they testily replied that luncheons are "business meetings where personal topics like families and children are off-limits." Apparently, however, discussion of the football team's win/loss record was not regarded as inconsistent with the purpose of a "business meeting." In fact, the catalyst that triggered this uncomfortable situation may well have been gender. The new member was a woman. All the rest were men. As long as she talked about football like "one of the boys," everything was fine, but the mention of children may have provoked the men's stereotype of a "female" topic.

This example illustrates one of the ways in which groups exert pressure for conformity to norms. Methods for producing this pressure include the following:

1. Delay action toward the deviant, allowing for self-correction.
2. Joke humorously with the deviant about the violation.
3. Ridicule and deride the violation.
4. Seriously try to persuade the deviant to conform.
5. Engage in heated argument with the deviant.
6. Reject or isolate the deviant.

Bormann (1969) indicated that these methods actually reflect several stages of pressure toward conformity. If conformity does not occur after delaying action, the group might engage in humor. Should deviance still continue, the group would move to ridicule. As pressure toward conformity progresses through these steps, the amount of communicative action directed at the deviant increases until, at stage six, attempts to communicate cease.

Rules and norms are essential to group action for at least two reasons. First, they help to reduce uncertainty. When we understand the norms and rules in a situation, we can have more confidence about the appropriateness of our own actions and in our expectations of others. Second, some predictability is required for joint action and cooperation. In order to collaborate at all, we must have some shared expectations for one another's behavior. But norms also have some unfortunate effects as well. As Baird and Weinberg (1981) noted, norms can hamper group creativity and protect inefficient and archaic practices. Such practices may take the form of certain traditions or so-called sacred cows. Norms also enforce inequities within and between groups. They can be used as instruments of repression that primarily serve the interests of a privileged few. Nevertheless, norms and rules are ever-present in group interaction.

Values and Sense-Making

In chapter 2 we talked about the emergence of the Human Relations movement from the Hawthorne Studies. Evidence from the Hawthorne Studies suggested that work group relationships provide the primary context from which individual values and attitudes toward work and the organization are derived. One of the most important functions of group communication may be to provide the basic frames of reference from which individual members understand, enact, and justify the organization and its mission. This idea is getting renewed attention at least in part because of the interpretive movement in the study of organizational communication. As we noted in chapter 1, the interpretive perspective of organizational communication is concerned especially with the social construction of organizational reality through collective discourse. This topic will receive much more attention in chapter 10 on organizational culture. The point here is that the group, as "*the* unit of social life" (Jensen & Chilberg, 1991, p. 5), provides the basic "petri dish" for culturing the negotiated order of meanings and values. We know, for example, from Van Maanen's (1975) work on occupational communities (in chapter 6) that these shadowy structures not only cut across formal organizational structure but also give rise to and sustain powerful work values.

Another way to understand the values and sense-making function of groups is to examine the process of new member assimilation into the organization. This theme also has received a great deal of recent attention from scholars. Much of the attention given to the assimilation process is attributable to the efforts of Fredric Jablin. Jablin (1984, p. 594) began with the simple but powerful observation that "time may be a major independent variable affecting the development of organizational communication attitudes and behaviors" among individual organization members. The assimilation process provides a context in which to observe this development. Borrowing from earlier work by Van Maanen (1975) on organizational socialization, Jablin (1982; 1984; 1987) argued that assimilation involves three distinct stages:

1. *Anticipatory socialization,* which occurs prior to one's entry into an organization. This stage may actually begin during one's childhood as one acquires attitudes and values about work, organizations, and communication through the influence of family, schools, peers, part-time jobs, and the media.
2. *Encounter,* which begins when one enters an organization and is confronted with the reality of its expectations, policies, and practices.
3. *Metamorphosis,* during which the new member acquires new attitudes and behaviors or changes old ones in order to meet organizational expectations and becomes an accepted, participating member. Jablin goes a step further by distinguishing organizational assimilation from organizational

socialization. Organizational socialization generally is defined as "the process by which a person learns the values, norms and required behaviors which permit him or her to participate as a member of the organization" (Van Maanen, 1975, p. 67). But Jablin argues that assimilation also includes the process of *individualization* as well as socialization. Just as the organization attempts to influence and mold the new member, the new member may attempt to put his or her own stamp on the organization, create an individual identity within the organization, stake out a territory, or in some other way oblige the organization to adapt to the new member's goals, values, and needs.

Jablin (1987) concluded from his own findings and from those of other studies that the quality of the relationship with the immediate supervisor is a key factor in determining the nature of a new employee's assimilation experience, particularly in the encounter phase, but work group processes also may be very important in new member assimilation. Just to provide a few examples of this influence, we know that new organization members depend on peers for technical and social information (Comer, 1991), and they receive more help and attention from peers than they receive from immediate supervisors (Posner & Powell, 1985). We also know from recent work by Fulk, Schmitz, and Ryu (1995) that co-worker attitudes are more influential than supervisor attitudes in organization members' use of and feelings about technology.

Group Decision Making and Problem Solving

Many organizational groups exist primarily for decision-making and problem-solving purposes. Project teams, task forces, and committees typically serve such functions. Sometimes groups are created temporarily to deal with one special contingency. The members of such ad hoc groups work through to the solution of a particular problem, then disband and move on to other projects. The importance of group decision making to organizations has led researchers in small group communication to study these processes almost to the exclusion of any attention to other aspects of communication in group action (Littlejohn, 1992).

Group decision-making is a rule-bound process, but members often seem to be aware only tacitly of the norms, roles, and regularities that they enact in the process. Status and power factors are accepted implicitly without reflection or examination. Members often note the presence of conflict, but they do not seem to understand its nature. Certain patterns of interaction and ways of doing things are simply taken for granted. Thus, as Schein argued, groups are not always aware of their own processes for problem solving and decision making, even when these processes are inefficient and ineffective. Schein (1969) pointed out that groups typically make decisions in one of six ways, even though members may not recognize that their groups are operating in these ways:

1. *Lack of response.* This method is evident in a group when ideas are introduced, then immediately dropped without discussion. In effect, the ideas are vetoed by silence.

2. *Authority rule*. In this case, the power structure in the group places final authority for decision making with one person, usually the leader. The group may discuss an issue, share information, and suggest ideas, but the authority figure has the last word.

3. *Minority coalition*. Schein describes this method as a process of "railroading" decisions through a group by a vocal minority, especially a minority with a powerful member. When other members remain silent in the face of strong minority support for an idea, it can create the impression that the group has reached a consensus. In fact, most members may be opposed to the idea, but no one voices an objection for fear of disrupting what appears to be a consensus.

4. *Majority rule*. This is a familiar system of decision making through voting. Majority rule is typical of highly formal decision-making procedures. An issue or problem is discussed, then a policy or proposal is adopted or rejected on the basis of the percentage of members who favor it.

5. *Consensus*. When the members of a group are prepared to accept an idea, even though they may have some reservations about it, a group has a consensus. Schein is careful to point out that consensus does not necessarily mean that the group unanimously and enthusiastically endorses an idea. Consensus only implies that discussion of the problem has been open and all points of view have been considered. Although group members may not be in complete agreement, the solution or proposal falls within their range of acceptability.

6. *Unanimity*. This rare but ideal mode of decision making occurs when all of the members in a group are in full agreement on a point of view, proposal, policy, or problem-solution.

Schein regards consensus and unanimity as preferred modes of arriving at decisions. Although the processes required to achieve consensus can be inefficient and time consuming, the result is more effective implementation of the decision. Decisions that are made by authority, minority coalition, and majority rule may be arrived at quickly, but those members with other viewpoints may feel frustrated and have little incentive to support the decision. Why are some groups able to achieve consensus-based decision making, while others are not? The answer may have something to do in part with culture.

Decision Making and Culture

The contrast between different methods of arriving at decisions is easy to see when one compares the methods of traditional western organizations to those of Japanese organizations. As Ryutard Nomura, chairman of Japan's Triyo Industries, pointed out, the "bottom-up" consensus-based decision methods of Japanese organizations are painfully slow and cumbersome, but most decisions are implemented effectively because support has been developed among all essential participants during the decision-making process. In contrast, decisions are made quickly with traditional western methods such as reliance on centralized authority, but implementation is slow and uncertain. According to Nomura,

"Opposition and misunderstanding which inevitably arise emerge *after* the decision has been announced" (1981). One only has to examine the American political system to see that losing factions often are more interested in regaining power, winning the next decision, and stalling unwanted decisions than in cooperating with the winner.

Differences between cultures in their methods of group decision making can be explained in part by the degree to which a given culture is *individualistic* or *collectivistic*. As explained by Hofstede and Bond (1984, p. 419), people in individualistic cultures "are supposed to look after themselves and their immediate family only," while those in collectivistic cultures "belong to ingroups or collectivities which are supposed to look after them in exchange for loyalty." When Hofstede and Bond talk about ingroups, they are referring to people such as co-workers, colleagues, and classmates. Outgroups include strangers or anyone who is not specifically a member of an ingroup.

Gudykunst, Yoon, and Nishida (1987) argued that ingroup relationships are more intimate in collectivistic cultures than in individualistic cultures. Consequently, ingroup communication should be more personalized, better coordinated, and less difficult in collectivistic cultures than in individualistic cultures. Results from their study of ingroup communication among students from Korea (highly collectivistic), Japan (moderately collectivistic), and the United States (highly individualistic) supported this hypothesis. Ingroup communication was more personalized, better coordinated, and less difficult for the Koreans than for the Japanese, and more personalized, better coordinated, and less difficult for the Japanese than for the Americans.

These results do not necessarily mean that we should all initiate a cultural revolution in an effort to make American society more collectivistic. Individualistic values may offer some communicative advantages. Gudykunst, Yoon, and Nishida also found that American students had somewhat better experiences than the Japanese and Koreans with *outgroup* communication. Interaction with strangers was easier and better coordinated (though less personal) for American students. Infante and Gorden (1987) also have claimed that independent mindedness of organization members, a condition that can be troublesome in group interaction, is essential to productivity in American organizations.

Effective Group Decision Making and Task Performance

What distinguishes effective decision-making groups from ineffective groups? Social scientists have been interested in this question for several decades, but much of the research has been more concerned with comparing group performance to individual performance. These studies indicate that groups generally produce more and better ideas than do individuals working alone, but the evaluative judgments of groups are not as good as those of the very best individuals.

Research on the characteristics of interaction in decision-making groups has not yet provided a comprehensive picture of the differences between effective and ineffective groups, but several studies during the 1980s and 1990s have at least provided many of the pieces for this particular puzzle. A series of group effectiveness studies has been conducted by Randy Hirokawa and his colleagues. In one of his early investigations (1980), he assembled groups to study a problem for which experts already had devised a correct solution. All of the group interactions were recorded. Hirokawa distinguished between effective and ineffective groups on the basis of agreement between their solutions and the expert solution, then compared their recorded interactions. Surprisingly, Hirokawa found many more similarities than differences between effective and ineffective groups. Only one major difference occurred in the communicative behaviors and interaction patterns: *effective groups were much more attentive to the procedures used to solve the problem.* Specifically, one member would make a statement of procedural direction (e.g., "Why don't we set up some evaluation criteria?"), and the others would adopt this direction.

Hirokawa became concerned that he might not be finding differences between effective and ineffective groups because he was focusing on behaviors that might be irrelevant to group tasks and effective decisions. He tried to correct this problem in a 1983 study by examining only group communication acts that served one of five functions: (a) *establishing operating procedures,* (b) *analyzing the problem,* (c) *establishing evaluation criteria,* (d) *generating alternative solutions,* and (e) *evaluating solutions.* Results of the study indicated a positive relationship between effectiveness of a group's decision and the group's efforts to analyze the problem, but the relationship between effectiveness and attempts to establish operating procedures was *negative.* Moreover, there was no association between effectiveness and attempts to establish evaluation criteria, to generate alternative solutions, or to evaluate solutions.

In spite of these mixed findings, Hirokawa continued his work and gradually developed the idea that group interaction affects group decisions by shaping critical thinking. Hirokawa's position and others like it are known as vigilant interaction theory. This theory claims that the quality of group decisions depends on the group's vigilance [attentiveness] in interaction concerning four questions:

1. Problem analysis: Is there something about the current state of affairs that requires change?
2. Objectives: What do we want to achieve or accomplish in deciding what to do about the problem?
3. Choices: What are the choices available to us?
4. Evaluation: What are the positive and negative aspects of those choices? (Hirokawa & Rost, 1992, p. 269)

Over the years, Hirokawa and his colleagues gradually have accumulated extensive evidence to support the theory. The most recent study by Hirokawa and Rost (1992) is particularly important because it involved groups from a large utility company. Many group decision-making studies are laboratory experiments, but this study shows clearly that vigilant interaction theory applies to groups in real organizations. In the utility company groups, interaction that facilitated problem analysis and evaluation of both positive and negative features of choices led to high-quality decisions. Interaction that inhibited problem analysis, development of standards to assess choices, and evaluation of positive features of choices led to low-quality decisions.

Hirokawa recently has extended his studies of group effectiveness beyond decision making and problem solving to focus on the more general problem of work team performance. He and Joann Keyton (1995) studied work teams implementing drug abuse prevention programs in schools to identify factors perceived by team members to facilitate or inhibit team progress and to determine whether these factors actually had anything to do with team effectiveness. Hirokawa and Keyton found a dozen factors, some facilitative, some inhibitive, that distinguished between effective and ineffective teams. As you might suspect, team members reported that facilitating factors occurred more often in effective teams, while inhibiting factors occurred more often in ineffective teams. Fortunately, the one dozen factors can be reduced to four basic conditions that Hirokawa and Keyton say are necessary for team effectiveness:

1. motivated team members;
2. adequate time and informational resources for the task;
3. competent leadership;
4. direct organizational assistance (e.g., training).

Group Decision Development

In addition to Hirokawa's work on the differences between effective and ineffective group decision making, another important line of research has addressed the *stages* or *phases* of decision development within groups. One of the most complete treatments of this topic was developed by B. Aubrey Fisher (1970), who identified four stages in group decision-making processes: **orientation, conflict, emergence,** and **reinforcement.**

The orientation phase begins as the members of a group meet for the first time. The members experience uncertainty; they are not sure what to expect. Behavior is based on members' understanding of social norms regarding politeness and initiation of relationships. These norms are brought into the situation, since the group has evolved no rules of its own.

Politeness norms become less important as members acquire some familiarity with one another, and the group moves into a conflict phase characterized by disputes, disagreements, and hostility. The group gradually works through conflict, entering an emergence stage in which increased tolerance for ambiguity in opinions is reflected. Ambiguity at this point allows for face-saving and reconciliation of conflicts. Finally, the group moves to a reinforcement stage in which the members develop and endorse a decision. The idea of reinforcement implies that group members engage in a mutual process of justifying and committing themselves to the decision. For example, they might say, "This is the right decision because . . ." or "This solution is better than the other possibilities."

Many studies of group development, including Fisher's own studies, have examined the processes of groups during a relatively limited time frame (e.g., over several meetings or even in only one meeting). The results of these studies suggest that group development occurs in an orderly, linear fashion, proceeding from one step to the next. Fisher points out, however, that a phase model may not apply to all task-oriented groups. The limitations of phase models like Fisher's are reinforced in a series of studies by Marshall Scott Poole (1981, 1983a, 1983b). Poole found that the stages of decision development in small groups may follow any one of several possible sequences. He concluded that a "logical" or unitary sequence of problem-solving steps may provide normative expectancies that influence the group, but the group's actual course of action emerges from many complicated factors. In other words, groups in different situations act in different ways. Even when group decision making fits a phase model, the specific types and cycles of interaction within any given phase differ substantially from group to group.

Roles and Role Categories in Groups

Group action, whether it is effective or ineffective, is produced through member enactment of roles. George Kelly (1955) defined role as "an ongoing pattern of behavior that follows from a person's understanding [or misunderstanding] of how others who are associated with him or her in his or her task think" (p. 97). Simply stated, the enactment of a role depends on a person's interpretations of a given situation. It does not necessarily follow from others' expectations for what a person in the role is supposed to do.

Wofford, Gerloff, and Cummins (1979) attempted to clarify the idea of role by distinguishing between perceived, expected, and enacted roles:

The *perceived role* is the set of behaviors that the occupant of the position believes he or she should perform. The *expected role* is the set of behaviors that others believe he or she should perform. *Enacted role* is the actual set of performed behaviors. (p. 39)

There may be a high level of agreement among perceived, expected, and enacted roles, but the three frequently differ. Suppose that the members of a work group expect a supervisor to be a democratic leader, providing guidance and encouraging participation. The supervisor's perception of the leadership role, based on a belief in autocratic methods such as controlling decisions, dictating orders, and using punishment to gain compliance, is quite different from the members' expectations. Moreover, the supervisor's actual behavior—the enacted role—turns out to be a laissez-faire approach of "cool your heels on the desk and leave things alone," in which the supervisor actually relinquishes much of the leadership responsibility. As we shall see later, disparities among expected, perceived, and enacted roles can be significant sources of conflict in groups.

Any role is enacted. It is not only defined by others' expectations for appropriate behavior, but it is also defined by the perceptions, capabilities, and choices of the person who enacts it. Even so, there do seem to be some types of roles that frequently occur in task groups. A classic description of typical task group roles that Benne and Sheats developed in 1948 is still widely accepted today. Their description includes the following:

Task Roles

Initiator: defines problem, contributes ideas and suggestions, proposes solutions or decisions, offers new ideas.
Information seeker: asks for clarification, promotes participation by others, solicits facts and evidence.
Energizer: prods members into action.
Orienter: keeps group on track, guides discussion.
Secretary: keeps track of group progress, remembers past actions.

Maintenance Roles

Encourager: provides support, praise, acceptance for others.
Harmonizer: resolves conflict, reduces tension.
Comedian: provides humor, relaxes others.
Gatekeeper: controls communication channels, promotes evenness of participation.
Follower: accepts others' ideas, goes along with others.

Self-Centered Roles

Blocker: interferes with progress of group by consistently making negative responses to others.
Aggressor: attacks other members in an effort to promote his or her own status.
Dominator: monopolizes group time with long, drawn-out monologues.
Deserter: withdraws from group discussion by refusing to participate, engages in irrelevant conversations.
Special-interest pleader: brings irrelevant information into discussion, argues incessantly for his or her own point of view.

As you read the descriptions, most may have seemed familiar to you from your own experience in group activities. It is very likely that you have seen some, if not all, of these roles enacted in task groups. Sometimes a particular individual consistently will enact one of these roles, but Benne and Sheats do not mean to imply that any given member has only one role. Generally, the actions of a given member will reflect some of these roles but show little or no evidence of others, and more than one member may enact any given role.

Among the roles that may occur in groups, organizational groups generally are characterized by leadership roles that are exercised in relation to member (follower) roles. The subjects of leadership, leader-member relations, and hierarchical superior-subordinate relationships are addressed in the next chapter.

Summary

Groups constitute the most obvious and, perhaps, most important organizational subsystems. Communication within and between groups can be channeled toward cooperation or conflict. In either case, group action must be understood as joint action. A group not only serves the functions of a larger system, but it also strives to survive within that system. Hence, the goals of different organizational groups are not always consistent with one another or with the goals of the larger system. Groups, like living organisms, appear to move through stages of development. In some cases, the stages seem orderly and sequenced, but activities of many groups take on cyclical characteristics. Interaction in groups is a rule-bound process based on normative expectations and role enactment. Group members are accorded varying levels of power and status within the group. One of the most important functions of group communication may be to provide the basic frames of reference from which individual members understand, enact, and justify the organization and its mission. Interpretive research especially has created renewed interest in this aspect of group process.

Most communication research on small group processes has been concerned with decision making. Hirokawa's studies are fairly typical of research in this area. Few consistently reliable differences have been found between effective and ineffective groups, although recent studies suggest that communicative behaviors involving evaluation of opinions, evaluation of alternatives, decisional premises, and the styles of influential group members may explain some of the differences.

Group activity is carried out through the enactment of member roles. There are many different kinds of roles, and they may be enacted by different members at different times. Some of the more important categories of roles include task roles, maintenance roles, and self-centered roles.

Discussion Questions/ Activities

1. Observe a group in a decision-making process. What kinds of communicative behaviors seem to influence the group's effectiveness? Can the group's decision-making process be characterized by any of the models or procedures described in this chapter?
2. Do you think that group memberships within an organization play an important role in shaping individual members' values? Can you provide some examples to support your conclusion?
3. Some organizational scholars have argued that prescriptive models of group decision making are undesirable and should be avoided. Do you agree with this position? Why or why not?

Additional Resources

Books

Goldberg, A., and Larson, C. E. (1975). *Group communication: Discussion processes and applications*. Englewood Cliffs, NJ: Prentice-Hall.

Hwang, C. L., and Lin, M. J. (1987). *Group decision making under multiple criteria: Methods and applications*. Berlin: Springer-Verlag.

Shonk, J. H. (1992). *Team-based organizations: Developing a successful team environment*. Homewood, IL: Business One Irwin.

Swap, W. C., et al. (Eds.). (1984). *Group decision making*. Beverly Hills, CA: Sage.

Web Sites

http://infolabwww.kub.nl:2080/w3thesis/Groupwork/gains_and_losses.html
   Study of factors that lead to group process gains and losses.
http://medg.lcs.mit.edu
   The M.I.T. Clinical Decision Making Group

References

Baird, J. E., Jr., and Weinberg, S. B. (1981). *Group communication: The essence of synergy* (2nd ed.). Dubuque, IA: Wm. C. Brown.

Beckhard, R. (1969). *Organization development: Strategies and models*. Reading, MA: Addison-Wesley.

Benne, K. D., and Sheats, P. (1948). Functional roles of group members. *Journal of Social Issues, 4*, 41–49.

Blumer, H. (1969). *Symbolic interactionism: Perspective and method*. Englewood Cliffs, NJ: Prentice-Hall.

Bormann, E. (1969). *Discussion and group methods*. New York: Harper & Row.

Comer, D. R. (1991). Organizational newcomers' acquisition of information from peers. *Management Communication Quarterly, 5*, 64–89.

Fisher, B. A. (1970). Decision emergence: Phases in group decision making. *Speech Monographs, 37*, 53–66.

Fulk, J., Schmitz, J., & Ryu, D. (1995). Cognitive elements in the social construction of communication technology. *Management Communication Quarterly, 8*, 259–288.

Goldhaber, G. M., Dennis, H. S., III, Richetto, G. M., & Wiio, O. (1979). *Information strategies: New pathways to corporate power.* Englewood Cliffs, NJ: Prentice-Hall.

Gudykunst, W. B., Yoon, Y., & Nishida, T. (1987). The influence of individualism-collectivism on perceptions of communication in ingroup and outgroup relationships. *Communication Monographs, 54,* 295–306.

Hirokawa, R. Y. (1980). A comparative analysis of communication patterns within effective and ineffective decision-making groups. *Communication Monographs, 47,* 312–321.

Hirokawa, R. Y. (1983). Group communication and problem-solving effectiveness II: An exploratory investigation of procedural functions. *Western Journal of Speech Communication, 47,* 59–74.

Hirokawa, R. Y., & Keyton, J. (1995). Perceived facilitators and inhibitors of effectiveness in organizational work teams. *Management Communication Quarterly, 8,* 424–446.

Hirokawa, R. Y., & Rost, K. M. (1992). Effective group decision making in organizations: Field test of the vigilant interaction theory. *Management Communication Quarterly, 5,* 267–288.

Hofstede, G., & Bond, M. (1984). Hofstede's culture dimensions: An independent validation using Rokeach's value survey. *Journal of Cross-Cultural Psychology, 15,* 417–433.

Homans, G. C. (1950). *The human group.* New York: Harcourt Brace Jovanovich.

Infante, D. A., & Gorden, W. I. (1987). Superior and subordinate communication profiles: Implications for independent-*Journal, 38,* 73–80.

Jablin, F. M. (1982). Organizational communication: An assimilation approach. In M. E. Roloff and C. R. Berger (Eds.), *Social cognition and communication* (pp. 255–286). Beverly Hills, CA: Sage.

Jablin, F. M. (1984). Assimilating new members into organizations. In R. N. Bostrom (Ed.), *Communication yearbook 8* (pp. 594–626). Beverly Hills, CA: Sage.

Jablin, F. M. (1987). Organizational entry, assimilation, and exit. In F. M. Jablin, L. L. Putnam, K. H. Roberts, & L. W. Porter (Eds.), *Handbook of organizational communication: An interdisciplinary perspective* (pp. 679–740). Beverly Hills, CA: Sage.

Jensen, A. D., & Chilberg, J. C. (1991). *Small group communication: Theory and application.* Belmont, CA: Wadsworth.

Kelly, G. A. (1955). *The psychology of personal constructs.* Vol. 1. New York: Norton.

Lippitt, G. L. (1982). *Organization renewal: A holistic approach to organization development* (2nd ed.). Englewood Cliffs, NJ: Prentice-Hall.

Littlejohn, S. W. (1992). *Theories of human communication* (4th ed.). Belmont, CA: Wadsworth.

Nomura, R. (1981). West learns Japanese ways: Executives wear workclothes. *Neihon Keizai Shimbum.* Translation Service Center, the Asia Foundation.

Poole, M. S. (1981). Decision development in small groups I: A comparison of two models. *Communication Monographs, 48,* 1–24.

Poole, M. S. (1983a). Decision development in small groups II: A study of multiple sequences in decision making. *Communication Monographs, 50,* 206–232.

Poole, M. S. (1983b). Decision development in small groups III: A multiple sequence model of group decision development. *Communication Monographs, 50,* 321–341.

Posner, B., & Powell, G. (1985). Female and male socialization experiences: An initial investigation. *Journal of Occupational Psychology, 58,* 81–85.

Schein, E. (1969). *Process consultation: Its role in organization development.* Reading, MA: Addison-Wesley.

Secord, P. F., and Backman, C. W. (1964). *Social psychology.* New York: McGraw-Hill.

Simon, H. A. (1957). *Administrative behavior.* New York: Free Press.

Van Maanen, J. (1975). Breaking in: Socialization to work. In R. Dubin (Ed.), *Handbook of work, organization and society* (pp. 67–120). Chicago: Rand McNally.

Weick, K. W. (1976). Educational organizations as loosely coupled systems. *Administrative Science Quarterly, 21,* 1–19.

Wofford, J. C., Gerloff, E. A., and Cummins, R. C. (1979). Group behavior and the communication process. In R. S. Cathcart and L. A. Samovar (Eds.), *Small group communication: A reader* (3rd ed.). Dubuque, IA: Wm. C. Brown.

CHAPTER 8
LEADER-MEMBER RELATIONSHIPS

Most organizational theorists believe that leadership is a central factor in the effectiveness of groups as well as organizations. We assume that leadership is required in order to initiate structure, to coordinate activities, and to direct others toward the accomplishment of group goals. The preoccupation with leadership is driven in part by a long-standing desire to identify the means of achieving organizational effectiveness through managerial control. Attention to the quality of leader-member relationships initially came about to some extent through the human relations assumptions that superiors gain compliance from subordinates by promoting interpersonal relationships and satisfaction of social needs. Later on in the 1960s and 1970s, emphasis shifted to the basic theme in human resource development theory that the role of leaders and superiors is to create the proper climate for the development of subordinates' abilities and to facilitate that development. In either case, *the study of leader-member relations in our culture has been preoccupied with revealing strategies for leaders and superiors to use in communicating with subordinates for accomplishment of organizational objectives.*

It should not escape your attention at this point that we are tying the leader-member relationship closely to the superior-subordinate relationship. The very idea of organization not only implies coordinated action, including divisions of labor and role specialization, but also a hierarchy of authority in which those who occupy higher positions are accorded more status, privilege, and power than those who occupy lower positions. In chapter 4, we described emerging alternatives to traditional systems of hierarchy, but it is still generally true in the organizational world that a person at any given level of the organization is **subordinate** to an immediate **superior**–the person to whom you report, from whom you take orders–the boss, or, if you prefer, your leader. Eisenberg, Monge, and Farace

(1984) argued, "Of the communication processes that operate in organizations, the most important include those that regulate interaction between superiors and subordinates" (p. 261).

If you conducted a library search on the ideas that we will discuss in this chapter, some would show up under the topic of leadership. Others would show up under superior-subordinate communication. A few would show up under supervision. These certainly are not just different terms for the same thing. For example, we can associate leadership with almost any type of organization, but we do not generally think about supervision except within work organizations. Nonetheless, the exercise of leadership, of the superior role, or of supervision involves the direction of others' activities and their responses to that direction. These are the basic issues with which we are concerned in this chapter. Consequently, you will see references to each of these terms in our discussion, depending on usages in the literature from which the ideas are taken.

Theories of Leadership Behavior

Despite the overwhelming belief in the importance of leadership in organizations, no one has been able to develop a uniformly accepted theory of leadership behavior (Koehler, Anatol, & Applbaum, 1981). Over the years, we have attempted to distinguish leaders from nonleaders on the basis of personality traits, to identify and describe ideal styles of leadership, and to determine the kinds of situations under which any given type of leadership behavior is likely to be effective or ineffective. Some scholars have even argued that "leadership" and "management" involve two different and sometimes inconsistent forms of behavior (Bennis, 1976a, 1976b).

Leadership as Trait

The earliest theories of leadership attempted to distinguish leaders from nonleaders on the basis of certain personality traits. The list of distinguishing traits such as intelligence, responsibility, and others like them typically sounds as if it came from the pages of the Boy Scout or Girl Scout Handbook. Despite many efforts to identify a clear and consistent set of characteristics of leaders, results of the trait approach are mixed. Jennings (1961) argued that the trait school has "failed to produce one personality trait or set of traits that can be used to discriminate between leaders and nonleaders." On the other hand, Koehler, Anatol, and Applbaum believe that at least three specific traits are associated with effective leaders across a broad range of situations: intelligence, adjustment, and deviancy.

Leadership as Style

The stylistic approach to leadership behavior developed, in part, out of frustration with the earlier trait approach. As Koehler and colleagues pointed out, "Unlike the trait approach to leadership, the stylistic approach is concerned with what leaders do rather than the personal characteristics they possess" (p. 228). Two widely used models of leadership style were presented by White and Lippitt (1960) and by Blake and Mouton (1964).

White and Lippitt identified three basic styles of leadership that they labeled as **authoritarian, democratic,** and **laissez-faire.** Authoritarian leaders exercise strong control over decisions and tasks. They issue and enforce orders to ensure that their plans are executed in an acceptable manner. Democratic leaders are more oriented toward guidance than complete control of group activities. They share authority with subordinates and seek subordinate input in decision making. Laissez-faire leaders relinquish virtually all control of decisions and group processes to subordinates. Such leaders may remain available for consultation or problem solving but generally delegate all authority for tasks to subordinates.

A second and more widely used stylistic approach to leadership is presented by Blake and Mouton (1964, 1985), revised as Blake and McCanse's (1991) Leadership Grid®. Blake and Mouton (1964, 1985) argued that several basic managerial (i.e., leadership) styles can be identified according to their degree of concern for production and concern for people. Five of these styles can be located in the Blake and McCanse Leadership Grid® in which the two dimensions of concern form axes. Two additional styles are displayed graphically outside the grid because they involve manipulations of grid styles. As the phrase "concern for" implies, Blake and McCanse's concept of style is more *attitudinal* than behavioral. The Leadership Grid is presented in figure 8.1.

The 1,1, or **impoverished leader,** is theoretically the least effective. Given low concern for both production and people, the impoverished leader exercises little initiative and abdicates any responsibility for group outcomes. According to Blake and McCanse, the 9,1 **authority-compliance** and 1,9 **country club** leaders are not much more effective. The authority-compliance leader basically regards people concerns as obstacles to production accomplishment. This leader may use punitive and even abusive strategies to subordinate people concerns to the all-important goal of production accomplishment. In contrast, the country club leader thinks of nothing but people concerns. This leader strives primarily to maintain morale, satisfaction, and harmony among group members, even if production has to suffer in order to accomplish maintenance functions.

The 5,5, or **middle-of-the-road leader,** attempts to compromise and balance production and people concerns by relying on precedent and avoiding unproven risks. The middle-of-the-road manager may believe that **production** and people concerns are competing and contradictory aspects of group behavior. In order to cope with the contradiction, the middle-of-the-road leader settles for moderately harmonious group relationships and adequate, but not outstanding, task performance.

Two styles displayed outside the grid in figure 8.1 involve manipulations of grid styles. The **opportunist** adopts any grid style that is required to accomplish self-interest and self-promotion. Opportunists adapt to situations in order to gain maximum advantage, for example, using a 9,1 style to intimidate one person and a 1,9 style to gain the trust of another.

The **paternalistic** leader is characterized as a 9+9 because this person creates a combined style of controlling paternalism. The paternalist adopts level 9 concern for both people and production by rewarding loyalty with support and encouragement, but only so long as the follower's behavior meets the paternalist's expectations. The paternalist punishes those who deviate with monitoring and restrictions.

The Leadership Grid Figure

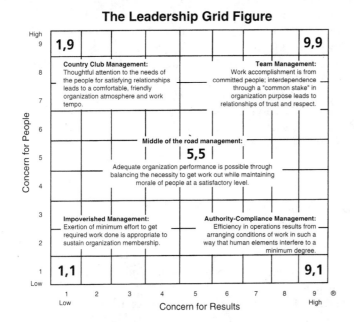

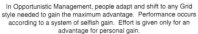

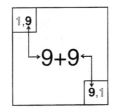

Figure 8.1
The Leadership Grid Figure for *Leadership Dilemmas—Grid Solutions*, by Robert R. Blake and Anne Adams McCanse. (Formerly the Managerial Grid figure by Robert R. Blake and Jane S. Mouton) Houston: Gulf Publishing Company, Page 29. Copyright 1991 by Scientific Methods, Inc. Reproduced by Permission of the owners.

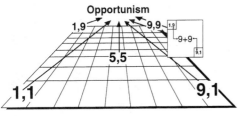

In Opportunistic Management, people adapt and shift to any Grid style needed to gain the maximum advantage. Performance occurs according to a system of selfish gain. Effort is given only for an advantage for personal gain.

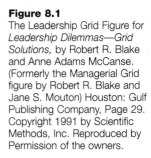

9+9: Paternalism/Maternalism
Reward and approval are bestowed to people in return for loyalty and obedience; failure to comply leads to punishment.

The ideal style for leadership effectiveness presumably is the 9,9 or **team leader.** Whereas the 5,5 leader sees production and people concerns as competing, the team leader believes that group effectiveness depends on integration of people needs with production objectives. This leader personifies the ideals of human resource development theory as described in chapter 2. Specifically, group effectiveness is presumed to depend on the extent to which individual members are able to develop, assume responsibility, and function as a team. The team leader concentrates on bringing about this form of development.

Some writers (e.g., Hersey & Blanchard, 1982) have claimed that the Leadership Grid is based on earlier studies of leadership behavior at the Institute for Social Research (ISR) in Michigan and at Ohio State University (OSU). The ISR studies identified two basic styles of leadership, job-centered and employee-centered. The OSU studies found two similar leadership variables—initiating structure and consideration. The OSU model regarded *both* variables as potential factors in a leader's behavior, whereas the ISR model viewed them as different styles. In either case, the job-centered and initiating structure factors represent a **task** dimension of leadership style, whereas employee-centered or consideration behavior represents a **maintenance** dimension. Despite the similarity of terms in all of these models, there are some important differences. The OSU and ISR models specifically are behavioral, whereas the Leadership Grid, as we noted earlier, is attitudinal. Moreover, Scientific Methods, Inc., the corporation holding the rights to the Leadership Grid, contends, "Blake and Mouton's research and writings are not based on either the ISR or the OSU studies" (Knause, 1990).

Situational Theory

Just as trait theories have been criticized for failing to produce clear distinctions between leaders and nonleaders, stylistic theory has been criticized for assuming that any one style of leadership can be effective in all situations. Situational or contingency theories of leadership argue that no one leadership style is ideal and that the circumstances of leadership will determine whether a particular style will be effective or ineffective.

Frederick Fiedler (1967) devised one popular contingency theory. Fiedler argued that the effectiveness of a leadership style will be influenced by three factors:

1. Leader-member relations, or the degree of confidence and trust that subordinates have in the leader.
2. Task structure, or the degree of certainty and routine as opposed to ambiguity and unpredictability in the task.
3. Position power, or the influence inherent in the leadership role (legitimate authority and ability to reward or punish).

Fiedler conducted a number of studies on directive and permissive styles of leadership under varying combinations of the three key situational factors. Results of these studies led him to propose a model of situational conditions under which each style would be most effective. Fiedler's model is presented in table 8.1.

The group and task characteristics identified by Fiedler probably are not the only factors that influence the effectiveness of a given leadership style. Eblen (1987) found that the relationship between leadership style and employee commitment varied across organizational contexts. Given the two basic leadership variables from the OSU studies, initiating structure and consideration, she found that consideration was positively related to employee commitment in hospitals, while initiating structure was positively related to commitment among employees in city government departments.

The gender of a leader also may mediate the effectiveness of a given style. Whether men and women actually differ in their styles of leadership is a subject of some dispute. Sally Helgesen (1990) popularized an argument that sex differences do occur in leadership style, and the differences clearly are to the advantage of women because their supportive and facilitative styles are more conducive to participatory and democratic work environments. Similarly, Fairhurst (1993) reported that women leaders have numerous ways of demonstating concern for

Table 8.1   Fiedler's Situational Model. From *A Theory of Leadership Effectiveness,* by F. Fiedler, 1967. New York: McGraw-Hill. Used by permission.

Group Situation

Condition	Leader-Member Relations	Task Structure	Position Power	Leadership Style Correlating with Productivity
1	Good	Structured	Strong	Directive
2	Good	Structured	Weak	Directive
3	Good	Unstructured	Strong	Directive
4	Good	Unstructured	Weak	Permissive
5	Moderately poor	Structured	Strong	Permissive
6	Moderately poor	Structured	Weak	No Data
7	Moderately poor	Unstructured	Strong	No relationship found
8	Moderately poor	Unstructured	Weak	Directive

relationships in their interactions with subordinates. On the other hand, comprehensive reviews of scholarly studies on this subject suggest that there simply are no substantial and reliable behavioral differences between female and male managers (e.g., Wilkins & Andersen, 1991). Other studies have revealed no basic differences between male and female leaders on any behaviors related to initiating structure or consideration (Nieva & Gutek, 1981).

Whether or not gender differences occur in leadership behavior, there is ample evidence that subordinates' *evaluations* of any given leadership behavior appear to depend on whether that behavior is exhibited by a male or a female. Studies by Wolman and Frank (1975), Hagen and Kahn (1975) and Bartol and Butterfield (1976) indicated that women who enact stereotypically "masculine" leadership behaviors are evaluated unfavorably by subordinates. On the other hand, women's stereotypically "feminine" enactments of leadership are associated with high levels of satisfaction among subordinates. This bias in subordinates' evaluations of leaders usually is attributed to sex role incongruence. As explained by Lamude and Daniels (1991):

When traditional sex role expectations for women are imported to the workplace, these expectations not only lead to the belief that women do not behave in the stereotypically masculine fashion associated with leadership, but also to the belief that they *should* not; that female enactments of "masculine" behavior are incongruent with sex role expectations. (p. 44)

Finally, there is some reason to believe that there are circumstances under which no style of leadership can be effective. For example, recall our brief discussion of Pettegrew's S.O.B. theory from chapter 3. Because resources in the hospital that Pettegrew studied were essentially "fixed," many administrative decisions resulted in "win-lose" reallocations of resources to different groups in the organization. Whether administrators were authoritative or participative in style had no effect on subordinates' perceptions of the administrators. Administrators inevitably were S.O.Bs.

Leader-Member Exchange Theory

Situational, as well as stylistic theories of leadership, also have one other very important limitation. They assume that leaders behave in a consistent manner toward all of the members within a group, exhibiting something like an "average leadership style" (ALS model). Graen (1976) challenged this assumption with a leader-member exchange (LMX) model, arguing that leaders discriminate significantly in their behavior toward subordinates.

Fairhurst and Chandler (1989) examined the LMX model in a qualitative study of interaction between one manager and three of his subordinates in the warehouse division of a large manufacturing company. One subordinate was an "in-group" member (worked under conditions of mutual trust, influence, and support with the manager), one was an "out-group" member (worked under conditions involving low trust and support along with exercise of the manager's formal authority). The third subordinate was a "middle-group" member, which fell between the conditions of the other two. Fairhurst and Chandler found both consistency and inconsistency in the manager's relationship with these three subordinates. The manager used indirect and ambiguous communication to exercise unobtrusive control with all three subordinates. As described by Fairhurst and Chandler, he was "a control-based manager who tries to appear noncontrolling and participative" (p. 230). At the same time, the manager's behavior and the patterns of interaction between the manager and subordinates clearly differed across in-group, middle-group, and out-group relationships. Both parties frequently challenged and disagreed with each other in the in-group relationship. The manager was somewhat more dominant in the middle-group relationship and exercised direct authority with the out-group subordinate. Interestingly, the out-group subordinate went to great lengths to maintain his out-group status with communicative behaviors that created social distance between the manager and himself.

In a more recent and larger LMX study, Waldron (1991) reported results that are only partially consistent with Fairhurst and Chandler's findings. In Waldron's study, in-group subordinates were able to communicate informally with their supervisors about subjects that had no relationship to the work. In Albrecht and Ropp's terms, we might say that these subordinates had multiplex linkages with the supervisors, "a kind of latitude not available to out-group members" (Waldron, p. 301). But some of the differences that Waldron found between in-groups and out-groups were so small that he believes subordinates in either group exercise little control in defining their relationships with their superiors, that superiors maintain power over in-group members as well as out-group members.

Fairhurst (1993), on the other hand, has continued to find marked differences in leader-member communication between in-groups, middle-groups, and out-groups. In a much larger study than the original Fairhurst and Chandler case, Fairhurst found that in-group communication emphasized supportiveness, collegiality, and similarity. Out-group leader-member exchange involved face threats and competitive conflict, implying "an openly contentious and adversarial relationship" (p. 345). Middle-groups reflected both accommodating and polarizing interactions.

One potential explanation for the inconsistency between the Waldron and Fairhurst studies may be that differences in relationship quality have more influence on subordinates' behavior than on leaders' behavior. Lee and Jablin (1995) found evidence of this when they were studying what supervisors and subordinates do to maintain their relationships under stressful circumstances, for example, when the relationship is deteriorating or when one party wants to escalate the relationship to a level that is too close for the other party's comfort.

Lee and Jablin found that supervisors' perceptions of the leader-member exchange quality (i.e, in-group vs. out-group) had no effect on the relationship maintenance strategies that they used with subordinates in any situation. This is consistent with ALS theory and with the results in the Waldron study. On the other hand, the quality of the leader-member exchange was very important to choices made by subordinates in communicating with their supervisors. Where relationship stress was caused by escalation, out-group subordinates were more likely than in-group subordinates to avoid communication. Where deterioration was occurring, out-group subordinates were more likely than in-group subordinates to use both direct *and* deceptive strategies to deal with the situation. You probably are asking, "How can that be?" It is a matter of timing. Since out-group subordinates' relations with leaders are rule driven and formal, they can call attention directly and openly to any deviation from the rules. If this does not solve the problem with the leader, the out-group member may turn to deception and distortion. This certainly looks like the kind of LMX in-group/out-group difference that Fairhurst has seen in her studies.

Leadership as Development

In many organizational and professional settings, integration and development of new members, especially in management, professional, and certain trade occupations occurs in mentor-protégé relationships. These relationships may be formal but often are informal. The new member becomes a protégé to an older or more established member who functions as a mentor. We know of no leadership theory that specifically includes mentoring as a dimension of leadership, but we are identifying it that way here because the mentor leads the protégé in a developmental sense. The mentor role entails teaching, guidance, counseling, appraisal, and other developmental activities, including sponsorship and promotion of the protégé's career advancement (Bolton, 1980; Shelton, 1981).

Although a mentor may also be a protégé's immediate superior, the mentor frequently occupies another role (e.g., a higher-level manager or a more experienced peer at the same level of the organization). Moreover, the mentor role is inherently different from the definition of the conventional role of an immediate superior, in which the relationship is based on task rather than on the objectives of career development.

Most studies of mentor-protégé relationships have focused primarily on determining how common they are in the work world and whether protégé participation in such relationships actually leads to career advancement (e.g., McLane, 1980; Shelton & Curry, 1981). One investigation by Daniels and Logan (1983) specifically analyzed the communicative features of mentor-protégé relationships. They restricted their study to female managers and professionals, comparing those who participated as protégés in career development (mentor-protégé) relationships with others who only had experience as subordinates in conventional superior-subordinate relationships. Daniels and Logan found that levels of supportiveness, influence, satisfaction, and overall communicative activity were perceived to be much higher in career development relationships than in conventional superior-subordinate relationships. They also found that the mentor's supportiveness and upward influence were both important to protégés' satisfaction with the relationship.

Motivation and Control

It is almost impossible in American culture to talk about the effectiveness of leadership and supervision without addressing motivation and control because the function of leaders and supervisors is the direction of others' activities toward organizational goals. Theories of leadership and supervisory communication are concerned at least implicitly with the problem of motivating subordinates. Even LMX theory, which begins with the premise that a leader's behavior is not the same with all subordinates, values the power of "transformative leadership" in high-quality LMX conditions where subordinates "move beyond self-interest" (Fairhurst, 1993, p. 321).

Some of the early work on the problem of motivation and control was driven by traditional human relations values and beliefs in the linkage between communication and effective supervision. In organizational communication, one important source of these values and beliefs is a series of graduate research projects directed by W. Charles Redding at Purdue University. These studies classified supervisors as effective or ineffective on the basis of ratings by higher-level managers, then examined the supervisors' communicative dispositions. Redding (1972) drew five major conclusions from these studies:

1. The better supervisors tend to be more "communication-minded." For example, they enjoy talking and speaking in meetings, they are able to explain instructions and policies, and they enjoy conversing with subordinates.
2. The better supervisors tend to be willing, empathic listeners; they respond understandingly to so-called "silly" questions from employees; they are approachable; and they will listen to suggestions and complaints, with an attitude of fair consideration and willingness to take appropriate action.
3. The better supervisors tend (with some notable exceptions) to "ask" or "persuade," in preference to "telling" or "demanding."
4. The better supervisors tend to be sensitive to the feelings of others. For example, they are careful to reprimand in private rather than in public.
5. The better supervisors tend to be more open in their passing along of information; they are in favor of giving advance notice of impending changes and of explaining the "reasons why" behind policies and regulations. (p. 433)

Although the Purdue studies were not directly concerned with the effect of superiors' communicative behavior on subordinate satisfaction and morale, the tone of Redding's conclusions bears a strong resemblance to the prescription that earlier human relations theorists offered: Management promotes compliance by promoting morale and satisfaction. Morale and satisfaction depend on effective interpersonal relations, namely, empathy, sensitivity to social needs, receptivity, and two-way communication—essentially the same communicative behaviors that the Purdue studies link with "effective supervision."

Satisfaction and Communication Climate

In a classic investigation closely related to the ideal of the Purdue studies, Jack Gibb (1961) made a more direct connection between superiors' communication and subordinate satisfaction by distinguishing between climates of supportive and defensive interpersonal communication. According to Gibb, a supportive climate leads to subordinate satisfaction and accuracy in communication, while a defensive climate leads to dissatisfaction and distortion of communication. He identified the communicative behaviors of superiors that trigger the development of these climates. The resulting model is summarized in table 8.2.

The influence of the Purdue studies, Gibb's model, and other studies such as those on communication openness (see findings in table 8.1) have continued in the 1980s through many investigations of factors in superior-subordinate communication that are related to subordinates' satisfaction with their job, superiors, and organizations. Most of these studies concern the relationship between some aspect of the superior's communicative behavior and subordinate satisfaction. Generally, these studies affirm the claim that supportive, "people-oriented" styles of communication promote satisfaction.

The Motivational Limits of Leadership and Supervision

The quality of communication between superiors and subordinates, whether understood in the context of supervision or the context of leadership, is important, but we do not want to leave the impression that morale and satisfaction are completely dependent upon the behavior of leaders and supervisors. Some researchers have tried to build a more comprehensive picture of the factors that influence satisfaction. An excellent example of this kind of work is a study by Eileen Ray and Katherine Miller (1991) who found that employee job satisfaction depends on a complex set of relationships among several factors. In their study, job satisfaction was negatively related to role ambiguity and positively related to fatigue that employees experienced. As role ambiguity increased, satisfaction went down, but to some extent, fatigue led to higher satisfaction. Apparently, satisfying work is tiring work. In turn, fatigue was related to perceived workload. Role ambiguity was positively related to perceived workload and negatively related to supportiveness of one's co-workers and supervisor. Interestingly, co-worker support was more important than supervisor support in lowering role ambiguity, and employee perceptions of their co-workers' supportiveness depended on the strength of the network links that they had with those co-workers.

Interestingly, some motivational theories in the human resource development era of the 1960s, 70s, and 80s also pointed to limits in the quality of leader-member relations to influence motivation and, thus, performance. The best

Table 8.2 Descriptions of Gibb's Defensive and Supportive Communication Climates. From "Defensive communication," by J. Gibb, 1961, *Journal of Communication, 11,* pp. 141–148. Used by permission.

Defensive	Supportive
1. *Evaluation:* To pass judgment on another; to blame or praise; make moral assessments of another or question his [or her] motives; to question the other's standards.	1. *Description:* Nonjudgmental; to ask questions which are perceived as requests for information; to present feelings, emotions, events which do not ask the other to change his or her behavior.
2. *Control:* To try to do something to another; to attempt to change behavior or attitudes of others; implicit in attempts to change others is the assumption that they are inadequate.	2. *Problem Orientation:* To convey a desire to collaborate in solving a mutual problem or defining it; to allow the other to set his [or her] goals and solve his [or her] own problem; to imply that you do not desire to impose your solution.
3. *Strategy:* To manipulate another or make him or her think that he or she was making his or her own decisions; to engage in multiple and/or ambiguous motivations; to treat the other as a guinea pig.	3. *Spontaneity:* To express naturalness; free of deception; a "clean id;" straightforwardness; uncomplicated motives.
4. *Neutrality:* To express a lack of concern for the other; the clinical, person-as-an-object-of-study attitude.	4. *Empathy:* To respect the other person and show it; to take his [or her] role; to identify with his [or her] problems; to share his [or her] feelings.
5. *Superiority:* To communicate that you are superior in position, wealth intelligence etc.; to arouse feelings of inadequacy in others; to express that you are not willing to enter into joint problem solving.	5. *Equality:* To be willing to enter into participative planning with mutual trust and respect; to attach little importance to differences in ability, worth, status, etc.
6. *Certainty:* Dogmatic; to seem to know the answers; wanting to win an argument rather than solve a problem; seeing one's ideas as truths to be defended.	6. *Provisionalism:* To be willing to experiment with your own behavior; to investigate issues rather than taking sides; to solve problems, not debate.

example of this is Frederick Herzberg's (1966) motivator-hygiene theory. Like a number of other motivational theories of the 1960s, motivator-hygiene theory is based on Abraham Maslow's (1954) need hierarchy, but Herzberg added two novel and unique features to his theory:

1. Satisfaction and dissatisfaction are *not* opposite conditions. The opposite of satisfaction is simply the absence of satisfaction.
2. The factors that lead to job satisfaction and, therefore, to motivation are different from the factors that lead to job dissatisfaction.

Herzberg observed in his studies of organizations that six factors seemed to contribute to job satisfaction and motivations for high levels of performance. A different set of ten factors was related to job dissatisfaction. The satisfiers, called **motivators**, and the dissatisfiers, called **hygiene factors,** are as follows:

Motivators

Achievement
Recognition
Advancement
The work itself
Responsibility
Potential for personal growth

Hygiene Factors

Policy and administration
Technical supervision
Relationships with supervisor
Relationships with peers
Relationships with subordinates
Salary
Job security
Personal life
Work conditions
Status

According to Herzberg, failure to provide for organization members' hygiene needs will lead to job dissatisfaction and poor performance, but merely meeting these needs does not produce motivation to improve performance. In Herzberg's view, positive relationships between superiors and subordinates may prevent dissatisfaction, but relationship quality will not lead to better performance. Better performance depends on incorporating the six motivators into the work environment. Thus, as Wayne Pace explains:

A supervisor who does a good job of creating positive relationships with employees will be disappointed if he or she thinks that those employees will be motivated to work harder as a result. . . . To motivate employees, the supervisor will need to find ways to give employees greater freedom and more responsibility for doing their work, or at least give them more recognition for work done well. (1983, p. 89)

The Control Behavior of Superiors

It is well and good to discuss theories of leadership behavior and the motivational characteristics of supervisory communication, but recent studies have been more concerned with the actual patterns of communication reflected in compliance gaining and more concerned with factors that may influence a superior's choice of compliance-gaining strategies. In particular, Fairhurst, Green, and Snavely (1984a, 1984b) have examined the strategies that managers use to correct or control poor performance by employees. They have emphasized the importance of studying control as a process that occurs over time, rather than as a single event. For example, one of their studies (1984b) described bank managers' use of face support in attempts to correct or control subordinates' poor performance. Face support includes two factors: (1) the degree of approval and (2) the degree of freedom given to poor performers to define a corrective course of action. The researchers found two different patterns in managers' behaviors over as many as four attempts to deal with a poor performer. The first pattern was punitive, consisting of direct disapproval (criticism and reprimand) and no freedom (threats and orders) throughout the entire sequence of correction attempts. The second pattern involved reliance on questions to discover the source of the problem and to identify possible solutions in early attempts (problem-solving approach), but this strategy was abandoned for the punitive approach in later attempts.

Fairhurst and colleagues offered this very insightful conclusion from their study:

Branch and personnel administrators in the banks we studied advocated the use of the punitive approach only after the problem-solving approach . . . repeatedly failed. Yet, in the field, we find that the punitive approach predominates from the start for many while the problem-solving approach is used by some but is quickly abandoned. (p. 289)

In other words, the managers professed commitment to problem solving as a strategy, but they showed little reliance on this strategy in actual attempts to control poor performance. In short, they simply did not practice what they preached. Fairhurst and colleagues provide an interesting picture of the strategies that managers use for compliance gaining but little information that helps us to understand why they select these strategies. They do indicate that the choice of a control response probably depends upon whether the manager is closer to a "problem-solving" breakpoint or an "elimination breakpoint" in the control process. At the problem-solving breakpoint, the manager recognizes a performance problem and hopes that it can be corrected. At the elimination breakpoint, the manager has decided that the problem cannot be solved and that the employee is not worth retaining. But they also note, "There appears to be no 'formula' of necessary ingredients for determining whether a manager will issue a warning, choose only to 'counsel' the employee, request retraining, or whatever" (1984a, p. 587).

Other studies attempt to provide some insights on this issue, that is, what factors influence a superior's choice of tactics to gain compliance from subordinates? Some researchers have suggested that sex of the manager is a powerful factor influencing choice of compliance-gaining tactics. Conrad (1991) found that women tried longer than men to maintain prosocial strategies in conflict resolutions, but eventually turned to coercion in efforts to gain compliance, an outcome that is consistent with Fairhurst's findings. Hirokawa, Mickey, & Miura (1991) found that differences between men and women in choice of compliance-gaining tactics could be accounted for by **request legitimacy,** that is, managers' belief that they have a right or prerogative to make a request of a subordinate. Men and women differed only in situations where they had high request legitimacy, with male managers being somewhat more assertive and direct. Hirokawa and colleagues concluded that such differences are attributable to situational factors rather than to sex differences. In addition to request legitimacy, other factors clearly are related to managers' choices of compliance-gaining tactics.

Superiors' own perceptions of their supervisory skills also are related to strategies that they choose to manage conflicts with their subordinates. In particular, Conrad (1983) found that superiors who perceived their skills to be low were more likely to rely on autocratic (threatening or coercive) strategies, whereas those who expressed low self-confidence avoided use of participative conflict resolution. In addition to self-concept, trust is a factor in superiors' selection of strategies. Riccillo and Trenholm (1983) found that trusted subordinates are subjected to interpersonal persuasive strategies, whereas untrusted subordinates are subjected to coercion.

Another factor influencing the choice of compliance-gaining strategies is **locus of control**. Locus of control is said to be either *internal* or *external*. People who have external locus of control believe that they are victims of fate. Whether they attain desired goals or rewards depends on luck and circumstance rather than on their own efforts. People who have internal locus of control believe that they control their own destinies (i.e., they are largely responsible for what happens to them). Spector (1982) summarized several studies that found relationships between locus of control and choice of compliance-gaining or influence strategies. Generally, these studies indicate that superiors who have internal locus of control tend to rely on interpersonal persuasive strategies, whereas those who have external locus of control rely on threat and coercion.

The factor of locus of control in compliance gaining is especially interesting because a good theoretical model can be developed to explain what happens. External locus of control appears to be related to authoritarian personality characteristics. Authoritarians are unduly submissive to authority; hostile toward anyone who defies or disregards authority; and preoccupied with use of power, conformity, and enforcing rules. Since people who have external locus of control believe they are victims of fate, it makes sense that they would rely on higher authority to mediate their fate, to "take care" of them by enforcing the rules. This style of thinking would lead easily to use of threat and coercion as a defensive strategy.

Subordinate Behavior toward Superiors

So far in this chapter we have focused on the way in which leaders, supervisors, and superiors relate to subordinates, but subordinates also act toward their superiors in ways that affect the relationship and its outcomes. Historically, most of this research has addressed two themes, upward distortion and feedback. We have not seen a study in many years that has attempted to describe or explain subordinates' feedback to superiors, but Jablin reviewed and summarized some studies of this type in 1979. The studies indicated generally that subordinates provide more responsive feedback to superiors when the subordinates have role clarity, and superiors tend to improve their own performance after receiving feedback from subordinates.

Although most studies of upward distortion also occurred prior to Jablin's 1979 review, researchers in the 1980s have continued to show some interest in this topic. Early studies of upward distortion indicated that subordinates' mobility aspirations (desire for promotion and advancement) are *negatively* related to accuracy in upward communication, whereas subordinates' trust in superiors is *positively* related (Read, 1962). As mobility aspirations go up, accuracy goes down. Increased trust is associated with increased accuracy. Other studies suggest that distortion is more likely to occur in rigid, machinelike organizational climates than in open, "organic" climates (Young, 1978).

Studies in the 1980s have extended past research by attempting to identify other variables that influence distortion of upward communication. For example, Krivonos (1982) reviewed studies suggesting that subordinates are more likely to distort information when that information reflects unfavorably upon them. When he extended this research by distinguishing between task and nontask situations, he found that subordinates are more likely to distort unfavorable information in a task situation but actually seem to relay unfavorable information more accurately than favorable information in a nontask situation. According to Krivonos, distortion of unfavorable information occurs in task situations because superiors exercise more power over subordinates in such situations. The possible consequences of a "bad report" in a task situation are more ominous than they might be in a nontask situation. Since the nontask situation is less risky, subordinates might capitalize on "pratfall effect" by accurately reporting unfavorable information. Pratfall effect occurs when a person's admission of errors or mistakes actually increases his or her credibility with others.

More recently, scholars have turned their attention away from traditional topics such as feedback and upward influence in order to explore new themes on subordinates' behaviors in communicating with superiors. One new theme concerns subordinates' use of compliance-gaining strategies in upward communication. Put another way, we know that bosses are trying to manage their subordinates, but how does the subordinate manage the boss?

In one study of this topic, Lamude, Daniels, and White (1987) explored the influence of locus of control and situation on strategies that subordinates chose to gain compliance from superiors. Assuming that external locus of control is closely tied to authoritarian personality characteristics, Lamude and colleagues argued that an external subordinate is more likely to attempt compliance gaining with a superior in situations *only* in which the superior's intervention is needed to enforce rules that protect the subordinate's interests (e.g., a conflict with co-workers). In contrast, an internal subordinate may be inclined to attempt compliance gaining with a superior in any situation in which some goal can be achieved by influencing the superior.

Moreover, Lamude and colleagues argued that subordinates in general will be more likely to attempt compliance gaining with superiors who are perceived to be external in locus of control. Although such superiors are presumed to behave autocratically, their external orientation predisposes them toward compliance. Internals are presumed to be more resistant to compliance-gaining attempts (Spector, 1982).

Lamude and his colleages made some interesting predictions, but the results of the study did not turn out in quite the way that they had expected. First, subordinates showed high inclination to use some compliance-gaining strategies regardless of situation and locus of control factors. These strategies included liking (being friendly in the compliance-gaining attempt) and altruism (asking a person to act unselfishly).

Second, external subordinates were more likely to use threats and aversive stimulation (e.g., harassing the superior until the superior complies) with internal superiors than with external superiors. This finding is consistent with arguments that external subordinates are likely to rely on coercive strategies, but it is inconsistent with the expectation that external superiors are more likely to be targets for compliance-gaining attempts. It is possible that the risk of threatening an external, autocratic superior is too great for the external subordinate and that the internal superior is perceived as an easier target.

Third, internal subordinates showed high inclination to use aversive stimulation under various circumstances. This is surprising because theory suggests that internals avoid the use of coercive strategies in relationships with others. Internal subordinates, however, showed little inclination to use threat. One explanation may be that internals like to exert direct control over their environments. Since a threat merely forecasts a future consequence, it is not as direct as aversive stimulation in which one takes hostile action against a target and continues the action until the target complies. Locus of control literature generally paints a socially desirable picture of internals and attributes negative characteristics to externals, but internals show some inclination to do whatever they have to do in order to get what they want.

We want, for a couple of reasons, to return in closing to the LMX theory and the research that this theory has produced. First, several of the factors that we have just discussed in subordinates' behavior toward superiors may also have something to do with subordinates' perceptions of the the quality of leader-member exchange and whether they are working from an in-group or an out-group position. The study by Lee and Jablin on relationship maintenance certainly seems to indicate that this is an important consideration. Second, the "exchange" part of the LMX model envisions leaders trading resources in return for subordinates' performance. Although there is some inconsistency across studies over whether leaders treat in-groups and out-groups differently, defining that group context may not depend so much upon leader action as upon leader-member *interaction*. Both parties in the relationship determine to some extent what the quality of that interaction will be.

Summary

Leadership generally is regarded as essential to group and organizational effectiveness. Leadership and supervision by superiors is presumed to be necessary in order to initiate structure and direct subordinates toward organizational goals. Leadership itself has been studied as a trait and as a style in an effort to identify ideal leadership behaviors, but situational theorists suggest that no one approach to leadership is right for all situations. Advocates of leader-member exchange theory also have shown that leaders do not act in a consistent way toward all subordinates but treat different subordinates in different ways.

One pervasive issue in the study of leadership and supervision centers on motivation and control, that is, the means by which superiors are able to direct subordinates. Early human relations theory emphasizes particularly the connection between subordinates' satisfaction and subordinates' compliance with superiors, stressing especially the quality of supervisory communication in promoting satisfaction. The Purdue studies of effective supervision and Gibb's model of defensive and supportive communication both are testaments to human relations principles, providing evidence that effective supervision is correlated with positive, open, and receptive communication behaviors. It is *not* clear whether any of these factors in superior-subordinate communication is connected with task performance, and human resource development theories of motivation such as Herzberg's motivator-hygiene theory challenge the idea that the quality of superior-subordinate relationsips will motivate subordinates to perform better.

Although a climate of open, supportive, and trust-based communication may be the ideal in superior-subordinate relationships, managers' claims that they have adopted these ideals may be based more on wishful thinking than on fact. Recent studies of superiors' communicative behaviors in attempts at compliance gaining, influence, and conflict management with their subordinates suggest that coercive, threatening, autocratic, and punitive tactics are still quite common. Factors such as low self-esteem and confidence in one's supervisory abilities, external locus of control, and mistrust of subordinates continue to promote defensive styles of communication.

Subordinates' behaviors toward superiors also are far removed from a picture-perfect representation of openness and supportiveness. Studies continue to show that distortion is a common occurrence in upward communication and that various situational factors may contribute to this phenomenon. Moreover, although subordinates generally are in a less powerful position in the superior-subordinate relationship, they certainly are not powerless. They can and do attempt to influence their superiors and may well use some unsavory tactics such as threat and aversive stimulation in the process.

Discussion Questions/ Activities

1. Some scholars believe that the leader-member or superior-subordinate relationship is the most important level at which organizational communication occurs. What is the basis for this belief? Do you agree or disagree? Why?
2. Identify some of the reasons for researchers' preoccupation with the study of superior-subordinate communication.
3. After studying the chapter discussion, write a summary of what we think we know about leadership and superior-subordinate communication. Are there any problems with some of the conclusions that we have drawn?
4. What is the connection, if any, between effective leadership or supervision and performance of organization members?

Additional Resources

Books

Barge, J. K. (1994). *Leadership: Communication skills for organizations and groups.* New York: St. Martin's Press.
Stech, E. (1983). *Leadership communication.* Chicago: Nelson-Hall.
Ulrich, B. T. (1992). *Leadership and management according to Florence Nightingale.* Norwalk, CT: Appleton & Lange.

Web Sites

http://www.tmn.com/organizations/Leadership/leader.html
    Leadership, Inc., developing leaders for the 21st century.

http://www.gtinet.com/l2000.htm
The Leadership 2000 project of the Breakpoint Company.
http://styx.uwa.edu.au/csd/LDPwomen.html
Leadership Development Center for Women

References

Albrecht, T. L., & Ropp, V. A. (1984). Communicating about innovation in networks of three U.S. organizations. *Journal of Communication, 34,* 78–91.

Bartol, K. M., & Butterfield, D. A. (1976). Sex effects in evaluating leaders. *Journal of Applied Psychology, 61,* 446–545.

Bennis, W. (1976a). Leadership—A beleaguered species. *Organizational Dynamics, 5,* 3-16.

Bennis, W. (1976b). *The unconscious conspiracy: Why leaders can't lead.* New York: American Management Association.

Blake, R. R., & McCanse, A. A. (1991). *Leadership Dilemmas-Grid® Solutions.* Houston: Gulf Publishing.

Blake, R. R., & Mouton, J. S. (1964). *The managerial grid.* Houston: Gulf Publishing.

Blake, R. R., & Mouton, J. S. (1985). *The managerial grid III: The key to leadership excellence.* Houston: Gulf Publishing.

Bolton, E. (1980). A conceptual analysis of the mentor relationship in the career development of women. *Adult Education, 30,* 195–207.

Conrad C. (1983). Supervisors' choice of modes of managing conflict. *Western Journal of Speech Communication, 47,* 218–228.

Conrad, C. (1991). Communication in conflict: Style-strategy relationships. *Communication Monographs, 58,* 135–155.

Daniels, T. D., & Logan, L. L. (1983). Communication in women's career development relationships. In R. N. Bostrom (Ed.), *Communication yearbook 7* (pp. 532–553). Beverly Hills, CA: Sage.

Eblen, A. L. (1987). Communication, leadership, and organizational commitment. *Central States Speech Journal, 38,* 181–195.

Eisenberg, E. M., Monge, P. R., & Farace, R. V. (1984). Coorientation of communication rules in managerial dyads. *Human Communication Research, 11,* 261–271.

Fairhurst, G. T. (1993). The leader-member exchange patterns of women leaders in industry: A discourse analysis. *Communication Monographs, 60,* 321–351.

Fairhurst, G. T., & Chandler, T. A. (1989). Social structure in leader-member interaction. *Communication Monographs, 56,* 215–239.

Fairhurst, G. T., Green, S. G., & Snavely, B. K. (1984a). Managerial control and discipline: Whips and chains. In R. N. Bostrom (Ed.), *Communication yearbook 8* (pp. 558–593). Beverly Hills, CA: Sage.

Fairhurst, G. T., Green, S. G., & Snavely, B. K. (1984b). Face support in controlling poor performance. *Human Communication Research, 11,* 272–295.

Fiedler, F. (1967). *A theory of leadership effectiveness.* New York: McGraw-Hill.

Gibb, J. (1961). Defensive communication. *Journal of Communication, 11,* 141–148.

Graen, G. (1976). Role-making processes within complex organizations. In M. D. Dunnette (Ed.), *Handbook of industrial and organizational psychology* (pp. 1201–1245). Chicago: Rand McNally.

Hagen, R. L., & Kahn, A. (1975). Discrimination against competent women. *Journal of Applied and Social Psychology, 5,* 362–376.

Helgesen, S. (1990). *The female advantage: Women's ways of leadership.* New York: Doubleday.

Hersey, P., & Blanchard, K. (1982). *Management of organizational behavior: Utilizing human resources* (4th ed.). Englewood Cliffs, NJ: Prentice-Hall.

Herzberg, F. (1966) *Work and the nature of man.* New York: Collins.

Hirokawa, R. Y., Mickey, J., & Miura, S. (1991). Effects of request legitimacy on the compliance-gaining tactics of male and female managers. *Communication Monographs, 58,* 421–436.

Jablin, F. M. (1979). Superior-subordinate communication: The state of the art. *Psychological Bulletin, 86,* 1201–1222.

Jennings, E. (1961). The anatomy of leadership. *Management of Personnel Quarterly, 11,* 2.

Knause, C. (1990, March). Letter stating the position of Scientific Methods, Inc., on the origin of the managerial grid.

Koehler, J. W., Anatol, K. W. E., and Applbaum, R. L. (1981). *Organizational communication: Behavioral perspectives* (2nd ed.). New York: Holt, Rinehart & Winston.

Krivonos, P. D. (1982). Distortion of subordinate to superior communication in organizational settings. *Central States Speech Journal, 33,* 345–352.

Lamude, K. G. & Daniels, T. D. (1991). Mutual evaluations of communication competence in superior-subordinate relationships: Sex role incongruency and pro-male bias. *Women's Studies in Communication, 13,* 39–56.

Lamude, K. G., Daniels, T. D., & White, K. (1987). Managing the boss: Locus of control and subordinates' selection of compliance-gaining strategies in upward communication. *Management Communication Quarterly, 1,* 232–259.

Lee, J., & Jablin, F. M. (1995). Maintenance communication in superior-subordinate relationships. *Human Communication Research, 1995, 22,* 220–257.

Maslow, A. H. (1954). *Motivation and personality.* New York: Harper & Row.

McLane, H. J. (1980). *Selecting, developing, and retaining women executives.* New York: Van Nostrand Reinhold.

Nieva, V. F., & Gutek, B. A. (1981). *Women and work: A psychological perspective.* New York: Praeger.

Pace, R. W. (1983). *Organizational communication: Foundations for human resource development.* Englewood Cliffs, NJ: Prentice-Hall.

Ray, E. B., & Miller, K. I. (1991). The influence of communication structure and social support on job stress and burnout. *Management Communication Quarterly, 4,* 506–527.

Read, W. H. (1962). Upward communication in industrial hierarchies. *Human Relations, 15,* 3-15.

Redding, W. C. (1972). *Communication within the organization: An interpretive review of theory and research.* New York: Industrial Communication Council.

Riccillo, S. C., & Trenholm, S. (1983). Predicting managers' choice of influence mode: The effects of interpersonal trust and worker attributions on managerial tactics in a simulated organizational setting. *Western Journal of Speech Communication, 47,* 323-339.

Shelton, C. (1981, July). Mentoring programs: Do they make a difference? *National Association of Banking Women Journal,* p. 25.

Shelton, C., & Curry, J. (1981, July). Mentoring at Security Pacific. *National Association of Banking Women Journal,* p. 25.

Spector, P. E. (1982). Behavior in organizations as a function of employees' locus of control. *Psychological Bulletin, 91,* 482–497.

Waldron, V. R. (1991). Achieving communication goals in superior-subordinate relationships: The multi-functionality of upward maintenance tactics. *Communication Monographs, 58,* 289–306.

White, R., & Lippitt, R. (1960). *Autocracy and democracy.* New York: Harper & Row.

Wilkins, B. M., & Andersen, P. A. (1991). Gender differences and similarities in management communication: A meta-analysis. *Management Communication Quarterly, 5,* 6–35.

Wolman, C., & Frank, H. (1975). The solo woman in a professional peer group. *American Journal of Orthopsychiatry, 45,* 164–171.

Young, J. W. (1978). The subordinate's exposure of organizational vulnerability to the superior: Sex and organizational effects. *Academy of Management Journal, 21,* 113-122.

CHAPTER 9

INFORMATION TECHNOLOGY AND COMPUTER-MEDIATED COMMUNICATION

Outline

Charly McNab developed a passion for rock climbing, rappeling, and hiking as a college student. She and some of her climbing friends took a big gamble after graduation in 1980 when they decided to start a catalog sales company in order to market everything from rope and carabiners to helmets and boots to sleeping bags and tents for climbers and hikers. From modest beginnings, Sundance Mountain Gear had become a reasonably successful, worker-owned company, but Charly and her thirty worker-owner partners never imagined how computers and information technology would affect the way they do business today. Charly thought it was a big deal ten years ago when the company got a 1–800 number and began for the first time to process more orders by phone than from the tear-out order form in the catalog. In those days, not one person in the Sundance partnership had any working knowledge about computers. Even with the 800 number, customer service still took down orders with pencil and paper, official letters and memos were pounded out on typewriters, and the most important means of immediate communication with vendors and with customers was the telephone.

The technological revolution at Sundance began just a few years ago when Julio Camacho, a newly-hired catalog designer who had taken some college classes in management information systems, professed absolute amazement that

Sundance had not at least computerized the process for handling orders. If telephone and mail orders were entered into a computer as they arrived, according to Julio, credit card purchase authorizations could be done immediately, processing of orders would speed up, and the company would always know at any time the inventory of any item that it stocked. Charly and the other partners immediately saw the advantages, and the computerization of Sundance began.

Now we can fast-forward to the present—to this morning, in fact. When Charly got to her office this morning, the first thing that she did is the first thing that she always does these days. She turned on the personal computer (PC) on her desk and logged onto Sundance's World Wide Web server (another very powerful PC) to see how many times the company's Website "homepage" and "on-line electronic catalog" had been accessed since yesterday. Putting up a computer dedicated exclusively as a World Wide Web site, then getting that site set up properly so that customers could use their own computers to find out about Sundance Mountain Gear were time consuming, but it paid off. The Sundance Web server gets more than 1,000 "hits" each week from people all over the U.S. and from several foreign countries. The next step is to make it possible for customers to place their merchandise orders through World Wide Web, but problems with protecting the security of credit card transactions on the Web have delayed this step.

Charly left the Web server to check her electronic mail (e-mail). Since her departure from the office yesterday, several messages had come in, including a few from other members of the company, some from customers around the country, one from the company that prints the Sundance catalog, and one marked "urgent" from a mail order company that competes with Sundance. Notes from competitors being unusual, Charly read this message first. The other company had just seen a newspaper report that a bill had been introduced in Congress to outlaw rock climbing in national forests. Such an action could, of course, affect the business of companies that sell climbing gear.

Since Sundance also subscribes to a computer service that offers access to "on-line" newspapers, Charly never buys a "paper" newspaper anymore. She moved out of e-mail and logged her computer onto the subscription computer service. She searched recent news reports for references to national forests and, sure enough, turned up the article. It was so alarming that she decided to write immediately to her Congressional representative about opposing the bill, but she could not remember the Congressperson's e-mail address. Fortunately, the computer service company also provides browsing software that can look for just about anything on the World Wide Web, including Congressional e-mail addresses. In less than a minute, Charly found the one for which she was looking, GEORGIA6@HR.HOUSE.GOV, the e-mail address for Newt Gingrich.

This was just the beginning of Charly's day. Before she left her office at closing time, she sent several more e-mail messages, left voice mail messages for people who were unavailable when she called them by telephone, accessed other computers in the Sundance local area network on several occasions for information that she needed to complete some monthly reports, and had a telephone conference with two of her partners to discuss material that they all had displayed simultaneously on their computers. The two partners in question were at a trade show in another state.

In order to tell this story, we had to invent Sundance Mountain Gear and Charly McNab, but we assure you that Sundance and Charly closely resemble a real company and a real person. Congressman Gingrich's e-mail address also is real (at least at the time of this writing), and it is certainly true that our description of Charly's workday experience with information technology is getting to be fairly typical for organizations of all sizes in many different countries around the world. Despite the pervasiveness of sophisticated information technology in today's organizations, authorities vary considerably in their opinions about the effects of this technology on work and on people.

Some observers believe that contemporary information-processing technology has little effect on organizational life other than improved efficiency and productivity. Others claim that this technology, especially in its more sophisticated forms, brings about profound changes within organizations and the society at large (Gratz & Salem, 1984; Olson, 1982). Creation of new jobs, elimination of some old jobs, changes in management functions, and higher levels of stress usually are included in the list of potential changes. Bjorn-Andersen (1981) pointed out that an even more compelling issue, however, should draw the attention of social scientists to this technology:

One of the most important questions concerning this technology is whether there is a change in human relationships and in the way we handle complex interpersonal interaction. (p. 56)

In this chapter, we will describe some of the major developments in contemporary information-processing technology and the possible effects of its introduction on organizational structures and communication.

Types of Information Systems

Contemporary information-processing technology occurs in several forms. All of these forms have one thing in common. They are electronic and computer based. Otherwise, they are quite different. Each form represents a technological advance over the forms that preceded it. Because the history of this technology is short but very active, older as well as newer forms can be found in today's organizations. It is important to distinguish among the various types of information technology because the influence of technology on organizational communication depends, in part, on the form of the technology. Thierauf (1978) identified five major types of contemporary information-processing technology: (1) computerized accounting, (2) integrated data processing, (3) integrated management information systems, (4) real-time management information systems, and (5) distributed processing.

Computerized Accounting

The earliest large-scale electronic computers were invented in the late 1940s. The first-generation commercial versions of these machines were acquired by businesses in the 1950s (Sanders, 1974). In these early years, the business vision of the role of computers in organizations was limited to **computerized accounting**. The computer was regarded as nothing more than a highly efficient calculator, a new hunk of machinery used by the accounting department. The computer was not used as a management decision-making tool, and its potential as a communications medium was unimagined.

Integrated Data Processing

By the 1960s, just about everyone had begun to recognize the value of information as an organizational resource, and software designers developed **integrated data-processing systems** that unified data from logically related organizational subsystems such as human resources, finance, machinery, and materials. With integrated data processing, information could be stored in one place but retrieved by authorized users from many different locations.

Integrated Management Information Systems

Integrated data-processing systems allow some use of computers in decision making, but the applications are confined primarily to areas such as production scheduling, ordering, and inventory control. The next step was creation of **management information systems** or **MIS.**

As described by Thierauf (1978), MIS is "a system designed to provide selected decision-oriented information needed by management to plan, control, and evaluate the activities of the organization" (p. 16). MIS makes two improvements in integrated data processing. First, MIS produces reports with information arranged in exactly the way that managers need it for decision making. Second, it automates routine decisions such as reordering products when inventory is reduced to a certain level.

Real-Time MIS

A conventional MIS is subject to one problem that also occurs with integrated data processing. Data for such systems are processed in "batch" form. This means that information is accumulated over a period of time, then entered into the computer all at once. As a result, users of conventional MIS sometimes work with the computerized equivalent of yesterday's news. This limitation can be overcome with **on-line, real-time systems.**

An on-line system has the capability for continuous entry of and access to data through remote terminals. The system serves users in real time when data are entered into the computer as soon as they exist and become immediately available to potential users (Greenless, 1971). On-line and real-time characteristics are important features of **time-sharing systems** in which two or more users at different remote terminals have virtually simultaneous access to a computer.

The principles of time sharing, provision of reports tailored to the user's decision-making needs, and computerization of routine decisions not only provide us with real-time MIS for business management but also with systems that we use throughout daily life to meet many personal needs, for example, making deposits and withdrawals from automated teller machines (ATMs), booking airline reservations by computer, checking a circulation data base to find out whether a book is available at the university library, or purchasing merchandise with a credit card. When such systems are accessed by telephone, voice synthesis technology can even provide the illusion of an "artificial person" on the other end of the transaction. For example, if you do not know how to use the bus system in some of America's more progressive cities, just call the transit office and tell the operator where you are and where you want to go. In a matter of seconds, the transit authority computer will tell you with a synthesized voice where and when to board the bus, what transfers to make, and where to get off.

Distributed Processing

Despite the differences between integrated data processing, integrated MIS, and real-time MIS, all of these systems often operate with **centralized processing.** Centralized processing means that all operations are performed by one large computer complex. Even though input/output devices (terminals and printers) may exist at various locations in an organization, all rely on the central processing unit (e.g., a mainframe computer). Whatever the advantages of centralized processing may be, it is not very adaptive to the needs of different departments or units. **Distributed processing** is one way to solve this problem. Figure 9.1 provides a comparative diagram of centralized and distributed systems.

According to Thierauf, the basic concept of distributed processing is simple: "Small computers, located near the data, do much of the processing and send only summary information to headquarters" (p. 4). These small machines can be deployed at locations such as departments, field offices, or profit centers that require some form of electronic data and information processing. Burnett (1975) described three ways to use them:

1. To control communication through a network by a large computer.
2. To communicate with other machines in a network and to perform local computing functions.
3. To link small machines together in a network in which any given computer performs a specialized function and can be called on by other computers in the system for performance of that function.

Originally the small machines in distributed processing systems were minicomputers. Today very powerful PCs also are used to accomplish the functions of distributed processing. These machines not only have "stand alone" capabilities such as word processing and file management but also the speed and capacity to be used as powerful communications devices. PCs in offices and homes allow organization members to be linked together and to the world beyond the organization in complex information networks.

The Information Network: LANs, WANs, and the Internet

The "newest" organizational application of information technology involves a convergence of several information technologies in electronic networks. Within the organization itself, there may be a **wide-area network** (WAN) with hundreds

Figure 9.1
Examples of information-
processing systems.

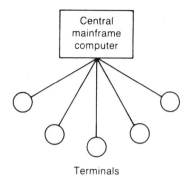

Central
mainframe
computer

Terminals

Centralized Processing

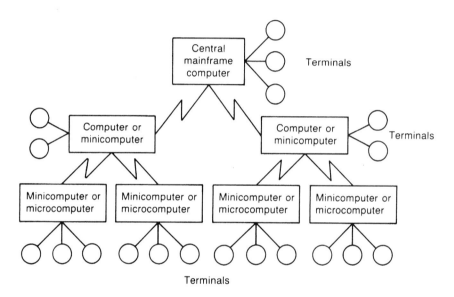

Central
mainframe
computer

Terminals

Computer or
minicomputer

Terminals

Computer or
minicomputer

Minicomputer or
microcomputer

Minicomputer or
microcomputer

Minicomputer or
microcomputer

Minicomputer or
microcomputer

Terminals

Distributed Processing

or even thousands of users. This WAN may very well provide a bridge to the out-side world of the **Internet** and **World Wide Web.** One may also find many **local-area networks** (LANs) that connect only users within a specific group (e.g., a department within a company). While the effects of technologies such as MIS are important, the use of LANs and WANs may have much more impact on human communication in organizations because such networks provide the basis for complex **computer-mediated communication systems.**

LANs and WANs

We already have described the concept of on-line real-time systems that afford time-sharing access to a central computer through remote terminals. We also

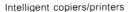
Intelligent copiers/printers

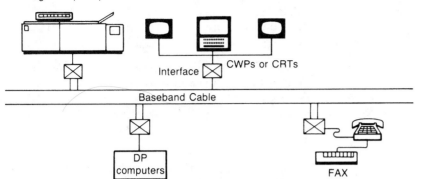

Figure 9.2
Elements in an information bus.

noted the capability of minicomputers to communicate with one another in distributed processing systems. Given these basic capabilities, the next logical step is to allow system users to communicate with one another through terminals in a distributed system. In effect, the placement of powerful PCs in LANs and WANs creates a highly connected network of information-processing devices that have **multimode capability**—in Meisner's words, "the capability to transport audio, video, and digital information" within and between organizations (1980, p. 151). The basic elements in such a system are illustrated in figure 9.2.

LANs and WANs provide much of the technology that is required for the Sundance Mountain Gear story at the beginning of this chapter to become a reality. These systems are implemented through cable that can accommodate not only remote terminals and microcomputers but also telephones, television, graphics devices, and other information-processing tools. In this form, electronic information processing literally becomes a communications medium that can complement or potentially replace other forms of communication. For example, consider Danowski's (1983) list of communication applications that are possible with current technology:

computer messaging (private electronic mail)
computer conferencing (group communication through terminals)
computer bulletin board
computer newsletter (periodic on-line message distribution to a large group)
data base access (both internal and external)
voicegrams (telephone messages computer-stored and transmitted)
teleconferencing (audio, video, or both)

LANs also provide a medium for the use of **groupware,** a form of software that, according to G. Berton Latamore, "holds the potential to vastly improve business communication and interaction" (1988, p. 72). Latamore noted that groupware packages combine electronic mail with individual and group scheduling, note taking, and a directory of group projects. With groupware, if you wish to schedule a group meeting, for example, you can call up each participant's electronic calendar, find an open time, schedule the meeting, and then send an announcement by electronic mail simultaneously to each person within a few minutes. Without groupware, the same task would require individual telephone calls and follow-up memos to each group member and might take hours to complete.

Barnes and Greller (1994) note that groupware allows people in different locations to work simultaneously on the same project:

With groupware, each computer screen becomes the participant's blackboard or the flip-chart located at the staff conference. Simply put, groupware simulates the experience of a group working in the same room, but the group participants are in different geographic locations. Moreover, unlike the blackboard or flip-chart, the collaborative work product produced with groupware can be printed, stored, copied, re-read, or forwarded from and to other people. (p. 136)

In its most sophisticated form, groupware provides **group decision support systems.** Both academic journal and popular magazine articles often abbreviate this as GDSS. As described by Jensen and Chilberg (1991), GDSS software for group conferencing by computer not only provides for creating, exchanging, and printing computer messages, but also for decision-making and voting procedures. For example, GDSS software may include a menu that allows the group to choose from different problem-solving or decision-making procedures. Driven by this software, the computer system guides the group through each step of the selected procedure.

A good example of GDSS is a program called Software Aided Meeting Management (SAMM) that was developed at the University of Minnesota. As described by Poole and DeSanctis (1992), SAMM is designed specifically to promote participative and democratic group decision making. It not only provides for public and private messaging, but also includes tools for analyzing problems and evaluating solutions.

GDSS systems generally are used in facilities like the Meeting Environment or Decision Room (MEDR) lab at the University of Arizona (Robinson, 1993). MEDR can accommodate up to thirty-two people working on a group project. The facility consists of sixteen PCs arrayed around a U-shaped table and a large projection screen, all of which are networked together. According to Barnes and Greller, GDSS systems often combine computer, video, audio, and telecommunications capabilities.

Internet and World Wide Web

During Bill Clinton's 1992 presidential campaign and in the early days of his administration, we often heard Vice President Al Gore talking about the administration's intentions of expanding access to the so-called "information superhighway." That "superhighway" is the Internet, which actually began in 1969 but did not acquire its current name until 1983. The Internet is a complicated system of telecommunications linkages of major computer facilities worldwide (Santoro, 1994). Anyone with access to such a major computer facility, typically at a university, corporation, or government agency, potentially has a gateway to the Internet. Access to the Internet also can be obtained through commercial computer services such as CompuServ, America Online, and Prodigy. In the Sundance Mountain Gear example, Charly McNab used a commercial computer service to find Newt Gingrich's e-mail address.

Although the Internet has been around in some form for many years, it was the mind-boggling increase in the use of personal computers during the 1980s that brought people to awareness and use of the Internet in the 1990s. *Newsweek* magazine reported in November, 1995 that 37 million Americans now have access to the Internet, and the average user spends more than 5 hours per week on the Internet. In December of the same year, *Newsweek* declared that 1995 was "The Year of the Internet."

Why are 37 million Americans interested in spending an average of 5 hours per week on "The Net," why is *Newsweek* so excited about it, and why should anyone in organizational communication be interested? The answer is the power of Internet access to connect a person or an organization very quickly with other people, information, and other organizations all over the world. This is why Gerald Santoro (1994) claimed, "The Internet is quite possibly the most important technical creation since the computer itself" (p. 73).

To begin with, Internet extends e-mail and computer conferencing beyond the immediate boundaries of the organization's LANs or WANs. Anybody with an Internet e-mail address can send messages to and receive messages from anyone else on the network. Similarly, one may subscribe to so-called listservers that automatically send information on a subject to all members of the listserve group or one may subscribe to newsgroups which use an electronic bulletin board system of posting and replying to messages. In 1994, according to Santoro, there were at least 6,000 such groups available on Internet, and the number is still climbing.

One may also use services known as Telnet, FTP (file transfer protocol), and Gopher to connect to databases and files of information that any organization or institution cares to make available on the Internet. You not only can read the information in the files but also print files at your own printer or have them sent to your e-mail address. For example, we know of an American consulting company doing business in Southeast Asia that monitors several Internet newsgroups to keep up on events in Malaysia and Singapore and regularly uses so-called gopher servers to get publicly available information from government agencies and research institutes in both countries. The major attraction of all of these tools is immediacy. Just as it took Charly McNab only a minute to find Newt Gingrich's e-mail address with a search protocol on World Wide Web, the consulting company to which we referred has immediate access to information on the other side of the world that affects its ability to do business there.

World Wide Web (WWW) presently is the most sophisticated of Internet applications. In our example at the beginning of this chapter, Sundance Mountain Gear put up a site on the World Wide Web by setting up a powerful PC server that could be accessed by anyone on the Internet. When you access a Web site, you are presented with a so-called "homepage" that in most cases will contain some graphics and text. Some of the items in the text are highlighted. You can use a PC mouse to point and click on those highlighted items, each of which is a gateway to another page with more information (text, graphics, video, and/or audio) and links to still more pages.

The WWW homepage for Sundance no doubt would look something like the example from Perception Inc. in figure 9.3. This company manufactures and distributes high-performance kayaks for use on whitewater rivers. Perception's

Figure 9.3
WWW homepage for
Perception Inc.

Perception's way of better serving kayaking enthusiasts on the Internet.

Christmas <u>Greetings</u>

Our <u>Mission</u> is FUN!

touch the water

Select a topic below to jump to information about different boats, events, people and more.

[<u>Perception</u> | <u>Aquaterra</u> | <u>Gear</u> | <u>Events</u> | <u>Survey</u> | <u>Catalog</u> | <u>Kids</u> | <u>Links</u> | <u>Olympics</u> | <u>People</u>]

Perception/Aquaterra is located in Easley, <u>South Carolina</u> just outside of Greenville.

Perception, Inc. * P.O. Box 8002 * 111 Kayaker Way * Easley, South Carolina 29641 USA

Tel: 803/859-7518 * Fax: 803/855-5995

Last Updated: 12 13 95
© copyright 1995 Perception, Inc.
Author: Ward Hammond <u>ward@kayaker.com</u>

address on WWW is http://www.kayaker.com/perception/. When you access the site, you see the Perception logo followed by a greeting (Christmas, in this case, for the month of December). Halfway down is a list of highlighted topics. If you click on Events, you jump to a calendar of events sponsored by a number of kayaking and canoeing organizations. If you click on Perception, you jump to an electronic, on-line catalog of all of the kayaks that Perception manufactures, complete with pictures and technical descriptions. Each highlighted term is a gateway to another page of information, including Catalog, where you can ask Perception to send its paper-medium catalog to you. Perception sells its kayaks only through factory-authorized retail dealers, but the company is nonetheless using its Web site to market its products and to provide a lot of other information to the community of whitewater kayakers, many of whom not only surf waves in rapids but also surf the Internet.

The accessibility of information on WWW is as mind-boggling as the explosion of PC use itself. Universities, government agencies, nonprofit organizations, and even many commercial companies in countries from America to Singapore are putting up Web sites. On WWW, you can do a lot more than just find out where to buy a whitewater kayak. You can find out what is going on in Congress or contact your Congressperson by accessing the homepage for the United States House of Representatives (http://www.house.gov/welcome.html). You can get information from the Web sites that we have provided in the "Additional Resources" sections at the end of each chapter in this book, or access any one of ten million other Web sites around the world. According to *Newsweek* in November, 1995, at least 18 million Americans had used WWW during August to October, and 14 percent of those users had purchased products or services over the WWW.

Technological Effects on Structure and Work

The emergence of electronic information-processing technology has been greeted with dire predictions about its ultimate effects on organizations and society in general. Some experts have argued that the technology will eliminate many jobs, resulting in unemployment rates of 10 percent to 15 percent, the redefinition of the basic concept of management, the provocation of widespread worker resistance and the demands for more job security, and the creation of a more controlled social order (Barron & Curnow, 1979). Others point out that massive unemployment and other undesirable side effects of electronic information-processing technology are not occurring at present and are unlikely to occur in the future (West, 1981).

In the face of this debate, communication scholars are confronted with two critical questions. Do organizations use new technologies to alter structures, staffing, and job functions; and what are the communicative implications of these changes? More to the point, do organization members alter the content and patterns of interaction with one another through use of this technology, especially when it is employed as a communications medium? Before we try to answer these questions, we need to consider several factors that hamper any effort to assess the impact of information technology on organizations.

First, the technology is relatively new. Despite articles in popular magazines about the arrival of the "paperless office," electronic information technology is still a long way from becoming the dominant means for handling information in organizations. Davenport (1981) pointed out the following:

We live today in a paper information age. In every area of business and commerce, government, law, education, and health, our transactions are mainly paper documents. We have letters, memoranda, reports, specifications, executive orders, written policies, documentation, notes. . . . We are swamped with paper. (p. 1)

Even with the advent of PCs and the World Wide Web, Davenport's claim is still true. Use of e-mail, groupware, and electronic publishing on the Web are beginning to undercut the old technology of paper and ink, but until electronic information-processing technologies essentially displace paper as the medium of information storage and transmission, the effects of these technologies on communication will be difficult to assess.

Second, much of the impact (both positive and negative) of information technology depends on the extent to which it is automated rather than merely mechanized. West (1981) distinguished sharply between mechanization and automation. **Mechanization** involves the operation of a machine to accomplish a job that was formerly done manually (e.g., using a calculator rather than pencil and paper for computations). **Automation** means much more—the capability of the machine *to regulate itself* and to be put into operation with a set of instructions that it can execute without operator intervention. West claims that contemporary information technology has yielded neither the benefits nor the negative consequences that many have predicted because the systems implemented to date fall short of automation. Although true automation has affected dramatically the manufacturing of products such as automobiles, it has not affected information industries in the same way.

Third, as we pointed out earlier, the effect of the technology depends on the form in which it occurs. Where personal computers are used only as stand-alone devices for tasks such as word processing, or larger computers are used for little more than accounting or for highly routine decision applications, the effects on organizational structure and communication may be negligible. In contrast, MIS, distributed-processing, and computer-mediated communication systems may result in extensive organizational change (House, 1971; Sanders, 1974). This problem is complicated by the variety of labels that writers use when discussing the technology. Terms such as *electronic data processing, computer-based systems,* and *automated information processing* are employed almost interchangeably and with no specific referent. When a writer offers predictions or reports the results of studies about the effects of technology on organizational life, those effects are difficult to evaluate unless one clearly understands the form of technology with which the writer is concerned. For example, Rice and Bair (1984) provide an excellent summary of thirty-one studies "on office automation impacts" (p. 210). Each of these studies is concerned with one or more forms of computer-based information processing (e.g., word processing, electronic mail, and data base applications). An uninformed reader who assumes that "office automation" means only one thing might be quite confused by the various findings produced in these studies because the results of any given study only make sense when they are understood within the context of the form of technology considered in that study.

Finally, assessing the impact of technology on organizational structure and communication is difficult because there is some disagreement over the degree to which technology operates as a *causal* force in determining change. Some experts such as Rogers (1988) subscribe to a hypothesis of technological determinism, namely, "that certain social changes result from technological innovations" (p. 438). Others (e.g., Olson, 1982) reject the **technological determinism** hypothesis, pointing out instead that changes are a result of choices made by humans in their adoption and use of technology, not as a result of the technology itself. Even though we have spoken so far in this chapter with causal terminology (effects, impact, etc.), we are inclined to agree with Olson that social changes result from human choice rather than technological force.

Despite these limitations, we can draw some conclusions about the general consequences of innovations in information technology for organization structure, staffing, job functions, and communication. The remainder of this chapter includes a review of some claims as well as research findings regarding these consequences.

Changes in Organizational Structure

To what extent do organizations alter their structural characteristics through the use of information technology? This has been a hotly debated question among management, information-processing, and communication experts since the late 1960s. The focal point of the argument centers on the extent to which new technologies foster centralization or decentralization of authority and decision making. If you recall the relationships described earlier in this book between communication and centralization (or decentralization), you will see immediately that this is an important question for communication scholars.

Centralization School

Before the arrival of more sophisticated forms of information technology, decentralization of authority and decision-making power clearly was a trend in American organizations (Sanders, 1974). While the trend developed in part from the influence of human resource and organization development theory, the primary force behind decentralization was much more utilitarian. Top managers, faced with greater complexity in organizations and with environments that demanded rapid response to new conditions, were virtually compelled to delegate authority to lower levels of management. Lower-level managers were closer to immediate problems and to the information required to solve these problems.

The basic argument of experts who predict a return to centralization (i.e., recentralization) rests on the fact that the new technology, especially in the form of MIS, creates the potential for top managers to recover delegated authority (Emery, 1964). Without a handy computer, a top manager might have to wait for information to trickle up from lower levels or could be obliged to transpose large quantities of information from unusable to usable forms. Given a desktop PC with access to data through LANs and WANs, the top manager has information at a fingertip not only for strategic decisions concerning broad plans, goals, and objectives but also for tactical decisions involving day-to-day organizational functions. Advocates of the centralization view claim that top managers not only will use technology to recover authority delegated to middle managers during the decentralization trend, but they also will extend their control over decisions into operational areas, bypassing middle managers who are now responsible for such functions.

Decentralization School

Some experts reject the claim that electronic information-processing technology leads to recentralization of authority. They argue instead that trends toward decentralization already in progress will be reinforced by information technology. Since top management's ability to monitor lower-level activity is greatly enhanced through technologies such as MIS, these managers will be more willing to delegate authority and to allow major decision making at lower levels (Sanders, 1974). Casbolt and Cherry (1983) argued that decentralization will be even more pronounced as distributed-processing systems take hold in organizations:

Traditionally, information in the organization has been controlled in an unintegrated fashion by service functions such as Data Processing, Personnel, Controller, and Office Services. Often these functional areas are politically antagonistic. As data processing departments evolve to information resource management, the traditional walls of mystique and control are broken down. Managers become more responsible for their own information needs as DDP [distributed data processing] is implemented. Shared decision making and joint accountability create an interdependent cycle. (p. 3)

The arrival of PCs also has fueled the fires of the decentralization school (Danowski, 1983). Writers such as Hiltz and Turoff (1978) and Naisbitt (1982) argued that the capabilities of personal computers will lead inevitably toward a "network" society with revolutionary implications for organizational life. According to Danowski, some authorities, in line with Rogers' technological determinism hypothesis, actually see the personal computer as an *agent* of social change. We cannot say to what extent the presence of the personal computer in and of itself creates social change, but there is no question that millions of people in America and millions more in other countries already are participating in the network society.

Neutrality School

A few observers have claimed that electronic information-processing technology, in and of itself, will not result in any particular form of structural change in organizations. Instead, the technology can be used to support moves in the direction of either centralization or decentralization. Management philosophy and the environment in which the organization operates will determine whether organizational structure becomes more or less centralized as a result of technological innovations. The technology "can be effective (or ineffective) in either a centralized or decentralized mode" (Kanter, 1972, p. 22). This position is similar to the view expressed by Olson.

Research Findings

Even though experts have speculated a lot about the effects of information technology on organizational structure, relatively little field research has been conducted in an effort to identify the kinds of changes that are occurring. Danowski (1983) concluded from his review of studies during the 1960s and early 1970s, "The dominant theme in this research was the effects of mainframe computing on centralization of organizational structure" (p. 13). Studies by Vergin (1967) and Brink (1969) are typical of those in this group. Brink interviewed leading business executives in a number of organizations. Vergin interviewed data-processing managers, system analysts, department managers, and senior executives in eleven Minnesota companies that ranged in size from 89 to 23,000 personnel.

Executives in Brink's study insisted that electronic information processing technology had no impact on organizational structure in their companies. Even though they would not rule out the possibility of *future* impact resulting from MIS, they claimed that changes in organizational structure are driven by management philosophy and organizational circumstances. This finding supports the view of the neutrality group.

In contrast, Vergin concluded from his study, "Undoubtedly, the largest and most visible organizational change resulting from computer use in the eleven firms was a move toward recentralization of decision making" (p. 65). Although the technology may be used to support either centralization or decentralization, organizations in Vergin's study chose the path of greater centralization. In particular, managers elected to recover decision-making authority that had previously been delegated to lower levels.

Vergin did qualify his findings by pointing out that changes associated with recentralization were less dramatic than some forecasters had predicted. Moreover, structural changes seemed to be confined primarily to organizations with integrated data processing or some form of MIS. Virtually no changes occurred in organizations that employed computers as little more than accounting tools.

According to Danowski, the tendency toward centralization as a result of computer technology is best reflected in research by Whisler (1970), who produced a complete book from his studies. Some of Whisler's major findings include the following:

1. Computerization led to many structural changes including creation of new departments, elimination of others, and functional reorganization of departments.
2. Decision making was consolidated and generally moved to higher levels in organizations with increased quantification of information used in decisions.
3. Control became more centralized, and computers were used to monitor employee behavior.
4. Interpersonal communication increased during the process of computerizing, but face-to-face communication declined after computerization was completed. Employees used computers for communication and spent more time working alone.

While the studies by Brink, Vergin, and Whisler are quite dated, more recent investigations by European researchers have produced similar results. Bjorn-Andersen (1981) concluded from studies of European organizations that technological innovations in information processing typically were followed by greater centralization. In particular, interdependence fostered among organizational units by integrated-processing systems—the same kind of interdependence that Casbolt and Cherry associate with distributed processing—actually had the effect of "limiting the discretion of individual managers" (p. 53). Bjorn-Andersen concluded from his studies that the introduction of sophisticated information-processing technology in an organization is followed by more rules, more policies, more methods, and more procedures. At the same time, day-to-day orders and advice from higher-level to lower-level managers *decrease*.

Bjorn-Andersen also noted marked separation between information system *planners* and system *users*. Even where information technology did not directly foster centralization, control of the system and knowledge about the system were centralized. In effect, "The system planner defines the need for information, designs the system, handles the programming, and implements the system. The user is often an astonished spectator" (p. 55). Although use of distributed-processing systems might correct this problem (Casbolt & Cherry, 1983), management has to make a conscious decision to adopt and support a distributed system. Other studies by Roveda and Ciborra (1981) of five types of organizations in Italy produced results that differ somewhat from Bjorn-Andersen's findings. They observed evidence of centralization *and* decentralization occurring simultaneously, although in different levels or areas of the organization. Centralization of production control through integrated-processing systems was "often accompanied by delegation of decision power and autonomy to work groups" (p. 134). While control of the information-processing system itself was centralized and moved further up the organizational hierarchy, system failures and other unanticipated contingencies required an ability "to work in an 'informal' group, where hierarchical levels disappear and different personal expertise and know-how have to be integrated in ad hoc problem solving" (p. 134). But Roveda and Ciborra reported one major finding that fits some of the dire predictions of the centralization school. Supervisory and middle-management functions typically were "made redundant or emptied of control power" (p. 134).

The results of both American and European investigations are somewhat ambiguous. Although one must exercise caution in comparing American organizations with their European cousins, the study by Roveda and Ciborra is especially interesting because it suggests that centralization and decentralization may be interrelated. A move toward centralization in one application of information technology results in decentralization of some other application.

Effects on Staffing and Job Functions

An issue closely related to the centralization controversy is the extent to which electronic information-processing technology results in unemployment and redefinition of job functions. Barron and Curnow pointed out in 1979 that 65 percent of all occupations are concerned directly with acquisition, processing, and/or distribution of information. Even moderate increases in processing efficiency through electronic systems could result in high levels of unemployment for workers in such occupations.

While clerical and secretarial occupations would bear the brunt of personnel reductions, managerial positions are not immune from possible effects. Since much activity at middle-management levels is concerned with manipulating information rather than with decision making per se, integrated data processing and MIS could reduce the number of managers as well or, at least, redefine their jobs substantially. Especially in areas in which top managers use information technology to recentralize authority, middle managers would be eliminated. Those who survive would find that some of their functions are taken over either by a computer or by higher levels of management.

Other scholars argue that claims of massive unemployment are unwarranted. In particular, advocates of the decentralization view argue that information technology will create many new jobs and that middle-management roles will be enhanced, with less need to attend to routine matters and more opportunity for creative problem solving (e.g., see Emery, 1964; Sanders, 1974).

Research Findings

Studies to date lend some support to both of the positions described previously. For example, large-scale personnel reductions have not resulted from innovations in information technology. West (1981) almost seemed unhappy with the situation when he pointed out, "There are more clerical workers today than ever before. . . . We're not going to pick up a lot of savings in reduction of personnel [by adopting new information technology]" (p. 115). Vergin found in his study that no middle managers were terminated or downgraded in salary as a consequence of "the shift in duties to the computer" (p. 64).

On the other hand, job functions in many organizations clearly have been redefined by integrated data processing, MIS, and distributed processing. Clerical and secretarial personnel have become terminal operators and word processors rather than typists and paper shufflers. Middle-management functions also have changed. European researchers report loss of control, power, and discretion in management functions, although Bjorn-Andersen found that *staff* managers (those in support functions) gained influence as information gatekeepers. Vergin's study of United States companies indicated that computers had taken over some management functions in each organization that he examined. Moreover, some managers were moved to lower echelons of the organization, even though they retained their old salary levels. Changes in managerial job functions are not necessarily negative, at least as perceived by managers who are users of the new technologies. In a survey conducted by Millman and Hartwick (1987) of 151 middle managers from fourteen large organizations, most respondents indicated that new information technologies had enriched their jobs by making their work more important and interesting.

Staffing Implications for Communication

Technological effects on employment and job definitions, whether real or imagined, have several communication-related implications. If personnel believe that their jobs are jeopardized by electronic information processing, there could be extensive resistance to adoption of the technology accompanied by demands for more job security. Even job redefinition, especially at the management level, is likely to be resisted. Since middle managers highly value participation in decision making, Vergin argued that any serious use of information technology to recentralize decision making at top levels could result in "serious revolt [by middle managers]" (p. 68). The reaction of middle management might be like the militant unionism of the 1920s and 1930s, which resulted, in part, from scientific management and elimination of worker participation in planning.

Gouldner and Alvin (1955) pointed out that subordinates can use various upward communication strategies to exert pressure against downwardly imposed policies and changes. Top management's unilateral attempts to impose technological innovations could be met by some of these strategies if subordinates believe that the technology works against their interests. Consequently, organizations must consider communication planning in connection with decisions to implement information technology.

What kind of communication program should accompany the adoption of technological innovations? Brink (1969) concluded from his study that worker acceptance of information technology was greatest when management took two steps: (1) provided assurances that technology would not endanger job security and (2) kept the promise implied in these assurances. As we already have seen, Brink's second step may be difficult to honor, and the first step should not be undertaken without the second. Wherever computer technology is used as more than a mere calculator, some change is almost inevitable. A simplistic internal public relations program designed to sell the technology to personnel may be woefully inadequate. Instead, the communication program should be based on active involvement of and consultation with those groups of organization members that will be affected by the change. The successful adoption of computer-mediated communication systems requires a "commitment to the effort of communicating differently" (Mabry & Allen, 1995, p. 28). This kind of commitment generally requires participation, especially since the most important factor that seems to influence member perceptions and use of such technology is the social influence of co-workers (Fulk, Schmitz, & Ryu, 1995).

Organizational communication scholars traditionally argue that acceptance of change is more likely to occur when all parties affected by the change are able to participate in decisions and plans that lead to the change. Vergin's findings on adoption of information technology support this argument. He found that technological change occurred with less resistance in organizations that encouraged relevant departments to participate in both the design of the information system and in the planning for its implementation. Opposition and resistance were strongest in those organizations in which decisions about the system were made primarily in a centralized data-processing department without the participation of system users and others affected by the innovation. As one might also expect, training and support also influence organization members' receptiveness to and use of new technologies (Gardner & Gunderson, 1995).

Communicating in the Computer-Mediated Environment

Changes in organizational structure, staffing, and job definition as a result of technological innovation certainly raise issues with which communication scholars should be concerned. These issues are secondary, however, to a more central question that we have not addressed fully—Bjorn-Andersen's question about the changes in complex human interaction that may occur in the wake of technological innovation. This question is important now because many large organizations have implemented computer-mediated communication systems in LANs and WANs. What are the effects of this technology on communicative behavior? We already have provided some general answers to this question in the discussion of LANs, WANs, and the Internet, but this section provides more specifics and implications.

Changes in Patterns and Practices

Meisner claims that computer conferencing and teleconferencing through LANs and WANs will substantially reduce the number of face-to-face meetings that now occur in organizations. On average, face-to-face meetings consume about 40 percent of the managerial workday. Voicegrams can reduce the problem of "telephone tag" that affects over 70 percent of business phone calls (Meisner, 1980). Telephone tag occurs when Person A calls B, B is not available, A leaves a message, then B later returns the call only to discover—as you probably have guessed—that A is not available! Other capabilities such as word processing on microcomputers, computer messaging, and computer newsletters can increase efficiency and accuracy in the composition and transmission of letters, memos, and other documents. Moreover, computer-based group decision support systems allow groups to shape their interaction and to structure the entire process of problem solving by choosing from among features offered by a GDSS.

Several studies of computer-mediated communication systems appear to support these claims. For example, Rice and Case (1983) found that use of electronic messaging not only reduced paper and telephone traffic, but also increased work quantity and quality. Tapscott (1982) found changes in communication patterns and decreases in telephone usage and meetings. Steinfield (1983) reported improvements in the timeliness and accuracy of information as well as in general coordination of tasks. Conrath and Bair (1974) found that reductions in telephone and face-to-face communication were accompanied by increased upward communication. Similarly, Barnes and Greller reported that individuals and organizational groups are using computer-mediated communiation and groupware systems "as an alternative or supplement to face-to-face meetings, telephone conversations, memos and written correspondence" (1994, p. 131). Group processes under computer-mediated conditions are characterized by the presentation of many opinions and high-quality decisions (Garton & Wellman, 1995).

Some of the evidence regarding the influence of LANs and WANs on communication comes from popularized anecdotes and case studies. For example, Latamore (1988) reported excerpts of interviews with managers and secretaries from various companies about their experiences with LANs. A manager with Coca-Cola Foods claimed that her employees "want to live on the network" (p. 72). An assistant vice-president with Banker's Trust of New York reported, "LANs make people look at what constitutes logical work groups so they can work together more effectively" (p. 77). An executive secretary at Prudential-Bache R & D Funding Corporation said that the company's LAN "has had a huge impact. It has opened a new channel of communication and made me more effective, able to do more in less time and with less effort and more fun."

One of the most powerful communication-altering features of computerization is its potential to free the organization of time-space dependency (Barnes & Greller, 1994). When we think of a "real" organization, most of us think of people coming together in the same time and space to coordinate their activities toward some end. Networking through computers can abolish the organizational need for shared time and space. A "real" organization can now be enacted by people who are miles apart from one another and even working at entirely different times because they are working through an electronic network.

Limitations and Disadvantages

Despite the glowing accounts about the benefits of LANs as reported by Latamore, computer-mediated communication systems and group decision support systems do have limitations. First, some studies point to some undesirable results in the use of computer-mediated communication for group decision-making processes. Hiltz, Johnson, and Agle (1978) found that equality of member participation is greater in computer conferencing than in face-to-face meetings but that computer-mediated groups engage in less communication, have more difficulty achieving consensus, and require more time to arrive at decisions. Kiesler, Siegel, and McGuire (1984) and Rice (1982) reported similar results.

Such findings suggest that computer conferencing, even with all of the powerful features of GDSS, should not be substituted for face-to-face group meetings without first considering the relative advantages of each method. Keep in mind, though, that the two modes of meetings are not mutually exclusive. In the SAMM facility at the University of Minnesota, group members sit face-to-face around a horse-shoe shaped conference table, but each group member also has a computer keyboard and individual monitor. A high-resolution projector linked to the computer system can display public information on a large screen at the front of the room, but members can receive private messages at their own monitors (Poole & DeSanctis, 1992).

Second, computer-mediated communication heightens the potential for more "informal messages and 'short-circuiting' of the hierarchy . . . due to the remote nature of the electronic network" (O'Connell, 1988, p. 480). People can communicate directly rather than through levels of a hierarchy because it is so very easy to do it electronically. E-mail systems and electronic newsgroups also often make it possible to easily get a message to everyone on the network with a distribution list or with a posting. Reaching everyone in an organization via written memo requires physical duplication and distribution of that memo, but an e-mail distribution list allows instant distribution in a matter of a few keystrokes. And a paper poster can always be stripped from a bulletin board. An electronic posting may not be so easy to remove. To the extent that the political order of the organization is dependent on control of information, that order can be challenged with computer-mediated communication systems. Of course, whether this is an asset or a liability is largely a matter of perspective.

Use of computer-mediated communication also poses a paradox that we described earlier in this book. On the one hand, organizations are faced with a growing need to acquire, process, and distribute large quantities of information in the most efficient way possible. On the other hand, Goldhaber (1993) contends that organization members typically express a desire for more face-to-face interaction in the workplace—a somewhat inefficient means of handling information. He suggests that the explosion of information technologies may be producing a backlash, and O'Connell says that management actually will have to create "more opportunities for face-to-face contact to occur" (p. 480).

Other communication theorists express similar concerns. For example, Gratz and Salem (1984) are not so worried about interactive or conferencing capabilities but about long hours at terminals becoming a form of "human-machine" communication that steals time from human-to-human communication. Since human interaction is critical to the formation and stability of self and relationships with others, human-machine communication "has the potential for doing great harm to human relationships, even as our capability to handle information is expanded" (p. 100).

Karl Weick (1985) argued that contemporary information technology not only interferes with human interaction but also interferes with our ability to make sense of events in organizations:

The growth of electronic information processing has changed organizations in profound ways. One unexpected change is that electronic processing has made it harder, not easier, to understand events that are represented on screens. As a result, job dissatisfaction in the 1990s may not center on issues of human relations. It may involve the even more fundamental issue of meaning: Employees can tolerate people problems longer than they can tolerate uncertainty about what's going on and what it means. (p. 51)

According to Weick, dependence on incomplete, abstract, or even cryptic displays of information at a computer terminal denies people access to the kinds of data and actions that they usually employ to validate their observations. Sandra O'Connell (1988) raised a similar concern when she said, "Meaning for the computer is established through precisely defined code. Humans . . . establish meaning through context and interpretation" (p. 474). For example, a good deal of ordinary "sense making" occurs by affiliating and deliberating with others. We decide "how things are" by comparing our thoughts and feelings with those of other people and negotiating with them to arrive at "some mutually acceptable version of what really happened" (Weick, p. 54). But technology isolates us from affiliation and moves too quickly for deliberation. While Weick is worried that "extensive nonsocial interaction with a terminal can atrophy social skills" and lead to "clumsy interactions" (p. 60), he is more concerned that it will lead to gross distortions in our interpretations of reality unless people learn to "simply push back from their terminals and walk around" (p. 61) in order to interact with one another and to use their ordinary sense-making capabilities.

Suspicions and observations that computer-mediated communication is of lesser quality than face-to-face communication are attributed to the absence of **social context cues** in computer-mediated communication that help to define situations and relationships in face-to-face communication (Sproull & Kiesler, 1986). These cues include nonverbal behaviors, personal appearance, spatial arrangements, and other features of the environment. Computer-mediation by its very nature removes social context cues. The absence of these cues is presumed to cause fundamental differences between computer-mediated and face-to-face communication. But recent studies by Joseph Walther (Walther, 1992; Walther & Burgoon, 1992; Walther, 1994) indicate that differences between computer-mediated and face-to-face communication have more to do with the time available for relationship development and expectations of future interaction than with any inherent characteristics of the media. In particular, when people interact over an extended period of time, the characteristics of computer-mediated communication become more interpersonal than impersonal and there are fewer differences between computer-mediated and face-to-face communication.

Do contemporary information technologies threaten the quality of human organizational communication as well as organization members' sense-making capacities? No doubt, debate over this question will continue through the 1990s. Regardless of the final answer, reliance on these technologies certainly is increasing. Protests against their overuse are likely to fall on deaf ears in the management ranks of work organizations. If the trends identified thus far in research continue, we will all be networked out of sheer necessity, whether we like it or not.

Communication and Technological Skill

We do not wish to close this chapter with the implication that "human communication" and "information technology" are antithetical. For one thing, college graduates with majors in communication clearly understand the need to be proficient in the use of computer-based information technology. In a 1992 survey of communication degree recipients by Seibold and associates, respondents said that college training in "technologies must be required in such a way that even the most determined 'technophobe' cannot avoid learning these skills" (p. 28).

Some research suggests that communicative ability may be important in one's acquisition of new technology. Papa and Tracy (1988) studied the transition from one computer system to another in a large, multiline insurance company with specific attention to the relationship between each employee's communicative behaviors and his or her productivity with the new system. The transition involved a major change in the employee's tasks. According to their findings, "The more an employee was communicatively competent, a skillful listener, and talked frequently about the new task, the more productive that employee was likely to be using the new computer" (p. 17). Papa and Tracy also found that communicative competence and interaction frequency were negatively correlated with declines in productivity during the first week that the new computer was used and positively correlated with the speed with which employees returned to their past levels of performance. These findings may be particularly important, since those employees who were productive under the routine of the old system were not necessarily productive under the novel conditions of the new system.

Summary Electronic information-processing technology occurs in several basic forms, including computerized accounting, integrated data processing, integrated MIS, real-time MIS, and distributed processing. The most recent developments involve fully integrated audio, video, and digital information networks in LANs and WANs. These systems have many capabilities that can complement or replace other forms of communication with computer-mediated communication systems. Such capabilities include computer messaging, computer conferencing, teleconferencing, computer bulletin boards, computer newsletters, voicegrams, and database access. When personal computers are linked in LAN and WAN environments, they can make use of groupware that allows remote users to work on the same project and group decision support systems that can actually structure group decision making through software. Such networks also provide gateways to the so-called "Information Superhighway," that is, the Internet and World Wide Web, which literally create possibilities for global communication and access to information.

Changes in organizations as a consequence of information technology innovations depend to some extent on the form of the technology. Where computers are used only for accounting functions, few changes appear to occur. Other systems may foster various changes. In particular, use of the technology as a means for centralization or decentralization of decision making and authority has occupied the attention of management theorists. Some predictions and studies suggest that top managers use the technology to recentralize authority that they delegated in earlier decades. Others claim that MIS and distributed systems in particular foster decentralization. Some European research suggests that both conditions may follow as consequences of technological change. Advocates of the so-called neutrality position claim that information technology may be used for either centralization or decentralization.

Although the impact of technology on centralization is not entirely clear, studies consistently suggest that jobs are redefined as a consequence of electronic information processing. Although the technology may not eliminate jobs, it may be perceived as a threat to job security. Effects on staffing and job definitions mean that organizations must consider the kinds of communication strategies that they will employ in gaining acceptance of technology. Research on this problem seems to indicate that acceptance is greatest under conditions of active participation in decisions related to the technological change.

Most of the technological implications for organizational communication are linked to computer-mediated communication systems in LANs and WANs. Research on the use of these technologies has produced both positive and negative results. Suspicions and observations that computer-mediated communication is of lesser quality than face-to-face communication are attributed to the absence of social context cues in computer-mediated communication, although some studies indicate that computer-mediated communication becomes more interpersonal than impersonal when it occurs over an extended period of time. Generally, however, theorists believe that these contemporary technologies will change the character of complex human interaction in organizations.

Discussion Questions/ Activities

1. Given the different forms of electronic information-processing technology described in this chapter, which ones do you think are most likely to affect organizational communication? What kinds of changes, if any, are likely to occur as organizations adopt these technologies?
2. Some studies have found that adoption of electronic information technology is followed by organizational changes that have features of both centralization and decentralization. Can you think of some ways in which this might occur?
3. Have a discussion with someone who works in an organization that uses advanced systems of information technology. How does this person feel about the technology? Does this person feel that the technology has a particular effect on organizational communication?

Additional Resources

Books

Chesebro, J. W., & Bonsall, D. G. (1989). *Computer-mediated communication: Human relationships in a computerized world*. Tuscaloosa, AL: University of Alabama Press.
Kaye, A. R. (Ed.). (1992). *Collaborative learning through computer conferencing: The Najaden papers*. Berlin: Springer-Verlag.

Romiszowski, A. J. (1992). *Computer-mediated communication: A selected bibliography.* Englewood Cliffs, NJ: Educational Technology Publications.

Thierauf, R. J. (1989). *Group decision support systems for effective decision-making: A guide for MIS practitioners and end users.* New York: Quorum Books.

Web Sites

http://cscc.clarion.edu/resorse.htm
   The Center for the Study of Computer Mediated Communication
http://www.lib.umich.edu/chouse/inter/59.html
   Computer-Mediated Communication Clearinghouse
http://shum.cc.huji.ac.il/jcmc/jcmc.html
   The Journal of Computer-Mediated Communication

References

Barnes, S., & Greller, L. M. (1994). Computer-mediated communication in the organization. *Communication Education, 43*, 129–142.

Barron, I., & Curnow, R. (1979). *The future with microelectronics.* Milton Keynes, England: The Open University Press.

Bjorn-Andersen, N. (1981). The impact of electronic digital technology on traditional job profiles. In *Microelectronics, productivity, and employment.* Paris: Organisation for Economic Cooperation and Development.

Brink, V. Z. (1969, January–February). Top management looks at the computer. *Columbia Journal of World Business,* 77–103.

Burnett, G. J. (1975). Computer options: Large centralized computers versus minicomputers. In F. W. McFarlan & R. Nolan (Eds.), *The information systems handbook.* Homewood, IL: Dow Jones-Irwin.

Casbolt, D. M., & Cherry, J. (1983). *The decentralization of an organization's information center: Organizational change issues and answers.* Paper presented at the annual meeting of the International Communication Association. Dallas.

Conrath, D. W., & Bair, J. (1974). The computer as an interpersonal communication device: A study of augmentation technology and its apparent impact on organizational communication. *Proceedings of the Second International Conference on Computer Communications.* Stockholm, Sweden, 121–127.

Danowski, J. A. (1983). *Organizational communication: Theoretical implications of communication technology applications.* Paper presented at the annual meeting of the International Communication Association. Dallas.

Davenport, L. L. (1981). Technology and the communication society: An informal overview. In M. Lehman & T. J. M. Burke (Eds.), *Communication technologies and information flow.* New York: Pergamon Press.

Emery, J. C. (1964). The impact of information technology on organization. *Proceedings of the 24th annual meeting, Academy of Management.*

Fulk, J., Schmitz, J., & Ryu, D. (1995). Cognitive elements in the social construction of communication technology. *Management Communication Quarterly, 8*, 259–288.

Gardner, W. L., III, & Gundersen, D. E. (1995). Information system training, usage, and satisfaction. *Management Communication Quarterly, 9*, 78–114.

Garton, L., & Wellman, B. (1995). Social impacts of electronic mail in organizations: A review of the research literature. In B. R. Burleson (Ed.), *Communication yearbook 18* (pp. 434–453). Thousand Oaks, CA: Sage.

Goldhaber, G. M. (1993). *Organizational communication* (6th ed.). Dubuque, IA: Brown & Benchmark Publishers.

Gouldner, A. W., & Alvin, W. (1955). *Patterns of industrial bureaucracy.* London: Routledge & Kegan Paul.

Gratz, R. D., & Salem, P. J. (1984). Technology and the crisis of self. *Communication Quarterly, 32,* 98–103.

Greenless, M. (1971). Time-sharing computers in business. In W. G. House (Ed.), *The impact of information technology on management operation.* Princeton, NJ: Auerbach.

Hiltz, S. R., Johnson, K., & Agle, G. (1978). *Replicating Bales' problem-solving experiments on a computerized conferencing system. Report 8.* Newark, NJ: New Jersey Institute of Technology, Computerized Conferencing and Communications Center.

Hiltz, S. R., & Turoff, M. (1978). *Network nation.* Reading, MA: Addison-Wesley.

House, W. G. (Ed.). (1971). *The impact of information technology on management operation.* Princeton, NJ: Auerbach.

Jensen, A. D., & Chilberg, J. C. (1991). *Small group communication: Theory and application.* Belmont, CA: Wadsworth.

Kanter, J. (1972, April). The impact of computers on the business operation. *Data Management, 20–23.*

Kiesler, S., Siegel, J., & McGuire, T. (1984). Social psychological aspects of computer-mediated communication. *American Psychologist, 39,* 1123–1134.

Latamore, G. B. (1988, October). Why everyone works smarter when they're connected. *Working Woman,* 72–81.

Mabry, E. A., & Allen, M. (1995, May). *A performance theory of computer-mediated communication in organizations.* Paper presented at the annual meeting of the International Communication Association. Albuquerque, NM.

Meisner, N. B. (1980). The information bus in the automated office. In N. Naffah (Ed.), *Integrated office systems: Burotics.* Amsterdam: North-Holland.

Millman, Z., & Hartwick, J. (1987). The impact of automated office systems on middle managers and their work. *MIS Quarterly,* 478–489.

Naisbitt, J. (1982). *Megatrends: Ten new directions transforming our lives.* New York: John Wiley & Sons.

Newsweek, November 13, 1995, 14.

Newsweek, December 25, 1995, 21–30.

O'Connell, S. E. (1988). Human communication in the high tech office. In G. M. Goldhaber & G. A. Barnett (Eds.), *Handbook of organizational communication* (pp. 473–482). Norwood, NJ: Ablex.

Olson, M. H. (1982, December). New information technology and organizational culture. *MIS Quarterly,* 21–30.

Papa, M. J., & Tracy, K. (1988). Communicative indices of employee performance with new technology. *Communication Research, 15,* 524–544.

Poole, M. S., & DeSanctis, G. (1992). Microlevel structuration in computer-supported group decision making. *Human Communication Research, 19,* 5–49.

Rice, R. E. (1982). Communication networking in computer conferencing systems: A longitudinal study of group roles and system structure. In M. Burgoon (Ed.), *Communication yearbook 6* (pp. 925–944). Beverly Hills, CA: Sage.

Rice, R. E., & Bair, J. H. (1984). New organizational media and productivity. In R. E. Rice (Ed.), *The new media: Communication, research, and technology.* Beverly Hills, CA: Sage.

Rice, R. E., & Case, D. (1983). Computer-based messaging in the university: A description of use and utility. *Journal of Communication, 33,* 131–152.

Robinson, M. (1993). Computer supported co-operative work: Cases and concepts. In R. M. Baecker (Ed.), *Readings in groupware and computer-supported cooperative work* (pp. 29–49). San Mateo, CA: Morgan Kaufman.

Rogers, E. M. (1988). Information technologies: How organizations are changing. In G. M. Goldhaber & G. A. Barnett (Eds.), *Handbook of organizational communication* (pp. 437–452). Norwood, NJ: Ablex.

Roveda, C., & Ciborra, C. (1981). Impact of information technology on organisational structures. In *Microelectronics, productivity and employment.* Paris: Organisation for Economic Cooperation and Development.

Sanders, D. H. (1974). *Computers and management in a changing society* (2nd ed.). New York: McGraw-Hill.

Santoro, G. M. (1994). The Internet: An overview. *Communication Education, 43,* 73–86.

Seibold, D. R., Bauch, C. M., Grant, S. J., Nguyen, K. T., Saeki, M., Schnarr, K. L., Solowczuk, K. A. (1992). Communication/information technologies and university education: A survey of alumni about workplace technologies. *ACA Bulletin, 81,* 19–31.

Sproull, L., & Kiesler, S. (1986). Reducing social context cues: Electronic mail in organizational communication. *Management Science, 32,* 1492–1512.

Steinfield, C. (1983). *Communicating via electronic mail: Patterns and predictors of use in organizations.* Unpublished doctoral dissertation, University of Southern California.

Tapscott, D. (1982). *Office automation: A user-driven method.* New York: Plenum Press.

Thierauf, R. J. (1978). *Distributed processing systems.* Englewood Cliffs, NJ: Prentice-Hall.

Vergin, R. C. (1967, Summer). Computer-induced organizational changes. *MSU Business Topics,* 61–68.

Walther, J. B. (1992). Interpersonal effects in computer-mediated interaction: A relational perspective. *Communication Research, 19,* 52–90.

Walther, J. B. (1994). Anticipated ongoing interaction versus channel effects on relational communication in computer-mediated interaction. *Human Communication Research, 20,* 473–501.

Walther, J. B., & Burgoon, J. K. (1992). Relational communication in computer-mediated interaction. *Human Communication Research, 19,* 50–88.

Weick, K. E. (1985). Cosmos vs. chaos: Sense and nonsense in electronic contexts. *Organizational Dynamics, 14,* 51–65.

West, J. M. (1981). Some questions about the new office technology. In M. Lehman & T. J. M. Burke (Eds.), *Communication technologies and information flow.* New York: Pergamon Press.

Whisler, T. (1970). *The impact of computers on organizations.* New York: Praeger.

Part Two
Case Studies

This unit concludes with three case studies than can be used to illustrate concepts of communication function, structure, relationships, and technology. Questions with each case indicate appropriate uses.

The Circle of Misunderstanding

John Andriate likes to boast that he got his education in the "college of hard knocks." Andriate quit high school during his junior year to enlist in the military during the Korean conflict. After his discharge in 1953, he spent five years holding odd jobs in grocery stores before he persuaded his two brothers to join him in a produce business (supplying fresh fruits and vegetables to supermarkets).

Although you would never have guessed it from the condition of the company's facility (a run-down, ramshackle warehouse), Andriate Brothers Produce had become, over the years, a very successful company with massive amounts of reserve cash. Everybody in town knew the Andriates, so when John contacted Kanarick & Associates Accounting about the possibility of assuming full-charge bookkeeping for Andriate Brothers, it seemed that Kanarick & Associates was routinely taking on just one more well-established client.

Andriate met with Kate Malone, the supervisor for accounting services at Kanarick. He told her that he and his brothers had "handled the books during spare time" for many years but that the size of the company had begun to make this task impossible. Andriate wanted an accounting firm to take over the job. Malone, a CPA and an experienced supervisor, questioned Andriate about the condition of his company's accounting system. Andriate said, "We've got a basic ledger and complete tax and payroll records. Everything is up-to-date, so you should be able to just take it over."

Normally, Kate would personally examine a company's set of books before quoting a fee for providing a monthly bookkeeping service. Sometimes, Kanarick & Associates would have to set up a completely new system because the client's books had been poorly maintained or had not complied with the law. But Kate was preoccupied today. She was leaving town late that afternoon for a week-long workshop, and she knew that John Andriate was not the sort of fellow who waited for answers. Kate said, "Okay, the basic service charge will be $500 per month, assuming that the condition of your system is as you describe it. We'll set up a service contract as soon as I get back from my trip."

Malone introduced Andriate to Bob Plax, a 25-year-old bookkeeper at Kanarick. Plax worked part-time at Kanarick while pursuing an accounting degree at the local college. Malone instructed Plax to arrange an on-site meeting at Andriate Brothers for the next day. Bob was instructed to review the condition of the books and to take possession of all records required to set up the service.

When Plax arrived at Andriate Brothers the next day, he was visibly dismayed at the conditions he found. There was no general ledger. The only "accounting system" was the transaction record in the company checkbook. All income and expenses went through the same account. Tax records, payroll records, invoices, bills, and receipts were piled in old produce boxes along the walls of John Andriate's office. The boxes were labeled by year, but the material in each box was in complete disarray. Plax looked at the boxes, hung his head, and sighed in disgust. Andriate saw his reaction and started the following exchange:

"What's the matter, kid? You got a problem?"
"Well, Mr. Andriate, it is not a problem for me, but *you've* got a mess here."
"What do you mean, I got a mess? It's all here, just like I said. The ledger's in the
    checkbook and the records are in the boxes. Look, everything for this year is right
    here in this box."
"Mr. Andriate, a lot of small businesses just don't understand these things. We're going
    to have to do a lot to sort this out."
"Sort out what? What's to sort out?"
"Well," Plax replied, "let me give you some examples of things you probably don't know
    about. You'll need a double-entry accounting system, a complete reorganization of
    your records by function, and a P & L statement. The worst of it is that you're in
    the middle of the FY, so we'll have to completely reconstruct your records for the
    past six months."
"The only thing getting reconstructed here is how much all this is gonna cost. Nobody
    mentioned this stuff when I talked to your boss," Andriate replied.
"Mr. Andriate, we didn't know how disorganized you were when you talked to my boss."
"Look, kid," said Andriate sharply, "I got no time for this. You want the business or not?
    If you do, then pack up what you need, get back to your office, and do what needs
    to be done."

Plax assembled everything that he needed and returned to his office. He figured that he should check with somebody. Since Kate Malone was out of town,

Plax went to the supervisor of the auditing department (a separate unit from the accounting department) and explained that he had run into problems at Andriate Brothers. The auditing supervisor asked whether Andriate understood the situation . . . that the cost of setting up the system was going to be much higher than anticipated and that the additional cost would be added to the service contract. Plax replied, "Yeah, I guess so. He told me to take the records and do whatever needs to be done." The auditing supervisor barely looked up from a report that he had been reading during the conversation and said, "Well, go ahead with it and check in with Kate as soon as she gets back."

Plax worked diligently day and night for the rest of the week—more than seventy hours altogether—to organize an up-to-date set of books for the Andriate account. He hoped that Kate Malone would be impressed and that Andriate would be easier to deal with if Kanarick gave him quick and efficient service. Besides, this was a good chance for Plax to show Kanarick & Associates why the firm should hire him as a full-time accountant after his graduation.

On the day Malone returned to the office, Plax proudly displayed his work on the Andriate account. Malone responded, "This really looks great, Bob, but I'm a little surprised to see it. Does Andriate know that we had to do all of this?"

Plax replied, "Well, he hasn't seen it and the auditing supervisor told me to go ahead."

Malone seemed satisfied. She prepared and mailed the service contract that she had promised to Andriate. The contract included the $500-per-month service charge, plus a $1,400 setup fee for the work that Plax had done.

Two days later, Kate Malone received a phone call from an angry Andriate. He was in no mood for explanations. He insisted that the setup fee was totally unexpected and way out of line. "I'm gonna pay this setup cost so I can feel like I'm doin' right, but I'm gonna spread the word on you people. I want that kid of yours to bring back the new books *and* my records, then I don't wanna hear from you people ever again!"

1. At what points are there problems with ambiguous communication or with information adequacy in this case?
2. What difficulties with communication function and structure contribute to the difficulty in this case?
3. Do Plax and Andriate use different "codes"? How does this contribute to the problem?
4. What (if anything) could Plax have done to minimize or prevent the problem that developed in this situation?

Developing Human Resources at Anderson Medical Center

Tom Benson was delighted to learn that he had just been named director of the new department of human resource development (HRD) at Anderson Medical Center. The new department consolidated all training and development in the 750-bed, 2,200-employee hospital. Before HRD was created, training was split among three departments: personnel, which handled job-related and safety training for support (nonhealth care) staff; in-service education, which was responsible for nurses, orderlies, and other health care personnel; and management services, which identified training needs and conducted training programs for line administrators and managers.

The new department pooled the old in-service education and management services departments and removed all training functions from personnel. Tom knew that the people in the personnel department were glad to be rid of the training function, since they believed that their real responsibilities were hiring, negotiating labor contracts, and administering the benefits and safety programs. He was not so sure about the feelings of former in-service education director, Clara Carson, and former management services chief, Bob Roth. Carson was a registered nurse with more than fifteen years of nursing experience and ten years as an in-service education director. Roth was a retired military officer who believed firmly in the human relations principles espoused by Dale Carnegie during the 1930s.

Carson and Roth both had received hefty salary increases along with their "promotions" as Benson's new associate directors, but Benson suspected that they might be displeased by the new arrangement. After all, Benson was thirty-three years old, had a Ph.D. in organizational behavior, and was much younger than either Carson or Roth. Also, he had been brought in "from the outside" to start up and manage the new HRD department, although he had worked as a consultant to Anderson Medical Center for more than a year. In fact, the decision to create HRD developed out of needs assessment research that Benson had done for the hospital. Tom had never directly suggested that this be done, but when the chief administrator decided to make HRD a reality, he was happy to be offered the position of director.

The other members of the new HRD department included two registered nurses who had worked for Carson at in-service education; a program developer; a human relations trainer from the old management services group; and two technical trainers, formerly with the personnel department. Benson knew that the new members of HRD would experience some disorientation while the department was being organized. Prior to the change, their roles and jobs had been defined clearly. Now, everything was unclear. On the first day of HRD's operations, Benson called Roth and Carson in for a meeting. He asked them whether they had any reservations about the new department and their roles in it. Carson asserted that she was "happy as a clam." Roth said that he was looking forward to learning about the idea of basing training programs on formal needs assessments, though he still thought that tapes of Norman Vincent Peale speaking on the "Power of Positive Thinking" were the best training programs that money could buy. Benson was not entirely pleased with these answers, but he let the matter drop.

Benson then discussed his ideas for the first few months of HRD's existence. Since they, rather than the hospital administrators, were the experts on training and development, HRD would have to develop its own statement of mission, objectives, and functions within broad guidelines laid down by top administration. Benson suggested that the department should continue with "business as usual" during the first few weeks. Members would continue with the training projects that already were underway in the in-service education, management services, and personnel departments before HRD was created. During this same time frame, HRD would work on a mission statement. After all current projects were completed, HRD would set up a list of new project priorities and develop some general plans for their execution. Carson and Roth praised the plan.

The three broke up their own meeting and reconvened with the entire group. Benson explained the general plan. Outside of some casual jokes about the uncertainty over job functions, no one expressed any concerns. The two training specialists from the personnel department did seem somewhat remote and withdrawn. Even so, the group hammered out a schedule for completion of projects already underway, then set up a series of six meetings over the next three weeks in order to develop a mission statement. Benson asked everyone to consider two questions before the first planning meeting: "Who are we and what do we do?" Members spent the rest of the day organizing their new offices.

Planning Meeting 1

Benson was surprised to discover at the first planning meeting a few days later that no one had given much thought to his questions. In general, members simply said, "I know what *I* do, but I have no idea what anyone else here does." Benson was uncertain about how to proceed. He had planned on a lively discussion. Carson finally said, "Look, I'm really confused by this whole question." The remark was followed by nods of agreement all around the table. Roth, agitated over the lack of progress, suggested that Benson prepare his own version of a functional organizational plan for HRD to use as a "springboard for discussion" at the next meeting.

Planning Meeting 2

Benson began by laying out a functional organization chart. The idea was simple. Carson and the two registered nurses would still have responsibility for all health care delivery training. Roth, along with his two former staffers and the technical trainers from personnel, would cover all nonhealth care areas from top administration to cafeteria workers. All projects would be reviewed by the entire group as it worked toward developing a model for collecting data on training needs, translating that data into training objectives, and designing training and development programs. At this point, one of Carson's nurses became angry at the idea of collaborating with nonnurses on training programs designed for nurses. Roth, perceiving the remark to be directed at him, said that he was not very pleased about trying to work with "a gaggle of geese like hard-headed nurses." Carson attacked Roth for his lack of professionalism, announced that she was late for a training seminar, and then left the meeting, remarking that she hoped the next meeting would yield some productive ideas. With the meeting in shambles, Benson asked all members to think through their concerns and ideas about the plan, then write them down for discussion at the next meeting.

A few days after the meeting, Benson discovered that the director of personnel had asked the hospital administrator, "What in the world is going on at HRD? If they can't get their act together, maybe we ought to recover our trainers and just pick up where we left off." The administrator replied, "Well, let's give it a couple of months. If things aren't under control by then, we'll have to make some changes."

1. How would you characterize Benson's style of leadership in this situation? In light of situational theories of leadership, could Benson get more effective results by changing his approach?
2. Given what you read in the chapter about basic concepts in group dynamics, explain why this group is not developing as a group.
3. Does research on small group decision-making processes provide any insights that might help to explain why HRD is having problems and how these problems might be corrected? Explain your answer.

The New System

A large, American corporation has a training facility in the midwest where it trains approximately 50,000 people each year. Most are company employees, but the company also does contract training for smaller corporations. Logistical requirements for the training of these personnel include the managing of classrooms and equipment, the coordinating of housing and meals, the scheduling of faculty, the booking of participants, and the arranging of inbound and outbound transportation. At any time, a potential exists for 15,000 people to make a request to hold a meeting or a training session. Each request involves all aspects of managing the facility. For example, suppose that the vice-president of marketing wants to hold a workshop for all marketing representatives. The following actions would have to be taken:

1. A request would be made to the facilities management specifying number of attendees and room preference.
2. If the request is approved and space is available, detailed information would be provided to answer the following questions:
   a. Number of rooms? Layout of each?
   b. Number of attendees?
   c. Equipment needs (always a big production for marketing)? When? What?
   d. Special meals/events if appropriate (i.e., banquet on the last night or cocktails before dinner)?
   e. The names of attendees and faculty? When will they arrive? How long will they stay, and when will they need transportation to the airport?
   f. Charge number: How to bill? Whom to bill?
3. Participants register with the registrar (one designated for each school). They communicate their arrival day/time and departure information by a registration form. This information is entered on a computer, which is accessed only by the registrar. A request for information about attendees is made by telephone.
4. Details about A through F are communicated by the person requesting the program to the facilities management. The information is keyed into a computer system that is accessed only by the facilities management. That office prints copies of the completed request form and routes the form to the requestor for confirmation. Copies also are given to support staff, including Audio Visual Department, Room Set-up, Materials/Distribution, and Catering, when appropriate. Any requests for information or changes are made by telephone or by a revised form.

Two years ago, the company began designing a computer system that would enable all departments to access the same information through their computer network. The design phase required one year, and implementation was expected to take six months. This system would affect all of the 500 people working at the Training Center. The goal of the system was to save time and, consequently, money. It would cut down on the number of telephone calls and the amount of paperwork. It would also increase the accuracy of information. Each person working directly in the Center would have access to the system at his/her desk. People outside the Center (e.g., those who requested programs or others who frequently needed information) would also have access. They would be able to input and review. Everyone would be able to use the computer at his/her desk to review information, to check for accuracy, or to check the status of the project. Departments no longer would be dependent on someone else to do their job. If a change was necessary, they could get on the system and make it themselves, rather than requesting that the change be made and then double-checking.

The potential benefits—and potential complications—of the system were substantial. Generally, the implementation of the new system was handled proactively and effectively. Users were involved in the design phase by being interviewed for suggestions. A steering committee was formed, which included one or two people from each area. These committee meetings kept people informed of progress and provided a forum to discuss major issues. Decisions were made in those meetings and then implemented.

Once the system was operational, each area chose two or three people to get involved in a user acceptance test. This was an opportunity to both train end-users and to get feedback about the system. The people managing the design and implementation of the system were always accessible and continuously consulted users for information. Despite these safeguards, problems arose during and after the change.

The conversion required substantial overtime. It took longer than expected for people to learn how to use the system fully. Ironically, in a division of the company that specializes in the provision of training programs, the only form of training provided to division employees for the change to the new system was a user's manual.

Some employees experienced computer anxiety. They were afraid of making mistakes that would affect hundreds of other people. It actually became more difficult to expedite "special" or "rush" requests for programs that did not fit into the routine of the system design. When problems arose, some Center personnel used the limitations of the new system as an excuse not to solve the problem.

1. Are there any surprises in the case? That is, given what you read in chapter 9, would you expect to see both the benefits and the problems that this company experienced with its new information system? Why or why not?

2. Evaluate the company's steps in designing and implementing the system. Was the process an effective way of meeting potential resistance to change?

3. What, if anything, could the company have done differently to make the implementation more successful?

PART THREE
DYNAMICS OF
ORGANIZATIONAL
CULTURE

COMMUNICATION AND ORGANIZATIONAL CULTURE

In chapters 5 through 8, we concentrated on the idea that organizational communication can be understood by examining its functions, structure, and the relationships in which it occurs in an organization. These concepts have been employed for many years in the study of organizational communication (even though Farace, Monge, and Russell's version of structural functionalism was not published until 1977). More recently, an entirely different way of studying organizations has provoked a great deal of interest. The basic idea in this new approach is that organizations can be studied with the same concepts and methods that are used to study cultures.

While the study of culture is a long-standing tradition in the field of anthropology, the concept of **organizational culture** is a relatively recent development. Many scholars and practitioners have become intrigued with the idea that organizations have cultural features. Some even assert that an organization literally *is* a culture and that organizational communication is a *performance* of this culture (Pacanowsky & O'Donnell-Trujillo, 1984). One very popular cultural perspective of organizations is presented in Deal and Kennedy's (1982) *Corporate Cultures.* Wright's (1979) *On a Clear Day, You Can See General Motors,* Maccoby's (1976) *The Gamesmen,* and Kanter's (1977) *Men and Women of the Corporation* also have been called studies of organizational culture. What comes to mind when you think about the word *culture?* Do you think of the history, values, beliefs, language, and modes of expression as part of the culture of a particular people or nation? Or do you think of culture as their customs, folklore, and artifacts? If you associate any of these elements with culture, you have at least some sense of the concepts that have been used to study and understand cultures. In this chapter, we will describe the concept of organizational culture; traditionalist, interpretivist and critical-interpretivist perspectives of culture; and some communication-based methods of studying organizational culture.

The Concept of Organizational Culture

In a fundamental sense, a culture exists when people come to share a common frame of reference for interpreting and acting toward one another and the world in which they live. This common frame of reference includes language, values, beliefs, and interpretations of experience. It is reflected in customs, folkways, communication, and other observable features of the community, including rites, rituals, celebrations, legends, myths, and heroic sagas (Bormann, Howell, Nichols, & Shapiro, 1982).

For many years, anthropologists have used the concept of culture to study nations, communities, and even tribal groups, but the discipline of anthropology has never settled on a uniform definition of culture. The term is used in several different ways. The same problem occurs in organizational studies. Although there is consensus among scholars in various fields that the concept of culture can be applied to organizations, there are different ways of defining organizational culture.

Eisenberg and Goodall (1993), two organizational communication scholars, define culture primarily in terms of *practices* rather than values. Claiming that anthropologists have rejected the idea of culture as shared meaning, they say that "nothing in the culture metaphor requires that values be shared" (p. 152). In contrast, anthropologist W. A. Haviland (1993) says the following:

> Culture consists of the abstract values, beliefs, and perceptions that lie behind people's behavior. . . . They are shared by members of a society, and when acted on, produce behavior considered to be acceptable within that society. (p. 29)

Haviland's definition of culture differs sharply from the conception presented by Eisenberg and Goodall, but these positions are not as contradictory as they might appear to be at first glance. Just as shared meaning is essential to communication, Haviland makes it clear that shared values are essential to culture. The claim that anthropologists have rejected this idea may be overstated. Even so, the presence of enough commonality in meaning and values to sustain communication and culture still leaves plenty of room for ambiguity, conflict, pluralistic ignorance, and false consensus among many different organizational groups and constituencies. Organizational culture arises from a dynamic tension and interplay among these groups. Culture may depend on shared values, but it is also an ongoing dialogue among diverse subcultures (Clifford, 1983; Eisenberg & Goodall, 1993).

The concept of subcultures is particularly important to consider when attempting to describe an organization's culture. The stance we adopt here is that an organization's culture is not a monolithic form controlled from above by managers and owners. Although managers and corporate owners play an important role in shaping or influencing an organization's culture, it is also necessary to examine the role employees play in creating and sustaining culture through their interactions with one another at work. In order to clarify the stance we take here let's consider one of Clifford Geertz's (1973) observations in the book *The Interpretation of Cultures*. Geertz (1973) argued that "man is an animal suspended in webs of significance he himself has spun . . . culture [is] those webs" (p. 5). As webs, cultures are spun continuously as people within a social system interact with one another and create their own rules and norms. Interestingly, the webs spun by cultural members are both confining and mobilizing. Just as a web confines a spider's movement to the area traversed by the web, an organization's culture restricts worker actions to those considered acceptable by the norms and rules within the system. Webs, however, are not only confining; they also make movement for the spider possible. This is also true of the webs spun by employees interacting with one another at work. The webs spun within an organization empower employees to act in ways legitimized by their collectively created culture.

We would like to extend Geertz's metaphor by describing an organization's culture as a collection of interconnected webs. These interconnected webs represent subcultures within the organization. Each subculture is somewhat unique because of the particular workers who comprise it; however, because the subcultures are interconnected and embedded within a single organization, they also share certain characteristic features and commonly held meanings or interpretations.

Traditionalist, interpretivist, and critical-interpretivist scholars have written about and produced studies of organizational culture, but these three groups understand organizational culture in very different ways. To the Traditionalist, a culture is something that an organization *has*—a set of characteristics that the organization possesses. The interpretivist and the critical-interpretivist see culture as what the organization *is*—the essence of organizational life. While the *pure* interpretivist, however, is content to describe an organization's culture, the critical-interpretivist describes and evaluates cultures by focusing on power struggles among competing groups. The basic differences among the three approaches to organizational culture are summarized in table 10.1.

Traditionalist Perspective

According to Smircich (1981), traditionalism (also called functionalism) always has been concerned with the actions that organizations can take to ensure their "continued survival in an essentially competitive situation" (p. 3). This translates into discovering the right combinations of organizational variables that promote effectiveness. Consequently, traditionalist research is characterized by studies of variables such as structure, size, technology, leadership, and communication. Eventually, traditionalists added cultural variables to those that they typically study in recognition that organizations not only produce goods and services but also produce "cultural artifacts, e.g., stories, myths, legends, rituals, that are distinctive" (p. 3).

The kinds of artifacts that Smircich identified are, in effect, the concrete, objective features of a culture. Traditionalists study these artifacts in much the same way that they would study any other observable feature or organizational behavior. In line with their traditional concern for regulation of organizational processes, traditionalists usually want to know how to develop and change an organizational culture in order to make the organization more effective. Strategies for change usually emphasize managerial control over the observable features of culture (e.g., goals, practices, language, rites, rituals, sagas, and the content of orientation and indoctrination programs).

Deal and Kennedy's *Corporate Cultures,* a very popular book in business circles during the early 1980s, provides an interesting example of the traditionalist viewpoint. Deal and Kennedy regard organizational culture as a kind of identity

Table 10.1 Comparison of Traditionalist, Interpretivist, and Critical-Interpretivist Orientations to Organizational Culture.

	Traditionalism	**Interpretivism**	**Critical-Interpretivism**
Goals	Develop and change organizational culture to produce organizational effectiveness	Describe organizational culture according to the meanings that it makes possible to members	Describe and critique organizational culture according to meanings generated by members to uncover sources of oppression in systems of language, meaning and organizational structure, and identify paths to member emancipation
Definition of Culture	Artifacts of organizational life such as stories, myths, legends, and rituals	Common interpretive frame of reference; a network of shared meanings	Sites of power struggle revealed through discourse and organizational structure and focused on the interests of managers, employees, and external constituents
Activities	Promote managerial control over cultural artifacts through management of symbolism	Study meanings and themes in members' organizational sense making, as revealed in symbolic discourse	Critique the power struggles among managers, employees, and external constituents for the purpose of revealing paths to emancipation for the oppressed

for a corporation. Management is supposed to develop and foster commitment to this identity by propagating desired beliefs and informal rules that influence behavior, by celebrating desired organizational values through rites and rituals, and by creating legends through sagas that glorify the adventures, exploits, and successes of organizational heroes.

According to Deal and Kennedy, corporate executives should try to build a "strong" culture for two reasons. First, organizational effectiveness can be increased simply by letting employees know what is expected of them. A strong culture provides this information both formally and informally. Second, a strong culture "enables people to feel better about what they do, so they are more likely to work harder" (p. 16). For example, the use of rites, rituals, and sagas helps to legitimize and justify various forms of organizational behavior by answering such questions as the following: Who are we? What do we do? Why are we here? (Bormann et al., 1982).

What is a strong culture? For Deal and Kennedy, strong culture means a highly cohesive organization in which members are fully committed to organizational goals. In their words, a strong culture exists only when "everyone knows the goals . . . and they are working for them" (1982, p. 4). It follows, then, that organizations characterized by competing values and divided loyalties have "weak" and fragmented cultures.

Interpretivist Perspective

Like the traditionalist, the interpretivist also is concerned with uncovering the frame of reference shared by organization members, but the interpretivist understands this frame of reference in a different way. Smircich (1981) describes the difference between traditionalist and interpretivist ideas about organizational culture:

Social action becomes possible because of consensually determined meanings for experiences that to an external observer may have the appearance of an independent rulelike existence. What looks like an objective and real world to the [traditionalist] researcher is seen by the interpretivist researcher to be a product of interaction processes whereby meanings for experience are negotiated and then continually sustained through the course of interaction. (pp. 5–6)

In other words, the observable, tangible world of social action (i.e., behavior) is based on organization members' sharing of subjective meanings. To the interpretivist, organizational culture is understood only as a network of shared meanings. Consequently, the interpretivist describes organizational culture according to the meanings that it makes possible for its members and the ways in which the culture itself is enacted or "performed" through communication (Pacanowsky & O'Donnell-Trujillo, 1982).

Interpretive studies of organizational culture are characterized by an explicit focus on symbols and themes that are revealed in symbolic discourse (communication). According to Smircich, these themes "show the ways the symbols are linked into meaningful relationships and . . . they specify the links between values, beliefs, and actions" (p. 7). Presumably, the interpretive researcher is primarily concerned with revealing these linkages rather than with connecting organizational culture with traditionalist concerns for organizational efficiency and effectiveness.

Critical-Interpretivist Perspective

The most recent development in understanding and studying organizational culture has been to combine the theories and methods associated with the interpretivist and critical perspectives (see, e.g., Barker, 1993; Barker & Cheney, 1994; Papa, Auwal & Singhal, 1995, 1996). Critical-interpretivist researchers start with the premise that organizations are places where members develop shared and conflicting meanings to accomplish individual and organizational goals. Of course, this stance is not radically different than that advocated by many interpretivists. What separates the two interpretivist approaches is that critical-interpretivists also view organizations as places of struggle over competing meaning systems. In this power struggle certain groups (e.g., managers and owners) are privileged, meaning they receive the majority of the benefits associated with organizational membership. Other groups (e.g., nonmanagement personnel) are disadvantaged, meaning they receive fewer benefits while absorbing a higher level of the costs associated with organizational membership.

In order to clarify the approach taken by critical-interpretivists, let's consider an example. A group of managers within a large manufacturing company has become worried over a downturn in sales during the past year. These managers and their subordinates meet to decide how to address the problem of diminishing sales. During this meeting the two groups decide mutually that in order to remain competitive in their industry and meet the demands of consumers, worker performance must increase in terms of quantity and quality of output. The managers are happy to receive the agreement of their workers on this issue, and the workers accept the fact that they must work more diligently in order to receive positive performance evaluations and contribute to organizational goals. Whose interests, however, are being served best by this decision? The increase in task performance does not bring with it an increase in pay because that would increase the organization's overhead costs.

Furthermore, not only are these workers required to work more diligently, there is an expectation that they work overtime (without increased pay) in order to meet performance goals. Contrasting this expectation for higher worker output, managers do not increase their level of task performance. Their job is to oversee the workers to ensure that performance goals are met. The critical-interpretivist researcher would draw attention to the imbalances created by the new work rules.

One question that would be posed by this researcher is, Why don't managers and workers share equally in the burden of increased performance? Another question to be asked is, Who receives most of the economic benefits of increased production? If the organization generates more income from increased worker performance, shouldn't workers receive a share of this added income? Of course workers must surrender some of their individual goals in order to receive the benefits (e.g., salary, prestige, power, etc.) of organizational membership; however, at what point are the benefits of membership outweighed by the costs of continued participation? By addressing such questions and making employees aware of alternative interpretations of the rules and norms they create and sustain for one another, potential paths to empowerment and emancipation may be identified. For example, how can new technological equipment increase task performance without requiring workers to work overtime? How can manager contributions to increased performance expectations reduce the pressure placed on their subordinates? Thus, through focusing on worker conversations and interpreting their experiences, stories and metaphors, the critical-interpretivist identifies sources of struggle between opposing groups and opportunities for change and empowerment for the oppressed.

Merging Perspectives

The more researchers attempt to describe organizational culture, the more they recognize that a combination of forces accounts for the emergence and evolution of culture over time. This combination of forces can perhaps best be accounted for by turning to the work of traditionalists, *and* critical-interpretivists. Although this stance is not advocated by the majority of researchers who examine organizational culture, this view is not a new one. In one of the first articles written about organizational culture in the field of communication, Pacanowsky and O'Donnell-Trujillo (1982) argued that a quantitative assessment of employee perceptions about aspects of organizational communication could be combined with in-depth examinations of employee interpretations of organizational rites, rituals, stories, myths, and metaphors. The quantitative assessment of employee perceptions of communication factors is more consistent with the traditionalist approach, while the qualitative assessment of employee interpretations is more consistent with the interpretivist approach.

One compelling reason for combining traditionalist and critical-interpretivist approaches to organizational culture analysis is to improve the accuracy of the overall cultural assessment that is offered. Traditionalists often use survey questionnaires with objective items to tap employee perceptions of communication in their organizations. These questionnaires, which can be completed relatively quickly by employees, do not require a great amount of time to administer and score. Because of the ease associated with survey administration and scoring, hundreds or thousands of surveys can be distributed and examined. The results obtained from these surveys can then be used to guide the observations and questions subsequently asked by the critical-interpretivist researcher. Also, critical-interpretivist researchers can use the results obtained from survey questionnaires to guide their selection of certain groups of employees for in-depth interviews. The purpose of these in-depth interviews is to gain a more complete understanding of the struggles over competing meaning systems that are present within the organization.

In-depth interviews and detailed observations of employees at work take a substantial amount of time, thereby limiting the number of employees that can be included in any critical cultural analysis. Indeed, it is rare for a critical-interpretivist researcher to interview as many as 100 employees. This raises an important question. How can the critical-interpretivist researcher feel confident in the questions he or she asks and in the particular employees chosen for interviews? By relying on results obtained from survey questionnaires, critical-interpretivist researchers can feel more confident in the decisions they make in the field.

In advancing our argument for merging perspectives we purposefully exclude *pure* interpretivists from consideration. We do so because a comparison of interpretivism with critical-interpretivism shows that both approaches use similar methods of communication analysis and both take the stance that culture is the essence of organizational life. What separates the two approaches is the critical-interpretivists' belief that competing meaning systems create power struggles within organizations. Since we believe that power struggles exist in all organizations (an issue explained more fully in chapter 12), we turn to the more embracing approach to cultural analysis that is provided by critical-interpretivists. So in order to understand how researchers from these two perspectives can make important contributions to our understanding of organizational culture, let us return briefly to the premises linked to each one.

As explained earlier, traditionalists are usually concerned with how to develop and change an organization's culture in order to make the organization more effective. Strategies for development and change emphasize managerial control over the observable features of a culture such as rites, rituals, stories, metaphors, and work practices. The stance we advocate here is that this approach yields important insights into an organization's culture. Clearly, managers or owners of an organization have an incentive for creating and sustaining a culture that preserves their interests for profit and organizational survival. For example, Shockley-Zalabak and Morley (1994) point out that the founders of an organization "create a set of personal values that results in the development of the initial organizational rules specifying the way organizations should and should not be" (p. 353). Among the many important concerns of founders is how to create a productive work culture that allows the organization to survive and earn profits. Of course, such concerns are not exclusively negative for employees. The founders could decide that on-site day-care facilities meet the needs of working mothers and fathers *and* reduce worker lateness and absenteeism linked to child care needs. Such decisions and actions are a central part of an organization's culture and can be examined from the traditionalist perspective.

Critical-interpretivists, on the other hand, believe that organizational culture emerges primarily through the practices and interactions of people at work. As employees talk with one another they form and sustain interpersonal relationships that influence how they view working for an organization. Some of these conversations may focus on rules and norms created by company founders or particular managers while other conversations deal with performing specific work tasks. During the course of the work day employees also talk about social matters, personal problems and after-work activities. Importantly, all of these conversations shape worker experiences, and excluding them from consideration would result in an incomplete picture of any organization's culture. As employees talk with one another they figure out how to cope with company rules, they learn to enjoy or despise their co-workers, and they form judgments about the value of continuing their organizational membership. Thus, critical-interpretivists provide us with information that is vital to understanding how workers understand organizational culture.

Critical-interpretivists also draw our attention to the struggles that exist among different groups and organizational members. Organizations are places where resources, rewards, and punishments are distributed differentially depending on one's place within the system. Company owners and managers receive more of the monetary rewards and are more likely to have favorable working conditions. Nonmanagement employees compete over what rewards remain after managers and owners have received their share, and they have to accept directives received from management in order to receive rewards and to advance within the company. The critical-interpretivist draws attention to the fact that the distribution of resources, rewards, and punishments creates struggles among organizational members and groups. Some members and groups are more likely to receive benefits while others are more likely to absorb costs. The struggles that occur among these members and groups constitute a central feature of organizational life that cannot be ignored. Based on the preceding observations, we argue that any holistic description of an organization's culture needs to draw upon the theories and methods linked to traditionalism and critical-interpretivism.

Barker and Tompkins (1994) provide us with an excellent example of a study that merges the traditional and critical-interpretivist perspectives. They examined characteristics of worker identification (e.g., loyalty) with self-managed work teams. Working within the traditionalist framework, the authors administered a thirty-three-item questionnaire to sixty-eight employees of a small manufacturing company. This questionnaire tapped worker levels of identification with their work teams and with their organization.

In addition to administering their questionnaire, Barker and Tompkins integrated observations and interviews with employees that took place over a two-and-a-half-year period. The approach they took is referred to as *ethnographic data collection.* Before continuing to describe their study, let's take a moment to describe the practice of *ethnography.* This form of data collection and assessment involves a written representation of selected aspects of an organization's culture based primarily on field study (see, e.g., Patton, 1990; Van Maanen, 1988). When studying employee behavior in the field, researchers engage in what is called *participant-observation.* As participant-observers, researchers attempt to interpret cultural members' experiences from *their* frame of reference rather than offering objective or detached assessments of those experiences. Also, participant-observers recognize that their presence within an organization can alter members' perceptions of their surroundings and can influence their behavior. Keeping these challenges in mind, *ethnographers* try to offer interpretations that reflect how employees perceive their organizational experiences. How do ethnographers accomplish this goal? Ethnographers offer detailed observations of employee behavior in task and social settings. They focus on employee stories, accounts, and metaphors, and they examine their rites and rituals as they are performed. In addition, ethnographers involve themselves in conversations with organizational members, and they conduct in-depth interviews to gain insight into member perceptions and experiences.

In the Barker and Tompkins (1994) study, Barker was primarily responsible for ethnographic data collection. Over a two-and-a-half-year period he spent a total of 275 hours at the small manufacturing company that was the focus of the study. He conducted thirty-seven in-depth interviews that ranged from as short as forty-five minutes to as long as two hours. Barker also observed and recorded team and company meetings, and examined company memos, flyers, newsletters, and in-house surveys. Based on this extensive process of data collection and analysis, three conclusions were drawn: (a) workers identify more strongly with their work teams than with their company, (b) long-term workers identify more strongly with both their team and company than do short-term workers, and (c) team-based systems of worker surveillance and control are more powerful than bureaucratic systems of control.

Studying Organizational Culture

Although the methods of traditionalism and interpretivism can be combined in studying organizational communication (see, e.g., Barker & Tompkins, 1994; Faules, 1982; Gioia & Pitre, 1990; Papa, Auwal & Singhal, 1995; Shockley-Zalabak & Morley, 1994), many of the ideas associated with the study of organizational culture are new to traditionalism. Traditionalism usually is concerned with developing general knowledge about relationships among organizational communication variables with data drawn from many types of organizations (e.g., the relationship between openness and job satisfaction in superior-subordinate communication or the effects of different problem-solving methods on group effectiveness). The methods usually are quantitative and statistical. There are some *qualitative* traditionalist studies of organizational culture, but these studies are scientific classifications of observable cultural variables. So how can traditionalists attempt to describe central aspects of an organization's culture?

Chiles and Zorn (1995) recently published a study that combined quantitative and qualitative data collection techniques within a traditionalist framework to describe one aspect of an organization's culture, namely, employee perceptions of empowerment. The authors administered a six-item empowerment questionnaire to forty employees of a large manufacturing company. The degree to which employees felt empowered was tapped quantitatively by questions such as (a) I have the authority to make decisions that need to be made; (b) management trusts me to make decisions that need to be made; and (c) I have the opportunity to use my judgment for problem solving. In addition to these questionnaires, Chiles and Zorn conducted in-depth interviews with the same forty employees to gain a more complete understanding of worker definitions and experiences with work place empowerment. The qualitative component of their study was to analyze the content of the interview responses to identify factors that employees perceived as important in empowerment. The authors found that employee feelings of empowerment were influenced strongly by their perception of the organization's overall culture. Specifically, the more they felt hindered by the culture to act based upon their own expertise, the less likely they were to feel empowered. Also, the more positive verbal recognition employees received from their supervisors, the higher their feelings of empowerment tended to be.

Despite the fact that traditionalists can derive important insights about an organization's culture, there are limitations associated with this approach. Studies of organizational culture are intended to reveal the meanings and interpretations of organizational life made possible by a cultural frame of reference or to understand the process by which culture is created, transmitted, and changed through communication. Given this focus, interpretivist or critical-interpretivist methods are more appropriate for examining organizational culture.

Before turning to a description of the methods used by interpretivists and critical-interpretivists, a final note on studying organizational culture seems in order. The studies conducted by Barker and Tompkins (1994) and Chiles and Zorn (1995) show some of the complexities associated with describing and evaluating an organization's culture. Both studies involved hundreds of hours of observations, interviews, conversations, and data analysis. The time and effort expended by these researchers was necessary to gain accurate insights into employee perceptions of organizational culture. Logging hundreds of hours of data collection and analysis, however, may not yield cultural descriptions that are reflective of every employee's interpretations. This is true for two primary reasons.

First, as discussed earlier, within any large organization there are likely to be many subcultures. For example, in a huge multinational corporation such as General Motors with plants and offices located across the world, can there be a single corporate culture? Certain common cultural features may be found in many of the plants and locations, but each separate facility also exhibits cultural features that are unique to the particular collection of people working there. Cultural researchers need to take this fact into consideration before attempting to provide an overarching description of an organization's culture.

Second, although organizational cultures are collectively created by organizational members, these cultures are interpreted by individuals. For example, let's consider two employees (Jim and Mary) who work in the collections department of a large retail store. Mary has several close friendships with her co-workers. In addition, Mary has a congenial working relationship with her supervisor. Jim, on the other hand, is an isolate who rarely interacts with co-workers. Furthermore, Jim has a history of conflict with his supervisor. Although Jim and Mary work in the same department, their interpretations of departmental and organizational culture may be quite different because they have different experiences at work. This example does not negate the value of conducting an organizational cultural analysis; rather, it shows the complexities associated with the process and the restrictions researchers must recognize when drawing their conclusions.

Now that we have considered the difficulties associated with cultural analysis, let's turn to some of the major methods of examining culture from the interpretivist and critical-interpretivist perspectives. We will describe five methods that rely on analysis of organizational communication: fantasy theme analysis, narrative analysis, metaphor analysis, analysis of rites and ceremonies, and analysis of reflexive comments.

Fantasy Theme Analysis

Fantasy theme analysis is based on Ernest Bormann's symbolic convergence theory of communication. Symbolic convergence occurs when groups create rhetorical visions of their social world and what it is like to be in that world. As applied to organizations, a rhetorical vision is a view held by organization members "of the organization and its relationship to the external environment, of the various subdivisions and units of the organization, and of their place in the scheme of things" (Bormann, 1981, p. 6). These visions arise from shared fantasies involving creative interpretation of events and fantasy types, that is, common themes that reflect beliefs, goals, and values. How does one identify fantasies and rhetorical visions in an organization's life? Bormann has devised a system of fantasy theme analysis to address this question. Bormann, Howell, Nichols, and Shapiro said, "A good way to discover the symbolic world of a group is by collecting dramatic messages, stories, histories, and anecdotes that they tell and retell" (1982, p. 83). This may be done by observing and listening to members interact with one another, by interviewing organization members, by examining the organization's official written record (mission statements, official memos, reports, and newsletters), and even by using the unofficial written record (underground newsletter, songs, or graffiti).

Once the materials are gathered, they are subjected to a **script analysis** in which organizational life is treated as a drama with characters acting in scenes. The messages, stories, and other materials are examined to identify the following features:

1. Heroes, villains, and their goals and values.
2. The action line, including the things that characters do to achieve their goals.
3. The scene where the action takes place and the forces that are presumed to control the action.

After analyzing a number of stories and messages in this way, the researcher should be able to identify common themes that, like the moral of a story, reflect shared fantasies and rhetorical visions within the organization. One may then be able to understand the values that prevail within the organization or within its various groups and the realities of organizational life as members construct and understand them.

One example of the application of fantasy theme analysis to organizational communication is a study conducted by Bormann, Pratt, and Putnam (1978) of male response to female leadership in a female-dominated organization. The case was a laboratory company operated by college students—nine males and thirteen females. Conflicts over authority and power in the company led to a restructuring of its formal system, but the "real" organization ultimately was enacted through an informal communication network that was dominated by the women. Only two of the nine men fully accepted the situation. Two others actively attempted to achieve leadership positions, but were blocked by the women. The other men withdrew as much as possible from active participation. They disconnected from the network and did as little work as possible. As Bormann and colleagues put it, "They were goldbricking" (p. 150).

When Bormann and colleagues analyzed the discourse and dialogue of company members, they found fantasy themes that seemed to explain what had occurred in the male response to female leadership and in the female response to challenges. First and foremost, they identified "the recurrence of fantasy themes which linked leadership with male potency" (p. 154), portraying and dramatizing males under female domination as symbolically castrated. These themes were related to dramatization of a double-bind theme among the men: A male who challenges female leadership is a chauvinist pig, while a male who accepts female leadership is a castrated eunuch. Most of the men in the company opted for withdrawal as the only plausible response to this paradox. Others took up a portrayal of the women as mother. Those men "who merged with the group accepted dependency on the mother and on the female leadership" (p. 155).

Narrative Analysis

Bormann's fantasy theme analysis views stories as an important part of an organization's culture. These stories are interpreted by linking them to fantasy themes or rhetorical visions that exist within the organization. A more generic approach to examining organizational stories or *narratives* is provided by Walter Fisher (1978, 1984, 1985, 1987). Fisher believes that human reasoning is a process of using symbols to guide thinking. Furthermore, he argues that a person's reasoning is displayed in the narratives or stories that he or she tells.

Fisher (1984) contends that storytelling is central to the human experience. In other words, we make sense of the world around us by translating our experiences into stories or narratives that we share with others. In organizations employees justify decisions and offer reasons for their actions by telling stories to co-workers. Also, a person's values can be detected in the stories he or she tells (Meyer, 1995). Indeed, a number of researchers have suggested that stories are told by employees to indicate how others should act or not act within an organization

(Brown, 1990; Kirkwood, 1992; Mitroff & Kilmann, 1976). In order to show how narratives can play a central role in shaping an organization's culture, let's turn to a story told by a Grameen Bank field worker in Bangladesh. This story was reported to Rahnuma Shehabuddin (1992) and it focuses on how a group of female loan recipients empowered themselves against a moneylender (a powerful village resident who charges poor people exorbitant interest rates for loans):

A money-lender threatened to break the legs of a [Grameen] bank worker who walked along the path in front of the former's house every week on his way to the centre meeting. When they heard about this, the thirty loan recipients at the centre showed up at the money-lender's house. They told him that he could threaten the bank worker only if he himself was prepared to lend them the money they needed on the same terms as the Grameen Bank did. The money-lender, of course, was not willing to give up his exorbitant interest rates, but he promised to stop harassing the bank workers as well as the members who no longer came to him for money. So you see, there is power in numbers: Thirty landless women can intimidate a wealthy man if they join forces. (Shehabuddin, 1992, p. 83)

This story has been told many times by employees and loan recipients of the Grameen Bank, and it serves two central purposes. First, it is unlikely that the thirty women mentioned in the story would have ever confronted the powerful money lender prior to their affiliation with the Grameen Bank. Their membership in the Grameen empowered them to feel confident in their strength to collectively oppose an oppressive force, and in sharing the story they remind each other of what they can accomplish by working together. Second, field workers share this story with one another to show how their efforts can help transform the lives of the poor so they are no longer taken advantage of by powerful village citizens. Thus, the workers' commitment to helping the poor is strengthened by a story that shows how their efforts make a real difference in people's lives.

Further insight into organizational storytelling was provided in a recent article by John Meyer (1995). Meyer attempted to discern the values that were embedded in stories told by nineteen employees of a day-care center. A total of 555 stories were told in these interviews showing how prevalent storytelling is in some organizations. Also, upon analyzing the content of the stories, Meyer uncovered ten different organizational values. This finding underscores how many different types of messages or themes can be detected through listening to the stories employees tell. The ten organizational values discovered by Meyer were (a) people should show concern for others' needs and feelings; (b) people should plan for work tasks and activities in advance; (c) people should communicate information as quickly or as appropriately as possible; (d) there should be opportunities to influence events and make decisions; (e) conflict should be handled by talk among the persons involved; (f) people should be personal and easy to get along with; (g) messages should be sent clearly and repeated to ensure accuracy; (h) people should derive intrinsic rewards from their work, doing more than should be expected for their jobs; (i) people should be given flexibility and independence on the job; and (j) people should respect and follow directives of those above them in the decision hierarchy.

All organizational stories present the listener with the narrator's version of a particular experience. So by asking employees to recount those stories that have been influential in their affiliation with an organization, we can gain insight into what they view as an important encounter, how they make sense of their membership, and how they want others to understand their experiences.

Metaphor Analysis

Susan Koch and Stan Deetz (1981) believe that metaphors are at the heart of an interpretive process "that continually structures the organization's reality" (p. 16). Familiar phrases such as "the game of life," "hard as a rock," "working at a snail's pace," and "running like a well-oiled machine" are all metaphorical statements. The game, the rock, the snail's pace, and the machine are metaphors for other things.

Koch and Deetz argue that metaphors anchor our understandings of experience. When we speak metaphorically of life as a game and organizations as machines, these metaphors reflect our interpretations of life and of organizations. Since interpretation not only depends on language but many other factors as well, metaphors may not be as powerful as Koch and Deetz suggest. Cohen (1977) summarized a number of studies suggesting that some forms of interpretation and thinking can occur without any particular reference to language. If this is the case, the metaphors that people use sometimes may be little more than convenient figures of speech. Nevertheless, common metaphors that occur in organizational communication could provide important clues to the meanings that members hold for their experiences.

Metaphor analysis begins by recording the talk of organization members in interviews and discussions. Data also may be obtained from written records. Interview questions should be free of any metaphors that might bias results. For example, "Tell me how the organization *operates*" might prompt the interviewee to answer with "machine" metaphors.

The next step is to isolate metaphors by examining all of the statements in the data. This process is complicated and depends on the researcher's familiarity with different types of metaphors and on the researcher's ability to recognize them in statements. Metaphors may be created in several ways, but four of the most common rely on **spatial orientation, activities, substances,** or **entities.** For example, "I have authority *over* this matter" relates the idea of authority to a spatial orientation, *over.* "We're breathing new life into the company" relates an organizational process to a well-known biblical metaphor for the activity of creation, *and* it relates the organization to the substance of a living organism. "We're just one big, happy *family* at Burger Queen" relates the organization to the entity, *family.*

After metaphors are identified, they are worked through progressively until it is possible to identify all of the main or "root" metaphors used in the organization. In many cases, subcultural divisions yield more than one main metaphor. We observed this condition firsthand in a large research laboratory in which conflicts between a technical training department and a human resource development department seemed to be related to differences in root metaphors. The technical training group understood itself as a family, whereas the human resource development group characterized itself as a small business. The technical trainers spoke in terms of being a good neighbor to others in the laboratory "community." The supervisor was regarded as the head of a household. The human resource group described its function as "marketing services" to "client" groups in the laboratory. The supervisor was "the boss," who controlled and coordinated the business. The business group regarded the family group as unprofessional. The family group regarded the business group as rigid, competitive, and cold. Simply identifying these metaphors did not resolve the conflicts between the two departments, but it did seem to help members to make more sense of the conflicts.

One good example of the scholarly application of metaphor analysis is a study by Smith and Eisenberg (1987) of labor-management conflict at Disneyland. Late in 1984, the conflict culminated in a twenty-two day strike by unionized employees. This is an interesting work because, as Smith and Eisenberg put it, "Disneyland occupies a special place in the American psyche" (p. 367). Moreover, the Disney corporation has used its success and strong public image as a foundation for becoming a consultant to other companies on management methods and employee relations. Yet, the study by Smith and Eisenberg revealed a somewhat troubled state of affairs in fantasyland. Smith and Eisenberg began their study in 1983 through eight interviews with Disneyland managers. Later, in 1985, they conducted intensive audiotaped interviews of thirty-five hourly employees, who were men and women of various ages and lengths of employment and who represented six different divisions of Disneyland operations. In order to analyze the interviews, they applied what they describe as a "semantic sorting process in which coherent patterns or clusters of meaning emerged around specific metaphorical expressions" (p. 371). In effect, this means that they examined all of the metaphorical expressions in the interview transcripts for shared understandings that could be characterized with a root metaphor. Smith and Eisenberg provide an example of this process:

Expressions [used by interviewees]:
"The cast members"
"The show"
"Our costumes"
"The Disney image"
"The Disney role"

Shared understanding:
Disneyland has actors, costumes, and stories to be enacted on stage and an audience to be entertained.

Organizational entailment:
Disneyland puts on a show.

Root metaphor:
Disneyland is a drama.

Smith and Eisenberg found two root metaphors, namely, *drama* and *family* that characterized employees' experiences at Disneyland. They applied both of these metaphors to interpret various aspects of the labor-management conflict. Disney himself played a primary role in shaping the drama metaphor and supporting it with the image of Disneyland as an oasis for friendly family entertainment. This vision was adopted thoroughly by employees. After his death, the management philosophy began to shift, at least as it was perceived by employees. In response, employees cast themselves as defenders and caretakers of Disney's founding vision, but they revised their interpretation of that vision by *extending* the concept of family to Disney employees. Friendliness not only referred to employee-customer relationships (the original intention), but it also referred to relationships among employees themselves (the new interpretation). In short, Disneyland not only provided family entertainment, it *was* a family itself. This new interpretation was one that even Disney himself "may not have fully endorsed [and it] led ultimately to conflict with management" (p. 373).

As explained by Smith and Eisenberg, the family metaphor was accepted uncritically by most employees and by many managers. It was believed to characterize employee relationships and the management-employee relationship. But with increasing competition from other theme parks, take-over attempts, high-level corporate resignations, and greater operating costs, management gradually placed a rather unfamily-like emphasis on the bottom-line, including a wage freeze and elimination of benefits in its efforts to operate at a profit. Management tried to redefine the family metaphor (e.g., family life sometimes is hard and families sometimes have to make sacrifices), but employees rejected management's new idea of family. Management's bottom-line view "was perceived by many as constituting a breach of Disney's caring philosophy" (p. 374).

Another very important feature of this particular study occurs in the way in which Smith and Eisenberg draw conclusions from their analysis. You may recall from chapter 1 that interpretive approaches to organizational communication regard the organization as a negotiated order composed of pluralistic interests. These approaches generally attempt to avoid the managerial bias of functionalism and the worker-oriented bias of critical theory. The interpretivist point of view clearly is reflected in Smith and Eisenberg's efforts to find a way for management and labor groups at Disneyland to share a common understanding of their organization:

A conscious reconsideration of the drama metaphor might help reconcile management with employees, and past with present. An appeal of the drama metaphor lies in its ability to subsume some of the interpretations of both management and employees; it simultaneously retains the image of the park as *family* entertainment and permits a *business* orientation. (p. 378)

Analysis of Rites and Ceremonies

Harrison Trice (1985) has been largely responsible for drawing our attention to the importance of rites and ceremonials in describing organizational culture. A rite brings together a number of discrete cultural forms (e.g., customary language, metaphors, stories, ritualized behavior, settings) into "an integrated, unified public performance" (Trice & Beyer, 1984, p. 654). Ceremonies connect several rites into a single occasion or event. In order to clarify this perspective, let's consider an example.

In a large computer manufacturing company, sales representatives compete for an award that is given twice a year to the top seller. Since this award has been given twenty times during the past ten years, it has become a ritualized event.

When the award is made, all of the sales representatives in the company gather together to congratulate the top performer. During the award ceremony the national sales manager praises the sales representative's performance, encourages other sales representatives to follow his or her example, and presents the award winner with a bonus check. Furthermore, stories are told about the diligent work necessary to receive this award, and metaphors are used comparing the winners to tireless warriors who refuse to be beaten by competitors. Such an event can be considered an organizational rite because it connects a number of cultural forms such as stories, metaphors, and symbols (e.g., bonus checks) to a single event.

Trice and Beyer (1984) identified six different rites that can be linked to organizational ceremonies: (a) rites of passage, (b) rites of degradation, (c) rites of enhancement, (d) rites of renewal, (e) rites of conflict reduction, and (f) rites of integration. A rite of passage occurs when employees move into roles that are new to them. An example would be successfully completing the basic training program of the U.S. Army. Rites of degradation dissolve the power associated with an organizational identity such as occurs when a person is fired from his or her job. Rites of enhancement provide public recognition for an employee's accomplishments as shown by our sales representative example. Rites of renewal refurbish social structures by improving their functioning. For example, a developmental program that trains managers to be more effective administrators could be considered a rite of renewal. Rites of conflict reduction reestablish equilibrium in an organization beset by destructive arguments between certain members or groups. A collective bargaining session would exemplify this type of rite. Finally, rites of integration "revive common feelings that bind members together and commit them to a social system" (Trice & Beyer, 1984, p. 657). An annual office Christmas party would be representative of an integration rite.

Trice and Beyer (1984) argue that an examination of organizational rites and ceremonials is a comprehensive form of cultural analysis because the researcher focuses on events that bring a number of different cultural forms together. Rather than focus on stories or metaphors told by individual employees about many varied experiences, the researcher who observes an organizational ceremony is exposed to how different cultural forms are used in a given setting for a particular purpose. They also argue that this type of cultural analysis is very efficient since "identifying, observing, and even participating in [ceremonies] does not require sustained access over time" (Trice & Beyer, 1984, p. 664). In order to show the usefulness of this approach to cultural analysis, let's consider an example.

As part of their field study of the Grameen Bank in Bangladesh, Papa, Auwal, & Singhal (1995) observed local branch office meetings attended by bank field workers and loan recipients. These meetings can be viewed as ceremonials that bring together a number of different rites. One of the first items of business addressed in these meetings is loan repayment. The members either repay their loans, or explain to the field worker why they could not repay. Since weekly repayment is considered the norm, failure to repay is considered a failure. A rite of degradation is linked to the failure to repay as members are criticized by the bank worker for not meeting their financial obligations. Furthermore, since the loans of other center members are jeopardized when one member does not repay, the loan defaulter also receives criticism from his or her fellow members. Rites of enhancement can also occur during these meetings. For example, if a loan recipient builds a new house with a loan received from the bank, the other center members will visit the house and complement the owner for working so diligently to afford it. Rites of conflict reduction can take place when the field worker attempts to manage conflicts among loan recipients concerning failed business ventures. Finally, rites of integration are performed. For example, the members perform physical exercise drills as part of these meetings and they shout slogans that reaffirm their commitment to the bank's programs. This rite of integration is linked to the belief that members must act together so they can move forward together out of poverty and toward financial independence.

Papa, Auwal, and Singhal (1995) derived three important insights from their examination of the weekly loan meetings. First, the potential for public criticism served as a powerful motivating force for loan recipients to repay their loans in a timely manner. Second, high levels of organizational commitment were displayed by both loan recipients and bank field workers. Third, genuine camaraderie was shown among loan recipients and workers who shared in one another's successes.

Analysis of Reflexive Comments

Analysis of reflexive comments is a technique originally described by Harre and Secord (1972). It has been applied in organizational communication studies by Tompkins and Cheney (1983), Cheney (1983), and Geist and Chandler (1984). Like other interpretive methods, this technique focuses on language and discourse in order to reveal meanings and understand human behavior.

What is a **reflexive comment?** To begin with, we human beings generally are not only aware of our actions in social situations, but we also *know* that we are aware. We are both actors and observers of our own actions. This is reflexiveness. It allows us to make comments in the form of explanations, justifications, criticisms, and so forth about our own behavior. If we make a comment about an anticipated action, it is a **plan.** If it is about ongoing action in the present, it is a **commentary.** If it is a statement made after the occurrence of an event or action in a way that justifies or gives reasons for the occurrence, it is an **account.** According to Tompkins and Cheney, these comments reveal "the meanings and interpretations actors assign to items in their environment and the rules . . . that they follow in monitoring their social behavior" (p. 129).

Analysis of reflexive comments may be conducted in various ways. Cheney used analysis of accounts (after-the-fact comments) in a study of the relationship between identification and decision-making processes. He began with the assumption that identification as "the process by which individuals link themselves to elements in the social scene" (p. 342) is acted out in organizational decision making. For example, decisions or evaluations of alternatives might be based on identification with the entire organization, a department, or even a specific individual. Cheney's procedures were developed to explore the extent to which identification helps to explain decision making. Cheney collected accounts through moderately scheduled interviews (i.e., interviews in which major questions are preplanned, but follow-up questions intended to probe interviewee answers are generated spontaneously in the interview). Questioning proceeded through five steps:

1. The employee's role(s) in the organization (i.e., duties, decision making, responsibilities).
2. "Accounts" for specific decisions.
3. "Accounts" for decision-making practice (especially useful when an employee does not isolate specific episodes).
4. The employee's identifications.
5. Actions by the company that either foster or discourage identification with the organization. (p. 349)

The accounts obtained from interviews were analyzed in order to identify decision premises (the reasons or factors taken into account that influence a decision), the sources of decision premises (person, group, or other authority from which premises are acquired), and targets of identification (people, groups, or organizational units with which an employee identifies). Cheney used this information to answer questions about the relevance of organizational values and goals in employees' evaluations of decision alternatives, about overlap between identification targets and sources of decision premises, about changes in identification and decision making as length of employment increases, and about the influence of organizational policy on identification and decision making.

Geist and Chandler (1984) used reflexive comments to study the exercise of influence in group decision making, although the major purpose of their investigation involved a test of five claims made by Tompkins and Cheney regarding the value of account analysis:

1. Accounts express decisional premises or rules.
2. Accounts point to the sources of rules.
3. Accounts enumerate social units for whom the decision maker was prepared to give accounts at the time of making the decision.
4. Accounts reveal identification targets.
5. Accounts help to explain the nature of the identification process. (pp. 136–139)

In their investigation, Geist and Chandler videotaped weekly staff meetings of a psychiatric health-care team, then transcribed the tapes in order to analyze decisions related to the care and treatment of patients. Instead of soliciting accounts through interviews with organization members, Geist and Chandler attempted to locate reflexive comments in a record of *ongoing group interaction*. They did this by examining any statement that a group member made that revealed the member's values or targets of identification. Consequently, their data appeared to include not only accounts but also plans and commentaries. They concluded that analysis of reflexive comments will serve all five of the functions that Tompkins and Cheney claimed.

Summary

In a fundamental sense, a culture exists when people come to share a common frame of reference for interpreting and acting toward one another and the world in which they live. This common frame of reference includes language, values, beliefs, and interpretations of experience. It is reflected in customs, folkways, artifacts, communication, and other observable features of the community, including rites, rituals, celebrations, legends, myths, and heroic sagas.

Although there is consensus among scholars in various fields that the concept of culture can be applied to organizations, there are different ways of understanding organizational culture. Traditionalists study cultural artifacts in much the same way that they would study any other observable feature of organizational behavior. In line with their historic concern for regulation of organizational processes, traditionalists usually want to know how to develop and change an organizational culture in order to make the organization more effective. To the interpretivist, organizational culture is understood only as a network of shared meanings. Consequently, the interpretivist describes organizational culture according to the meanings that it makes possible for its members and the ways in which the culture itself is enacted or "performed" through communication. Critical-interpretivists also describe culture according to the meanings it makes possible for members; however, their focus is on the struggles that occur over competing meaning systems. In these struggles there are certain groups more likely to receive rewards or benefits from organizational membership, whereas other groups are more likely to absorb costs. Both interpretivists and critical-interpretivists use methods such as fantasy theme analysis, narrative analysis, metaphor analysis, and analysis of rites and ceremonials and reflexive comments to gain insight into organizational culture.

Bormann (1981) defines a fantasy as a "creative and imaginative interpretation of events" that includes both real and imagined elements. He believes that symbolic convergence occurs through sharing of fantasies within groups. Group fantasies provide the basis for and reinforce common beliefs, goals, values, and wishes within a group.

Fantasy themes are identified through a script analysis in which organizational life is treated as a drama with characters acting in scenes. Messages, stories, and other materials including written records, jokes, songs, and even graffiti are examined to identify heroes, villains; the action line, including the things that characters do to achieve their goals; the scene where the action takes place and the forces that are presumed to control the action.

Narrative analysis focuses on the stories told by organizational members. These stories are told for a variety of reasons. Employees justify their decisions or actions through stories as well as give insight into their values. Stories are also told to indicate how members should act or not act within an organization. Finally, organizational stories provide researchers with insight into how employees make sense of their membership and how they want others to understand their experiences.

Metaphor analysis assumes that metaphors anchor our understandings of experience. Metaphor analysis begins by recording the talk of organization members in interviews and discussions. The next step is to isolate metaphors by examining all of the statements in the data. Three of the most common types of metaphors rely on spatial orientation, activities, or substances and entities.

Rites and ceremonials are activities that bring together a number of different cultural forms (e.g., customary language, metaphors, stories, ritualized behavior) in a single setting. Trice and Beyer (1984) identified six different rites that can be linked to organizational ceremonies: rites of passage, rites of degradation, rites of enhancement, rites of renewal, rites of conflict reduction, and rites of integration. This form of analysis is valuable in terms of its efficiency and its insight into member perceptions of organizational culture because it allows researchers to observe a single event that displays a number of different cultural forms.

Reflexive comments are statements of explanation, justification, criticism, and so forth, that we make about our own action. According to Tompkins and Cheney (1983), these comments reveal "the meanings and interpretations actors assign to items in their environment and the rules . . . that they follow in monitoring their social behavior" (p. 129). Organizational communication researchers have gathered reflexive comments through use of moderately scheduled interviews with organization members and by taping and transcribing comments from group meetings.

While interpretivist or critical-interpretivist methods appear to be best suited for the study of organizational culture, the traditionalist concept of managerially planned cultural change has gained great popularity. The idea of controlling and changing organizational culture through unilateral management direction is controversial because an organizational culture is influenced by many different forces. In particular, diversity of the workforce is changing organizational cultures whether managers intend it or not. Thus, in the next chapter we will deal specifically with the issues of cultural control, cultural change, and workforce diversity.

Discussion Questions/ Activities

1. Write a brief characterization of the culture at your college. Identify some of the major rites, rituals, myths, legends, and other symbolic artifacts of this culture. What do these artifacts reveal about the meaning that members of the college community have for their experiences?
2. What are some of the essential differences among the traditionalist, interpretivist, and critical-interpretivist perspectives of organizational culture? Are the goals of the three perspectives compatible or incompatible?
3. Studying culture sounds like a problem for an anthropologist. Why should the field of organizational communication be interested in organizational culture?

Additional Resources

Books and Articles

Czarniawska-Joerges, B. (1994). Narratives of individual and organizational identities. In S. A. Deetz (Ed.), *Communication Yearbook 17* (pp. 193–221). Thousand Oaks, CA: Sage.

Gahmberg, H. (1990). Metaphor management: On the semiotics of strategic leadership. In B. A. Turner (Ed.), *Organizational symbolism* (pp. 151–158). Berlin: Walter de Gruyter.

Knuf, J. (1993). "Ritual" in organizational culture theory: Some theoretical reflections and a plea for greater terminological rigor. In S. A. Deetz (Ed.), *Communication Yearbook 16* (pp. 61–103). Newbury Park, CA: Sage.

Philipsen, G. (1992). *Speaking culturally: Explorations in social communication*. Albany, NY: State University of New York Press.

Singelis, T. M., & Brown, W. J. (1995). Culture, self, and collectivist communication: Linking culture to individual behavior. *Human Communication Research, 21,* 354–389.

Smith, R. C., & Turner, P. K. (1995). A social constructivist reconfiguration of metaphor analysis: An application of "SCMA" to organizational socialization theorizing. *Communication Monographs, 62,* 152–181.

Web Site

http://www.umich.edu/~winner/intro.htm
Organizational culture survey instrument

References

Barker, J. R. (1993). Tightening the iron cage: Concertive control in self-managing teams. *Administrative Science Quarterly, 38,* 408–437.

Barker, J. R., & Cheney, G. (1994). The concepts and practices of discipline in contemporary organizational life. *Communication Monographs, 61,* 19–43.

Barker, J. R., & Tompkins, P. K. (1994). Identification in the self-managing organization: Characteristics of target and tenure. *Human Communication Research, 21,* 223–240.

Bormann, E. G. (1981). *The application of symbolic convergence communication theory to organizations.* Paper presented at the SCA/ICA Conference on Interpretive Approaches to the Study of Organizational Communication. Alta, UT.

Bormann, E. G., Howell, W. S., Nichols, R. G., & Shapiro, G. L. (1982). *Interpersonal communication in the modern organization* (2nd ed.). Englewood Cliffs, NJ: Prentice-Hall.

Bormann, E. G., Pratt, J., & Putnam, L. (1978). Power, authority, and sex: Male response to female leadership. *Communication Monographs, 45,* 119–155.

Brown, M. H. (1990). Defining stories in organizations: Characteristics and functions. *Communication yearbook 13* (pp. 162–190). Newbury Park, CA: Sage.

Cheney, G. (1983). On the various and changing meanings of organizational membership: A field study of organizational identification. *Communication Monographs, 50,* 342–362.

Chiles, A. M., & Zorn, T. E. (1995). Empowerment in organizations: Employees' perceptions of the influences on empowerment. *Journal of Applied Communication Research, 23,* 1–25.

Clifford, J. (1983). On ethnographic authority. *Representations, 1,* 118–146.

Cohen, G. (1977). *The psychology of cognition.* London: Press.

Deal, T. E., & Kennedy, A. A. (1982). *Corporate cultures: The rites and rituals of corporate life.* Reading, MA: Addison-Wesley.

Eisenberg, E. M., & Goodall, H. L., Jr. (1993). *Organizational communication: Balancing creativity and constraint.* New York: St. Martin's Press.

Farace, R. V., Monge, P. R., & Russell, H. M. (1977). *Communicating and organizing.* Reading, MA: Addison Wesley.

Faules, D. (1982). The use of multi-methods in the organizational setting. *Western Journal of Speech Communication, 46,* 150–161.

Fisher, W. R. (1978). Toward a logic of good reasons. *Quarterly Journal of Speech, 64,* 376–384.

Fisher, W. R. (1984). Narration as a human communication paradigm: The case of public moral argument. *Communication Monographs, 51,* 1–22.

Fisher, W. R. (1985). The narrative paradigm: An elaboration. *Communication Monographs, 52,* 347–367.

Fisher, W. R. (1987). *Human communication as narration: Toward a philosophy of reason, value, and action.* Columbia, S. C.: University of South Carolina Press.

Geertz, C. (1973). *The interpretation of cultures.* New York: Basic Books.

Geist, P., & Chandler, T. (1984). Account analysis of influence in group decision making. *Communication Monographs, 51,* 67–78.

Gioia, D. A., & Pitre, E. (1990). Multiparadigm perspectives on theory building. *Academy of Management Review, 15,* 584–602.

Harre, R., & Secord, P. F. (1972). *The explanation of social behavior.* Totawa, NJ: Littlefield, Adams.

Haviland, W. A. (1993). *Cultural anthropology* (7th ed). Fort Worth, TX: Harcourt Brace Jovanovich.

Kanter, R. M. (1977). *Men and women of the corporation.* New York: Basic Books.

Kirkwood, W. G. (1992). Narrative and the rhetoric of possibility. *Communication Monographs, 59,* 30–47.

Koch, S., & Deetz, S. A. (1981). *Metaphor analysis of social reality in organizations.* Paper presented at the SCA/ICA Conference on Interpretive Approaches to Organizational Communication. Alta, UT.

Maccoby, M. (1976). *The gamesmen: The new corporate leaders.* New York: Simon & Schuster.

Meyer, J. C. (1995). Tell me a story: Eliciting organizational values from narratives. *Communication Quarterly, 43,* 210–224.

Mitroff, I. I., & Kilmann, R. H. (1976). On organization stories: An approach to the design and analysis of organizations through myths and stories. In R. H. Kilmann, L. R. Pondy, & D. P. Slevin (Eds.), *The management of organization design, strategies, and implementation* (pp. 189–207). New York: Elsevier North-Holland.

Pacanowsky, M. E., & O'Donnell-Trujillo, N. (1982). Communication and organizational cultures. *Western Journal of Speech Communication, 46,* 115–130.

Pacanowsky, M. E., & O'Donnell-Trujillo, N. (1984). Organizational communication as cultural performance. *Communication Monographs, 50,* 126–147.

Papa, M. J., Auwal, M. A., & Singhal, A. (1995). Dialectic of control and emancipation in organizing for social change: A multitheoretic study of the Grameen Bank in Bangladesh. *Communication Theory, 5,* 189–223.

Papa, M. J., Auwal, M. A., & Singhal, A. (1996). *Organizing for social change within concertive control systems: Member identification, discursive empowerment, and the masking of discipline.* Paper presented at the annual meeting of the Eastern Communication Association. New York, NY.

Patton, M. Q. (1990). *Qualitative evaluation methods.* London: Sage.

Shehabuddin, R. (1992). *The impact of Grameen Bank in Bangladesh.* Dhaka, Bangladesh: Grameen Bank.

Shockley-Zalabak, P., & Morley, D. D. (1994). Creating a culture: A longitudinal examination of the influence of management and employee values on communication rule stability and emergence. *Human Communication Research, 20,* 334–355.

Smircich, L. (1981). *The concept of culture and organizational analysis.* Paper presented at the SCA/ICA Conference on Interpretive Approaches to Organizational Communication. Alta, UT.

Smith, R. C., & Eisenberg, E. M. (1987). Conflict at Disneyland: A root-metaphor analysis. *Communication Monographs, 54,* 367–380.

Tompkins, P. K., & Cheney, G. (1983). The uses of account analysis: A study of organizational decision making and identification. In L. L. Putnam & M. E. Pacanowsky (Eds.), *Communication and organizations: An interpretive approach* (pp. 123–146). Beverly Hills, CA: Sage.

Trice, H. M. (1985). Rites and ceremonials in organizational cultures. *Research in the Sociology of Organizations, 4,* 221–270.

Trice, H. M., & Beyer, J. M. (1984). Studying organizational cultures through rites and ceremonials. *Academy of Management Review, 9,* 653–669.

Van Maanen, J. (1988). *Tales of the field: On writing ethnography.* Chicago: The University of Chicago Press.

Wright, J. P. (1979). *On a clear day, you can see General Motors.* Grosse Pointe, MI: Wright Enterprises.

CHAPTER 11

CULTURAL CONTROL, DIVERSITY, AND CHANGE

Outline

In chapter 10 we defined the concept of organizational culture and considered how it is studied in the field of organizational communication. Among the issues raised in the last chapter was management's interest in promoting a productive work culture in which employees labor in pursuit of organizational goals such as survival and profit. Also, we drew attention to the existence of subcultures within organizations. Management's interests in controlling culture and the needs and concerns of various subcultural groups form the essence of this chapter. Our purpose in this chapter is to focus on the struggles for cultural control that exist among various groups in organizations and some of the major factors in workplace diversity that influence these struggles.

Cultural Control

It should certainly be clear from the last chapter that organizational culture involves much more than simply defining the work process and roles of the organization. Consequently, many different forces and constituencies attempt to shape culture, sometimes by design, sometimes by accident. One aspect of this struggle is management's attempt to create and sustain a productive work culture. Another aspect of this struggle relates to the increasing diversity of the workforce in the U.S. Over the last twenty years women, racial and ethnic minorities, and the physically challenged have joined organizations in increasing numbers. The increased presence of these various group members has brought with it an increase in struggles for power within organizations. An important part of this power struggle is creating and sustaining a workplace culture that meets the needs of diverse members. Each group wants to be recognized, respected, and empowered to accomplish individual and organizational goals. Each group also has interests and views that can influence the overall culture of the organization. Given these observations, this chapter will proceed as follows. First, we will examine the concept of cultural control. Cultural control will be viewed both from the perspective of management's interests and the interests of various employee groups. Second, we will examine the issue of workplace diversity. In this section, we consider the needs and concerns of women, racial and ethnic minorities, the physically challenged, and employees of different age groups. Finally, we offer our reflections on the likely changes that will result in organizational culture as the needs of diverse members are integrated into the workplace.

Limits of Managerial Action

There are a number of ways to address the issue of cultural control. One way is to focus on management's attempts to control organizational culture. Indeed, when the traditionalist concept of organizational culture was first popularized, it was so novel and attractive that it quickly became the newest cure-all in corporate America's search for excellence. Many management and communication consultants began to talk to their clients about "changing corporate culture" with an emphasis on managerial control of the culture's objective features. However well-intentioned this idea may be, the concept of cultural change through management direction has been questioned. For example, the October 17, 1983, issue of *Fortune* magazine carried this revealing cover headline: "The Culture Vultures: Can They Help Your Company?" The cover story inside pointed out that change in organizational culture involves many factors that are *not* controlled by unilateral management decisions (Uttal, 1983). As the "vulture" metaphor implies, the article took an uncharitable view of consultants who are telling executives to attempt large-scale change in organizational culture.

Eisenberg and Goodall (1993) also provide us with insight into the traditionalist perspective on changing organizational culture. They make reference to a financial firm in Boston that "bought" a culture from a consulting firm. Managers within this firm were provided with slogan buttons and award plaques to distribute to employees at appropriate times. A new policy of casual dress at work was also instituted. The employees were forced to comply with this culture, even though many considered it a corporate joke. Eventually, the new culture was abandoned, "but not until after it had seriously damaged the organization through turnover and ill-will among employees toward the managers" (Eisenberg & Goodall, 1993, p. 150).

The preceding example shows what can happen when culture is treated as a commodity—something that can be bought and sold to naive workers. Managers can pursue a number of different options, however, in their attempt to influence or control an organization's culture. For example, in chapter 4 we explained that systems of concertive control emerge within decentralized organizations when top management produces a value-based corporate vision that is intended to serve as a guide for member behavior and decision making. The value and factual premises linked to this vision statement are accepted by employees in exchange for incentives such as continued employment, wages, and salary (Papa, Auwal, & Singhal,

1996). Workers then exhibit their identification with this corporate vision when, in making a decision, they perceive the organization's values and interests as relevant in evaluating the alternatives of choice (Tompkins & Cheney, 1983).

Deal and Kennedy's (1982) ideal of a strong culture certainly has intuitive appeal, but it is important to realize that the culture of an organization arises from and can be changed by many complex economic, technological, and social forces. As we approach the turn of the century, organizational cultures are, in fact, being reshaped by such forces. Although managers and, for that matter, all organization members should plan for these changes, the changes will occur whether or not management wants them.

A more embracing view of cultural control is articulated by Dennis Mumby (1988, 1989). According to Mumby, the social construction of meaning in organizations does not occur separately from the power relations that exist among the different social groups that comprise it. Referring to Geertz's (1973) metaphor of the web, Mumby (1989) argues that the analysis of a cultural web should "be concerned not only with how it is constructed, but also with whose interests are served by virtue of that particular construction" (p. 292). Importantly, it is through communication that cultural meaning systems are created. Given the centrality of communication to the social construction of culture, what can managers do to exert their influence? Let's turn to the views of Linda Smircich (1983) to understand how managers can communicate in ways that control culture:

They may attempt to define interpretations and meanings that can become widely understood and shared by organization members so that actions are guided by a common definition of the situation. Those with power are able to influence the course of organizational development through control over valued resources and through use of symbols by which organization members mediate their experience. (p. 161)

Mumby (1989) extends this perspective by arguing that as employees talk with one another relations of domination are produced and reproduced. For example, a group of workers respond positively to a directive from their manager because they accept the fact that their cooperation is part of what it means to be a good employee. This does not mean, however, that culture always functions smoothly in an organization. The construction of culture through communication "involves a struggle over dominant interpretations of the myriad of discourses that make up a culture" (Mumby, 1989, p. 293). In other words, just because group A (e.g., management) wants group B (e.g., workers) to accept a given interpretation of a rule does not mean that group B will passively accept that interpretation. Indeed, it may offer a counter-interpretation that creates a struggle for power within the organization. The example presented by Eisenberg and Goodall (1993) in which employees forced management to abandon their "purchased culture" shows just how such a power struggle can take place.

Of course, managers and corporate owners are often able to influence the interpretations and meanings formed by their subordinates. As Mumby (1989) explains, "certain dominant groups are able to frame the interests of competing groups within their own particular world-view" (p. 293). Van Maanen and Kunda (1989) also advocate this view. They explain that senior managers influence work culture in the following ways: codification of values and beliefs, promotion of interaction and close ties among employees, taking care of newcomers through socialization activities, and carefully monitoring the extent to which corporate values, norms and practices are received and put into use by employees. It is in this context that *ideology* plays a key role in the meaning formations that emerge within organizations, so let's take a look at what is meant by this term.

Ideology

The concept of *ideology* refers to the body of ideas that reflect the social needs or worldview of an individual, group, or culture. There are two approaches to understanding ideology: *interest theory* and *strain theory*. From the perspective of interest theory, ideologies emerge "against the background of a continuous struggle between various groups who vie for power in society; the most powerful group is the one which is able to institutionalize its own particular world-view or ideology" (Mumby, 1989, p. 294). Obviously, managers are often able to institutionalize their ideologies because of their control over rewards and punishments that are meaningful to employees. Strain theory takes the perspective that people accept a particular ideology because it provides them with the means of dealing with the strains associated with a social role. So a subordinate may accept a manager's interpretation of a work rule because it both meets the manager's expectation of what "good performance is" (thereby enhancing the manager's evaluation of the subordinate), and it prevents a troublesome conflict from surfacing between the two organizational members.

When managers attempt to persuade workers to adopt certain values, norms, and ideas about what is good, important, and praiseworthy within an organization, they are engaging in a form of ideological control (Alvesson, 1993). The ideologies advocated by management justify certain principles, actions, and feelings and discourage others (Alvesson, 1987; Czarniawska-Joerges, 1988). For example, managers within an organization may persuade workers to internalize a commitment to producing products of high quality. They are persuaded to do so because the production of high-quality products helps to ensure organizational survival, increases corporate profits, and results in positive employee performance evaluations.

Although managers are often able to influence ideology formation within organizations, resistant meanings can also surface. As Giddens (1979) argues, all power relations are reciprocal. He uses the term *dialectic of control* to account for this phenomenon. What Giddens means by this is that every social actor within a system has the capacity to exercise power and control. Even if managers within an organization dominate ideology formation, counter-meanings can surface to challenge their dominance. One group can not impose an ideology on another without expecting some sort of challenge. As Mumby (1989) argues, alternative, resistant interpretations are always possible.

Organizational Culture and Diversity

The emergence of alternative, resistant ideologies is more likely to occur when an organization employs members who have different perspectives or worldviews. This is where the issue of *workplace diversity* comes into play. The commonly held interpretation of workplace diversity is that diversity exists when an organization employs members of different demographic characteristics. The demographic characteristics most often linked to programs of workplace diversity are gender, race and ethnicity, age, and physical ability. So a diverse organization is one that employs (a) men and women, (b) members of African, Asian, European, and Latin American descent, (c) young, middle-aged, and older workers, and (d) people with a range of physical abilities and challenges. We would like to add a component to the diversity definition, however, namely, that diversity involves not only variation in demographics but also variation in modes of thinking, feeling, and acting.

We certainly believe that all people should have equal access to organizations. Indeed, many of those who champion workplace diversity point to the historical discrimination that made it difficult for women, members of racial and ethnic minorities, older workers, and physically challenged people to find meaningful employment. When an organization opens access to members formerly denied entry, that is just part of what workplace diversity is, however. As mentioned in chapter 4, contemporary organizations operate in an increasingly complex and global environment. In order to succeed in this environment, organizations need creative thinkers who approach issues or problems from a multiplicity of perspectives. So diversity is not just about different demographic characteristics; it is about differences in thinking and behavior that can help firms to compete in a global economy (Conrad, 1994; Cox, 1993; Gardner, Peluchette, & Clinebell, 1994). An organization that employs people from different demographic backgrounds does not experience the benefits of diversity if all these diverse members think and behave the same way. Differences in worldviews or differences in approaches to problem solving are what organizations need to thrive in a rapidly changing world. Of course, an organization is more likely to experience the benefits of diversity if it employs people with different demographic characteristics. But what needs to be promoted within corporate walls are differences in thinking and behavior. Now that we have provided our views of what workplace diversity is, let's turn to a discussion of how workplace diversity can influence and change organizational culture.

The agents of change in organizational culture include not only top management but also middle- and lower-level management, various labor groups, the divisions and departments of the organization, occupational groups, political coalitions, the community, and the environment in which the organization functions. These agents sometimes work in harmony, sometimes conflict sharply, and generally coexist in a dynamic tension and interplay that shape the culture of the organization. To say that the culture of an organization is based on a commonly held frame of reference for interpreting and acting toward one another does not mean that everyone in the organization is the same or that members have the same values and commitments. This point is especially important because the most undeniably relentless source of change at the moment is the increasing diversity of people who make up the workplace. Many leaders in business, industry, education, and government began for the first time to pay serious attention to this issue with the 1987 publication of *Workforce 2000*, a study that predicted radical changes in the composition of the twenty-first century American workplace due primarily to the entry of vast numbers of women and minorities into the labor market. No one expected in 1987 that these changes **would start occurring before the turn of the century.** In fact, *Workforce 2000* is already arriving in the 1990s. Accommodating the concerns of these new members and dealing with the problems that arise from differences between the new and old as well as between different groups of the new have transformed the problem of "changing corporate culture" from cultural engineering to diversity management **and learning how to value diversity.** A review of some of the key issues brought on by diversity of gender, race, ethnicity, physical ability, and age in the workplace illustrates just how complex **the process of valuing and managing** diversity will be and how attention to communication will figure into the process.

Gender

As college students we can remember seeking summer employment in companies where it was, however illegally, still tacitly understood that "only able-bodied men need apply." Those days are over forever. In 1992, women comprised 46 percent of the total American labor force (Bureau of Labor Statistics, 1992), and by 2005 they are expected to constitute 48 percent (*Occupational Handbook,* 1994–1995). The transformation of the workplace from a predominantly male to a mixed gender environment has compelled organizations to address and make decisions about issues such as company-sponsored day care, redesign of benefits, and creative work scheduling. Three of the most important issues are the prevalence of sexual harassment, the "Glass Ceiling," and the contentious question of differences between women and men in styles of leadership and communication.

Sexual Harassment

We can cite the numerous studies on sexual harassment, but the results generally are consistent. Sexual harassment is pervasive in the American workplace, and women usually are the victims. Wagner (1992) summarizes several surveys in which 70 to 90 percent of working women report having experienced conditions that constitute sexual harassment according to the Equal Employment Opportunity Commission definition.

Under the EEOC definition, illegal sexual harassment takes two forms: *quid pro quo* and hostile environment (Wagner, 1992). *Quid pro quo* (this for that) harassment occurs when employment conditions such as raises, promotions, or job security are contingent upon sexual favors. *Quid pro quo* may be overtly coercive ("If you want to keep your job, you'd better put out") or covertly suggestive ("Let's fly to Vegas for the weekend and discuss your future with the company").

Harassment in the form of a sexually hostile environment is more complicated. It may include behavior such as sexual propositions, sexual jokes, lewd comments, displays of pornographic materials, fondling, and even nonsexual actions directed at a person because of that person's sex, but it must be unwelcome and constitute an environment that a *reasonable person* would regard as offensive. Moreover, while one instance of *quid pro quo* may be enough to sustain an allegation of sexual harassment, hostile environment usually requires repetition or a general pattern of behavior.

When does a hostile environment exist? In 1986 the United States Supreme Court adopted the standard of offensiveness to a "reasonable person." In recent years this standard has been changed to "reasonable woman" by some lower courts. Women tend to differ from men in their interpretation of harassment situations, and the intent of the "reasonable woman" standard is to privilege the female interpretation over the male interpretation (Wagner, 1992). Thus, the behavior alone does not constitute harassment. Harassment is defined by a combination of behavior, the circumstances under which it occurs, and its effect on women. If the sexualized condition of the workplace is unwelcome (i.e., neither solicited nor desired) and a reasonable woman would be offended by it, it probably constitutes a "hostile environment."

Sexually hostile environment so defined casts a broad net, and one study of sexual harassment court cases occurring after 1986 found that 75 percent involved hostile environment claims. At least one case, *Robinson v. Jacksonville Shipyards,* has generated heated debate over whether this net has become too broad.

Jacksonville Shipyards apparently had every condition that might conceivably be construed as sexually hostile: everything from sex-oriented conversations, pornographic literature, and display of nude pinups to sexual taunting and hazing. Some of this behavior was specifically targeted at the six female employees in the 850-person company. Some of it was not, but all of it contributed to the environment. When the women complained about that environment, the situation actually got worse. So one of the women, Lois Robinson, took legal action.

The sexual taunting that was directed toward Robinson was so outrageous that we will not print it in this text. We can tell you that the most explicit lyrics in songs by controversial rock and rap music artists just about match some of the comments to which Robinson was subjected. In ruling on Robinson's case, however, the court not only responded to actions targeted at Robinson but also ordered fundamental changes in other areas of male behavior at the shipyard, including tight restrictions on the kinds of photographic and reading materials that could be brought into the workplace.

The American Civil Liberties Union (ACLU) initially argued that the court's application of the "reasonable woman" standard in *Robinson* is so sweeping in its restrictions that the remedies violate First Amendment rights. *Glamour* magazine (April, 1992) reported that the Florida ACLU, led by Robyn Blumner, was seeking to overturn the decision in *Robinson*. Nadine Strossen, ACLU's national president, told the 1992 convention of the Speech Communication Association that the national ACLU opposes some aspects of the *Robinson* decision but accepts others. At that time, the national ACLU and its Florida chapter apparently agreed that mere offensiveness does not warrant prohibition of behavior; behavior must be *targeted* at the offended party in order to qualify as sexual harassment. In April, 1993, however, the national ACLU board voted after a heated and divisive debate to abandon the targeted behavior concept in favor of a broader definition of harassment and, according to *The New York Times,* took the position that "Courts should make it easier for women to bring harassment complaints" (Lewis, 1993, p. 12). A court test of the ACLU position may help to clarify what does—or does not—constitute sexual harassment. Such a test may be provided when the Supreme Court hears *Harris v. Forklift Systems,* where a lower court ruled that sexual jokes were not harassment because they caused neither harm nor interference with job performance. For the moment, it is very clear that you cannot do something such as put a pornographic photo with a sexual proposition couched in vulgar language on a co-worker's office desk to taunt that person. Whether you can play songs with explicit lyrics on your portable CD for your own amusement during lunch break remains to be seen.

Glass Ceiling

Women not only constituted 46 percent of the workforce in 1992 but also held 42 percent of all management positions (Bureau of Labor Statistics, 1992). Yet, while half of all entry-level managers are female, women fill only 3 percent of senior executive positions, a miniscule share of upper-management jobs that reflects little change from the 1 percent share held by women in 1981 (Segal, 1992). Thus, women can see the top, but they are still excluded from positions there—a condition known as the "Glass Ceiling."

Is the Glass Ceiling a result of *de facto* sex discrimination or a condition that exists only because large numbers of women are still in the process of gaining the experiences that ultimately will bring promotions and parity in senior management? Opinions vary. Marion Sandler, president of Golden West Financial Corporation, says, "It's the power structure that doesn't allow women entry." But Carleton Fiorina, a vice president with AT&T responds, "I've never felt that my sex has been a disadvantage to me. . . . No one can expect to be handed power." Both women were quoted in a 1992 *Business Week* article by A. T. Segal, and both probably are reflecting accurately their personal experiences. In either case, Segal makes the point that the 1990s should be "a breakout decade for women" (p. 74). That is to say, if the lack of parity really is attributable to factors other than sex discrimination, then we should see many more women assuming senior positions over the next few years because a critical mass of women will have the experience and accomplishments generally expected for admission to the top echelons of business, industry, government, and education. If a substantial change in female representation at senior management levels does not occur within the next few years, *de facto* sex discrimination will be the only plausible explanation.

As the situation stands at the moment, many women executives are frustrated with the Glass Ceiling. A Harris survey of 400 women executives in April, 1992, found that more than half of them feel that women's progress in American companies actually has slowed down and that women do not have the same chance as men to be promoted. Two out of every three women executives believe that a male-dominated corporate culture is an obstacle to their success, three out of four say women should take legal action against discrimination, and four out of five favor creating and using women's networks to help each other (Vamos, 1992).

Feminine Styles of Leadership and Communication

Are there general characteristics that can be said to define feminine styles of leadership and communication that one would expect to be more consistently exhibited by women than by men? If so, then such a difference between men and women suggests a more provocative question: Are these feminine styles more conducive than masculine styles to the effective management of organizations?

Whatever the behavioral similarities between men and women may be, there is one difference "on which virtually every expert and study agree: Men are more aggressive than women. It shows up in 2-year-olds . . . persists into adulthood. . . . And there is little doubt that it is rooted in biology" (McLoughlin, 1988, p. 56). It is this difference that prompts questions about the possibility of gender differences in leadership and communication styles.

Sally Helgesen (1990) not only contends that women do differ from men in their ways of leadership but also calls this difference "the female advantage." Helgesen is neither the first nor the only scholar to advance this argument. During the 1980s, feminist theorists relied on the presumption of a "feminine difference" to promote an agenda for nonhierarchical, democratic, collective life in organizations (e.g., Ferguson, 1984). As early as 1979, Baird and Bradley found that employees perceived the communication styles of female managers to be more open and receptive than those of male managers and suggested that the findings for females are more consistent with the requirements of modern management methods. Burrell, Buzzanell, and McMillan (1992) also cite some studies of gender differences in conflict management where women are found to be less competitive, more accommodating, and more willing than men to share power and discuss diverse viewpoints.

If these findings point to a "feminine" style of leadership and communication, its elements would be more consistent than a competitive, aggressive "masculine" style with the human resource development ideal of participative management, but most studies report either no differences between men and women in leadership positions or that gender has a trivial, almost nonexistent influence on that behavior. In a recent and comprehensive review of quantitative studies on this question, Wilkins and Andersen (1991) stated, "It can be safely concluded that *there is no meaningful difference in the behavior of male and female managers*" (p. 27).

How does one explain the inconsistency of research findings on the question of gender differences in styles of leadership and communication? Burrell and colleagues suggest that quantitative studies of conflict management may simply fail to reveal important differences or that women may be obliged to subordinate their preferred feminine style to requirements of aggressive, male-dominated situations. This second explanation has been advanced by a number of feminist writers (Marshall, 1984, 1993; Natalle, Papa, & Graham, 1994; Sheppard, 1989). As Judi Marshall (1993) explains, male behaviors represent the norm to which organizational members must adapt. Women copy the behaviors of men in order to gain acceptance and succeed in their careers. If this is indeed the case, organizations are losing out on the benefits of gender diversity in the workplace. As argued earlier, the benefits of diversity are experienced only when diverse members are encouraged to think and behave according to their own unique perspectives.

The prevalence of sexual harassment, women's resentment about the Glass Ceiling, and a potentially divisive debate over which sex is best equipped for management make gender alone a confounding problem in the management of diversity. Sexual harassment must be addressed by active programs of prevention, investigation, and, where warranted, disciplinary action against offenders. Dialogue between women and men about the conditions and effects of harassment might also be appropriate, but such a dialogue would require that women's inter-pretations cannot automatically be privileged over men's interpretations in defin-ing harassment. Breaking the Glass Ceiling requires the same commitment to development of female management talent that has been devoted to male man-agement talent followed by equitable treatment in promotion practices. Importantly, developmental efforts targeted at women managers must recognize, value and promote the thoughts and behaviors that distinguish women from men. As for differences between women and men in communication, we need to create and sustain organizational cultures that value differences rather than supress them.

Women, Feminist Philosophy, and Cultural Change

Classifying values as "male" or "female" may involve a certain degree of stereo-typing, and members of either gender may internalize values attributed to the other, but feminist writers have argued that there are characteristic value differ-ences between men and women. We introduced three central values of feminist organization theory in chapter 4 (cooperative enactment, integrative thinking, and connectedness). We are expanding on feminist theory here to illustrate how diver-sity of ideas and values can enhance organizational cultures.

Marshall (1993) explains that male values are characterized by "self-assertion, separation, independence, control, competition, focused perception, rationality, analysis, clarity, discrimination, and activity" (p. 124). The underlying themes linked to male values include a self-assertive tendency, a desire to control the envi-ronment, and a focus on personal and interpersonal processes. Female values are characterized by "interdependence, cooperation, receptivity, merging, acceptance, awareness of patterns, wholes and contexts, emotional tone, personalistic percep-tion, being, intuition, and synthesizing" (p. 124). The underlying themes linked to these values are openness to the environment, interconnection, and mutual devel-opment. Buzzanell (1993), another feminist scholar, argues that four feminist themes are relevant to organizational communication: cooperation; caring and con-cern for relationships and community; viewing humans as significant holistic beings; and recognizing the value of pursuing possibilities and alternatives.

When such themes are considered in light of the moral and ethical teachings of major religious movements such as Judaism, Islam, Christianity, and Buddhism, it is obvious that the supporting values of caring, respect, human dignity, and coop-eration are hardly unique to twentieth-century feminist theory. Yet institutionalized religions often seem to function as cold bureaucracies. The point of feminist the-ory is to escape from the entrapments of a bureaucratic life-world that feminists regard as male constructed. So how would an organization that embraced feminine values be different from an organization that espoused only male values? Also, what are the potential advantages to embracing feminine values?

By focusing on the values and themes identified by Marshall (1993) and Buzzanell (1993, 1994), we can gain some insights into what working for a "fem-inist" organization would be like. First, workers would be encouraged to cooper-ate with one another to reach individual and organizational goals rather than to compete against one another for limited rewards. In order to encourage such a cooperative environment, organizational members may need to think of structures other than pyramids with multilayered hierarchical forms of control. For example,

Peters (1987) has proposed organizational structures that resemble circles with permeable boundaries and self-designing functional linkages. Alternatively, Weick and Browning (1991) discuss the possibility of self-organizing forms that evolve as the environment changes. Finally, Buzzanell (1994) recommends engaging in consensus processes for negotiating decisions where there is minimal rule use, little differentiation among members, and value-based rather than reward-based incentives.

Part of creating a cooperative environment within an organization is placing an emphasis on interconnections between people and groups. Feminists believe that people are more likely to accomplish their goals through working cooperatively with others. Thus, people from different departments may be encouraged to work collaboratively on a problem because each member has some specific expertise or a unique perspective on how the problem should be addressed. The concept of mutual development can also be linked to cooperation and interconnectedness. Feminists posit that workers can grow and develop together if a supportive environment is created in which they are encouraged to combine their talents with others to reach mutual goals. This perspective is in stark contrast to the ethic of "competitive individualism" that dominates most bureaucracies. As Buzzanell (1994) explains, "At the heart of the competitive orientation is the need to excel over others, to stand out against the performance of others, and to distinguish oneself publicly by seeing others fail" (p. 345).

In order for a cooperative environment to exist within an organization, all members must exhibit care and concern for relationships with others. This means sustaining an organizational culture in which members care about one another's needs and concerns and provide help for each other. In this cooperative culture, workers recognize that their professional development and their satisfaction with the organization are tied to establishing and sustaining helpful and caring relationships with others.

The sort of cooperative workplace culture envisioned by many feminists is not one which privileges any particular ideology over any other. So conflict between members is an expected reality (an issue discussed more extensively in chapter 13). Rather than supress conflict because it interferes with "getting the job done," feminist researchers advocate bringing conflict out into the open and re-evaluating issues in a search for common ground (Putnam, 1990). Furthermore, for conflict to be managed successfully, organizational members need to learn threat-reducing strategies, integrative decision making, and nondefensive conflict-reduction techniques (Pearson, 1981). The emphasis on reducing threats and engaging in nondefensive communication, however, does not mean supressing emotions in the workplace. On the contrary, emotions are one of the ways in which we view the world. As Ferguson (1984) explains, "We need the connection to the world that emotion allows in order to reflect on and evaluate the world" (p. 199). Thus, feminist theorists emphasize the importance of sustaining organizational environments in which members can express their emotions (Mumby & Putnam, 1992).

Another aspect of feminist philosophy that has implications for organizational communication theorizing is viewing human beings as significant holistic beings. For example, women recognize that the boundaries between work life and personal life are fluid. This means that the workplace is an arena for work *and* personal relationships and that members must have time to balance family/personal needs with work needs (Chester & Grossman, 1990). For example, in the attempt to help professors balance work and family roles, Harvard University has recently implemented two policies. First, faculty members in the Arts and Sciences may request up to six months of relief from teaching with full pay for each child they have (up to two children). In addition, for each child they have, faculty members can put off the review for their next promotion for a year (Wilson, 1995).

Care and concern for the community and the environment are also linked to feminist philosophy. Devoting resources (e.g., personnel and money) for community development projects, homeless shelters, child abuse programs, and battered women's shelters are some of the ways that organizations can help improve the communities in which they operate. Also, feminists advocate paying careful attention to the potentially damaging effects of organizational operations on the environment. For example, many feminists argue that science which neglects social responsibility is unacceptable (Schiebinger, 1987). Given this stance, it would be considered unacceptable for a timber company to harvest an old growth forest without considering the impact of its efforts on local wildlife. Also, if some environmentally sound harvesting was performed by the timber company, it would be considered imperative to replace the trees that were harvested with seedlings to promote new growth in the forest.

Finally, one of the greatest strengths of feminist philosophy is its emphasis on enlarging what is considered possible within organizations and encouraging creative thinking about alternatives (Buzzanell, 1993). This aspect of feminist philosophy links up with our earlier observation about diversity in thinking and behavior. The diverse organization embraces differences rather than rejects them. Every employee should be encouraged to submit new ideas and approaches for accomplishing tasks. Discussions that challenge the very nature of what the organization is and what goals it should pursue need to occur on an ongoing basis. Only through considering all possibilities and alternatives can organizations remain responsive to their environment and change to meet new demands.

In this general overview of key aspects of feminist philosophy, one can see the possibilities for organizational change as women's voices are allowed to resonate more clearly within corporations. One of the key problems confronting women and organizational communication researchers is how to "surface repressed voices and how to enable them to express themselves in the face of dominant groups embedded within current power structures" (Poole, 1994, p. 272). Now that we have considered the possibilities for cultural change that are linked to women's participation and integrating aspects of feminist philosophy into the workplace, let's turn to a discussion of racial and ethnic diversity in organizations.

Race and Ethnicity

If women are concerned about breaking through the Glass Ceiling, members of racial and ethnic minority groups are worried about getting through the door of the workplace and being able to remain once they have arrived. The condition of minorities is reflected rather ironically in the fact that 97 percent of all *female* managers are white. Only 1 percent are African American, and 2 percent are members of other minorities (Baskerville, 1991). Alvin Poussaint, a Harvard psychiatrist, said in 1992 that African Americans as a group actually are worse off today than at any other time since the 1960s. While affirmative action programs have helped "millions of African-Americans to enter the mainstream economy," millions more have been left in the ghetto (Morganthau et al., 1992, p. 21). In 1982, Sir Arthur Lewis warned that "extended joblessness . . . will destroy the black American community unless something drastic is done to ease it" (Board of Economists' Report, 1992, p. 196). By 1992, a decade after Lewis' warning, the situation was so serious that 43 percent of all African American children lived in poverty and nearly one-fourth of young black men were in jail, on probation, or on parole (Morganthau et al., 1992). The only good news for African Americans is that their representation in the workforce is expected to increase 28 percent by 2000. The numbers of Asians and Hispanics in the workforce is projected to increase by 81 percent and 75 percent, respectively (Myers & Lambert, 1990). Collectively, these three groups will account for 35 million workers by 2000.

Employment projections for Native Americans do not even appear in any of the data that we have seen. Although two million people in this country are legally identified as Native Americans, they are treated in many respects as America's invisible people. We did find out that about 21,000 business firms in this country are owned by Native Americans, compared with over 422,000 by Hispanics, 424,000 by African Americans, and over 2.6 million by women (Bureau of the Census, 1992). Even when the relatively small size of the Native American population is taken into account, Native Americans are far worse off than other minorities and women in business ownership, and we suspect that the same may be said for Native American employment in general.

As for those minorities who are at least not invisible, there is a real possibility that they will confront insidious forms of racism, hostility, and even hatred as their numbers increase in the workplace. While everyone would like to think that the kind of racism that embroiled Cincinnati Reds' owner Marge Schott in controversy late in 1992 is no longer typical in America, former baseball commissioner Fay Vincent reportedly said that the Schott incident proves that baseball reflects the racism that exists throughout our society. It was convenient in the 1960s and 1970s to see racism only as a southern problem, but racially motivated murders in the East and race riots in the West belie that myth. From New York to Cincinnati to Los Angeles, bigotry tears at the community fabric in every region of the nation.

A report by Charlene Solomon (1992a) on hatred in the workplace paints a despicable picture of the treatment that often is accorded to racial and ethnic minorities and to people of gay and lesbian sexual orientations. The behaviors range from racial slurs (not only in conversations but also in hate mail, graffiti, and even hate faxes) to sabotage of computer files or work projects, and even outright physical assaults.

All three authors of this text have observed personally these kinds of behaviors in organizations. For example, one of us was involved in a consulting project with a nationally prominent insurance company when a group of white managers joked in the office lunch room on Martin Luther King Day. One manager said to his two collegues that instead of celebrating Martin Luther King Day, they should be celebrating James Earl Ray Day (Ray was King's assassin). This comment was said loudly enough to be overhead clearly by some African American employees who responded by laughing nervously. The unfortunate pervasiveness of such clear bigotry has led many researchers to paint a rather bleak picture of workplace culture in the U.S. Indeed, Howard Erlich of the National Institute Against Prejudice and Violence says, "The workplace probably is going to be the major site of ethnoviolent conflict throughout the 1990s" (Solomon, 1992a, p. 30).

Solomon offers four basic recommendations that organizations can implement in order to prevent or at least reduce hatred in the workplace:

1. Have clear standards for acceptable behavior and monitor the culture for unacceptable behaviors that require intervention, especially those with the potential to escalate into violence.
2. Supervisors need to be able to call upon a management team for help. This team might consist of human resources, security, and employee assistance staff.
3. Have a consulting psychologist available.
4. Provide counseling or additional training for "toxic" supervisors who provoke high levels of frustration and hostility among employees.

Controversies and Possible Solutions

Ethnic and racial minority group members in the U.S. have reported a number of significant problems in workplace culture that need to be addressed by managers, consultants, and researchers. For example, one African American executive in the transportation industry reported that his new boss greeted him at their first meeting with the statement: "The South should have won the war" (Leinster, 1988, p. 118). More pervasive, however, is dealing with the assumption that minority group members can not perform as well as their white colleagues or, if they do perform at high levels, it is considered surprising. H. Naylor Fitzhugh, former PepsiCo vice-president, provided an excellent example of dealing with these assumptions. He recalled a business colleague congratulating him for his ideas and then "just as often saying, 'It's hard to remember you're black.' Now that's hardly a compliment" (Leinster, 1988, p. 118).

Other minority group members focus on the pressure of being under constant observation. For example, consider the comments of Gary Jefferson, an African American, who is vice-president of the Midwest Region of United Airlines. He stated, "It's always catastrophic when a black fails. Individual blacks have got to be allowed to fail without everybody thinking that all blacks screwed up. Whites are allowed that" (Leinster, 1988, p. 118).

Part of the rage felt by many minority group members is related directly to their experiences in U.S. organizations. Cose (1993) recently interviewed an African American corporate attorney who shared a story reflective of his workplace experiences. Despite having brought millions of dollars into the firm the year before, he felt he was not receiving his due. To make his point he referred to an experience that happened a few days earlier. When he arrived at work early one morning, he entered the elevator with a white junior staff attorney. When the two attorneys exited the elevator on the same floor, the white attorney turned around and blocked the path of the African American, saying, "May I help you?" He tried to pass, only to be stopped again with the same question, this time in a louder voice. The African American spat out his name, identified himself as a partner in the firm, and the junior staff attorney quickly stepped aside. Sadly, this successful African American attorney no longer expects praise, honor, or acceptance from his white collegues. Rather, he concluded, "Just make sure my money is at the top of the line. I can go to my own people for acceptance" (Cose, 1993, p. 56).

Although African Americans have been burdened by particularly humiliating experiences in U.S. organizations, other groups have suffered as well. In newly diversified organizations, many problems can arise that influence different racial and ethnic groups, and women as well. In an ethnography entitled "It's Like a Prison in There," Zak (1994) addresses the communication problems that can occur in newly diversified organizations. Zak included an example from the vehicle maintenance unit of a large company. This unit had recently become more demographically diverse by hiring people from different racial and ethnic groups and class levels as well as integrating more women. Unfortunately, leading veteran employees (mostly white males) asserted their power through horseplay and shoptalk that was traditionally used to maintain hierarchy and control in this workplace. In response to the conflicts that surfaced between the newcomers and the veterans, management increased its surveillance of the workers and enforced punitive policies, which led to a fragmented and dysfunctional organization. Zak attributed this outcome to management's failure to promote "communication processes through which shared or negotiated meaning and agreed-upon language and behaviors appropriate to the new workplace could be constructed" (p. 282). Indeed, in this study Zak found that worker race, ethnicity, and gender accounted for differences in language and behaviors among the employees. Until these workers figure out how to understand their differences and similarities, their problems will likely continue.

In dealing with problems and controversies such as those described above, managers need to keep in mind the many reasons that support workplace diversity programs. Companies need to diversify their workforce "to best utilize the country's labor pool and to lure a changing consumer base" (Lowery, 1995, p. 150). J. T. Childs Jr., director of workforce diversity at IBM stated, "It [workplace diversity] may have been a moral issue 30 years ago. Today, it is a strategic issue" (Lowery, 1995, p. 150). Conrad (1994) also addressed this issue when observing that diversity in the workplace will help American organizations compete successfully in a global economy.

Affirmative Action Misconceptions

Perhaps one of the greatest controversies surrounding the hiring, development, and advancement of racial and ethnic minorities in U.S. companies is the issue of *affirmative action*. The term "affirmative action" was coined by President Lyndon B. Johnson in 1965 when he issued Executive Order 11246. This order prohibited federal agencies from contracting with firms that were not committed to affirmative action. What was meant by this term was that companies must engage in "vigorous efforts to bring people of color into jobs from which they had previously been excluded" (American Civil Liberties Union, 1995, p. 1).

The American Civil Liberties Union (ACLU) has discussed four major misconceptions that have been associated with affirmative action over the years. First, affirmative action is often linked to quota systems. In fact, quotas are illegal. In some organizations, however, biased hiring and promotion practices have been so pronounced that courts have had to exercise their power under the Civil Rights Act of 1964. Hiring goals and timetables have been included among the enforced remedies. These goals and timetables estimate the number of women and minority group members who would be hired if there were no discrimination. Although some affirmative action critics insist on calling these mechanisms "quotas," such a stance can not be justified. Hiring goals and timetables are "flexible, remedial instruments of *inclusion,* while quotas were used historically to *ex*clude members of some ethnic groups from workplaces and educational institutions" (American Civil Liberties Union, 1995, p. 2).

Another misconception associated with affirmative action is that it promotes preferential treatment. It is true that preference programs have been created for affirmative action purposes. Berkman (1995) discusses a Library of Congress study that yielded a thirty-two-page list of laws and regulations granting preferences based on race, gender, national origin, or ethnicity. Some preference programs, for example, a gender preference policy used by the Federal Communications Commission in awarding radio station licenses, are being overturned by courts (Veraldi, 1993). But one may question whether such programs really are preferential in the usual sense of the word. The ACLU says that affirmative action is "an equalizer that accommodates people whose gender and color have long been viewed as proxies for incompetence" (American Civil Liberties Union, 1995, p. 2). In order to clarify this point, let's consider an example.

Two job candidates, one African American and the other white, apply for the same position. On paper their credentials are identical; however, they have earned those credentials through very different life experiences. From birth, the African American has had to contend with various forms of racial discrimination. Conversely, the white was raised in a society that favors whites, giving him a built in advantage from birth. Arguing that these two candidates have the same credentials glosses over the fact that the African American applicant traveled a much harder road to get where he is. These applicants are also different in the way they are perceived by those who will interview them. Indeed, many African American applicants are often given less interview time than white applicants with similar credentials (American Civil Liberties Union, 1995).

Also, about 80 percent of executives get their jobs through networking, and about 86 percent of available jobs are not listed in classified advertisements (Blumrosen, 1995). Unfortunately, people of color have been excluded from these networks because they are comprised mostly of white men. As a result, the African American applicant confronts a hiring process that privileges whites and does not test the full range of skills he or she may possess. Thus, affirmative action policies attempt to balance a scale that is tipped sharply in favor of the white candidate.

A third misconception associated with affirmative action programs is that they force employers to hire and admit unqualified people just because they are nonwhite or female. In fact, affirmative action has never been about hiring people *solely* because of their color or sex without concern for their abilities. "Rather, affirmative action guidelines require employers to make a conscientious effort to find and train *qualified* people, based on job-related standards" (American Civil Liberties Union, 1995, p. 2).

A final misconception associated with affirmative action is that reverse discrimination penalizes white males. There are two responses to this misconception. First, "Restructuring a discriminatory status quo to create a nondiscriminatory environment isn't reverse discrimination, but it may feel that way because something is being lost: White people are losing the favoritism they have enjoyed for so long" (American Civil Liberties Union, 1995, p. 2). Second, affirmative action abuses are relatively rare. One recent study conducted from 1990 to 1994 found that the problem of reverse discrimination is not widespread and that when it does occur, the courts have provided relief (Blumrosen, 1995). Furthermore, the courts have found that many people claiming reverse discrimination were actually disappointed job applicants who were less qualified for the job than the chosen female or minority applicant (Blumrosen, 1995).

A somewhat sarcastic treatment of the issue of reverse discrimination was provided by Bruning (1995):

White people love to torture themselves with the belief that when a black presents himself at an employment office, the cheering begins. Bosses tremble with excitement, kick white applicants out the door, take the honored new arrival to lunch at a four-star restaurant, enroll him in the executive health club and eagerly inquire as to his starting date. Of course, the black individual is allowed to set his salary and dictate the terms of his benefit package. Then someone runs out and leases him a BMW, and, bingo, the guy is on his way to wealth and power, and all because he has had the incredible good fortune to be born black in America! (Bruning, 1995, p. 9)

Sarcasm aside, racism in the U.S. is real and it must be handled in a variety of ways including some form of affirmative action. In 1995 the U.S. Supreme Court argued that the federal government must narrowly tailor its programs to survive strict judicial scrutiny. What this means is that courts will now carefully at an organization's past history of discrimination and how precisely its affirmative action efforts are targeted. This prevents employers from enacting programs that automatically advantage or disadvantage individuals because of their race or gender. As Susan Estrich (1995) recently argued, if we can look at affirmative action as a matter of narrowly remedying past injustices and helping those who need a helping hand, there is at least a possibility that more Americans will support these programs.

Affirmative action represents only one part of the process of integrating racial and ethnic minorities into the workplace. Other efforts are also needed for organizations to receive the benefits of having a diverse workforce. For example, in order to successfully manage diversity, groups must be willing to share power (Allen, 1995). This means that people who have historically had access to power (e.g., white males) must be willing to relinquish some control to others. Also, those groups historically excluded from positions of power (e.g., those of African, Asian, and Latin American descent) must refrain from actions that simply reverse the power imbalances that formerly existed. Once an organization is able to sustain a cultural environment in which all members have equal access to power, the advantages of workplace diversity will surface clearly. Instead of focusing on how the organization can socialize the individual to fit within a pre-existing culture, minority group members can be encouraged to innovate their work roles by engaging in behaviors that are more consistent with their cultural heritage (Allen, 1995; Van Maanen & Schein, 1979). In such a cultural environment, diversity is truly valued.

One way that organizations have attempted to grapple with the challenges of an increasingly diverse workforce is to institute programs that value diversity. These programs, usually organized by human resource departments, emphasize that people who are different should be able to maintain their cultural and ethnic identities in a pluralistic society. For example, Black and Mendenhall (1990) argue that employees need three broad skill dimensions to interact effectively with members of different racial and ethnic backgrounds: (a) skills related to the maintenance of self, mental health, psychological well-being, stress reduction, and feelings of self-confidence; (b) skills related to the fostering of relationships with people of different cultural backgrounds; and (c) cognitive skills that promote a correct perception of the other culture.

On the more specific issue of race relations training, Foeman (1991) contends that interpersonal processes must be emphasized to create a productive work culture where diversity is valued. In her review of race relations training programs, she found that successfull programs, tend to espouse five interpersonal objectives. First, trainees need to discuss race related issues in order to clear up misunderstandings and myths linked to positions on controversial subjects. Second, each racial group needs to articulate its views on issues that concern it about the workplace. Third, these views need to be examined carefully by all members. Fourth, each racial group needs to find validity in the perspectives advanced by members of other racial groups. Finally, the perspectives advanced by each racial group must be valued and used so that all organizational members can work more effectively toward common goals.

Although many race relations training programs are improving the nature of inter-racial communication within organizations, further research is necessary to help promote understanding and racial harmony in the work place. As Kim and Sharkey (1995) noted, people from different racial and cultural backgrounds "bring different meanings, value assumptions, and discourse styles into the workplace conversation" (p. 33). These differences can lead to communication breakdowns and they can threaten a common orientation to organizational goals (Fine, 1991). Workers must learn to become more openminded and accepting of other people's viewpoints. Also, workers need to manage conversations with diverse members more sensitively by taking the time to listen and ask questions to check for understanding (Martin, Hecht, & Larkey, 1994). This is where additional research by organizational communication scholars is necessary. Specifically, research is needed to test and evaluate the effectiveness of race relations training programs within organizations.

There are two key issues that must be addressed in order to effectively integrate and value the contributions of racial and ethnic minorities in the workplace. First, people from different racial and ethnic backgrounds have life experiences that influence the way they think, talk, and behave. In order for people from these different backgrounds to work productively together, instructional programs are needed to increase each group's understanding of the other groups' behaviors and worldviews. Second, once intergroup understanding exists, the key to profiting from diversity is to value it. This means integrating the perspectives and behaviors of racial and ethnic minorities into the workplace so no single ideology silences the voices of those who can make important and meaningful contributions. Also, valuing diversity means that minority group members are a part of the organization's leadership team. When minority group members are fully integrated and empowered in organizations, the advantages of their membership will be felt more clearly. Merging different worldviews together can help to promote creativity in decision making. Tapping diverse national and international markets requires employing organizational members who understand the needs that exist within these markets. So although organizations will undergo changes in integrating and empowering minority group members, there are many benefits associated with these changes.

Physical Abilities

There are at least 43 million Americans with disabilities (Solomon, 1992b). Until 1992, most were effectively kept out of employment because employers had done very little to accommodate the workplace to their needs. The federal government intends to change this situation with the implementation of the Americans with Disabilities Act (ADA), "the most sweeping civil rights legislation since 1964" (Solomon, 1992b, p. 70). The ADA requires employers to make "reasonable accommodations" for the workplace needs of the disabled and prohibits discrimination against the disabled "in regard to *all* employment practices" (Barlow & Hane, 1992, p. 53).

Defining "reasonable accommodation" is, like defining sexual harassment, a process that probably will be worked out in the courts, but it is generally clear that making these accommodations will require close attention to job descriptions, supervisors' responsibilities, employee etiquette, and training programs not only for the people with disabilities but also for those who need to know what kinds of accommodations to make and how to make them.

According to Solomon, Patricia Morrissey, vice president of Employment Advisory Services, has observed rather astutely that effectiveness in complying with the ADA will center on the quality of interaction that occurs between disabled employees and those who are receiving them into the workplace. Morrissey emphasizes courtesy in interviews, provision of appropriate orientation, adapting one's communicative behavior to the nature of the disability, and assuring that the people with disabilities have appropriate access to information, tools needed for work, and physical facilities.

We would add to Morrissey's list that organization members in general can provide acceptance and support for the people with disabilities (or, for that matter, toward any other historically excluded group) as they assimilate into the workplace. The disabled endure much derision in our society, and the physically abled often react to the presence of people with disabilities with great discomfort, so sensitivity and respect will be required by all in the workplace if the people with disabilities are to realize the promise of the ADA.

Age

Age is the final major factor that is likely to present difficulties in the management of diversity. Bradford and Raines (1992) observed that the workplace of the 1990s is inhabited by three basic age groups: Traditionals, Baby Boomers, and Baby Busters. The values and needs of these three groups are not especially compatible, and organizations will need creative reconstructions of the workplace and of work processes in order to maximize the effectiveness of each group and achieve reasonable levels of mutual tolerance.

Bradford and Raines' descriptions of these three groups suggest to us that many of the potential age difficulties reside in the groups' attitudes toward one another. Traditionals, born between 1925 and 1945, are influenced by the history of catastrophic events such as the Great Depression and World War II. They tend to regard Baby Boomers as disrespectful, too blunt, yet also too "warm and fuzzy." They regard Baby Busters as impatient and unethical. Traditionals include people like former president George Bush.

Baby Boomers, born between 1946 and 1964, comprise the awesomely enormous post-World War II generation that created or, in the case of younger Boomers, grew up under the influence of the 1960s counterculture. They tend to see Traditionals as too cautious, too conservative, and inflexible, and they regard Baby Busters as selfish and manipulative. Bill and Hillary Rodham Clinton, as well as Tipper and Al Gore, are members of this generation.

Baby Busters, born between 1965 and 1975, are in numbers a much smaller generation than the generation of Boomers that preceded them. Solomon (1992c) says that Baby Busters are "not a monolithic group that can be defined by one set of principles; they're different in significant ways from the generations that came before them" (p. 52). Baby Busters do tend to bring a new set of concerns to the workplace, especially an emphasis on quality of work life, including the work environment and the nature of the work itself. They see Traditionals as rigid, old, and over-the-hill and regard Boomers as disgustingly "New Age" workaholics.

Although they are children of the counterculture, Boomers nonetheless tacitly accept many conventions that Traditionals hold as bedrock principles of work life. Baby Busters are much less likely to accept these conventions, so the arrival of Busters in the workplace presents a new set of management issues and opportunities. According to Bradford and Raines, Busters are turned off by inflexible time schedules, workaholism, and close supervision. They like to learn new things, expect praise, and want work to be fun. Rather than pressuring Busters to convert to traditional behavior, many organizations are trying to figure out how to meet their needs creatively.

Taken collectively, gender, race, ethnicity, ability, and age differences in the workplace of the twenty-first century present an almost overwhelming array of issues, questions, and novel conditions not only for management but for all organization members. It will be difficult to work through and resolve some of the issues, but diversity is not just a condition to be treated as a management problem. It is also a management opportunity. Moreover, diversity management is not just an activity to be carried out by management. All organization members will have to learn in a real sense how to manage and value diversity. Responses to some issues will be dictated by legislation and court rulings, others by the construction of management policy. We hope most will be worked out through the sort of dialogue that Mary Parker Follett envisioned among all organizational constituencies.

Summary

The influx of women, racial and ethnic minorities, and the physically challenged into the workplace continues to impact the nature of corporate culture in the U.S. In this chapter we addressed the challenges faced by different demographic groups, the contributions each group can make to organizational success, and the ways these different groups can change organizational culture by their presence and empowerment. Women face challenges such as sexual harassment and the Glass Ceiling, while racial and ethnic minorites continue to face entry and advancement barriers in many companies. Also, acts of hatred are still targeted at different minority group members while they are at work. The physically challenged face problems of access and accommodation in many companies, but the Americans with Disabilities Act seems to be ópening many doors that were formerly closed to this group. Age differences among employees also pose challenges when people of different ages must work together on projects.

In order for companies to reap the benefits of diversity, the members of different demographic groups must be valued and empowered. This means valuing and empowering women and men, racial and ethnic minority group members, the physically challenged, and workers of different ages. What corporate leaders and managers need to recognize is that the members of these various groups have different ways of viewing issues, problems and work procedures based on their particular worldviews. These differences offer limitless possibilities for creativity and innovation in the workplace as the members of different groups are empowered and encouraged to work together. Also, the globalization of the economy requires hiring people who represent the varied markets that companies are attempting to tap. There is no better way to find out about the needs and concerns of different market groups than to hire people from these groups and rely upon their expertise and experience. Organizations that value diversity by employing and empowering members of different demographic groups will experience significant changes in corporate culture as different worldviews are integrated into companies formerly dominated by a single perspective. The payoff for this diversity, however, will eventually become clear. Remember the statement we quoted earlier from J. T. Childs, Jr., director of workforce diversity at IBM: "It [workplace diversity] may have been a moral issue 30 years ago. Today it is a strategic issue."

Discussion Questions/ Activities

1. What kinds of cultural diversity issues have you encountered in your own experience? Were these issues handled effectively by everyone involved? What do you think organizations can do to address the problems and opportunities of diversity?
2. To what extent do you think leaders and executives can really control and direct organizational cultures? In your own organizational experiences, what are some of the important factors that have shaped the organizational culture?

3. How would you assess the prospects for constructing or reconstructing organizations according to feminist principles? Will this be easier to do in some kinds of organizations than in others? What are some of the factors that might influence the effectiveness of feminizing organizations?

Additional Resources

Articles/Books

Calas, M., & Smircich, L. (1991). Voicing seduction to silence leadership. *Organization Studies, 12,* 567–601.

Gilligan, C. (1982). *In a different voice.* Cambridge, MA: Harvard University Press.

Nkomo, S. M. (1992). The emperor has no clothes: Rewriting "race in organizations." *Academy of Management Review, 17,* 487–513.

Orbe, M. P. (1995). African-American communication research: Toward a deeper understanding of interethnic communication. *Western Journal of Communication, 59,* 61–78.

vanDijk, T. A. (1993). Stories and racism. In D.K. Mumby (Ed.), *Narrative and social control: Critical perspectives* (pp. 121–142).

Wharton, A. S. (1992). The social construction of race in organizations: A social identity and group mobilization perspective. *Research in the sociology of organizations, 10,* 209–264.

Web Sites

http://www.umich.edu/~itdtq/managing_diversity.html
University of Michigan, Information Technical Division, Diversity Management Program

http://www.sddt.com/~columbus/Files/ran950913.html
Ransom & Associates' statement on diversity management

http://www.occ.com/occ/WomenMinority.html
Career resources information for women and minorities

References

Allen, B. J. (1995). "Diversity" and organizational communication. *Journal of Applied Communication Research, 23,* 143–155.

Alvesson, M. (1987). *Organization theory and technocratic consciousness.* Berlin: de Gruyter.

Alvesson, M. (1993). Cultural-ideological modes of management control: A theory and a case study of a professional service company. In S. Deetz (Ed.), *Communication Yearbook 16* (pp. 3–42). Thousand Oaks, CA: Sage.

American Civil Liberties Union. (1995). *Affirmative action: Still effective, still needed in the pursuit of equal opportunity in the '90s.* New York: American Civil Liberties Union Press.

Baird, J. E., Jr., & Bradley, P. H. (1979). Styles of management and communication: A comparative study of men and women. *Communication Monographs, 46,* 101–111.

Barlow, W. E., & Hane, E. Z. (1992, June). A practical guide to the Americans with Disabilities Act. *Personnel Journal,* 53–60.

Baskerville, D. M. (1991, August). Breaking through the glass ceiling. *Black Enterprise,* 37.

Berkman, H. (1995). Many 'tentacles' to race-based federal policies. *National Law Review, 17,* A1, A29.

Black, J. S., & Mendenhall, M. (1990). Cross-cultural training effectiveness: A review and theoretical framework for future research. *Academy of Management Review, 15,* 113–136.

Blumrosen, A. A. (1995). *Affirmative action programs and claims of reverse discrimination.* New York: American Civil Liberties Union.

Board of Economists' Report (1992, June). *Black Enterprise,* 195–202.

Bradford, L. J., & Raines, C. (1992). *Twentysomething: Managing and motivating today's new work force.* New York: Master Media, Ltd.

Bruning, F. In defence of affirmative action. *Maclean's,* March 20, 1995, 9.

Bureau of the Census (1992). *Statistical Abstract of the United States, 1992.* Washington, DC: U.S. Department of Commerce.

Bureau of Labor Statistics. (1992, September). *Employment and earnings.* Washington, DC: U.S. Department of Labor.

Burrell, N. A., Buzzanell, P. M., & McMillan, J. J. (1992). Feminine tensions in conflict situations as revealed by metaphoric analyses. *Management Communication Quarterly, 6,* 115–149.

Buzzanell, P. M. (1993). Feminist approaches to organizational communication instruction. In C. Berryman-Fink, D. Ballard-Reisch, & L. H. Newman (Eds.), *Communication and sex-role socialization* (pp. 525–553). New York: Garland.

Buzzanell, P. M. (1994). Gaining a voice: Feminist organizational communication theorizing. *Management Communication Quarterly, 7,* 339–383.

Chester, N. L., & Grossman, H. Y. (1990). Introduction: Learning about women and their work through their own accounts. In H. Y. Grossman & N. L. Chester (Eds.), *The experience and meaning of work in women's lives* (pp. 1–19). Hillsdale, NJ: Lawrence Erlbaum.

Conrad, C. (1994). *Strategic communication: Toward the twenty-first century* (3rd ed.). Fort Worth, TX: Harcourt Brace Jovanovich.

Cose, E. Rage of the privileged. *Newsweek,* November 15, 1993, 56–63.

Cox, T., Jr. (1993). *Cultural diversity in organizations: Theory, research and practice.* San Francisco: Berret-Koehler.

Czarniawska-Joerges, B. (1988). *Ideological control in nonideological organizations.* New York: Praeger.

Deal, T. E., & Kennedy, A. A. (1982). *Corporate cultures: The rites and rituals of corporate life.* Reading, MA: Addison-Wesley.

Eisenberg, E. M., & Goodall, H. L., Jr. (1993). *Organizational communication: balancing creativity and constraint.* New York: St. Martin's Press.

Estrich, S. (1995). Counterpoints: An apt compromise on affirmative action. *USA Today,* 9 May, p. 9A.

Ferguson, K. E. (1984). *The feminist case against bureaucracy.* Philadelphia: Temple University Press.

Fine, M. G. (1991). New voices in the workplace: Research directions in multicultural communication. *Journal of Business Communication, 28,* 259–275.

Foeman, A. K. (1991). Managing multiracial institutions: Goals and approaches for race-relations training. *Communication Education, 40,* 255–265.

Gardner, W. L., Peluchette, J. V. E., & Clinebell, S. K. (1994). Valuing women in management: An impression management perspective of gender diversity. *Management Communication Quarterly, 8,* 115–164.

Geertz, C. (1973). *The interpretation of cultures.* New York: Basic Books.

Giddens, A. (1979). *Central problems in social theory.* London: Macmillan.

Helgesen, S. (1990). *The female advantage: Women's ways of leadership.* New York: Doubleday.

Kim, M. S., & Sharkey, W. F. (1995). Independent and interdependent construals of self: Explaining cultural patterns of interpersonal communication in multi-cultural organizational settings. *Communication Quarterly, 43,* 20–38.

Leinster, C. Black executives: How they're doing. *Fortune,* January 18, 1988, 109–120.

Lewis, N. A. (1993). At A.C.L.U., free speech balancing act. *The New York Times,* 4 April, Sec. 1, p. 12.

Lowery, M. (1995, February). The war on equal opportunity. *Black Enterprise,* 148–154.

Marshall, J. (1984). *Women managers: Travellers in a male world.* Chichester: John Wiley.

Marshall, J. (1993). Viewing organizational communication from a feminist perspective: A critique and some offerings. In S. Deetz (Ed.), *Communication Yearbook 16* (pp. 122–143). Newbury Park, CA: Sage.

Martin, J. N., Hecht, M. L., & Larkey, L. K. (1994). Conversational improvement strategies for interethnic communication: African American and European American perspectives. *Communication Monographs, 61*, 236–255.

McLoughlin, M. Men vs. women. *U.S. News & World Report,* August 8, 1988, 50–56.

Morganthau, T. et al. Losing ground. *Newsweek,* April 6, 1992, 20–23.

Mumby, D. K. (1988). *Communication and power in organizations: Discourse, ideology and domination.* Norwood, NJ: Ablex.

Mumby, D. K. (1989). Ideology & the social construction of meaning: A communication perspective. *Communication Quarterly, 37,* 291–304.

Mumby, D. K., & Putnam, L. L. (1992). The politics of emotion: A feminist reading of bounded rationality. *Academy of Management Review, 17,* 465–486.

Myers, S., & Lambert, J. (1990). *Managing cultural diversity: A trainer's guide.* Solana Beach, CA: Intercultural Development.

Natalle, E. J., Papa, M. J., & Graham, E. E. (1994). Feminist philosophy and the transformation of organizational communication. In B. Kovacic (Ed.), *New approaches to organizational communication* (pp. 245–270). Albany, NY: State University of New York Press.

Occupational Handbook 1994–1995. Washington, D.C.: U.S. Government Printing Office.

Papa, M. J., Auwal, M. A., & Singhal, A. (1996). *Organizing for social change within concertive control systems: Member identification, discursive empowerment, and the masking of discipline.* Paper presented at the annual meeting of the Eastern Communication Association. New York, NY.

Pearson, S. S. (1981). Rhetoric and organizational change: New applications of feminine style. In B. L. Forisha & B. H. Goldman (Eds.), *Outsiders on the inside: Women & organizations* (pp. 55–74). Englewood Cliffs, NJ: Prentice-Hall.

Peters, T. (1987). *Thriving on chaos: Handbook for a management revolution.* New York: Knopf.

Poole, M. S. (1994). Afterword. In B. Kovacic (Ed.), *New approaches to organizational communication* (pp. 271–277). Albany, NY: State University of New York Press.

Porn at work: Is it legal? (1992, April). *Glamour,* 130.

Putnam, L. L. (1990, April). *Feminist theories, dispute processes, and organizational communication.* Paper presented at the Arizona State University Conference on Organizational Communication: Perspectives for the 90s. Tempe, AZ.

Schiebinger, L. (1987). The history and philosophy of women in science: A review essay. In S. Harding & J. E. O'Barr (Eds.), *Sex and scientific inquiry* (pp. 7–34). Chicago: University of Chicago Press.

Segal, A. T., et al. Corporate women. *Business Week,* June 8, 1992, 74–78.

Sheppard, D. L. (1989). Organizations, power and sexuality: The image and self-image of women managers. In J. Hearn, D. L. Sheppard, P. Tancred-Sheriff, & G. Burrell (Eds.), *The sexuality of organization* (pp. 139–157). London: Sage.

Smircich, L. (1983). Studying organizations as cultures. In G. Morgan (Ed.), *Beyond method: Strategies for social research* (pp. 160–172). Beverly Hills, CA: Sage.

Solomon, C. M. (1992a, July). Keeping hate out of the workplace. *Personnel Journal,* 30–35.

Solomon, C. M. (1992b, June). What the ADA means to the disabled. *Personnel Journal,* 70–72.

Solomon, C. M. (1992c, March). Managing the baby busters. *Personnel Journal,* 52–58.

Strossen, N. (1992, October 31). The first amendment in the communication century. Speech presented at the Speech Communication Association convention, Chicago, IL.

Tompkins, P. K., & Cheney, G. (1983). The uses of account analysis: A study of organizational decision making and identification. In L. L. Putnam & M. E. Pacanowsky (Eds.), *Communication and organizations: An interpretive approach* (pp. 123–146). Beverly Hills, CA: Sage.

Uttal, B. The corporate culture vultures. *Fortune,* October 17, 1983, 66–72.

Vamos, M. N. (Ed.) Business Week/Harris executive poll. *Business Week,* June 8, 1992, 77.

Van Maanen, J., & Kunda, G. (1989). Real feelings: Emotional expression and organizational culture. In B. M. Staw & L. L. Cummings (Eds.), *Research in organizational behavior*. Vol. 11, (pp. 87–113). Greenwich, CT: JAI.

Van Maanen, J., & Schein, E. H. (1979). Toward a theory of organizational socialization. *Research in Organizational Behavior, 1,* 209–264.

Veraldi, L. (1993). Gender preferences. *Federal Communications Law Journal, 45,* 219–245.

Wagner, E. J. (1992). *Sexual harassment in the workplace.* New York: AMACOM-American Management Association.

Weick, K. E., & Browning, L. D. (1991). Fixing with the voice: A research agenda for applied communication. *Journal of Applied Communication Research, 1,* 1–19

Wilkins, B. M., & Andersen, P. A. (1991). Gender differences and similarities in management communication: A meta-analysis. *Management Communication Quarterly, 5,* 6–35.

Wilson, R. (1995). Colleges help professors balance work and family. *Chronicle of Higher Education, 62*(12), 17 November, A24.

Workforce 2000—Work and Workers for the 21st Century. (1987) Indianapolis: The Hudson Institute.

Zak, M. W. (1994). It's like a prison in there. *Journal of Business and Technical Communication, 8,* 282–298.

We began this text with the simple observation that organizations are constituted through communication. The constitutive function of communication, however, depends upon the manner in which it is used to exercise one of the most pervasive phenomena in organizational life—**power.** Russell (1983) claims that power is *the* fundamental concept in the social sciences, analogous to the place of energy in physics. The importance of power in organizational life was once expressed quite neatly, though somewhat grimly, by W. Charles Redding during some informal comments to members of the International Communication Association's organizational communication division. "We must not forget," said Redding, "that organizations run on subservience." In effect, subservience means being submissive or acting as a servant. Consequently, organizational power is tied to **status.**

Traditional Views of Status and Power

In hierarchically structured organizations, differences in members' status and power are a simple fact of life. These differences, in large part, create the "top to bottom" character of contemporary organizations. Even within groups, different members are accorded varying degrees of power and status. Just as some members of a group have more power and status than others, some groups within an organization have more prestige and are better able to exert influence than other groups.

    Status refers essentially to the rank or importance of one's position in a group. Traditionally, power has been regarded as any means or resource that one person may employ to gain compliance and cooperation from others (Secord & Backman, 1964). As Dahl (1957) expressed it, power is the capacity of actor A to get actor B to do what actor B would not otherwise do. Traditional views of power also recognize that it involves the ability to control the agenda or plan of action in a situation, to suppress issues in discussions and decision making that would pose a challenge or create controversy (Bachrach & Baratz, 1962). Status and power should not be regarded as traits that are inherent in a particular position. Generally, it is more appropriate to think of status and power as conditions that other members of the group accord to a person in a given position. The two conditions are closely related. The ability to exercise power enhances status; status enhances the ability to exercise power.

Types of Power

Status distinctions facilitate the use of power by people in higher positions to secure compliance from those in lower positions. In part, the power that actor A has over actor B is determined by B's dependence on A (Emerson, 1962). Status distinctions create barriers that reduce the dependency of those in higher positions upon those in lower positions. Such barriers help to maintain a power difference that favors the higher position.

French and Raven (1959) provided an analysis of social power that has become a classic model for classifying the forms of power applied in organizational relationships. They described five basic types of power: reward, coercive, referent, expert, and legitimate.

Reward and **coercive power** are closely related. The former involves the ability to control and apply rewards, either directly or indirectly, whereas the latter is based on the ability to control and apply punishments. One's reward or coercive power over others depends on at least two factors. First, those things that can be controlled or mediated (e.g., salary increases, promotions, work assignments, demotions, suspensions, terminations) must be perceived as rewards or punishments by others. Second, a person has these forms of power only to the extent that he or she is perceived as being willing and able to apply or at least mediate rewards and punishments. As Secord and Backman (1964) pointed out, "If a supervisor has seldom rewarded or punished an employee, either directly or indirectly, his or her reward and coercive power is likely to be weak" (p. 275).

Referent power depends on identification. Identification sometimes is defined as the desire to be like another person. In this sense, actor A has referent power with actor B to the extent that B wishes to be like A. The concepts of identification and referent power, however, are somewhat more complex. According to Kelman (1961), identification involves a desirable, satisfying, and self-defining relationship with another person or group. Consequently, a given individual or group has referent power with a person to the extent that this person engages in certain behaviors because these behaviors maintain the relationship or the definition of self that is anchored in the relationship. One form of identification occurs when one person literally models another's behavior. A second form involves different but complementary behaviors. Identification also occurs when a person adopts the attitudes and values of a self-defining group.

Expert power is based on the perception that a person possesses some special knowledge that is required to solve a problem, perform a task, or decide on a course of action. A person wields expert power with others if they follow his or her course of action in the belief that the individual "knows more" than they do about what should be done in the situation.

Legitimate power is based on acceptance of internal norms and values regarding authority and the right to exercise authority. People accept influence from someone in a certain position because they believe this person has the right to exercise the authority accorded to that position. For example, a company president might create a team leader position for a project group and decree that the position has certain status and powers. Functionally, however, status and power depend on group members' acceptance. In other words, the team leader exercises legitimate power only to the extent that team members accept the leader's authority to exercise control over the members' behavior.

Power in the View of Critical Theory

Traditional theories of power have tried to describe the forms of power that occur in social processes and have emphasized social exchange explanations for the operation of power. The result is an appealing—but somewhat sterile—view of power that fails to account for the connection between power and communication, while ignoring the dark side of the subservience to which Redding called attention.

Peter J. Frost, a prominent professor of industrial relations at the University of British Columbia, has advanced four propositions about power that are not explicit in traditional treatments of the concept:

1. Organizational life is significantly influenced by the quest for and exercise of power by organizational actors, which constitute the political activity of organizations.
2. Power exists both on the surface level of organizational activity and deep within the very structure of organizations.
3. Communication plays a vital role in the development of power relations and the exercise of power.
4. The manipulation and exercise of power is expressed, in the sense both of actions and relations, as organizational games. (1987, p. 504)

Particularly with respect to communication, Frost points out that communication provides the means for the development and exercise of power. In turn, power creates and shapes communication structure and rules. With respect to power and politics, "the communication medium is never neutral" (Frost, p. 507).

In chapter 1, we provided an introduction to critical theory as a perspective of organizational communication that differs from both traditionalism and interpretivism. Critical theory is the perspective that focuses explicitly on a communicative and symbolic approach to power.

For the critical theorist, power is confounded with domination and oppression—conditions in the structure of society and in organizations that scholars should reveal and criticize. But critical theory does something that goes beyond mere complaining about societal oppression. As Dennis Mumby explained, it attempts to show how symbolism can "potentially legitimate dominant forms of organizational reality . . . restricting the interpretations and meanings that can be attached to organizational activity" (1987, p. 113).

Power and Legitimation

Critical theory has its roots in the works of Marx, but real development and articulation of modern critical theory began in Germany during the 1930s at the University of Frankfurt's Institute for Social Research, known more simply as "The Frankfurt School" (Farrell & Aune, 1979). Whatever Marx's original notions about history and society, Soviet-style communism had refined Marxist theory into a purely materialistic philosophy. Like the early machine metaphor of traditionalism, materialism reduced explanations for social process to machinelike causal relations that were divorced from questions of human consciousness and values. The Frankfurt School aimed at creating a form of neo-Marxism that addressed dominance and oppression in terms of values and morals (McGaan, 1983). Since the 1960s, this effort has been best reflected in the works of Jurgen Habermas (1968, 1979). The difference between traditional Marxism and Habermas's brand of neo-Marxism is explained clearly by Lee McGaan:

The traditional Marxist argument is that the West will fall as a result of economic collapse brought on by an uncontrollable cycle of inflation and recession. This will lead to class consciousness by workers and bring the revolution. Habermas has shown that . . . the real source of difficulty for capitalistic societies involves problems of **legitimation** [emphasis added]; . . . the crisis faced by institutions in the West comes from challenges to the legitimacy of power and function of capitalistic structures. . . .

What Habermas did in developing the concept of a legitimation crisis was to shift the traditional Marxist critique of society from the positivistic and material to the conceptual and moral. Critical theory in this light looks not at the economic relations undergirding social institutions. Instead, it focuses on the conceptual structures which justify the existence of institutions and the relation of those legitimations to real human interests. (p. 5)

In fact, since western capitalism has managed to remain more or less intact despite the doomsaying of traditional Marxist theory, one of the more interesting issues addressed in modern critical theory concerns why this has happened. While dominance can be achieved through force and coercion, and force and coercion are not unusual in organizations, the maintenance of power in capitalist organizations depends in large part on its legitimation (i.e., the manner in which its use is justified and accepted). Thus, as Robert McPhee (1985, p. 1) pointed out, some of the most prominent examples of modern critical research "concentrate on a single question: how is it, given the alienated and exploitative nature of work in capitalist organizations, that workers cooperate with management, labor at their jobs, and forego resistant stances, without the constant presence of coercion and threat?"

Power and Organizational Structure

In an effort to answer this question, critical theory focuses on the intricate relationships between power and organizational structure. The idea of organizational structure in critical theory is not quite the same thing as the traditionalist concepts that we presented in chapter 6. There, we considered structure in terms of formally designated lines of authority and divisions of labor and in terms of communication networks. But you may also remember the basic definition of a *system* that we presented in chapter 3; namely, it is a set of elements and the *rules* that define the relationships among those elements. Structure is realized through these rules, and this is the concept of structure with which critical theory is concerned.

What is the relationship between structure and power? As explained by Stewart Clegg (1975), power arises from the **deep structure rules** of organization and is achieved by controlling those rules. Deep structure rules include shared unquestioned assumptions that guide our social actions. The organizational rule system provides what Clegg characterizes as a "mode of rationality" by shaping and directing the ways in which we think and act. In this sense, power resides in the "socially structured and culturally patterned behavior of groups and practices of institution" (Lukes, 1974, p. 22). From the traditional viewpoint, power may be the ability of actor A to get actor B to do what B otherwise would not do. But from the vantage point of critical theory, there is nothing quite so powerful as the assumption within a group that things are or should be a particular way. As Lukes (1974) observed, it is "the supreme exercise of power to get another or others to have the desires you want them to have . . . to secure their compliance by controlling their thoughts and desires" (p. 23).

Mumby and Stohl (1991) also address the issue of power structures but their approach is somewhat different from Clegg's. They argue that within organizations there are struggles between different interest groups "to create a meaning system in which certain views of the world are privileged over others" (Mumby & Stohl, 1991, p. 318). The dominant group is the one that is best able to create and sustain a meaning system that serves its own interests. More specifically, Mumby and Stohl claim that discourse (e.g., conversations, written interaction) functions to structure systems of *presence* and *absence* within the organization. What they mean by this is that certain views of what is acceptable within the organization are organized into everyday practices, while other alternative views are organized out (or absented). For example, in most organizations members are expected to make decisions according to rational procedures intended to produce optimal outcomes. Within such organizations, "rationality is given primacy (made present) over emotionality (absented) as a legitimate model of organizational experience" (Mumby & Stohl, 1991, p. 319; also see Mumby & Putnam, 1992).

Power, Symbols, and Systematic Distortion

Obviously, different rule systems provide us with different ways of organizing our behavior. Thus, Dennis Mumby noted, "Domination involves getting people to organize their behavior around a particular rule system" (1987, p. 115). Borrowing from Gramsci (1971), Mumby says, "The process of hegemony works most effectively when the world-view articulated by the ruling elite is actively taken up and pursued by subordinate groups" (p. 123). **Hegemony** refers to a relational system where one group is dominant over others. In organizational settings, such dominance occurs when a group in power (e.g., managers) convinces the oppressed group (e.g., subordinates) to identify the dominant group's interests as it's own (Williams, 1977).

How does this occur? How is it that people are induced to adopt and, perhaps more importantly, *maintain* a rule system or mode of rationality that actually disadvantages them? This is where symbols and discourse come into play, particularly in a condition that critical theorists refer to as **systematically distorted communication.**

Systematically distorted communication is a bit like magic. It is illusory. It distorts the reality of a situation. In effect, systematically distorted communication legitimizes hegemony *by making it appear to be something other than what it really is.* In developing the concept of systematic distortion, Habermas (1979) distinguished between communicative action and strategic action. Communicative action is intended to achieve mutual understanding and agreement as a basis for consensual action. Communicative action is joint action. Strategic action is a unilateral attempt at achieving one's own goals and aims. Strategic action may be open. Let's suppose that you are presenting a new policy proposal to a management group. You expect some opposition and you want one of your friends in the group to be very vocal in supporting your proposal. If you say this to your friend in an "upfront," nondeceptive manner, you have been openly strategic. But let's suppose, in an effort to get your friend's support, you say something like this instead: I really dread this meeting today. I think Bill and June are going to give me some trouble about this proposal. You remember how those two really tried to stab you in the back last year. You know, they actually went around outside of meetings trying to line up support to torpedo that new marketing plan you introduced. I remember how most of us in the group supported it and you got it approved, but those two sure tried to kill it.

In this case, your strategic action is *latent.* Although all of the information in your statements may be factual, your real intentions are obscured. There is a "hidden agenda" in the action. If you have deliberately tried to deceive your friend about your intentions, you have engaged in manipulation. Systematically distorted communication also arises from latent stategic action, but it is more complicated than manipulation. In manipulation, one person deceives the other. In systematically distorted communication, "at least one of the participants deceives *himself* or *herself* about the fact that the basis of consensual action is only apparently being maintained" (Habermas, 1979, p. 208).

In organizations, hegemony may be legitimized through systematically distorted communication in various ways, but systematic distortion in its most basic form can be found in the political functions of organizational **ideology.** As explained earlier, an ideology is a set of assumptions and beliefs that comprise a system of thought. Ideology provides the structure for an organization's mode of rationality. In other words, ideology is central to an organization's deep structure. Giddens (1979) contends that ideology functions politically in three ways to privilege the interests of one group over another. A concise summary of Giddens' claims is adapted from Mumby (1987):

1. *Representing sectional interests as universal.* Although the real organization may consist of competing constituencies and conflicting interests (e.g., management versus labor, staff versus line), ideology can tell us, "We're all in this together" (i.e., that the interests of one group are the interests of all).

2. *Denying or transmuting contradictions.* From the vantage point of critical theory, capitalist society and organizations within capitalist society are

fraught with fundamental contradictions. The ownership of the means for producing goods and services is private, yet, in organizations, the production is accomplished through a social process. Ideology can obscure the fundamental nature of these contradictions by making them appear to be nothing more than social conflict. Thus, ideology tells us that decision making is purely rational, when, in fact, it is political, or that we are "all equal here," when, in fact, we are not.

3. *Naturalizing the present through reification.* In effect, reification means that we make a socially constructed reality appear to be concrete (i.e., objective, fixed, and immutable). Ideology reifies meaning by telling us, "This is the way things are." As we pointed out in earlier chapters, the most obvious example of this probably is the concept of organizational hierarchy itself. It is taken to be concrete and as the natural order of things, but it has its existence only in shared meanings that shape our actions to fit the idea.

Mumby has added a fourth function, *control,* to Giddens' list of three. Perhaps the control function already is implied in Giddens' list, but Mumby wants to make it clear that ideological control is not so much a matter of one group's domination over another as it is the ability of a group or class to make the interests of other groups appear to be consistent with its own. We think it is also important to specifically connect Mumby's idea of control with systematically distorted communication. *Members of dominated groups participate in their own oppression through self-deception by identifying with and actively consenting to the system of hegemony.* When this occurs, we have, as Gramsci (1971) suggested, the condition under which hegemony works best.

One of us was involved in a consulting project with a large accounting and investment firm in which we were able to observe firsthand how employees can participate in their own oppression through self-deception. In this firm there were three women who had reached the rank of partner (out of twenty-one total partners). Two of the women, who had young children at home, realized that they could no longer meet the demands of heavy workloads that often resulted in sixty-hour workweeks. They felt that their children's needs were being sacrificed so the firm could continue to make money. After presenting their concerns to the other partners, a deal was struck in which the women were able to reduce their workweek to an average of thirty hours. Of course, with the reduction in hours came a 40 percent reduction in their share of the firm's profits. At first glance, it may seem that these women had struck a good deal. But did they really? Another way of interpreting their actions is to argue that they accepted without question the fact that partners must work sixty hours a week in order to retain full partner status. Couldn't the women have posed other questions such as the following: Why do we have to work sixty hours a week to retain partner status? Can't we promote more accountants or investment analysts to partner status so we can reduce the workload for all of us? Unfortunately, these women struck a deal that was based on their unquestioned acceptance of what a fair workload is for partners. If they had questioned these perceptions of fair workload, perhaps they could have negotiated a forty-hour workweek, retained full-time partner status, and spent more time with their children.

Limits of Ideological Manipulation

Advocates of the theory of hegemony, as we have described it so far, contend that power in organizations works through *ideological manipulation* (Witten, 1993). What this means is that the dominant group manipulates and structures the interests of the oppressed group. This manipulation is accomplished through convincing the oppressed group that its interests can best be served by adhering to the values and behaviors advocated by the dominant group.

Although the concept of ideological manipulation is linked to some critical theorists, other theorists criticize this perspective. Specifically, Abercrombie, Hill, and Turner (1980) observe that ideological manipulation is predicated on the Marxist notion of *false consciousness*. False consciousness refers to a condition in which the less powerful members of a social system ignorantly subscribe to the dominant control of more powerful members. The less powerful members accept this control because they uncritically accept the positions advocated by the dominant group as being in their best interests.

One good reason for discomfort with the notion of false consciousness is its contradiction with Giddens' (1979) description of the *dialectic of control*. As you will remember from chapter 11, Giddens argued that every social actor within a system has the capacity to exercise power and control. An interesting example of the dialectic of control in action was reported in a study by Hancox and Papa (1996). They conducted their study in a manufacturing organization that uses a monetary incentive system to reward employees for high levels of performance. The "bonus pay" received by high performers comes out of annual company profits. The positive side of this incentive system is that the employees are paid at rates three times higher than the average for workers in U.S. manufacturing companies. The negative side of this system is that the employees sometimes have to work six or seven days a week to meet production goals. The pressure to produce at high levels also creates equipment hazards that have resulted in severed fingers, burns, and visual injuries.

Given the preceding description, how do employees within this manufacturing organization exhibit control over management? Recently, the company operated at a financial loss due to poor performance from subsidiaries located in Europe. Since no profits were recorded for the year, bonuses were not scheduled to be paid. Certain managers within the company began to float the rumor that bonuses would not be paid because of the financial loss. Worker reaction to this rumor was emotional and forceful. For example, many employees indicated that violence would erupt if the bonus was not paid and that the majority of the laborers would quit their jobs. As one employee with thirty years experience stated, "People think that maybe somebody's gonna come in here with a gun if he doesn't like what he hears [on bonus day]" (Hancox & Papa, 1996, p. 22). Echoing this sentiment, an employee with twenty-nine years experience explained that too many of the employees rely on the bonus to pay their everyday bills. So if a particular employee does not receive the bonus he expects, "This might break this guy and he's likely to come in with an autoloader on bonus day and wipe everybody out" (Hancox & Papa, 1996, p. 23). Finally, dealing with the issue of a massive walkout, an employee with twenty-six years experience explained, "The average worker would walk out because they would find it very difficult to justify their presence there. They would probably lose 40% of their employees immediately" (Hancox & Papa, 1996, p. 22).

What was management's response to these worker statements? Well, despite the fact that bonuses had never before been paid when the company lost money, the owners borrowed 50 million dollars in 1993 so they could still provide performance bonuses to qualifying employees. Of course, it is difficult to prove that management's decision to take out the loan was predicated only on the basis of worker statements. A case can be made, however, that these statements had their intended impact. As one worker with twenty-nine years experience put it, "That bonus keeps all your good workers here, and keeps people from leaving. That is the reason they borrow money to pay the bonus" (Hancox & Papa, 1996, p. 24).

As the above example shows, employees have the ability to empower themselves even in organizations where managers attempt to engage in ideological manipulation. Does this mean that workers are always aware of management's attempts to manipulate them? Of course, this claim can not be made either. Sometimes management is successful in its attempts to manipulate workers; other times workers realize what is going on and empower themselves. In still other instances, workers recognize that they are being manipulated but they decide that the rewards associated with continued organizational membership outweigh the costs of continued manipulation. So within organizations, power and structure are related but the nature of that relationship is sometimes more complex than it seems at first glance.

Critical Theory in Organizational Communication Research

Critical theory has produced some outstanding studies of power in work and organizational settings (e.g., Burawoy, 1979; Clegg, 1975; and Edwards, 1979), but it has begun only recently to exert influence in the study of organizational communication. One good example of this kind of research is a study by Mumby on the political use of *narratives,* literally, the use of story-telling in organizations. Mumby (1987) examined a story that purportedly was widely disseminated in the IBM Corporation and that was told and retold by many members of this company. The story concerns an incident between IBM's chairman, Thomas Watson, Jr., and an IBM employee named Lucille Burger. While the exact form and content of the story might vary somewhat from one telling to another, the basic form published by Martin, Feldman, Hatch, and Sitkin (1983, pp. 439–440) goes this way:

Lucille Burger, a twenty-two-year-old bride weighing ninety pounds, whose husband had been sent overseas, had been given a job until his return. The young woman was obliged to make certain that people entering security areas wore the correct clear identification. Surrounded by his usual entourage of white-shirted men, Watson approached the doorway to an area where she was on guard, wearing an orange badge acceptable elsewhere in the plant, but not a green badge, which alone permitted entrance at her door. "I was trembling in my uniform, which was far too big," she recalled. "It hid my shakes, but not my voice. 'I'm sorry,' I said to him. I knew who he was alright. 'You cannot enter. Your admittance is not recognized.' That's what we were supposed to say." The men accompanying Watson were stricken; the moment held unpredictable possibilities. "Don't you know who he is?" someone hissed. Watson raised his hand for silence, while one of the party strode off and returned with the appropriate badge.

Mumby (1987) demonstrates how this story can plausibly accomplish all of the political functions of ideology, how the story is, in effect, an instance of systematically distorted communication. Although every statement in the story may be factually correct, the story nonetheless obscures and mystifies the actual conditions of organizational life at IBM.

As interpreted by Mumby (1987), the story implies that sectional interests are transcended by rules that are designed for the benefit of all, but it obscures the fact that the rules are "created *by* the corporate elite (of which Watson is head) to protect their own interests" (p. 121). The rules at issue in this story "are in place for the benefit of people like Watson, and not for people like Lucille Burger" (p. 121). Moreover, the story denies a fundamental contradiction and is, itself, a contradiction. It portrays Watson as an ordinary person who must obey Burger in her official capacity as an enforcer of the rules yet also makes him "a larger-than-life figure about whom fables are told" (p. 122). More to the point, it is the fact that Watson really *is* an exception that makes the story compelling. Watson wisely used the occasion to make a dramatic statement about corporate rules by deferring to a relatively low-echelon employee. In fact, he could have walked right by Burger without any consequences at all.

Mumby argues that this story provides a very good instance of reification simply because it can be recounted over and over again as a statement not only about rules but also about the rationale for enforcing them, not to mention latent statements about sex roles and status differences. In particular, Mumby says, "The story serves to reify ideologically the organizational rule system itself. . . . Lucille Burger's single-minded adherence to the rules reflects not so much a heightened sense of corporate loyalty, but rather an enforcing of the rules *because they exist*" (p. 123). Finally, the story serves the control function because it is not only recounted by high-level executives but throughout the company as "an example of 'intellectual and moral leadership'" (p. 123). The story itself is actively recounted by employees, and its ideology is taken up and adopted by employees. Its illustration of Burger's commitment to the system is identified and equated with the legitimacy and appropriateness of that system.

Mumby's study of the Watson-Burger story suggests three goals for critical scholarship, which are adapted from Deetz (1982):

1. *Richer understanding of naturally occurring events.* Deep structure elements of meaning are largely taken for granted. They shape our actions without much conscious reflection, examination, or questioning. Critical research attempts to produce insights not only for scholars but also for organization members themselves by calling attention to the deep structure of meaning systems. This is similar to the idea of "consciousness-raising."
2. *Criticism of false consensus.* When we deceive ourselves through systematically distorted communication, the result is false consensus. As Deetz expresses it, false consensus "is reached by the power of definition rather than open discussion" (p. 140). If illusions and the conditions that

make them necessary can be overcome, it is possible to have open dialogue among different organizational groups and constituencies. Returning to Habermas (1979), the task of the critical theorist is to identify and criticize strategic action in order to move toward communicative action in society.

3. *Expansion of the conceptual base from which organizational members think and work.* Organization members need to learn how to engage in communicative action in order to have a better understanding of organizational life and to expand their concepts and languages in order to grapple creatively with the problems that confront them.

In chapter 4 we described sytems of concertive control in organizations. Studies focusing on such systems have yielded interesting insights into the nature of power in organizations (Barker, 1993; Barker & Cheney, 1994; Papa, Auwal, & Singhal, 1995, 1996). In order to understand how power operates within concertive control systems, we need to return to two concepts discussed in chapter 4: *identification* and *discipline.* As you will remember, workers exhibit their identification with an organization when, in making a decision, they perceive the organization's values or interests as relevant in evaluating the alternatives of choice (Tompkins & Cheney, 1983). Such worker perceptions lead to the conclusion "What's good for the organization is also good for me." In addition, in systems of concertive control, workers show their identification with the organization and their work team by establishing and sustaining disciplinary techniques that allow workers to accomplish goals that they have created for themselves. These disciplinary techniques act as a powerful social force that governs and regulates worker behavior. In order to clarify how discipline acts as a powerful social force in organizations, let's turn to an example reported by Papa, Auwal, and Singhal (1995) in their study of Grameen Bank workers:

Atiquar Rahman is a Grameen bank field worker who works on the outskirts of Dhaka [Bangladesh]. He told us about the pressure he feels from fellow field workers to retain a high loan recovery rate. When he experienced problems with loan recovery in a particular center (four members had ceased loan repayment), he felt personally responsible to solve the problem. The four members had taken out a loan for a rickshaw repair business. However, they soon discovered that they could not compete with the more established repair businesses in Dhaka. Rahman met with the non-paying members and attempted to persuade them to resume loan repayment. When that did not work he offered to help them move their business to an area where they could compete. Rahman eventually wound up working on rickshaw repairs himself to help the loan recipients keep their business functioning. (pp. 208–209)

In interpreting this story, Papa, Auwal, and Singhal (1995) noted that the loan repayment records of Rahman's centers were posted on a wall behind his desk for all the other field workers to see. Rahman felt incredible guilt when he returned to the branch office at the end of a long day without having received any loan repayments from the delinquent borrowers. He felt that he was failing as a field worker, and he became most upset when he compared his loan recovery record to the posted records of his co-workers. He even considered quitting his job because he felt incapable of meeting the high standards his co-workers had established.

Why did Rahman identify so strongly with the standards established by his co-workers? First of all, he was part of establishing the standards. Second, sustaining these high standards allows the Grameen Bank to sustain its position as one of the most successful social and economic development organizations in the world. Rahman felt that he was part of this success until experiencing problems with loan recovery in one of his bank centers. Third, discipline acts as a social force in the Grameen Bank due to the carefully designed system of monitoring and evaluating worker performance. Papa, Auwal, and Singhal (1996) explain this system as follows:

The monitoring and evaluation of worker performance became particularly clear to us in the branch offices when field workers returned from their village centers. Although exhausted from a long day's work, bank workers would begin counting and recording loan repayments as soon as they sat down at their desks. Each member counted the money in full view of the other branch members and the branch manager. The pace of the counting and recording operations is fast and clearly stressful. As we learned in talking with a number of field workers, the stress they feel is linked to the immediacy of the evaluation they receive. Lagging performance is quickly discovered and corrected, and good performance is quickly rewarded. (p. 20)

Papa, Auwal, and Singhal (1996) note that the counting of loan repayments at the end of the day is similar to Foucault's (1979) three-fold disciplinary mechanism: *examination, hierarchical observation,* and *normalizing judgment.* The public counting of loan repayments is a form of daily examination for the workers. Hierarchical observation occurs as the counting of the money is performed in full view of the manager. The manager and the co-workers then offer a normalizing judgment in the feedback given to the worker about his or her performance. Workers who collect all outstanding loan repayments are praised. Those who fail to recoup all outstanding loan repayments are criticized and made to feel unworthy as a "team mate." Thus, the punishment workers receive is essentially communicative in form. Field workers criticize each other and make reference to the loan repayment records posted behind worker desks. In order to avoid this criticism and prove their strong identification with the bank's continued success, the workers labor long hours, and forego vacations to insure that members continue their loan repayments. Finally, Papa, Auwal, and Singhal explain that the workers accept these forms of discipline because of their strong identification with the bank. As one Grameen Bank worker, Shamsul Hoque, put it: "I feel like the engine of change. An engine that gets its fuel from the vision of Muhammad Yunus [Grameen's Managing Director] and water from the dreams of the poor and the landless" (Papa, Auwal, & Singhal, 1996, p. 19).

Thus, in concertive control systems power is embedded within a system of interaction among workers who identify strongly with an organization and its goals. What this means is that workers communicate with one another in ways that sustain the disciplinary system so that continued goal attainment is possible. Instead of a form of power in which a dominant group (e.g., management) enforces discipline upon workers, a concertive control system empowers workers to be their own enforcers. Since the workers themselves create the system of control, they are committed to sustaining it, despite the personal sacrifices entailed in continued organizational participation.

Reconceptualizing Power: The Feminist View

In chapter 2 we discussed Mary Parker Follett's (1982) distinction between power *over* others and power *with* others in organizational relationships and her use of "power with" as the basis for her concept of participation. Feminist theory has received attention in earlier chapters (4 and 11), but it is again relevant here because feminists have an interest similar to Follett's in distinguishing between power as a means of domination and power as "the ability to accomplish goals" (Iannello, 1992, p. 43). Feminists advocate the substitution of **empowerment** for power. Kathleen Iannello explains as follows:

> Power is associated with the notion of controlling others, while empowerment is associated with the notion of controlling oneself. Therefore, within organizations based on empowerment, members monitor themselves. In organizations based on power, there must be an administrative oversight function. (pp. 44–45)

In the feminist critique of modern organizations, the exercise of power as a means of domination over others is realized through hierarchy, and hierarchy is a fundamental instrument of patriarchal order. According to Kathy Ferguson, "Social relations between classes, races, and sexes are fundamentally unequal. Bureaucracy [hierarchy] . . . serves as a filter for these other forms of domination, projecting them into an institutional arena that both rationalizes and maintains them" (1984, p. 8).

Eliminating domination requires replacement of hierarchy with a collectivist, cooperative structure. In a **collectivist** as opposed to hierarchical organization, decisions and actions would be developed through participative dialogue to achieve action through consensus rather than action through top-down communication of orders from a central authority. Thus, feminist theorists such as Iannello (1992) speak of "decisions without hierarchy" (p. xi). The reformation of organizations into collectivist systems is a goal that appears to be common to most versions of feminist theory, but the attainment of this goal does pose a dilemma. As Hester Eisenstein expresses the problem, "A fundamental issue [is] unresolved for feminists, and that is how we get from the values we hold dear—of collective, non-hierarchical, democratic behavior—to the outcome we seek, of a peaceful world safe for women and others now subject to discrimination, victimization, and oppression, without sacrificing these values in the rush to seize and use power on behalf of feminist ends" (1991, p. 3).

Achieving organizational reformation seems to depend implicity in many feminist writings on the hope that women somehow will do a better job than men have done with the use of power. The potential difficulty in fulfilling this hope is reflected in Albrecht and Hall's (1991) study of innovation networks that we discussed in chapter 6. They found that core groups of elite insiders dominated the networks. While two-thirds of the outsiders—the disenfranchised—in Albrecht and Hall's study were women, women also comprised 75 percent of the elites— groups that manipulated the system to reinforce "their own relational positions of privilege, power, and influence" (1991, p. 557). If the quality of organizational life is to be made better for everyone, women and men alike must find an answer to the dilemma posed by Eisenstein.

Marshall (1989) discusses an alternative to hierarchy that addresses the concerns of Eisenstein. Specifically, she argues that organizations can structure themselves in *heterarchies* rather than hierarchies. As she explains, "A heterarchy has no one person or principle in command. Rather temporary pyramids of authority form as and when appropriate in a system of mutual constraints and influences" (Marshall, 1989, p. 289). An example of a heterarchy was observed by Wyatt (1988) in an ethnographic account of a weaver's guild. In this guild, there was a system of shared leadership, and all opinions expressed by members were respected. Two forms of leadership were present within the guild. First, there was a leader who focused on the overall operation of the guild. Second, task leaders were associated with specific weaving projects. This resulted in a pyramid of authority among the eight women who comprised the guild. They shared leadership of the entire group and rotated responsibility for tasks while sustaining flexibility in goals and values. In an evaluation of Wyatt's study, Mumby and Putnam (1992) observed, "Nestled in an environment of caring, members balance the demands of differing values, goals and relationships to make the group a place where all members feel comfortable and achieve their individual aims" (p. 475). In such an organizational environment the opportunities for worker empowerment are clear and meaningful.

Power and Conflict: Connected and Separate Phenomena

Power and conflict are often connected in the traditional management and conflict literature. Pfeffer's (1981) work is representative of this literature. According to Pfeffer, "Power follows from situations in which there is conflict" (p. 96). Why are power and conflict so closely intertwined? Well, when organizational members are interdependent, and those members have competing goals in an environment where rewards and resources are scarce, each member views the other as an obstacle to goal attainment. Hocker and Wilmot (1995), two conflict researchers, make this very point in their definition of interpersonal conflict: "Conflict is an expressed struggle between at least two interdependent parties who perceive incompatible goals, scarce rewards, and interference from others in achieving their goals" (p. 21). So when one person views another as an obstacle to goal attainment or the procurement of rewards, he or she will exercise power to try to get his or her way.

Are power and conflict always related? Well, it is difficult to envision a struggle between organizational members over scarce rewards or competing goals in which power would not be present. As people present their interpretation of a dispute and express their personal needs, they are clearly acting in an empowering manner. Empowerment, however, can exist without conflict. For example, Eisenberg (1994) discusses a form of employee empowerment that is linked to the promotion of *dialogue*. In establishing dialogue, all organizational members must have equal opportunities to present their ideas and opinions on important issues. Second, members must display empathy for differing ideas, opinions, and worldviews. Finally, the personal feelings and experiences of organizational members must be considered legitimate in making decisions. According to Eisenberg

(1994), dialogue both "limits defensiveness by reducing attacking communication and, more important, gives people insight into the ways in which others frame their opinions and behavior—the personal and cultural context that can help others seem different, yet sensible" (p. 282). It is certainly reasonable to assume that dialogue (as a form of empowerment) can exist in certain instances without the emergence of conflict.

Given the preceding observations, we feel comfortable with the following two conclusions about the relationship between power and conflict. When a conflict exists in which employees are struggling over scarce rewards and competing goals, there will be displays of power as each side tries to maximize its outcomes. There are forms of empowerment (such as dialogue), however, in which the expression of different viewpoints on an issue will not necessarily promote conflict. The reason for this is that when dialogue is promoted, the different parties to the discussion do not view one another as obstacles to goal attainment. Rather, when dialogue is promoted, organizational members exchange different perspectives on an issue until a potential decision emerges that meets the needs of *all* members. As the discussion evolves, members recognize that their commitment to and respect for one another will prevent a destructive conflict from surfacing in which one side tries to defeat the other. So a conversation can be sustained in which members help one another to reach goals that are mutually defined and important to all involved. Now that we have explained how power and conflict can be viewed as connected and separate phenomena, we will turn to a more developed description of conflict in organizations in the next chapter.

Summary

The function of communication in constituting organizations depends upon the manner in which it is used to exercise power, one of the most pervasive phenomena in organizational life. In hierarchically structured organizations, differences in members' status and power are a simple fact of life. Status refers essentially to the rank or importance of one's position in a group. Traditionally, power has been regarded as any means or resource that one person may employ to gain compliance and cooperation from others.

French and Raven provided an analysis of social power that has become a classic model for classifying the forms of power applied in organizational relationships. They described five basic types of power: reward, coercive, referent, expert, and legitimate.

Traditional theories of power have tried to describe the forms of power that occur in social processes and have emphasized social exchange explanations for the operation of power. The result is an appealing, but somewhat sterile, account of power that fails to account for the connection between power and communication and somehow seems to ignore the dark side of the organizational subservience. In the view of modern critical theory, power is confounded with domination and oppression—conditions in the structure of society and in organizations that scholars should reveal and criticize. Critical theory also attempts to show how symbols are used to legitimate dominant forms of organizational reality, thereby restricting the interpretations and meanings that members can attach to organizational actions. In the process, critical theory relies heavily on showing how ideological manipulation and systematically distorted communication sustain hegemony.

Feminist theory has contributed to the critique of power and domination by arguing for "empowerment" as a substitute for traditional concepts of power. Feminist theory calls for reforming organizations from hierarchical systems to collectivities or **heterarchies** that achieve action through consensus.

Finally, we looked at power and conflict as connected and separate phenomena. Power and conflict are connected when workers view one another as obstacles to goal attainment. The two phenomena can exist separately when workers mutually empower one another through dialogue. When dialogue is promoted, workers recognize how goals can be obtained through cooperation rather than by defeating their opposition. We will return to the issues of power and conflict at the beginning of the next chapter.

---

1. In what ways does the critical perspective of power differ from the traditional treatment of power?
2. Does the fact that our democratic society protects individual rights limit the application of critical theory to organizational communication? Why or why not?
3. What are the challenges of promoting dialogue in the workplace? Can you envision a problem-solving situation in which the promotion of dialogue would prevent a destructive conflict from surfacing? Have you ever had a conversation with another person that you would classify as a dialogue? If so, what happened in this conversation?

Discussion Questions/ Activities

Articles/Books

Additional Resources

Bradshaw-Camball, P. (1989). The implications of multiple perspectives on power for organizational development. *The Journal of Applied Behavioral Science, 25*, 31–44.
Clair, R. P. (1993). The use of framing devices to sequester organizational narratives: Hegemony and harassment. *Communication Monographs, 60*, 113–136.
Clegg, S. R. (1993). Narrative, power, and social theory. In D. K. Mumby (Ed.), *Narrative and social control: Critical perspectives* (pp. 15–45). Newbury Park, CA: Sage.
Deetz, S. A., & Mumby, D. K. (1990). Power, discourse, and the workplace: Reclaiming the critical tradition. In J. Anderson (Ed.), *Communication Yearbook 13* (pp. 18–47). Newbury Park, CA: Sage.
Giddens, A. (1993). *New rules of sociological method* (2nd ed.). Stanford, CA: Stanford University Press.
Salvador, M., & Markham, A. (1995). The rhetoric of self-directive management and the operation of organizational power. *Communication Reports*, 45–53.

Web Sites

http://www.arcticaid.org/2poke.HTM
    Example of grassroots organizing by an Arctic preservation group against ARCO
http://daedalus.com/didak/cccc95/tyanna.html
    Paper on Habermas
http://unp.unl.edu/up/habpas.htm
    Interviews with Habermas

References

Abercrombie, N., Hill, S., & Turner, B. S. (1980). *The dominant ideology thesis.* London: Allen and Unwin.

Albrecht, T. L., & Hall, B. (1991). Relational and content differences between elites and outsiders in innovation networks. *Human Communication Research, 17,* 535–561.

Bachrach, P., & Baratz, M. (1962). Two faces of power. *American Political Science Review, 56,* 947–952.

Barker, J. R. (1993). Tightening the iron cage: Concertive control in self-managing teams. *Administrative Science Quarterly, 38,* 408–437.

Barker, J. R., & Cheney, G. (1994). The concepts and practices of discipline in contemporary organizational life. *Communication Monographs, 61,* 19–43.

Burawoy, M. (1979). *Manufacturing consent.* Chicago: University of Chicago Press.

Clegg, S. (1975). *Power, rule, and domination.* London: Routledge & Kegan Paul.

Dahl, R. (1957). The concept of power. *Behavioral Science, 2,* 201–215.

Deetz, S. A. (1982). Critical interpretive research in organizational communication. *Western Journal of Speech Communication, 46,* 131–149.

Edwards, R. (1979). *Contested terrain.* New York: Basic Books.

Eisenberg, E. M. (1994). Dialogue as democratic discourse: Affirming Harrison. In S. A. Deetz (Ed.), *Communication Yearbook 17* (pp. 275–284). Thousand Oaks, CA: Sage.

Eisenstein, H. (1991). *Gender shock.* Boston: Beacon.

Emerson, R. M. (1962). Power-dependence relations. *American Sociological Review, 27,* 31–41.

Farrell, T. B., & Aune, J. A. (1979). Critical theory and communication: A selective literature review. *Quarterly Journal of Speech, 65,* 93–120.

Ferguson, K. E. (1984). *The feminist case against bureaucracy.* Philadelphia: Temple University Press.

Follett, M. P. (1982). Power. In E. M. Fox & L. Urwick (Eds.), *Dynamic administration: The collected papers of Mary Parker Follett.* New York: Hippocrene Books.

Foucault, M. (1979). *Discipline and punish: The birth of the prison* (A.S. Smith, Trans.). New York: Random House.

French, J. R. P., Jr., and Raven, B. H. (1959). The bases of social power. In D. Cartwright (Ed.), *Studies in social power.* Ann Arbor: University of Michigan Press.

Frost, P. J. (1987). Power, politics, and influence. In F. M. Jablin, L. L. Putnam, K. H. Roberts, & L. W. Porter (Eds.), *Handbook of organizational communication: An interdisciplinary perspective* (pp. 503–548). Newbury Park, CA: Sage.

Giddens, A. (1979). *Central problems in social theory.* Berkeley: University of California Press.

Gramsci, A. (1971). *Selections from the prison notebooks* (Q. Hoeare & G. Nowell Smith, Trans.). New York: International Publishers.

Habermas, J. (1968). *Knowledge and human interests* (J. Shapiro, Trans.). Boston: Beacon Press.

Habermas, J. (1979). *Communication and the evolution of society* (T. McCarthy, Trans.). Boston: Beacon Press.

Hancox, M., & Papa, M. J. (1996, May). *Employee struggles with autonomy and dependence: Examining the dialectic of control through a structurational account of power.* Paper presented at the annual meeting of the International Communication Association. Chicago.

Hocker, J. L., & Wilmot, W. W. (1995). *Interpersonal conflict* (4th ed.). Dubuque, IA: Wm. C. Brown.

Iannello, K. P. (1992). *Decisions without hierarchy: Feminist interventions in organization theory and practice.* New York: Routledge.

Kelman, H. C. (1961). Processes of opinion change. *Public Opinion Quarterly, 25,* 57–78.

Lukes, S. (1974). *Power: A radical view.* London: Macmillan.

Marshall, J. (1989). Revisioning career concepts: A feminist invitation. In M. B. Arthurs, D. T. Hall, & B. S. Lawrence (Eds.), *A handbook of career theory* (pp. 275–291). Cambridge: Cambridge University Press.

Martin, J., Feldman, M., Hatch, M. J., & Sitkin, S. B. (1983). The uniqueness paradox in organizational stories. *Administrative Science Quarterly, 28,* 438–453.

McGaan, L. (1983). *Critical theory and communicative action: An introduction to the work of Jurgen Habermas.* Paper presented to the Humanities Colloquium. Wabash College.

McPhee, R. (1985). *Four critical approaches to workplace power/control in organizational communication.* Paper presented at the annual meeting of the International Communication Association. Chicago.

Mumby, D. K. (1987). The political function of narrative in organizations. *Communication Monographs, 54,* 113–127.

Mumby, D. K., & Putnam, L. L. (1992). The politics of emotion: A feminist reading of bounded rationality. *Academy of Management Review, 17,* 465–486.

Mumby, D. K., & Stohl, C. (1991). Power and discourse in organization studies: Absence and the dialectic of control. *Discourse & Society, 2,* 313–332.

Papa, M. J., Auwal, M. A., & Singhal, A. (1995). Dialectic of control and emancipation in organizing for social change: A multitheoretic study of the Grameen Bank in Bangladesh. *Communication Theory, 5,* 189–223.

Papa, M. J., Auwal, M. A., & Singhal, A. (1996). *Organizing for social change within concertive control systems: Member identification, discursive empowerment, and the masking of discipline.* Paper presented at the annual meeting of the Eastern Communication Association. New York, NY.

Pfeffer, J. (1981). *Power in organizations.* Marshfield, MA: Pitman.

Russell, B. (1983). *Power: A social analysis.* New York: Norton.

Secord, P. F., & Backman, C. W. (1964). *Social psychology.* New York: McGraw-Hill.

Tompkins, P. K., & Cheney, G. (1983). The uses of account analysis: A study of organizational decision making and identification. In L. L. Putnam & M. E. Pacanowsky (Eds.), *Communication and organizations: An interpretive approach* (pp. 123–146). Beverly Hills, CA: Sage.

Williams, R. (1977). *Marxism and literature.* New York: Oxford University Press.

Witten, M. (1993). Narrative and the culture of obedience at the workplace. In D. K. Mumby (Ed.), *Narrative and social control: Critical perspectives* (pp. 97–118). Newbury Park, CA: Sage.

Wyatt, N. (1988). Shared leadership in the weaver's guild. In B. Bate & A. Taylor (Eds.), *Women communicating: Studies of women's talk* (pp. 147–175). Norwood, NJ: Ablex.

Conflict, as Putnam and Poole pointed out, is "an instrinsic part of organizational life" (1987, p. 550). Also, as we argued in the last chapter, conflict and power are inextricably related. While organizational action depends on the exercise of power, the exercise of power often leads to conflict (one exception being those situations in which employees mutually empower one another). In turn, conflict situations, by definition, involve interdependent actors who have the power to constrain or interfere with each other's goals. In a sense, conflict entails the exercise of power.

Most critical theorists are prepared to acknowledge that power is *not* simply imposed by dominant groups on subordinate groups or forced upon the oppressed by the elite. Subordinate groups must accept the legitimacy of the system of hegemony in order for it to work. More importantly, however, the legitimacy of institutional and organizational power can be challenged by these groups. In fact, Habermas's interest in the idea of legitimation was developed through his studies of student protest movements during the 1960s.

Mumby noted, "Even the ostensibly powerless can use organizational structure to their advantage" (1987, p. 114). When the less powerful assert their interests against those of the more powerful, or when persons or groups of roughly equal power find that their goals are incompatible, the result is **conflict.** Conflict is a common, yet widely misunderstood, phenomenon in group processes and intergroup relations. Classical theorists regarded conflict as an anomaly—an abnormal occurrence that was not supposed to happen under an organizational structure with exhaustive rules and a "fair day's pay for a fair day's work." Human relations theorists developed a better understanding of conflict in organizations, but even they regarded it as a negative and counterproductive force to be avoided (Dessler, 1980). As Redding (1985) noted, even the organizations of the 1980s are overwhelmingly characterized by a mentality of "go along in order to get along." Given the right situation and a good sense of timing, one can become an organizational hero by challenging the status quo, but more generally, anyone in conflict with prevailing organizational values or managerial prerogatives is quickly labeled a boat-rocker or troublemaker.

No one would deny that uncontrolled conflict can be harmful within groups and organizations. Richard Beckhard (1969) argued, "One of the major problems affecting organization effectiveness is the amount of dysfunctional energy expended in inappropriate competition and fighting between groups that should be collaborating" (p. 33). Conflict, however, has a functional as well as dysfunctional side. Contemporary organizational theorists stress the point that conflict is an inevitable and even necessary aspect of group and organizational processes (Janis, 1972; Goldhaber, 1993; Robbins, 1977). It should not be suppressed and avoided but confronted, managed, and resolved.

Conflict can bring to the surface issues that require resolution, relieve tensions, and lead to the development of new channels of communication (Koehler, Anatol, & Applbaum, 1981). Avoidance or suppression of conflict leaves underlying issues unresolved. These issues, like Schein's (1969) personal emotional needs, will continue to reemerge in forms that hamper the group's task efforts. Even when conflict is successfully suppressed, the effect may be poor decisions and solutions based on badly distorted conceptions of problems and situations.

Irving Janis (1972) identified a phenomenon known as "Groupthink" in which extreme efforts are made to suppress conflict and stop the input of any information that contradicts an established or dominant view. Individual group members surrender their own beliefs and begin to see things only from the group perspective. The group develops a dogmatic commitment to the "moral rightness" of its position and may even believe that it is being persecuted by enemies. Janis argued that the ill-fated Bay of Pigs invasion during John F. Kennedy's presidential administration was a product of "Groupthink." Virtually anyone outside Kennedy's cloistered group of advisors would have said that the concept of invasion to oust Cuba's Fidel Castro was misguided and unworkable, but suppression of competing views, avoidance of conflict, and a quest to gain consensus merely for its own sake resulted in a disastrous decision. Actions by members of the Nixon administration during the Watergate era and Jimmy Carter's ill-fated decision to attempt a military rescue of American hostages in Iran may also have been products of "Groupthink."

Janis also illustrated how the phenomenon figures into corporate decisions to continue marketing inferior or hazardous products. In a film on the development of "Groupthink," Janis showed how a pharmaceutical company arrived at a decision to market a drug with some extremely dangerous side effects by downplaying the importance and validity of studies demonstrating the hazards. The management team justified its decision by highlighting the benefits of the product and suggesting that those who had qualms about the drug were "not being team players." The group even developed a vision of itself as a heroic paragon of moral virtue in standing behind the product.

Sources of Conflict

Although it is possible to suppress conflict through "Groupthink," the suppression cannot go on indefinitely. Conflict arises from many sources within groups and organizations, including various forms of role conflict; value and goal differences; and competition for limited resources.

Role Conflict

As we already have noted, conflict may arise from discrepancies among expected, perceived, and enacted roles. If your perception and enactment of a role differ substantially from the expectations of other members in your group, you may soon find yourself in the midst of controversy and struggle over this discrepancy.

Sometimes role discrepancies are reflected in *intrarole* conflict. Intrarole conflict occurs when a person in a given role is subjected to competing expectations for that role. Professors, for example, frequently struggle with the realization that some students in a course prefer the teacher to function as a discussion leader and facilitator, whereas others regard discussion as a waste of time, preferring a dynamic lecturer instead. Group leaders face a similar situation when some members prefer a democratic style, whereas others clearly are more comfortable with a highly structured autocrat. *Interrole* conflict occurs when a person is placed in the position of making a choice between two or more competing roles that demand simultaneous performance. Members of organizations may have several different roles in various groups or may even be responsible for two or more roles in the same group (i.e., the member who wears several hats). Most organization members also have external role obligations (e.g., as a parent, spouse, community member). When mutually exclusive demands arise for enactment of different roles, the stage is set for conflict. If you are a member of two different committees that have scheduled meetings at the same time or the boss asks you to work late on a day when the baby-sitter wants you to pick up your children no later than 5:15 P.M., something has to give!

These first two forms of role conflict involve conflict only to the extent that an individual experiences the stress of mutually exclusive role requirements. Certainly, such conflicts are very important. Indeed, these forms of conflict probably will try your patience and your sanity on a daily basis throughout much of your organizational life. But the forms of conflict with which we are primarily concerned here are those that fit the definition of conflict advanced by Putnam and Poole as "the interaction of interdependent people who perceive opposition of goals, aims, and values, and who see the other party as potentially interfering with the realization of these goals" (1987, p. 552). The remaining sources of conflict all allow for conflict in this form.

Interpersonal role conflict involves competition between two or more individuals for the same role within a group. Such conflict may occur over the leadership position or for choice jobs within a work group. Even the presence of some system for designating role assignments (appointment, promotion, seniority) does not necessarily prevent interrole conflict. We once worked with a research group in which top management officially appointed the team leader. Some other senior team members felt that they were better qualified for the job. They continually undermined the leader's authority by telling junior team members to ignore his instructions on the grounds that the instructions were erroneous or inappropriate. Even in speaking with us, some of the senior team members would implicitly cast aspersions about the leader's competence. For example, they might say, "Joe's a nice guy, but decision making isn't his strong suit" and "Joe's appointment is just an example of the company's failure to promote qualified women." We do not know whether Joe was incompetent. We do know that most of the complaining senior team members had themselves been passed over for promotion to the leadership job. Under the circumstances, even the official sanction of top management could not guarantee Joe's authority in the situation.

Value and Goal Differences

Conflict is likely to occur when different groups or members within the same group have contradictory values and goals. This form of conflict sometimes arises between production and sales groups in manufacturing companies. The sales group, which is compensated on straight commission, wants rapid production for high-volume sales and quick delivery. The production group desires a slower pace that permits emphasis on quality. The two groups are most likely to clash when sales makes requests for special attention to "rush" orders or when production is slow in meeting schedules.

Conflicts arising from value and goal differences can be deep and very difficult to resolve. Problems and their solutions always seem to be value laden. There is a problem only to the extent that it is an obstacle to some valued condition. A solution is good or acceptable only to the extent that it fulfills valued conditions. When human values and the goals that arise from these values come into conflict, the result can be anything from rivalry and feuding to all-out warfare. One need only consider the violent reaffirmation of government control at Tianamen Square in the People's Republic of China or, conversely, the crumbling of East European communism late in 1989 and the resulting war in Bosnia to realize just how powerful conflicts over values can be.

Competition for Resources

Different groups and even members of the same group often must draw their resources from a common pool—money for raises or for new positions, supplies, staff support, and funding for projects. The economics of scarcity, which many organizations have been forced to face since the turbulence of the 1970s, has only compounded internal competition for resources. Simply stated, the organizational resource pie is only so large. If one group gets a larger piece, some other group must settle for a smaller one. When group A gets a new person, someone in group B is laid off in order to pay for it. When group B's paperwork receives special priority at the word-processing center, group A's work has to wait. Particularly when competing groups are interdependent, a denial of resources to one so that the other may have them heightens the potential for intergroup conflict and reduces cooperation.

Managing Conflict

Strategies for managing conflict can be organized into four categories: establishment of superordinate goals, problem restructuring, structural interventions, and conflict-resolution activities.

Superordinate Goals

Where conflict arises as a consequence of competing or contradictory values and goals, the establishment of goals and values that are superordinate to those of the competing parties may reduce conflict. According to Schein (1970), this mode of conflict management requires the identification of goals upon which competing parties can agree and of values that are mutually acceptable. Dessler (1980) also noted that the use of special incentive systems may reduce discrepancies between goals of competing parties. For example, some years ago, Sears had trouble understanding why its stores in a certain region would not cooperate with one another on sales and special promotions until someone pointed out that managers were rewarded solely on the basis of individual store performance. Sears started a new policy of rewarding managers not only for sales within their own stores but also for their production across all stores in a certain area. Reportedly, improvement in cooperation was immediate.

Problem Restructuring

Even when conflicting parties realize it is in their best interests to negotiate an outcome that is mutually beneficial to each side, deadlocks can occur over problem description. For example, in a typical management-labor dispute over wages, the following problem interpretations are likely. Management views the demand for higher wages as potentially threatening to organizational survival. Managers justify this stance because higher wages drive up production costs. Higher production costs both reduce profits and potentially require higher prices (reducing the competitiveness of the firm). Workers, on the other hand, view the problem as one of management greed. Managers, from the workers' perspective, receive an unfair percentage of the firm's profits. The workers believe that their wages should be increased because of the vital role they play in producing high-quality products. One way to remove such deadlocks is to restructure the problem. As Sycara (1991) observes, "Problem restructuring is the process of dynamically changing the structure of the conflict problem to achieve momentum toward agreement" (p. 1248). The first step in problem restructuring is for each side to put its desired outcome goals (both short-term and long-term) on the table. Once these goals are on the conflict table, the parties can search for relations among the goals that indicate a dovetailing of interests. According to Sycara, "By having access to information concerning goals and relations among them, [conflicting parties] can produce promising problem reformulations" (p. 1249).

How does problem restructuring work? Let's return to the example presented above. Management and labor can restructure the problem as one of production efficiency and innovation. If labor is willing to work with management on reducing the costs of production (through increases in efficiency and worker-recommended innovations), then higher wages can be paid without reducing corporate profits or increasing product prices. In order for such a solution to be reached, however, both management and labor must be willing to work together to figure out how their interests coincide with one another.

Structural Intervention

Structural interventions involve changes in group structure and relationships. These include third-party mediation or arbitration of a conflict (often by levels of management higher than those represented by the competing parties), reduction of interdependency between groups, reduced sharing of resources, exchange of competing personnel (competing parties are required to assume one anothers' roles), creation of integrators or liaisons between groups, and increased communication between conflicting parties.

Conflict-Resolution Activities

Conflict-resolution activities have been categorized in several ways. Lawrence and Lorsch (1967) suggested that three basic types of activities exist: confrontation, smoothing, and forcing. Confrontation involves a recognition of an attempt to work through and solve problems surrounding a conflict without suppressing or avoiding it. Smoothing is a form of avoidance or suppression—pretending that sources of conflict are not present in hopes that the conflict will dissipate on its own. Forcing involves an effort to bring the conflict to a resolution by soliciting third-party intervention. In this case, forcing is a type of structural intervention. According to Lawrence and Lorsch, effective organizations are more often characterized by confrontation than by smoothing and forcing.

Dessler's (1980) concise, but rather simple, conception of conflict management may imply that conflict management is straightforward and easily accomplished with the right techniques, but many complicated factors influence organization members' choice of strategies, including the level of the conflict itself and the ease with which conflicts can be resolved. Some of the more important factors are discussed in a recent analysis of research on interpersonal and intergroup conflict presented by Putnam and Poole (1987).

Interpersonal Conflict

Putnam and Poole note that most work on interpersonal conflict in organizations has centered on **conflict styles** in superior-subordinate relationships. Conflict style "refers to a characteristic mode or habitual way that a person handles a dispute" (p. 556). Models of conflict style vary somewhat, but most are consistent with an early model proposed by Blake and Mouton (1964) and revised by Hall (1969). The model, presented in figure 13.1, is based on two dimensions: concern for your personal goals in the conflict and the importance of your relationship with the other person in the conflict. Both are rated on a 1 to 9 scale (low to high). Your "style" of conflict presumably can be located by the coordinate of your

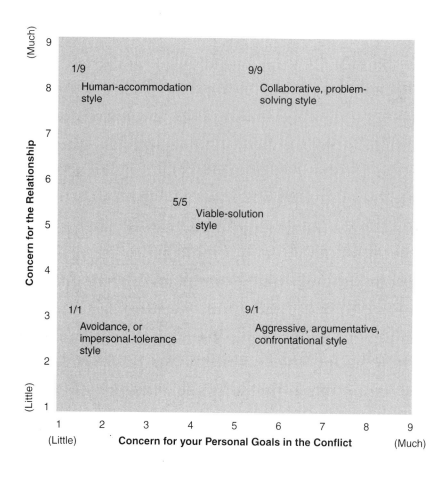

Figure 13.1
Conflict grid.
(From *Small Groups in Organizational Settings,* by R. Ross. Copyright 1989, Prentice-Hall, Inc. Reprinted with permission.)

Concern for the Relationship

(Much) 9

8 1/9
Human-accommodation style

9/9
Collaborative, problem-solving style

7

6

5/5
Viable-solution style

5

4

3 1/1
Avoidance, or impersonal-tolerance style

9/1
Aggressive, argumentative, confrontational style

2

(Little) 1

1   2   3   4   5   6   7   8   9
(Little)   Concern for your Personal Goals in the Conflict   (Much)

ratings on these two dimensions. Although there are eighty-one possible coordinates, each coordinate falls into one of five basic style categories.

The 1/1 Avoiding Style. This style is based on low concern for personal goals and for the relationship. The avoider refrains from arguing, withdraws from the situation, or otherwise tries to remain disconnected from the conflict.

9/1 Forcing Style. The forcer has high concern for personal goals in the conflict, but low concern for the relationship. Consequently, the forcer is aggressive, competitive, and confrontational in an effort to get his/her way.

1/9 Accommodating Style. When high concern for the relationship is coupled with low concern for personal goals, the result is an accommodating style. The accommodator glosses over differences or downplays disagreements in an effort to maintain the relationship.

9/9 Collaborating Style. The collaborator has high concern for personal goals and for the relationship. The collaborator faces the conflict directly and works toward an integrative solution. An integrative, or "win-win," solution embraces the goals of both parties in the conflict. Hence, the collaborating style often is viewed as the ideal in conflict management. Since this approach addresses the conflict directly, it is sometimes referred to as the *confronting* style.

5/5 Compromising Style. Given a moderate concern for personal goals in the conflict and a moderate concern for the relationship, the compromiser is willing to "split the difference" with the other party in the conflict, where each party gets something, but the end result probably is less than ideal for either. This is sometimes called the *viable solution* approach to conflict.

Generally, research suggests that several factors in the *relationship* between conflicting parties influence choice of conflict strategy. Superiors most often rely on forcing as a method of handling conflicts with their subordinates, although first-line supervisors are more likely than either middle- or upper-level managers to exhibit a collaborative style (Putnam & Wilson, 1982). Perhaps not suprisingly, subordinates tend to adopt avoiding, compromising, or accommodating styles in conflicts with superiors. Burke (1970) found that subordinates preferred for superiors to use a collaborative or confronting style, but superiors regarded collaborating as effective only when the issues are negotiable and conflicts of interest are low. According to Robbins (1978), forcing was regarded as the most effective strategy under conditions of incompatible goals or organizational endorsement of a particular solution. In this case, "organizational endorsement" probably is a euphemism for top-management insistence. Lawrence and Lorsch (1967) found that accommodating and compromising were acceptable strategies to subordinates, but superiors regarded these strategies as counterproductive. Organizational members in general have reported that the avoiding style is neither desirable nor effective (Burke, 1970).

Some studies, in particular Putnam and Wilson (1982), suggest that organization members adapt the conflict styles across different types of relationships. Although the concept of conflict style assumes that a person typically engages in a particular mode of action, one's actions in handling a conflict clearly depend on the relationship within which the conflict occurs.

Conflict style also appears to be influenced by *conflict issues*. Where conflict involves incompatible values, forcing is likely to occur. Compromising and accommodating are more likely when the conflict involves competition for scarce resources or personality differences. Putnam and Poole concluded that personality traits and contextual variables, such as organizational climate, leadership style, and communication climate, do not influence the selection of conflict strategies, although high levels of member commitment to the organization are positively associated with collaborative styles of conflict management.

The selection of conflict strategies also may be influenced to some extent by sex or gender, but the effect is unclear. Burrell, Buzzanell, and McMillan (1992) reviewed studies suggesting that women tend to assume noncompetitive and accommodating styles of conflict, but in their own investigation, they found that women regarded conflict as "war," which "corresponds to the traditional, also stereotypically 'masculine' construction of conflict interaction" (p. 132). Burrell and colleagues found that women do not necessarily prefer a destructive approach to conflict, but may engage in it because they have no other option. Similarly, Conrad (1991) found that women try longer than men to maintain prosocial strategies in handling conflict situations, but if the conflict wears on, both sexes ultimately turn to coercion in order to exact compliance from others. Finally, Papa and Natalle (1989) found that the key to discovering similarities and differences in the conflict behavior of men and women is to examine how their behaviors change over the course of a dispute. Specifically, they found that male-male conflict dyads used reason and assertiveness consistently over time, while female-female dyads shifted from high levels of assertiveness and reason to bargaining. Also, they found that when males and females were paired together, reason and bargaining were used throughout the interactions.

Researchers have begun to extend the study of interpersonal conflict in organizations beyond the narrow boundaries of conflict style in superior-subordinate relationships. One good example of such work is a study by Papa and Pood (1988) on coorientational accuracy and differentiation in conflict management within co-worker as well as superior-subordinate dyads in a large insurance company. Coorientational accuracy refers to "knowing where another person stands on an issue and what conflict tactics he or she prefers" (p. 401). Differentiation is "the process of clarifying differences in interactants' positions and pursuing the reasons behind those positions" (p. 401). Papa and Pood found that dyads entering a conflict with low coorientational accuracy spent much more time in differentiation than did high accuracy dyads. The finding is important because adequate differentiation is necessary in order to move conflict into an integration stage. According to Papa and Pood, "Dyads entering a conflict with low CA [coorientational accuracy] find it difficult to progress to the integration phase" (p. 418).

Another new direction in conflict research treats conflict management as a disputing process. This line of work directly challenges the adequacy of the two-dimensional basis for understanding conflict style that is presented in figure 13.1. This concept, derived from Blake and Mouton, has influenced most of the work on conflict styles, but Morrill and Thomas (1992) contend that it does not accurately characterize the kinds of conflict management behaviors that occur in organizations. Work by Morrill and Thomas suggests that conflict management behaviors are three dimensional, depending on aggressiveness, authoritativeness, and observability. Aggressiveness is one's willingness to achieve an outcome at the expense of the other party in the conflict. Authoritativeness is willingness to use social position in order to impose an outcome. Observability refers to the likelihood others outside the conflict will see or hear about the process.

A Competence-Based Approach to Interpersonal Conflict

One interesting development in conflict theory and research is a competence-based approach to describe how people can manage their disputes (Canary & Spitzberg, 1987, 1989; Spitzberg & Canary, 1985). Although this approach has typically been associated with personal relationships outside the organizational arena (e.g., marriages, friendships), recent work has shown its relevance to relationships within organizations (Papa & Canary, 1995; Papa & Papa, 1996).

The first feature of a competence-based approach to conflict management is to focus on the **impressions** of a person's communication behavior, not just the behavior itself. In other words, in conflict it is important to know how each person's behavior is perceived because any single behavior can be interpreted in a number of different ways. For instance, a threat can be perceived as inappropriate in certain instances, but appropriate in others (e.g., "If you do not complete this project by the deadline, your performance appraisal will suffer.").

The second feature of a competence-based approach is its focus on two behavioral criteria that are linked to communication quality: **appropriateness** and **effectiveness.** "Appropriateness refers to communication that avoids violation of relationally or situationally sanctioned rules, whereas effectiveness refers to communication that achieves the valued objectives of the interactant" (Papa & Canary, 1995, pp. 154–155). So the more appropriate and effective an interactant is, the more competent he or she is likely to be perceived. Importantly, "When two employees successfully manage a conflict in terms of appropriateness and effectiveness, not only is the immediate conflict issue resolved, the relationship between them is also preserved" (Papa & Canary, 1995, p. 157). Since relational preservation is necessary for people to work together productively, it is vital for organizational members to manage their conflicts in ways that are effective at the individual level and appropriate at the relationship level.

In order to explain how their competence-based approach is relevant to organizational members, Papa and Canary (1995) linked their discussion of competence to a **phase** model of conflict. Phase models describe the sequence of behaviors that people produce over time. Three conflict phases were described by Papa and Canary: **differentiation, mutual problem description, and integration.**

Differentiation refers to the process of people coming to terms with their differences in conflict. Sustaining this behavior during a conflict can be quite difficult. For example, during differentiation, emotional statements are likely as participants commit to positions (Apfelbaum, 1964). Also, differentiation can create uncertainty about the outcomes of the conflict and result in a heightened awareness of the consequences of not reaching a solution (Folger, Poole, & Stutman, 1993; Holsti, 1971; Smart & Vertinsky, 1977). So how can the pitfalls of differentiation be overcome? Papa and Canary (1995) argue that the key lies in **information sharing** (explaining your position on the issue of dispute) and **information seeking** (soliciting the other person's perspective).

Information sharing is important so each party to a conflict can understand the perspective advanced by his or her partner. Information seeking is important because it allows interactants to confirm the accuracy of their perceptions of a partner's views on the conflict issue (Papa & Papa, 1996). Also, without information seeking it may be difficult for each person to reach a clear understanding of his or her partner's views on the conflict.

In order to move from differentiation to integration, Papa and Canary (1995) argue that a middle phase must be enacted, namely, mutual problem description. In describing a conflict in mutual terms each party accepts responsibility for the conditions of the conflict and socially constructs the conflict in understandable terms. What this means is that each party accepts his or her role in creating and sustaining the conflict and the conflict problem is described clearly so each party understands what issues need to be negotiated. Mutual problem description also requires that the conflict problem is described as one requiring the efforts of each party to reach a mutually satisfying solution.

The final phase of conflict management is the integration phase. During this phase the parties remain focused on the problem and commit themselves to a solution that meets the goals of each party. According to Papa and Canary, six communication behaviors are linked to successful integration: (a) recognizing and postponing attributions, (b) maintaining cooperative tactics, (c) generating alternative solutions, (d) evaluating the positive and negative aspects of each proposed solution, (e) selecting and clarifying the solution to be implemented, and (f) establishing a monitoring system to determine if the solution is being implemented correctly. Let's take a brief look at each of these six behaviors.

Recognizing attributions refers to the fact that many people harbor biases regarding their attributions for causes of events (Bradbury & Fincham, 1990). For example, in dissatisfying conflicts, both parties "tend to attribute the causes of negative events to internal and stable features of the partner" (Papa & Canary, 1995, p. 166). A comment reflecting such a bias would be, "We are behind schedule because *he* is a slow worker." On the other hand, in satisfying conflicts the interactants are less likely to make such attributions. A statement reflecting this position would be "We are having financial problems because the cost of doing business has increased." So a first step in the integration phase is recognizing that "both parties to a conflict tend to think that the partner causes negative events, while (self-serving) biases preserve each person's own view of the self in conflict" (Papa & Canary, 1995, p. 167).

Maintaining cooperative tactics, the second part of Papa and Canary's integration phase, means enacting behaviors such as seeking a mutually beneficial solution, reasoning in a give-and-take manner, and compromising. Generating alternative solutions, the next integration step, is important for two reasons. First, it prevents disputants from identifying a solution too early in the process. Indeed, as Papa & Graham (1990) note, it is important to withhold the advancement of solutions until both parties agree on the nature of the problem. Second, when a number of solution alternatives are generated, it is more likely that a workable, mutual satisfying one will be identified. Once alternative solutions are identified, the disputants need to evaluate the positive and negative ramifications of each solution so the best one can be selected. Finally, a monitoring mechanism needs to be implemented. The reason a monitoring mechanism is necessary is to "prevent conflicting parties from undermining a solution by reverting to prior destructive behaviors" (Papa & Canary, 1995, p. 172).

Although the testing of this competence-based model in organizational settings is only in its early stages, there are some promising preliminary findings. Specifically, Papa and colleagues have found that their competence-based model can be applied to each of the four major arenas of organizational conflict: interpersonal, bargaining and negotiation, intergroup, and interorganizational. For example, in examining videotaped interactions of superiors and subordinates managing conflicts, Papa and Papa found that the competence-based model provided insight into how the disputes were managed successfully through each of three phases (differentiation, mutual problem description, and integration). They were also able to show how the successful collective bargaining agreement negotiated by players and owners of NBA teams in 1983 followed the competence-based model. This collective bargaining agreement resulted in the first player-owner partnership in professional sports. Future studies in organizational settings are necessary, however, to determine the extent to which this model offers opportunities for creative problem solving.

Coalitions and Intergroup Conflict

The large, complex organization provides a rich medium for the development of coalitions and the occurrence of intergroup conflict (i.e., conflict between different groups or units within the same organization). As Putnam and Poole (1987) point out, "When complexity increases, communication networks fragment and lead to different perspectives within units. If this condition is combined with high interdependence, conflict between units increases" (p. 575).

Intergroup conflict is affected by many contextual and structural factors in the organization. Factors as simple as physical separation of groups (e.g., different departments on different floors of a building or distances between field offices) may escalate conflict by making communication more difficult. Status distinctions between different groups also can lead to intergroup conflict (Dalton, 1959). As previously mentioned, competition for resources or ambiguous conditions in policy or authority may become sources of conflict. In the case of intergroup conflict, Zald (1981) found that groups increase their concern for equitable resource distribution in an effort to control their own destinies. Putnam and Poole also point out that " 'destabilizing' incidents, such as the departure of an executive or a financial crisis, often trigger struggles over the redistribution of power" (p. 576).

Not surprisingly, one of the major factors in intergroup conflict is the perception that groups have of their relationship. Those that see their relationship as competitive engage in misrepresentation, withholding of information, minimization of intergroup agreements accompanied by maximization of differences, discourse slanted favorably toward ingroup positions and unfavorably toward outgroup positions, and even charges of disloyalty against ingroup members who support positions taken by the outgroup (Walton, Dutton, & Cafferty, 1969; Blake & Mouton, 1964).

On the positive side, Thalhofer (1993) notes that intergroup conflict can be managed successfully if two conditions are present: **separateness** and **equal valuation.** The condition of separateness promotes the existence of separate, positive group identities. In other words, it is important to recognize that organizational members are likely to group together based on such factors as demographic (e.g., race, gender, ethnicity, age) and/or attitudinal similarities (e.g., comparable positions on issues). These various separate groups need to feel that their presence and contributions are respected within the organization. Also, in order for conflict to be managed successfully, an environment must be created where different group members recognize that their positions are equally valued in the intergroup environment. Thalhofer (1993) concludes that the conditions of separateness and equal valuation are particularly important for an organization to reap the benefits of an ethnically and racially diverse membership.

Much of the research on intergroup conflict is concerned with formal intact groups, but many of the more interesting conflicts in organizations may involve

coalitions that exist independently of the formal organizational structure. We touched briefly on the concept of organizational coalitions in chapter 6, saving the more detailed discussion for this chapter because coalitions are, by virtue of their very existance, agents of conflict. A coalition occurs when individuals band together in order to wield influence within the organization. Coalitional activity in large organizations seems to be as inevitable as the ebb and flow of the ocean tides, although the tides, unlike coalitions, are quite predictable. Stevenson, Pearce, and Porter say that a coalition has eight essential characteristics:

Interacting Group. Coalitions are considered to consist of members who communicate with one another about coalition issue(s) and potential coalition action.

Deliberately Constructed. Coalitions are explicitly constructed for a purpose. They can be distinguished from other informal groups by their self-conscious formation and design.

Independent of Formal Organization's Structure. A coalition is independent of formally designated groups such as departments, committees, or task forces. This does not mean that membership in coalitions and formally designated groups is necessarily mutually exclusive. . . . The formally designated structure of the organization may—but usually will not—coincide with a mapping of the network of coalitions within the organization.

Lack of Formal Internal Structure. Not only are coalitions independent of the formal structure of the organizations within which they are embedded, but they also lack their own formal structure. . . . Coalitions lack a hierarchy of formal, legitimate authority and are much more dependent on attempts at informal influence among members.

Mutual Perception of Membership. Coalitions, as with other nonformal groups, are likely to have fuzzy boundaries. Nevertheless, some reasonable consensus about who is a member and whose commitment is questionable would be expected.

Issue Oriented. Coalitions are formed to advance the purposes of their members. When their members cease to interact around these issues, the group no longer exists as a coalition.

External Focus. The issue that the coalition addresses must be external to the coalition. . . . The coalition forms to influence some external agent. This means that a coalition does not form merely so that its members may debate or argue some issue among themselves. It is created in order to get *other* organization members or groups to yield to its purposes through persuasion, coercion, or other means of influence.

Concerted Member Action. An integral part of the definition of coalitions is that they must act as a group, either through a group action . . . or through orchestrated member action. (1985, pp. 261–262)

Stevenson and colleagues also point out that many of the factors associated with intergroup conflict in general also may be linked with the formation of coalitions. They argue that coalitions are more likely to form in an organization when there is a major change in the allocation of resources or when some organization members believe that comparable others are receiving more favorable treatment. They also argue that coalition formation is more likely when there are opportunities for frequent interaction among organization members, and organization members have discretion in carrying out their job responsibilities. As the coalition itself becomes more visible, the issues pursued by the coalition also become more visible, and the likelihood increases that a "countercoalition" will form in order to block the aims of that coalition. Three examples of organizational coalitions that we have observed or read about will illustrate, however, that the forms, motives, and methods of coalitions may be very diverse.

1. The accounting department of a large manufacturing firm has always had a male manager. Historically, all of the professional accountants in the department had also been men, although the clerks and bookkeepers had been women. During the past few years, however, more women had entered the department as accountants. Now, about one-third of the accountants are female, and over one-half of the department employees are women. Apparently, the manager had a long history of sexual harassment, but the female clerks and bookkeepers had always been reluctant to take any action because they were in vulnerable positions and harassment was "just something you put up with." But the new professional women in higher-status accounting positions were not so willing to "put up" with the situation, particularly given new laws that allow for action against sexual harassment in organizations that allow it to occur. Under these new conditions, the women soon coalesced in order to support each other and pursue sexual harassment charges against the manager.

Eventually, the department manager was fired, but he was replaced by another male who was promoted from within the department. While most of the women were relieved by the change, two of the more influential female accountants were incensed that yet another man was given the manager's position. The two began to engage in a series of covert actions designed to redirect the coalition toward the replacement of the new manager with a female. Among other things, they initiated a biweekly "Women's Night Out," when all of the female members of the department met for dinner to discuss their work-related problems, but the primary purpose was to encourage all of the women to create problems for the new manager (e.g., taking maximum sick leave, making difficult requests for resources or work schedules, asking the manager continually to repeat or clarify directives, etc.) and, during managerial performance reviews, to turn in negative subordinate evaluations of their superior. The strategy worked. Frustrated and angry, the new manager resigned after less than twelve months in the position. He was replaced by one of the two coalition leaders.

2. During the 1980s public health issues surrounding the hazards of cigarette smoking expanded because of the concern for the dangers to smokers, which included the health risks to nonsmokers exposed to secondary smoke. Many companies were required to handle the problem of developing policies on smoking in the workplace. In some cases, top level executives or personnel managers surveyed employees to determine their opinions toward various options (e.g., open smoking, smoking only in restricted areas, or a complete smoking ban), then implemented policies that seemed to have the broadest support in the surveys. In other cases, policies developed only as a response to coalitional action among nonsmoking employees. These coalitions were visible only through the efforts of a few core members who were very vocal on the issue, but who were given more force by the tacit support of the "silent majority" of nonsmokers who outnumbered smokers by two to one. A coalition of this type can be very loose in the sense that most of its "members" engage in little or no direct interaction about the issue and may not even know each other. Yet, efforts to ban or restrict smoking in public areas and in the workplace have been so effective that Philip Morris Corporation, a major producer of tobacco products, has undertaken an active effort to promote "Smokers' Rights" groups throughout the country and to encourage countercoalitions to combat the actions of antismoking coalitions in organizations. *Philip Morris Magazine* even publishes what it calls a "Hall of Shame" list of companies that have imposed restrictions on workplace smoking.

3. In 1993, the president of Northern Arizona University allocated $200,000 to increase the salary of those faculty members who were identified as underpaid. Dozens of white male professors protested the distribution scheme for the raises. Their claim is that the method of distribution represented reverse discrimination. In fact, as many as seventy-six white male professors are expected to be part of a class action suit against the university. Their complaint is linked to a pay equity study completed by university administrators in 1993. In this

study it was determined that sixty-four white female professors, and twenty-seven minority professors were underpaid. Raises were given to all but six members of these two groups (annual raises ranged from $183 to $6,945).

Although 192 white male professors were also identified as underpaid, they received nothing. The administration claims it has corrected the problem by giving raises to all of the white male professors; however, the conflict remains. Many of the men are arguing that their raises were well below those paid to female and minority professors. As one professor stated, "If I had been a different race or sex, I would have received up to $6,900. What I was given retroactively was $1,200" (Wilson, 1995).

In the first case, the coalition is small, localized in a specific organizational unit, and works toward its objectives over a long period of time, sometimes overtly, sometimes covertly, with the concerted efforts of its members. In the second example, the coalition is large, with fuzzy boundaries. Status as a nonsmoker is the only specific defining characteristic of its members. Many of them may not really be "members" of the coalition, yet their presence in the organization and the policymakers' realization that they are nonsmokers tacitly lend force to the efforts of vocal core members. In the third example, the coalition is comprised of a group (white males) usually perceived as powerful in organizations; however, in this instance they are claiming to be disadvantaged by their status. Their path to resolving the conflict is formal and legal—filing a class action suit.

Bargaining and Negotiation

Bargaining and negotiation involve a special case of organizational conflict. Putnam and Poole state it as follows:

Bargaining constitutes a unique form of conflict management in that participants negotiated mutually shared rules and then cooperate within these rules to gain a competitive advantage over their opponent. . . . Bargaining, then, differs from other forms of conflict in its emphasis on proposal exchanges as a basis for reaching a joint settlement in cooperative-competitive situations. (1987, p. 563)

In chapter 2, we mentioned Mary Parker Follett's work on redefining traditional ideas of power and authority in order to achieve integration of competing interests. Follett's ideas directly influenced the development of classic bargaining theory. In particular, Walton and McKersie (1965) extended on Follett's work to classify bargaining processes in four categories: distributive, integrative, attitudinal structuring, and intraorganizational bargaining. Putnam and Jones (1982) narrowed the focus to distributive and integrative bargaining for purposes of communication research.

Putnam and Poole (1987) also suggest that much of the research on bargaining processes can be understood in terms of the distinction between distributive and integrative processes. A **distributive** bargaining situation "is one characterized by the existence or the appearance of fixed-sum (zero-sum) alternatives; one party must win and the other party must lose" (p. 172). In contrast, **integrative** bargaining "refers to situations where the potential outcomes can be expanded; inconsistent goals are combined to create a new alternative, one where neither side sacrifices his or her ultimate aims" (p. 172).

Distributive bargaining is characterized by deception, withholding of information, or the use of "disinformation" activities (i.e., directly disclosing information that obscures the negotiator's true objective). Bluffs, exaggerated demands, threats, and ambiguous cues are common in distributive bargaining. Negotiators conceal the strength of their positions, the outcomes that they really want, and the points that they are prepared to concede. Integrative bargaining is based on open communication, accurate disclosure of objectives, and sharing of information. Information is used for purposes of fact finding, problem definition, and generation of alternative solutions (Putnam & Poole, 1987).

How does one know the difference between accurate disclosure in an integrative situation and the misinformation of the distributive situation? In some cases, the circumstances themselves—the bargaining issue, the parties involved, and the resources at stake—will define the situation as distributive or integrative. For example, a local school board faced with a severe decline in tax revenues due to plant closings in the community enters negotiations with a teachers' union. The board, having exhausted all other possible options to reduce costs, must eliminate some teaching positions in order to balance its budget, but the union is absolutely committed to a "no lay off" clause in the new contract. The resulting environment is tense and distributive. In another school district on the other side of the state, the community is enjoying a strong period of economic expansion. Here, the issues between the board and the union are entirely different and both parties are seeking the best ways in which to use the abundant resources available to them.

But bargaining situations often are "mixed" rather than purely distributive or integrative. Moreover, Putnam and Jones contend that many bargaining situations are defined inappropriately as distributive. The situation is treated as a win-lose dilemma when, in fact, it is possible to achieve an integrative win-win settlement. Integrative strategies often do not appear until negotiators have gone through a lengthy period of distributive bargaining. In these situations, reciprocity is a critical factor in moving from distributive to integrative bargaining (e.g., when one party makes a concession and the other reciprocates). As we saw earlier in the study by Papa and Pood, differentiation also is critical for movement into integration stages of conflict, and differentiation appears to depend on coorientational accuracy. As Putnam and Poole point out, "integrative solutions emerge only after differences in perceptions of the problem are openly discussed" (p. 569).

Interorganizational Conflict: Examining Strategic Alliances

Interorganizational conflicts occur typically in the marketplace as "organizations attempt to carve out and maintain niches or domains" (Putnam & Poole, 1987, p. 581). The adoption of a communication perspective to study such conflicts is somewhat limiting since each competing organization will unilaterally pursue any action allowed by private and/or public regulatory agencies (Papa & Papa, 1996). There is, however, one type of interorganizational relationship that includes a mixture of motives to cooperate, compete, and engage in conflict. This type of interfirm relationship is called a *strategic alliance*. Parkhe (1991) explains that strategic alliances are "relatively enduring interfirm cooperative arrangements involving flows and linkages that utilize resources and/or governance structures from autonomous organizations for the joint accomplishment of individual goals linked to the corporate mission of each sponsoring firm" (p. 581).

Why do organizations enter into these strategic alliances? Well, when organizations began to downsize in the 1980s, many of them eliminated business functions that could no longer be executed competitively. For example, when IBM recognized that it could no longer manufacture computers competitively due to high labor costs in the U.S., it contracted with firms in Asia to take over much of its manufacturing function. IBM now defines itself as an engineering, design and marketing corporation, and it downplays its manufacturing role. In fact, Sherman (1992) reported that IBM had entered into 400 strategic alliances with companies in the U.S. and abroad as of 1991. Furthermore, Ernst and Bleeke (1993) report that the rate of strategic alliance formation between U.S. companies and international partners has been growing by 27 percent since 1985.

Why do strategic alliances create interorganizational conflict? Actually, strategic alliances offer opportunities for cooperation, competition, *and* conflict. Cooperation is necessary within the context of the specific agreement reached by the two firms. For example, a design and engineering firm contracts with a manufacturer to produce its products. The design and engineering firm pays for this service and expects that it will receive products from the manufacturer that meet its specifications. Competition may still exist between the two firms, however, regarding the marketing of products not covered by the alliance. Also, conflict occurs because each firm is motivated to uncover information from its partner that will increase its competitive advantage in the marketplace. In fact, in the consumer electronics industry, no U.S. manufacturer produces its own color television sets, VCRs, stereo equipment, or compact disc players. Unfortunately, the U.S. firms lost their competitive edge by unwittingly allowing critical technology to flow out of their corporations through poorly implemented alliance mechanisms. So all electronic products sold under the name of U.S. brands (e.g., Kodak, General Electric, RCA, Zenith, etc.) are made by their foreign alliance partners and imported into the U.S. (Lei & Slocum, 1992). Conflict between firms joined by a strategic alliance also occurs when there are differences in corporate culture. If the two firms linked by the alliance have substantially different cultures, it may be difficult for workers from the two organizations to work effectively together.

How can the conflicts likely to emerge in strategic alliances be prevented or how can their impact be lessened? A variety of recommendations have surfaced in the literature. First, the potential partners should discuss openly their mutual incentives for opportunism. In order to lessen opportunistic incentives, the firms can agree to institute punishments that are applied after a violation occurs. "These ex post deterrents consist of contractual safeguards, or stipulations in a formal partnership agreement, that inflict penalties for the omission of cooperative behaviors or commission of violative behaviors" (Parkhe, 1993, p. 804).

Of course, it is better to prevent violations of the alliance. So early in the negotiations to form an alliance, representatives of each firm should concentrate on how the partnership will enhance each firm's competitive position against *mutual* rivals (Shan, 1990). Indeed, by talking about the advantages of maintaining the partnership, each side may begin to recognize the value of cooperating rather than competing. This discussion should include a specific list of the economic benefits to be derived from the alliance and a description of the punishments linked to agreement violation (Parkhe, 1993).

The final part of promoting a successful strategic alliance is for the members of each organization to engage in frequent interaction and promote behavioral transparency. Frequent interaction between members is especially necessary as members of each firm learn to adapt to a different organizational culture. Also, frequent interaction allows the partners to perform periodic assessments of the outcomes of the alliance. Behavioral transparency refers to the speed and reliability with which partners learn about each other's actions. Frequent interaction and behavioral transparency can be promoted if the partners are willing to exchange workers. For example, in a recently formed alliance, IBM and BASF permanently transferred some staff and senior managers in charge of an alliance in order to improve their ability to conduct business with their partner. In describing this alliance, Jones (1992) concluded that "In the future, strong interpersonal linkages will be required to sustain learning and to provide the glue for keeping an alliance together" (p. 54).

Summary

Conflict is a common, yet widely misunderstood, phenomenon in group processes and intergroup relations. Classical theorists regarded conflict as an anomaly—an abnormal occurrence that was not supposed to happen. Contemporary organizational theorists stress the point that conflict is an inevitable and even necessary aspect of group and organizational processes. It should not be suppressed and avoided; instead, it should be confronted, managed, and resolved.

Conflict arises from many sources within groups and organizations, including various forms of role conflict, value and goal differences, and competition for limited resources. Various strategies for managing conflict can be organized into four categories: establishment of superordinate goals, problem restructuring, structural interventions, and conflict-resolution activities. Many complicated factors influence organizational members' choice of strategies, the level of the conflict itself, and the ease with which conflicts can be resolved. Some of the more important factors are examined in research on interpersonal and intergroup conflict. Most work on interpersonal conflict in organizations has centered on conflict styles in superior-subordinate relationships. Conflict style refers to a characteristic mode or habitual way that a person handles a dispute. A more recent development in studying interpersonal conflict in organizations looks at ways to sustain competent communication during conflict episodes. The competence perspective emphasizes how interactants can display relationally appropriate behaviors while also remaining effective in pursuing individual goals.

Much of the research on intergroup conflict is concerned with formal, intact groups, but many of the more interesting conflicts in organizations may involve coalitions that exist independently of the formal organizational structure.

Bargaining and negotiation involve a special case of organizational conflict. Communication research on bargaining processes usually is based on a distinction between distributive and integrative processes. Distributive bargaining involves the existence or the appearance of fixed-sum, win-lose situations. Integrative bargaining involves situations where the potential outcomes can be expanded or inconsistent goals combined in win-win outcomes. Distributive bargaining is characterized by deception, withholding of information, or the use of disinformation activities. Integrative bargaining is based on open communication, accurate disclosure of objectives, and sharing of information. Information is used for purposes of fact finding, problem definition, and generation of alternative solutions.

Strategic alliances provide opportunities and challenges for conflict management across organizational boundaries. In order to promote constructive conflict and prevent destructive conflict, the allied partners need to enact specific communication strategies. The partners must discuss incentives for opportunistic behavior and discourage such action by (a) focusing on the benefits of the alliance and (b) proposing potential punishments for violations of the agreement. The allied partners also need to engage in frequent interaction to promote understanding between organizational members. Finally, the activities of each side need to be observable so potential violations can be quickly detected and addressed.

Discussion Questions/ Activities

1. In what ways are power and conflict intertwined in organizations?
2. Are there any problems with a stylistic approach to the study of interpersonal conflict? Is one conflict style preferable to others? Why or why not?
3. Given the political nature of coalitions, under what conditions would it be ethically acceptable to form and work through coalitions in organizations? Are there circumstances under which coalitions might be unethical?
4. Assuming that integrative bargaining is superior to distributive bargaining, how does one move toward or encourage an integrative approach in the bargaining process? Can you think of any conditions under which distributive bargaining might be more effective than integrative bargaining?
5. Strategic alliances are sometimes formed between companies that have substantially different corporate cultures. How can these cultural differences be handled in a way that minimizes destructive conflict between the partners?

Additional Resources

Articles/Books

Cloven, D. H., & Roloff, M. E. (1995). Cognitive tuning effects of anticipating communication on thought about an interpersonal conflict. *Communication Reports, 8*, 1–9.

Friedman, R. A., & Podolny, J. (1992). Differentiation of boundary spanning roles: Labor negotiations and implications for role conflict. *Administrative Science Quarterly, 37*, 28–47.

Kolb, D. M., & Bartuniek, J. M. (Eds.). (1992). *Hidden conflict in organizations: Uncovering behind the scenes disputes.* Newbury Park, CA: Sage.

Natalle, E. J., & Papa, M. J. (1990). Gender and coorientational accuracy in conflict resolution. *International Journal of Group Tensions, 20*, 31–46.

Nicotera, A. M. (1994). The use of multiple approaches to conflict: A study of sequences. *Human Communication Research, 20*, 592–621.

Sitkin, S. B., & Bies, R. J. (1993). Social accounts in conflict situations: Using explanations to manage conflicts. *Human Relations, 46*, 349–370.

Web Site

http://www.cfe.cornell.edu/CPECM/cpecmhome.html
   Cornell University Conflict Management Program

References

Apfelbaum, E. (1964). On conflicts and bargaining. In L. Berkowitz (Ed.), Advances in experimental social posychology. New York: Academic Press.

Beckhard, R. (1969). *Organization development: Strategies and models.* Reading, MA: Addison-Wesley.

Blake, R. R., & Mouton, J. S. (1964). *The managerial grid.* Houston: Gulf Publishing.

Bradbury, T. N., & Fincham, F. D. (1990). Attributions in marriage: Review and critique. *Psychological Bulletin, 107,* 3–33.

Burke, R. J. (1970). Methods of resolving superior-subordinate conflict: The constructive use of subordinate differences and disagreements. *Organizational Behavior and Human Performance, 5,* 393–411.

Burrell, N. A., Buzzanell, P. M., & McMillan, J. J. (1992). Feminine tensions in conflict situations as revealed by metaphoric analyses. *Management Communication Quarterly, 6,* 115–149.

Canary, D. J., & Spitzberg, B. H. (1987). Appropriateness and effectiveness perceptions of conflict strategies. *Human Communication Research, 14,* 93–118.

Canary, D. J., & Spitzberg, B. H. (1989). A model of the perceived competence of conflict strategies. *Human Communication Research, 15,* 630–649.

Conrad, C. (1991). Communication in conflict: Style-strategy relationships. *Communication Monographs, 58,* 135–155.

Dalton, M. (1959). Conflicts between staff and line managerial officers. *American Sociological Review, 15,* 342–351.

Dessler, G. (1980). *Organization theory: Integrating structure and behavior.* Englewood Cliffs, NJ: Prentice-Hall.

Eisenberg, E. M. (1994). Dialogue as democratic discourse: Affirming Harrison (pp. 275–284). In S. A. Deetz (Ed.), *Communication Yearbook 17.* Thousand Oaks, CA: Sage.

Ernst, D., & Bleeke, J. (1993). *Collaborating to compete.* New York: McKinsey.

Folger, J. P., Poole, M. S., & Stutman, R. K. (1993). *Working through conflict* (2nd ed.). New York: HarperCollins..

Goldhaber, G. M. (1993). *Organizational communication* (6th ed.). Dubuque, IA: Brown & Benchmark Publishers.

Habermas, J. (1979). *Communication and the evolution of society* (T. McCarthy, Trans.). Boston: Beacon Press, 1979.

Hall, J. (1969). *Conflict management survey: A survey of one's characteristic reaction to and handling of conflicts between himself and others.* Monroe, TX: Telemetrics International.

Holsti, O. R. (1971). Crisis, stress, and decision-making. *International Social Science Journal, 23,* 53–67.

Janis, I. L. (1972). *Victims of groupthink.* Boston: Houghton Mifflin.

Jones, K. (1992). Competing to learn in Japan. *McKinsey Quarterly, 1,* 45–57.

Koehler, J. W., Anatol, K. W. E., and Applbaum, R. L. (1981). *Organizational communication: Behavioral perspectives* (2nd ed.). New York: Holt, Rinehart & Winston.

Lawrence, P. R., & Lorsch, J. W. (1967). *Organization and environment.* Boston: Division of Research, Graduate School of Business Administration, Harvard University.

Lei, D., & Slocum, J. W. (1992). Global strategy, competence-building and strategic alliances. *California Management Review, 26*(4), 81–97.

Morrill, C., & Thomas, C. K. (1992). Organizational conflict management as disputing process: The problem of social escalation. *Human Communication Research, 18,* 400–428.

Mumby, D. K. (1987). The political function of narrative in organizations. *Communication Monographs, 54,* 113–127.

Papa, M. J., & Canary, D. J. (1995). Conflict in organizations: A competence-based approach. In A. M. Nicotera (Ed.), *Conflict and organizations* (pp. 153–179). Albany, NY: State University of New York Press.

Papa, M. J., & Graham, E. E. (1990, June). *A test of the ecological validity of the functional perspective of small group decision-making.* Paper presented at the annual meeting of the International Communication Association. Dublin, Ireland.

Papa, M. J., & Natalle, E. J. (1989). Gender, strategy selection and discussion satisfaction in interpersonal conflict. *Western Journal of Speech Communication, 53,* 260–272.

Papa, M. J., & Papa, W. H. (1996). Competence in organizational conflicts. In W. R. Cupach & D. J. Canary (Eds.), *Competence in interpersonal conflict* (pp. 214–242). New York: McGraw-Hill.

Papa, M. J., & Pood, E. A. (1988). Coorientational accuracy and differentiation in the management of conflict. *Communication Research, 15,* 400–425.

Parkhe, A. (1991). Interfirm diversity, organizational learning, and longevity in global strategic alliances. *Journal of International Business Studies, 22,* 579–601.

Parkhe, A. (1993). Strategic alliance structuring: A game theoretic and transaction cost examination of interfirm cooperation. *Academy of Management Journal, 36,* 794–829.

Putnam, L. L., & Jones, T. S. (1982). Reciprocity in negotiations: An analysis of bargaining interaction. *Communication Monographs, 49,* 171–191.

Putnam, L. L., & Poole, M. S. (1987). Conflict and negotiation. In F. M. Jablin, L. L. Putnam, K. H. Roberts, & L. W. Porter (Eds.), *Handbook of organizational communication: An interdisciplinary perspective* (pp. 549–599). Newbury Park, CA: Sage.

Putnam, L. L., & Wilson, S. R. (1982). Communicative strategies in organizational conflicts: Reliability and validity of a measurement scale. In M. Burgoon (Ed.), *Communication yearbook 6* (pp. 629–652). Newbury Park, CA: Sage.

Redding, W. C. (1985). Rocking boats, blowing whistles, and teaching speech communication. *Communication Education, 34,* 245–258.

Robbins, S. P. (1977). Managing organizational conflict. In J. Schnee, E. K. Warren, & H. Lazarus (Eds.), *The progress of management.* Englewood Cliffs, NJ: Prentice-Hall.

Robbins, S. P. (1978). "Conflict management" and "conflict resolution" are not synonymous terms. *California Management Review, 21,* 67–75.

Schein, E. (1969). *Process consultation: Its role in organization development.* Reading, MA: Addison-Wesley.

Schein, E. (1970). *Organizational psychology.* Englewood Cliffs, NJ: Prentice-Hall.

Shan, W. (1990). An empirical analysis of organizational strategies by entrepreneurial high-technology firms. *Strategic Management Journal, 11,* 129–139.

Sherman, S. Are strategic alliances working? *Fortune,* September 21, 1992, 77–78.

Smart, C., & Vertinsky, I. (1977). Designs for crisis decision units. *Administrative Science Quarterly, 22,* 640–657.

Spitzberg, B. H., & Canary, D. J. (1985). Loneliness and relationally competent communication. *Journal of Social and Personal Relationships, 2,* 387–402.

Stevenson, W. B., Pearce, J. L., & Porter, L. W. (1985). The concept of "coalition" in organization theory and research. *Academy of Management Review, 10,* 256–268.

Sycara, K. P. (1991). Problem restructuring in negotiation. *Management Science, 37,* 1248–1268.

Thalhofer, N. N. (1993). Intergroup differentiation and reduction of intergroup conflict. *Small Group Research, 24*(1), 28–43.

Walton, R. E., Dutton, J. M., & Cafferty, T. P. (1969) Organizational context and interdepartmental conflict. *Administrative Science Quarterly, 14,* 73–84.

Walton, R. E., & McKersie, R. B. (1965). *A behavioral theory of labor negotiations: An analysis of a social interaction system.* New York: McGraw-Hill.

Wilson, R. (1995, November 24). Equal pay, equal work? *The Chronicle of Higher Education, 62*(13): A15–A16.

Zald, M. (1981). Political economy: A framework for comparative analysis. In M. Zey-Ferrell & M. Aiken (Eds.), *Complex organizations: Critical perspectives* (pp. 237–262). Glenview, IL: Scott, Foresman.

This part concludes with three case studies that may be used to illustrate concepts of organizational culture, cultural diversity, power, and conflict. Questions with each case suggest appropriate uses, but these cases are flexible and may be applied across a broad range of themes.

**Part Three
Case Studies**

Playing the Game

Hylton Villett

James reported for work at 8:58 A.M. on the first day of his first job after graduating from college. A bit nervous, James took the elevator to the second floor to meet Craig Adams, the CEO of Performa, Inc., a British multinational corporation operating in James' home country, Namibia. Because James had been recruited right out of college by a "head hunting" firm, he had never met Craig or anyone else at Performa.

"Good morning," James said to the receptionist. "I am James Page, a new employee here to see Mr. Adams." The receptionist informed Craig Adams, and Craig came out to the reception area to greet James. "Hi, James. Welcome to Performa," said Craig, as he extended his hand. "We are glad to have you join our team." "Thank you," replied James, "I certainly am glad to be here." Craig then invited James into Craig's office and offered him a seat.

"You know, James," Craig continued, "we are very proud of what we do here at Performa. We have championship teams in all of our departments." As he motioned to a wall of award certificates and plaques that Performa had received, he said, "Our record of winning speaks for itself. I'm sure that you will enjoy working with the guys in Marketing. We want every player at Performa to feel that he belongs to a dynamic team."

James had noticed that Craig was dressed very informally—not at all what he expected a CEO to look like. Just as he was going to ask about the dress code, the phone rang. "It's Rob," said Craig, "Let's get down there so you can meet the striker of Marketing." They got to the Marketing Department, an open-plan office, and Craig introduced James to Rob. "Come on, James," said Rob, "We're having a team meeting to review the playbook for our next game."

By now, James was a little confused. Striker? Playbooks? Games? What were these guys talking about? Rob took James to the Gameroom, a large area with one round table, a coffee maker, and some vending machines. Everyone was gathered around the table. After introducing James, Rob said, "Craig just informed me this morning that we're competing for a new contract against a couple of our arch rivals, and we've got to get together a good game plan to be sure we win it."

After Rob provided a few more details, other members chimed in. "To win this one, we're going to need some get setplays," said Dennis. "You're right about that," Peter replied, "We can't afford any dribbling. George, Tim, and I will be the midfielders on this one, and we'll make the pass to Dennis and Rob to strike up front."

The meeting continued on in this way for another hour. James knew that the terms came from the game of soccer, but he had never played soccer, nor did he follow the game, so talking about the work project in this way sounded like senseless chatter to him. He was baffled. Just as he decided to ask for some clarifications, Rob said, "Ok, I think we've all got our positions and plays, so lets take it to them." With that, everyone scattered, and James was left standing by himself.

In a few minutes, Pat returned. "Are you ready to roll?" Pat asked. "Roll?" said James. "Yes. We have to get out on the field to get some data. I'm taking you with me to show you how we do things." James was thankful that someone apparently was going to show him the ropes, but his optimism turned to dismay when Pat spent their time together talking about how their task would be to mark and charge the rival companies. The rest of the week continued in this way. By the end of the week, James understood no more about what he was supposed to do than he had understood when he arrived on his first day. He resigned from his new position, explaining to Rob that he did not think that he was cut out for this kind of work.

1. What can you infer about the organizational culture at Performa from the information in this case? Is this a "strong" culture or a "weak" one? How do you suppose it came to be constructed in the way that it is?
2. How would a feminist theorist critique the culture at Performa?
3. Is Performa the kind of company that promotes diversity? Why or why not?

Having an Attitude?

Hylton Villett

After graduating from college in 1985, Michael Miller got a job with Roberts Uranium, one of the largest uranium mining companies in Southern Africa. Michael started out in the Market Department where he worked his way up the career ladder, ultimately accepting a transfer to the Human Resource Development Department in 1990. Michael enjoyed the new challenge tremendously and got along very well with his colleagues and his supervisor, John Dammert. For the first time in five years, Michael was able to use the full range of his formal academic training, including design and presentation of training courses to first-line supervisors on supervision and problem solving. He performed very well in his new job and received a very good performance evaluation for his first year.

During 1991, Roberts Uranium experienced a progressive drive by the Mineworkers Union to unionize the company. The company tried to avoid recognition of the union, but the union won the certification election to represent the workers in bargaining with the company. Michael decided to become a union member. Soon after joining the union, Michael felt that his good relationship with his colleagues and especially with John Dammert was beginning to deteriorate.

The change did not worry Michael very much until the occasion of his next performance evaluation session with John. Here is a transcript of the meeting:

John: Michael, we've been working together for more than a year now, and I must admit that I am satisfied with your work. Your training courses have always been well prepared and well presented. However, we have noticed that you behave differently now than you did when you started here. Some of the course participants and your colleagues complain that you have an attitude problem which brings a lot of negativity to our department. As you know, positive interpersonal relations account for a large portion of this evalution, and it is very important for the type of work that you do. Michael, your attitude will affect your potential for promotion in this department. I think you should do something about it, or consider transferring to another department or resigning. I have no place for people with negative attitudes in my department, and I have no alternative but to give you a below average appraisal.

Michael: But . . . I do not have an attitude, and besides, this evaluation will not only affect my promotion, but also my immediate salary increase for this year. How do you justify this evaluation compared to the one that I received last year? I have been doing this job for more than a year now, and I definitely have improved. You said so yourself.

John: Michael, how do you expect me to give you an excellent evaluation in light of what is happening?

Michael: What *is* happening?

John: I feel that your attitude is seriously affecting the good working relationships in my department, and I cannot allow that.

Michael: Is this because I joined the union?

John: You can call it whatever you want, Michael. All I am saying is that since you joined the union, your attitude toward your work and colleagues has changed.

Michael: I disagree with you, and I will file a grievance against you to sort this out.

Michael stormed out of Dammert's office and went straight to the Industrial Relations Officer (IRO) to file a grievance against John. The IRO took Michael's statement of his complaint and later set up a grievance hearing with John Dammert's boss, Phil Burgess. Michael had always admired Phil and respected his opinion on HRD issues. Here is a partial transcript of the hearing:

Phil: Michael, according to this grievance dossier, you claim that you are being evaluated unfairly and that you are being victimized by John for being a member of the union. Why do you think this is the case?

Michael: First, I have improved so much in this job, and it is difficult to accept that I performed worse this year compared to last year. Second, although John did not say it explicitly, he implied that he has a problem with my union membership.

Phil: As you know, it is our company's policy not to discriminate against employees who join the union. However, I think you need to consider the pros and cons of being a union member and at the same time being a training officer. Think about it. You train supervisors who are at the forefront of daily union/management conflicts. How do you think the

	supervisors will accept training from a union member . . . someone from the other side?
Michael:	Well, I don't know.
Phil:	You know that I have been in the HRD field for over 20 years, and I can assure you that those supervisors view everything that you say with some skepticism. Don't you think so, too?
Michael:	Maybe they do.
Phil:	That is exactly what I think John was trying to tell you.
Michael:	He surely didn't express it to me in that way.
Phil:	Tell me, Michael, what is more important to you. Career advancement or union membership?
Michael:	Career advancement is very important to me.
Phil:	If that is the case, then your decision should be easy. You think about terminating your union membership, and I will speak to John about this situation and your salary increase for this coming year. Thereafter, I'd like for all three of us to meet and put this problem to rest.

Michael thanked Phil, shook his hand, and returned to his office.

1. Identify and describe the sources of conflict in this case.
2. Identify and describe the different conflict styles used by John and Phil.
3. Given the French and Raven model, what types of power are reflected in this case?
4. How would a critical theorist explain the discourse that occurred in this case and the way that the case turned out?

Diversity Dilemma

Harlin Lane was taken completely by surprise when Naguri Chofi marched up to his company cafeteria table in an obviously agitated and angry mood. Harlin, the company's operations manager, knew Naguri only as a very mildmannered and soft-spoken Kenyan who earned two degrees from a United States university, became a United States citizen, and joined the firm's research and development group about six months ago. He couldn't even imagine why Naguri had approached him in such an enraged state.

"Mr. Lane," Naguri began, "It is not my desire to make this your problem, but the motor pool of company cars is under your authority, and I want you to know that I am very upset that two employees from marketing who were going to the American Manufacturing Association convention last week in a company car refused to allow me to travel with them when I was assigned by my director to attend the same convention. I ended up taking my own vehicle at great expense, and I am sure, very sure, that the only reason these two white women refused me is because I am a black man. It is an affront to my dignity that they should do this. Something should be said to let them know what an injustice they have done."

Harlin took it all in, then said to Chofi, "Naguri, this is the first that I have heard of this, so I'm completely surprised by it. Can you give me a couple of days to look into it? I'll let you know what I find out and what response, if any, might be appropriate." "Yes," said Chofi, "I can accept that. I will call you two days hence, and I thank you for hearing my grievance."

After lunch, Harlin made a couple of phone calls to flesh out the details in Chofi's story. Apparently, the marketing department had reserved a company car for two employees to attend the AMA convention in another state. They would be driving in the evening and arrive at the convention very late at night. The director of research and development just happened to hear in a casual conversation that two people from marketing, Helen Barker and Juanita Garcia, were going to the convention. She had planned to send Naguri to the same convention, so she called the motor pool manager to add Naguri's name to the list of travelers who would be in the company car, and also notified one of the two marketing employees that Chofi would be joining them for the trip.

Chofi came to the motor pool at the appointed time, luggage in hand, but the two women refused to let him accompany them in the car, explaining that their department had checked out the car and they had no authorization to allow someone from another department to travel in the vehicle. The motor pool manager refused to intervene, saying that his only responsibility was to check out the vehicle, not decide who could travel in it. Chofi tried to call his director, but she was unavailable, and the two women from marketing left without him. Embarrassed and exasperated, Chofi walked to his own car and drove it to the convention.

When Harlin spoke with Barker and Garcia for some clarification, they indicated that their main reason for refusing Chofi was apprehension about traveling at night with an unfamiliar male. Helen and Judy were both in their early twenties and also fairly new employees. The convention was their first overnight travel for the company. They had never met Chofi before and felt that they might be putting themselves at risk. Harlin told the two women that he understood their concern, but he thought they could have handled the situation much more effectively by contacting a higher-level manager such as Lane for the authorization. He got the clear impression, though, that an authorization to take Chofi was the last thing that the women really wanted. He wondered, "If I were a woman, would I have done the same thing?" The facts having been made clear, Lane called Chofi and presented an acceptable face-saving fiction that the incident was just a misunderstanding, then told Chofi to submit a travel voucher for complete reimbursement of all of his expenses for the convention. Chofi thanked Lane for his graciousness and concern, but also added, "I don't believe this was a misunderstanding by these women. I have been in America long enough to know what racism is when I see it."

Later that week, Lane presented the situation in a management meeting for discussion. He hoped it would provide a basis for examining the company's growing workforce diversity and responding effectively to that diversity. The research and development director was incensed that her employee had been denied the right to ride in a company car. As she expressed it, "This incident just tells Chofi that he's a second class citizen, that he's automatically held in suspicion until he proves that he's above suspicion. It sure sounds like discrimination to me, and I think we owe him an apology." The marketing manager, also a woman, defended Helen and Juanita's decision. "Nobody even told me of the intention to send Chofi with my people, but I'm telling you right now that I wouldn't have allowed it if I had known. Compelling female employees to travel in a car at night with a man whom neither they nor I even know sounds to me like sexual harassment." The tension at that moment was so great that the whole subject was immediately dropped. Harlin left the meeting wondering when the next diversity crisis would occur.

1. What does this case say to us about the complexities of diversity and diversity management in organizations?
2. Given the circumstances of this case as presented, should Chofi have been allowed to travel with Barker and Garcia? Why or why not?
3. What, if anything, could have been done to prevent this situation from becoming an employee relations crisis? Apply ideas from the chapter on conflict to address this question.
4. What would you do to prevent similar situations from arising in the future?

PART FOUR
COMMUNICATION AND EXECUTIVE STRATEGY

STRATEGIC COMMUNICATION

Amy Stone, a new college graduate, recently was hired as an assistant dietitian at a large urban hospital. On her first day at work, she reported to the personnel office, where she was told that she, along with several other newly hired employees, would participate in a daylong orientation program. During the program, Amy and her companions saw a thirty-minute videotape about the history, services, and "caring tradition" of the hospital. They received copies of the employee handbook, along with a detailed review of hospital organization and policies. They also received a portfolio of information about employee benefits such as health insurance, pension plans, and credit union membership. They even got a personal welcome from the hospital administrator.

Later in the week, Amy got her first copy of the hospital's monthly magazine. The magazine was a slick professional production with stories about activities in several hospital departments, employee-of-the-month awards, an article by the administrator on the importance of delivering high-quality health care, and an "action line," in which designated managers answered questions and complaints from employees.

A few days after this, Amy noticed an advertisement in the city newspaper that the hospital had sponsored as a "public service." The ad described the growing need to control health-care costs and some of the factors that cause these costs to go up. One of these factors was competition among hospitals when too many serve the same community. According to the ad, competition in health care does not have the expected effect of reducing costs but actually causes the cost of health care to increase. Amy mentioned the ad to her supervisor and asked why the hospital was publishing such a statement, even if it was a public service. The supervisor told her that a large national health care corporation was trying to get a state permit to build a new hospital in the city. The hospital's top administrators decided to do an advertising campaign in hopes of creating public opposition to the new hospital.

Each of Amy's encounters (with the orientation program, the magazine, and the newspaper advertisement) is an obvious instance of public communication—the effort of a particular source or agent to communicate with a given audience or public. Each episode also includes features of **strategic** *organizational* communication that are less obvious. First, public communication in the organizational context can require a substantial commitment of resources: production facilities for newsletters, company magazines, and video programs; advertising space in print and electronic media; and salaries for the professionals who write, edit, and produce public communication programs. Second, top-level executives ultimately control these resources and use them for *strategic* purposes, in framing the organizational mission and directing the organization toward that mission. Although the content of public communication programs is influenced by employee groups, communities, special-interest groups, and in some cases, even legal requirements, those who control organizational resources also control the agenda for public communication. Consequently, we label these efforts as *strategic* communication in order to distinguish them from other forms of public communication.

When executives decide to commit resources to strategic organizational communication, they often have some form of public communication in mind. Generally, these forms may be classified as **internal** or **external.** Internal communication has become synonymous with the term *employee communications* (Williams, 1978). **Employee communications** is management's effort to provide information to and exert influence with organizational membership in general. External public communication traditionally has included advertising and public relations efforts designed to influence consumers, communities, special-interest groups, voters, regulators, and legislators.

In this chapter, we will describe various forms and examples of internal and external strategic communication. Although an organization's advertising and promotion of its products or services are a form of public communication, we will not be concerned with this activity. Instead, our treatment of external communication will focus on public relations functions and a recent transition in some major organizations in the U.S. away from traditional public relations to a concept known as **public affairs** and **issues management.** First, we will review some of the basic characteristics of strategic communication.

Characteristics of Strategic Communication

Public communication has been described as a process of *one communicating with many* (Wiseman & Barker, 1967). One person, who functions as a message source, creates and transmits a message to many others, who function as receivers.

Unfortunately, this intuitively obvious definition of public communication over-simplifies the idea of a "source" in strategic organizational communication activities and also fails to recognize the transactional character of communication.

The Source in Strategic Communication

Conventional definitions of public communication treat the source of messages as a specific individual. Although this may apply in some situations, messages intended for strategic communication in organizations often are originated and produced by organizational subsystems composed of many individuals. This point is illustrated in the following example.

Unitech Industries has never had a formal system for appraisal of employee performance. The personnel department has just developed a system for companywide appraisal of performance and then has persuaded management to adopt it. Since the new system will be used for decisions involving pay raises, promotions, and terminations, top management wants to ease potential employee concerns over the change in policy. At this point, top management decides to tell the communication department to develop an informational program that will explain to employees the appraisal system and the reasons for its adoption. Executives from top management, communication, and personnel groups will collaborate on deciding the content of the informational programs. After they decide what employees will be told, staff members in the communication department will write a series of articles based on these informational decisions and run the articles in the company newsletter.

In the Unitech example, top management makes the initial decision to provide employees with information on a policy change. Although the communication and personnel departments collaborate with top management on decisions about information provided to employees, in a real sense, it is management's message that is transmitted to the internal employee public. The communication department acts as a staff arm of management in producing and executing the informational programs. As the example indicates, strategic communication can be a complex process in which a number of units and individuals contribute to the dissemination of messages.

Strategic Communication as Transaction

Strategic communication, like other forms of public communication, usually is regarded as a linear process. Most of us seem to understand public communication in terms of a source-oriented view of presenting messages in ways designed to secure a desired response. Since the purpose of strategic communication often involves persuasion and gaining compliance, the image of the successful communicator is one of a person who has discovered some formula for using words to mold an audience like putty. This idea is quite misguided. Sources do gain compliance from receivers, but acceptance of an idea is an act that arises from the receivers' choices. No universal formula in public communication exists for guaranteeing that receivers' choices will be consistent with the intentions of the source.

Strategic communication programs arise out of executive objectives, but strategic communication, like other communication contexts, may be more appropriately characterized as a transactional process that merely takes on a deceptively linear appearance. Even though the "source" and "receiver" roles in any given episode of strategic communication may be relatively fixed, the people in these roles are participants in a process of creating shared meaning. They interpret the situation at hand, act within the situation, and influence one another simultaneously.

Internal Communication

Management often engages in efforts to disseminate messages and information through the entire structure of an organization to employees or other specific groups within the organization. This is *internal communication* or, as it is often called, *employee communications*. A 1978 survey of chief executive officers in major U.S. and Canadian corporations found that the majority regard employee communications as an important feature of their management plan and a contributor to organizational effectiveness and productivity (Williams, 1978).

The means for internal communication may include any of the following media and methods:

employee meetings
newsletters
internal magazines
manuals and handbooks
general memos
pay-voucher inserts
posters and bulletin boards
public-address systems
videotape, film, and slides
closed-circuit television

Some large organizations with ample resources for communication programs employ all of these systems. These days, of course, we can also add computer-mediated systems and Web sites to the list as a means of getting out strategic messages.

Organizational efforts at internal communication occur for many reasons. These reasons often are managerially biased in the sense that they represent management views and objectives. Whether this bias is appropriate or not, managerial bias influences the choice of topics and the content of messages involved in internal communication. Many of the conventional internal communication topics can be grouped under five functional areas: **orientation and indoctrination, safety and loss prevention, compensation and benefits, organizational change and development,** and **morale and satisfaction.**

Orientation and Indoctrination

Imagine that you are a new employee in a large organization. You have just been hired for a job in which you are well trained, but is your immediate task to gain knowledge about all that you want or need to know about the position and the organization? More than likely, it is not. You may arrive with a number of unanswered questions that range from "What is the company philosophy?" and "How does my job relate to the total organization?" to "When do I receive my first paycheck?" and "Where is the cafeteria?"

Many organizations provide answers to such questions through some type of formal orientation program. An orientation program may include topics that pertain to the organization as a whole (policies, procedures, operating philosophy, and structure), your specific position (scope of authority, job duties, work procedures), and other personal concerns.

Completion of orientation does not mean that you will never again be exposed to messages on organizational matters or your role within the organization. The maintenance and integration functions of communication that we described in chapter 5 often are carried out in part through a continuous program of public communication aimed at indoctrination and socialization of organization members. Such programs often are intended to build an organizational image with the internal employee public and to present and reinforce specific values, beliefs, and practices.

An example of an intensive orientation and indoctrination effort is reflected in programs conducted by Junior Achievement, Incorporated, a national nonprofit educational corporation. Junior Achievement franchises local program operations throughout the U.S. Typically, the only full-time paid staff members in these local programs are the executive directors, who work in relative isolation from the national office as well as from one another. This kind of isolation in combination with the franchise relationship means that the national office cannot directly control the executive directors of the local programs. Isolation also can have adverse effects on the directors' motivation and commitment to the goals of the national program. Consequently, the national office conducts an intensive two-week orientation program for all new field executives. Most of the content involves national policies and procedures along with methods and standards for local program operation, but the orientation also is an open attempt to cast the new executives in the national mold. The orientation is conducted with a group of new executives who are not only exposed to formal training but who are also placed in informal situations where they can interact, form friendships and alliances, and reinforce organizational values with one another. After they return to their own local offices, the national office continues indoctrination and reinforcement through frequent newsletters, bulletins, regional meetings, and occasional visits from internal consultants.

Safety and Loss Prevention

Organizations have two reasons for the promotion of safety and loss prevention. One is the conservation of organizational resources. The other is the welfare of organization members. Inventory shrinkages, theft of company property, and job-related accidents jeopardize both of these objectives, although it is probably fair to say that many organizations are more concerned with resource conservation than with member welfare because the former has a direct connection with costs and profits. Thus, many organizations make a conscientious effort to control losses and promote safe working practices through internal public communication.

For example, in the late 1960s, the Santa Fe Railway was plagued by a poor safety record. Accidents resulted in lost time and increased insurance risks. In an effort to improve, the Santa Fe management began a "Zero in on Safety" program that was promoted through internal publications, meetings between supervisors and top management, a safety film, employee-designed posters, and even a safety-incentive reward program. Within two years, Santa Fe's safety record advanced from nineteenth to first among the nation's large railroads (Industrial Communications Council, 1975). Even though it would not be appropriate to say that the public communication effort "caused" this improvement, the presence of the program clearly was a major factor in focusing attention on safety at Santa Fe.

In a limited sense, internal communication regarding safety is required by the Occupational Safety and Health Administration (OSHA). For example, OSHA requires the posting of warning and regulatory signs in hazardous work areas. But OSHA's authority under the 1970 Occupational Safety and Health Act focuses primarily on *compliance* with safety standards rather than on *promotion* of safety through communication programs. According to some safety and loss-prevention experts, any organization that really wants to promote safety and loss prevention "must go beyond OSHA compliance activities" (Peterson, 1975, p. 117). Strategic communication programs may form a major portion of these additional activities.

Compensation and Benefits

Whether or not work organizations wish to implement and maintain employee benefits, communication programs concerning employee benefits are virtually mandatory. The Employee Retirement Income Security Act, which became federal law in 1974, requires organizations to make full and understandable disclosure of employee benefit programs.

Benefit programs in large organizations can be very elaborate. In addition to basic health protection, life insurance, and pension plans, these programs may also include credit union participation, use of company recreation facilities, child-care services, family and personal counseling services, and profit-sharing plans. Development of a communication program that can effectively and efficiently provide information on benefit packages can also be complicated. Many organizations manage to incorporate information about benefits in orientation programs as a simple means of meeting legal requirements with new personnel. Changes in benefit packages, however, also require systematic dissemination of information to all personnel.

Organizational Change and Development

Change is a stressful process, even when it is desirable. This is especially true for organization members who do not participate in the basic decisions on such matters. When organizations undergo substantial change, many of the members may be very uncertain about the impact that the change will have on the organization and their positions within it. Members may need a great deal of new information in order to understand the purposes and effects of major change. In order to meet this need for information, management may authorize large-scale internal campaigns.

A classic instance of a massive, yet rapidly executed, internal public communication effort to cope with uncertainty over a major organizational change arose out of AT&T's divestiture agreement with the federal government in the early 1980s. In return for dismissal of a government antitrust suit, AT&T agreed to sell more than twenty of its operating companies, including Mountain Bell Telephone, a company providing telephone service in western states. Mountain Bell executives, who had some forewarning of the decision, were advised by AT&T one morning in January 1982 that the agreement with the government would be made public later *on the same day.*

Mountain Bell executives were concerned that company employees (more than 50,000) would get their first information about the decision on evening news programs. These executives understood that organization members can be very displeased and disconcerted when they don't receive important information within the organization before it appears in the media. Moreover, the situation was ripe with the possibility for morale-devastating rumors about the consequences of the change; in particular, the situation was ripe for rumors about massive layoffs, forced retirements, job changes, and transfers.

Mountain Bell attempted to mount an internal communication effort that would reach as many of its members as possible within the few hours remaining before the evening news programs. Obviously, tactics such as a special newsletter, a company magazine article, or an attempt to relay the message from level to level in the organization were useless in this situation. Instead, the company president appeared on Mountain Bell's internal closed-circuit television system to announce and explain the AT&T decision. All of the personnel who worked in offices with access to the television system were convened to hear the president's announcement. The presentation was reinforced later in employee meetings at all Mountain Bell locations. The one-day effort reached about sixty percent of the organization members.

Internal communication concerned with organization change sometimes occurs in the crisis atmosphere reflected in the Mountain Bell example, but it more often is an ongoing process intended to familiarize members with long-term goals, objectives, plans, and progress. Yet if you recall our discussion of information adequacy in chapter 5, these are precisely the kinds of topics on which many organization members think they are inadequately informed. Apparently, either many organizations do a poor job of public communication regarding organizational change and development or most members simply ignore the information.

Morale and Satisfaction

The final functional area in internal communication includes the promotion of morale and satisfaction among organization members. Messages concerned with any of the other four areas may serve this purpose, too, but promotion of morale and satisfaction includes many types of messages that are unrelated to these other areas. Messages that serve maintenance and human functions often fall into this group. For example, an employee-of-the-month column in a company magazine or notes about departmental accomplishments in the newsletter are instances of messages that have as their primary objectives the improvement of members' self-concepts, interpersonal relationships, and attitudes toward the organization.

External Communication

J. W. Hill (1977) argued that every private-sector corporation in contemporary America is faced with two tests: maintaining profitability and meeting the expectations and demands of society. A similar admonition can be offered to public-sector and nonprofit organizations by changing "maintaining profitability" to "providing services within budget" (although one wonders whether this will ever apply to the federal government!). In either case, contemporary organizations are faced with the problem of meeting societal demands.

Much has been written in recent years about growing public disenchantment with large corporations and institutions (Gallup, 1979). Hill believed that this problem developed, in part, because of public dependence on large organizations—dependence that brings about public frustration when such organizations fail to meet legitimate public needs and expectations. External communication is a means through which organizations can understand and respond to public expectations in ways that allow an organization to meet its other tests.

External communication occurs in at least three major forms: (1) *advertising and promoting products and services,* (2) *creating a desirable public image for the organization,* (3) *shaping public opinion on issues that are important to the organization.* In this text, we are concerned with the second and third functions. Traditionally, communication concerned with **image building** has been the responsibility of public relations practitioners. During the past twenty years, however, many organizations have expanded the concept of strategic communication to include a new function–the management of **public issues** and **public affairs.** In fact, some types of organizations exist solely for the purpose of advocating and gaining acceptance of positions on public issues. For example, virtually everyone has at least some familiarity with organizations such as the National Consumers Union, Public Interest Research Group, Sierra Club, National Organization for Women, and the Urban League. Frequently, public-interest organizations and special-interest groups challenge business and government policies when these policies adversely affect the environment, consumers, minorities, and communities. Some corporations have attempted to cope with these challenges by shifting away from image building to identifying and tracking public issues that concern the organization. An organization may try to change in order to respond to public criticism or it may try to influence public opinion on important issues by advocating its own position in the public arena (Sethi, 1982).

Public Relations and Image Building

Gerald Goldhaber (1993) described **image building** as a process of creating the identity an organization wants its relevant publics to perceive. Image building involves an organization's attempt to cultivate a public impression that a set of positively valued features defines the essential character of the organization.

Corporate and business concerns over image building date back to at least the mid-1950s, when the *Harvard Business Review* published a landmark article on business image (Gardner & Rainwater, 1955) and many major companies made definite efforts to change their corporate images (Finn, 1962). Typically, such changes are accomplished by developing and publicizing specific organizational characteristics and behaviors that are consistent with the image being cultivated. The art of image building usually is associated with the field of public relations. Clearly, it is inappropriate to equate the whole field of public relations with nothing more than image-building activity. In fact, Heath and Nelson (1986) indicate that the primary distinction between public affairs and public relations occurs in their relative focus on commercial or noncommercial concerns and in their power to direct corporate planning:

If public affairs is concerned primarily with the noncommercial aspects of corporate communication, public relations could be designated as being responsible for commercial communication, excluding paid product and service advertising . . . generally, public relations has no power to direct corporate planning departments. . . . (p. 27)

While Heath and Nelson point out that public relations functions may include activities such as media relations, marketing publicity, and internal communication, the process of image building has become, nonetheless, a major feature of public relations practice. For example, public relations has been defined as "the management function which evaluates public attitudes, identifies the policies and procedures of an individual or an organization with the public interest, and executes a program of action to earn public understanding and acceptance" (Cutlip & Center, 1964, p. 4). The second part of this definition, identifying an individual or organization with the public interest, lies at the heart of the image-building process. Hence, Scott Cutlip and Allen Center, whose text on public relations is a classic in the field, argued in 1964 that farsighted contemporary public relations practice is concerned with developing public appreciation of good organizational performance. Presumably, this appreciation is a public image of what the organization is or does.

Image building continues to be a major concern in many types of organizations. In the 1970s, Ford automobiles were humorously called cars that one must *Fix Or Repair Daily*, and Henry Ford II openly admitted in a segment of *Sixty Minutes* that the company had manufactured some bad products. Today, Ford works hard (at least in its corporate advertising) to be known as the company where "Quality Is Job One." When repairs on the Exxon *Valdez*, the ship that lost millions of gallons of oil when it ran aground in Prince William Sound, were completed in July, 1990, the ship was renamed the *Mediterranean* and sent to transport oil from the Persian Gulf. Exxon said that the ship was no longer needed on the oil run from Alaska to California, but Keeble (1991) claims, ". . . it's more likely that the company hoped the new name and assignment would wipe out the ship's former identity" (p. 260).

Big corporations are not the only organizations that worry about image. American labor unions, struggling with dramatic losses of membership during the

1970s, still are attempting to redefine their relevance to workers, while the National Democratic Party, demolished in three consecutive presidential elections, refurbished its image in order to achieve identification with voters and captured the White House in 1992, then lost both houses of Congress in 1994. Such examples remind us that image building also involves image maintenance, and maintenance always is a continuing process.

At times, it seems as if every public entity is in the image-building business. Even the notorious motorcycle club Hell's Angels has tried through a publicity campaign to shake its reputation as a loose assemblage of thugs and sociopaths and to replace it with a public view of the Angels as community-minded, upstanding citizens. Some months after being acquitted on charges of murdering Ronald Goldman and Nicole Brown Simpson, O. J. Simpson rolled out a television campaign in an attempt to rehabilitate his tarnished image.

Despite the prevalence of image building in public relations practice, serious questions exist about the real purposes served by such activity. When public relations is equated with public appreciation of good organizational performance, the equation presumes that the performance is, in fact, good. But what happens when performance is not good? Chandler (1988) provided an interesting answer to this question in his examination of annual reports issued by Fortune 500 companies. The annual report is a "colorful, expensive document that allows the organization almost total rhetorical flexibility in choosing how to describe performance and communicate that description to the organization's audience" (p. 5). Chandler studied the reports of twenty profitable companies as well as those of twenty unprofitable companies. He found, perhaps not surprisingly, that corporations attributed poor performance to external factors beyond management control (e.g., legal constraints, government regulation, poor economic conditions, unfair competition, or labor problems). In contrast, good performance was attributed to management decisions such as product innovations or new marketing strategies.

Public relations tools and strategies can provide valuable information to audiences, but they also can be instruments of concealment and deceit for covering up poor performance or downplaying harmful actions. More importantly, much of the emphasis on developing public image may have more to do with fulfilling the psychoemotional needs of managers and executives than with influencing public opinion. David Finn (1962) described the problem this way:

The recent interest of organizations and public figures in images–besides compensating for self-doubt and rationalizing overweening ambition–is also a search for meaning in a confused period of history. The fact that corporate images have turned out to be just another fictitious wardrobe for the Emperor who still walks naked in the streets is not important. The image is so tenacious, not because it dresses up the organization, but because it answers a basic need for finding a convincing purpose for the corporate enterprise.

Public Affairs and Issues Management

In recent years, several types of organizations, especially some large corporations, have moved beyond traditional image-building functions of public communication in order to deal more effectively with social and political issues that affect organizations and their relationships with various publics. This new and emerging concern often is identified by the label **public affairs** and **issues management.** Richard Armstrong (1981) noted that public relations and public affairs overlap to some extent, but corporate executives draw a line between the two functions. Unlike public relations, public affairs developed primarily out of concerns over issues that lead to laws and government regulations affecting organizations. Issues management is a principle vehicle through which public affairs can accomplish its objectives. As described by Arrington and Sawaya (1984), issues management involves foresight, policy development, and advocacy. Buchholz (1982) reported that 91 percent of the Fortune 500 companies have implemented issues management programs.

Organizations become involved in public affairs and issues management for various reasons. In the case of a public-interest or special-interest group, the principal purpose of the organization is to create public awareness of issues and to influence local, state, or federal government policies on these issues. These efforts at influence frequently challenge business and industrial organizations, which respond with their own attempts to influence public policy. Such attempts at influence not only arise from conflicts between business and public-interest groups, but they also arise among entire industries. Industry versus industry confrontations occurred several times during the 1980s. For example, in 1985, the federal government proposed to ease its standards for automobile fuel economy. Ford and General Motors, whose products did not on average meet 1984 standards, favored the reduction. Chrysler, a company that invested heavily in the technology required to meet the standards, opposed the change. Other recent examples include the furor created in the boxing industry when the American Medical Association called for a ban on the sport and the furor raised within the American Medical Association over the insurance industry's ideas for controlling physicians' fees!

Virtually every working organization in America is subject to some form of legal regulation that has an effect on operations and effectiveness. Heavily regulated industries and trade groups traditionally have relied on legislative lobbying to influence the regulatory process. The basic idea in lobbying is to obtain passage of laws that favor your industry or group and to ensure the failure of unfavorable legislation. But influencing legislative and regulatory processes poses two problems for industries and trade groups. First, many public issues do not become the objects of legislative action until they have grown, developed, and become politicized. In this case, lobbying is a *reactive* approach to a matter on which public opinion may already be frozen (i.e., not easily changed). Second, many organizations have used political and legislative influence strategies in ways that are almost exclusively self-serving, without regard for the real public interest in a situation. Hence, as the late J. W. Hill (1977) pointed out, failure to address public issues adequately is a major weakness in many organizations.

Public issues often represent adversity to executives and managers precisely because they raise challenges to the organization's established traditions and modes of operation. It is not surprising that managers avoid such issues until an effect on the organization seems inevitable. As Jones and Chase argued, "The

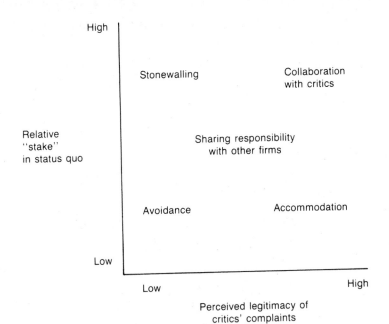

Figure 14.1
Modes of corporate response.
(From *Corporate Behavior and Social Change,* by J. E. Post, 1978, Reston, VA: Reston Publishing. Adapted by permission of John Wiley & Sons from "Conflict and conflict management," by K. Thomas, 1976, in M. Dunnette (Ed.), *Handbook of Industrial and Organizational Psychology,* Chicago: Rand-McNally.)

most significant explanation of the failure of business to gain respect for its positions on public issues is that corporate leadership either does not recognize or ignore the discernible trends which always precede issues" (1977, p. 3). James E. Post (1978) has developed a model of corporate responses to public issues that helps to explain how such failures occur.

Post characterizes organizational responses in light of two factors: (1) the organization's stake in maintaining the status quo (i.e., in continuing its current practices) and (2) the perceived legitimacy of public complaints against the status quo. According to Post's model in figure 14.1, organizations will avoid a public issue if both the stakes and perceived legitimacy are low. If the stakes are high and perceived legitimacy is low, organizations tend to "stonewall" with cover-ups, distortions, and other methods. Where stakes are low and perceived legitimacy is high, the organization attempts to accommodate critics through some form of change. If both the stakes and perceived legitimacy are high, the organization attempts to collaborate with critics.

Avoidance and stonewalling are based on a perception that the legitimacy of complaints arising from a public issue is low, but executives' *perceptions* of legitimacy may have little to do with the actual impact that a public issue may have on an organization. The only way to assess the importance of a public issue and to develop an appropriate response to the issue is through some means of tracking and monitoring the issue as it develops. This process is the central feature of issues management (Jones & Chase, 1977).

Raymond P. Ewing (1979) pointed out that issues management is concerned with "emerging issues whose definition and contending positions are evolving in the public arena and legislation or regulation is likely in a moving time frame of 18 to 36 months" (p. 15). He described several techniques that organizations can use to track and predict the development of such issues. Some of the more common techniques include the following:

1. *Trend extrapolation.* A factor or variable is measured over time and statistical forecasting techniques are used to project a trend from these measurements.
2. *Trend impact analysis.* This technique is a variation on trend extrapolation. After a trend is extrapolated, experts identify future events that would affect the extrapolation and the trend is modified in light of these events.
3. *Scanning.* A relatively simple technique in which issues that might affect an organization are identified and monitored by use of volunteers who regularly scan print and electronic media for useful information.
4. *Monitoring.* This method may be used in conjunction with scanning. Scanning identifies potential issues, while monitoring tracks these issues through systematic analysis of data. Monitoring may include public opinion polling and other forms of social science research.
5. *Scenario writing.* This technique begins by asking the question, "What would happen if X came to pass?" Given an assumption that X occurs, a chronological projection into the future is written. According to Ewing, some large organizations hire novelists and playwrights to develop and write such scenarios.

The kinds of tools that Ewing described help organizations to gather and interpret information on emerging public issues. Development of a meaningful information base on a public issue is only one component, however, of an issues management project. The other important component involves the use of this information in decision-making processes that lead to organizational action on the issue. This action typically takes one of two forms: organizational change or issue advocacy.

Issues Management and Organizational Change

Sometimes issues management may mean changing the organization and communicating with relevant publics about this change. A classic case of corporate change in response to public issues is reflected in the experience of Giant Food Corporation, which we discussed briefly in an earlier chapter. Giant operated many of its stores in urban inner-city areas. These urban communities were inhabited largely by minority groups who suffered the devastating effects of institutionalized racism–high unemployment, low education, poor housing, and, worst of all, little hope of real improvement in these conditions. Under the guidance of Paul Forbes, a private community relations consultant, Giant executives began to recognize that their customers also were members of a disenfranchised and increasingly frustrated segment of American society.

Many corporations that operated in inner-city areas during this period either didn't recognize or simply ignored the oppressive economic and social forces that mired these communities in a cycle of poverty. In the eyes of these communities, such companies were viewed as the agents of oppression–profiteers who took a great deal away, while returning nothing. Giant executives decided that they did not want this role for their company, but their actions went far beyond the simple mechanics of image building. The corporation undertook a careful study of inner-city problems, then responded with an equal employment opportunity program long before the federal government required such programs. Giant recruited minority job applicants and devised on-the-job training programs in order to merge corporate and community interests.

Sometime later, violence erupted throughout urban Washington, D.C., just after the assassination of Martin Luther King, Jr. The stores of many of Giant's competitors (who, according to Forbes, openly poked fun at Giant's community action programs) were demolished by riots and looting. The total damage to Giant Food facilities consisted of one broken store window. The company's stores had been defended and saved by community residents. The commitment to social change through corporate change resulted in a "payoff" for Giant Food not only because company property was protected but also because Giant had become a publicly valued member of the communities that it served.

Issues Management and Issues Advocacy

While organizational change is sometimes an appropriate response to public issues, another legitimate form of action is advocacy of the organization's positions on these issues. Public communication programs based on issues advocacy are quite different from the traditional image-building activities of public relations. As described by Prakesh Sethi, traditional image building is "usually rather general in scope and bland in character," whereas issues advocacy "addresses itself to specific controversial issues, presenting facts and arguments that project the sponsor's viewpoint . . . to try to influence political decisions by molding public opinion" (1982, p. 162). Sethi probably should have added that advocacy campaigns often are intended to preserve the organizational status quo.

One of the most obvious public issues that has generated considerable advocacy is the problem of environmental protection. Any organization that has a significant impact upon ecology because of its operations will have to answer to government and to the public at large. Some large industries have actively resisted environmental protection regulations. Others have taken a more realistic approach to the issue. For example, Public Service Company of New Mexico, an electric company operating in a region with a rapidly growing demand for power, decided to meet the increasing demand with coal-fired generating stations that require very expensive "scrubbers" to minimize air pollution. The costs of pollution control are passed on to the company's customers. Obviously, this means higher electric bills.

Rather than opposing the environmental protection laws that require control of air pollution, Public Service Company of New Mexico has taken a middle-of-the-road position on the issue. A major theme in the company's public communication campaigns is the need for balance between rates that customers pay for electricity and the cost of environmental protection. In advertising messages prepared primarily for its customers, the company affirms its own commitment to a clean environment, but it also argues that clean air cannot be attained without paying a price. The company suggests to customers that they, as voters, are really the ones who set environmental protection standards. In turn, as consumers of electricity, they will pay for their standards. The implication in this message is fairly obvious. If you want clean air, you had better be prepared to pay for it. If you want to control the rates you pay for electricity, then you have to control the clean air standards that the company is required to meet (see figure 14.2).

Of course, the outcome of an advocacy campaign may not be exactly what the advocate expects. A good example of an unanticipated outcome is reflected in the case of another environmental campaign waged by American Electric Power (AEP) in the mid-1970s. AEP, like PNM, wanted to present a case for coal-fired generating stations but got caught on the controversial issue of sulphur dioxide emissions from coal. According to Heath and Nelson (1986), AEP admitted that scrubber technology could control most of the emissions, but argued that disposal of sludge from scrubbers would destroy the land. While Sethi (1977) and Hush (1983) contend that the AEP campaign was very successful, AEP's use of fear appeals in the campaign drew the editorial wrath of the *Washington Post* and *New York Times,* and the Environmental Protection Agency (EPA) received more than 200 letters of protest about the campaign. The campaign failed to defeat interest in scrubber technology. EPA officials believed that their efforts to promote tougher clean-air standards "were strengthened by the AEP campaign, since the public learned more about scrubbers than it would have otherwise" (Heath & Nelson, p. 98).

Although some issues advocacy campaigns focus on a single issue that is salient to an organization, others are quite complex and involve several different types of public issues. Sethi (1982) provides an example of this kind of complexity in an extensive case study of advocacy campaigns conducted by Bethlehem Steel during the 1970s. Bethlehem executives identified six public issues that concerned their company and the steel industry in general:

1. Capital formation and federal tax reform.
2. Energy conservation.
3. Pollution and the environment.
4. Government overregulation.
5. Business concentration.
6. Steel imports and foreign trade policy.

You probably would not have to engage in much guesswork to figure out the company's positions on most of these issues. Obviously, the steel industry is not pleased with foreign competition because American steel companies have been decimated by cheaper foreign products. Furthermore, the use of the term "*over-regulation*" in issue 4 is a sure-fire giveaway of the company's position. According to Sethi (1982), Bethlehem budgeted $1.5 million in 1978 for advertising messages on these issues, but the company's problem was not as simple as just spending a lot of money to argue positions on these issues. For example, issues 4 and 6 put the company in a paradoxical situation. How can you argue against government regulation in one message, then ask for government intervention to control imports in another? Formulating argumentative strategies that resolved such problems required time and resources that went well beyond mere advertising costs.

ENERGY AND THE ENVIRONMENT:
HOW MUCH IS ENOUGH?

Figure 14.2
Example of issues advocacy advertising. (Reprinted by permission of Public Service Company of New Mexico.)

Balancing the need to develop adequate energy supplies with the need to maintain a clean environment in New Mexico is the constant challenge facing each of us. As the number of our customers increases and their demand for electricity grows, PNM must build generating plants and transmission lines to serve that demand. But at what cost to the environment? If steps are taken to reduce the effect on the environment, how much will you, the rate-payer, pay? And who will make the rules defining acceptable environmental standards? These are the questions facing all of us, you and PNM.

There is a strong link between environmental concerns and the economics of scarcity. Consider San Juan Generating Station. When increased demand necessitated additional electrical generation in New Mexico, coal was the obvious choice as a fuel source. Why? Because New Mexico is rich in coal resources. A power plant using natural gas would have been easier to operate, quicker to build and cheaper in the short run. The problem is that availability and price of future supplies of natural gas are in doubt. Besides, rather than being used as a boiler fuel, natural gas is better used for other societal needs, such as chemical and pharmaceutical purposes. Also, using the fuels we have reduces our nation's dependence on foreign imports.

Therefore coal, which we have in abundance, was chosen to be the boiler fuel at San Juan. But when burned, coal produces considerable pollutants—among these, fly ash and sulfur dioxide. These pollutants can have a major effect on air quality. To solve this problem, PNM constructed San Juan with "state of the art" pollution control equipment. Today the plant is a model for the electricity industry. But at a price. The sulfur dioxide scrubbers for the first two San Juan units, for instance, cost more than $120 million.

But environmental concerns at PNM extend beyond clear air. Energy development can also have a major impact on land, water and cultural resources. To make sure that PNM's activities have a minimum impact on the environment at the most reasonable cost, the company has a large environmental affairs department. Employing biologists, archaeologists, chemical engineers, land use planners, forestry and range specialists, atmospheric scientists, chemists and others, the department is charged with putting into action PNM's commitment to a clean and healthy environment.

Some of their work is nationally recognized as superior, such as the Chaco Canyon study recently featured on the PBS **Odyssey** program, or the department's long-term study of birds of prey; and, of course, San Juan Generating Station itself. But what is important is that PNM has demonstrated that energy development can go forward in harmony with the concern we all have of protecting our environment. Again, at a price. **Today, about 10 percent of your monthly electric bill goes to pay for environmental activities.** Should you pay more? Should you pay less? As a society, we need to agree on what environmental standards we want and how much we are willing to pay to meet them.

You, PNM'S customers, make the rules through your vote and through participating in the regulatory process. You pay to meet the environmental standards. And you benefit from those standards.

Please remember, all of mankind's activities affect the environment. That is unavoidable. Even the garden you planted drastically changed the ecology of your backyard. **The basic question then remains: how much is enough?** What standards do we as a society want for land use? For cultural resources? And how much are we willing to pay to meet these standards? Energy is produced for your use; therefore, consider the resources at your command and command them wisely.

This is the fifth of a series of six statements designed to confront the issues and concerns about energy: its availability, cost and impact. The entire series is being paid for by the stockholders of PNM, 5,300 of whom reside in New Mexico.

PNM
Public Service Company of New Mexico

If one takes the Bethlehem Steel, Public Service Company of New Mexico, and American Electric Power cases as typical examples of issues advocacy (and we believe that they are typical), then the social justification for issues advocacy seems questionable because the programs are one-sided and apparently self-serving. Indeed, the most controversial campaigns in this respect have been those run by Mobil Oil Corporation, one of the leading companies in issues advertising. Mobil's efforts to point out media bias against business, to protect the free enterprise system, and to chide the government for ill-conceived regulations and ineffective management have been described even by corporate executives of major American companies as "too strident" (Heath & Nelson, p. 81).

It is important to remember, however, that advocacy campaigns frequently are initiated in response to some specific challenge that is creating a public issue. In a pluralistic, free society, organizations, like individuals, have a right to speak out on issues. Hence, Mobil Oil contends that its campaigns are designed to promote the exercise of First Amendment rights, "to present our views and our ideas along with established facts to assist the public in making decisions" (quoted in Heath & Nelson, p. 81). Moreover, as we noted earlier, the growing sophistication of the advocacy concept often brings large organizations and entire industries into public conflict. Issues advocacy is no longer simply a case of a public-interest group versus a large corporation, but it is sometimes one corporation versus another or even one interest group versus another.

Recently, some issues advocacy campaigns have either eliminated or toned down their self-serving characteristics. In these cases, organizations are advocating positions that not only involve their interests but also involve the welfare of society as a whole. In the early 1980s, the W. R. Grace Corporation began a series of advocacy messages intended to encourage more efficient industrial production in the United States in the face of foreign competition. At one point, however, the Grace campaign became something of a public issue itself when the company was accused of anti-Japanese rhetoric in its messages. By 1985, Grace had moved its campaigns into an attack on the federal budget deficit and another call to efficiency, this time directed at the federal government. Yet W. R. Grace Corporation is not threatened directly by either foreign competition or the federal budget deficit. The selection of such issues for advocacy campaigns seems more dependent on the Grace executives' perception of public interest than on immediately tangible corporate interests.

The Grace Corporation experience also points out some of the obstacles to successfully mounting an issues advocacy campaign. In 1986, the company wanted to sponsor a highly controversial television message on the federal budget deficit. The advertisement portrayed a futuristic setting in which young people were conducting criminal court proceedings against former government officials. These officials in this America of the future had been charged with destroying the economy through their failure to halt deficit spending. Grace officials wanted to air the advertisement immediately after former President Reagan's State of the

Union Address, but all three of the major television networks refused to accept it. Some weeks later, Grace obtained limited access to air the message on network television.

Public Communication in Crisis Situations

Most of the concepts and examples of strategic communication that we have thus far considered in public relations and issues management presume that organizations have time to think through and carefully plan their strategies and messages. What happens when an organization must mount a major strategic communication effort in the midst of a crisis, especially a crisis that attracts the attention of national media? The answer to this question is sought after intensively by executives and leaders of many organizations around the world for a simple, but compelling reason. According to Bud Englehart, a public relations officer who has worked for companies such as Kraft Foods, Lockheed, and Mellon Bank, if you begin with the value of an organization and subtract from it the organization's material assets, "what you have left is the value that *perception* creates. . . . You can lose that value in a nano-second in a crisis" (1995, p. 27).

Barton (1993) defines a **crisis** as "a major, unpredictable event that has potentially negative results [and] may significantly damage an organization" (p. 5). Because a crisis can have devastating consequences for an organization, Williams and Treadaway (1992) add three other characteristics: urgency, observation by the media, and interruption of normal operations. Crises in this sense certainly are nothing new to corporations, institutions, and other types of organizational entities. Imagine the shock and horror that must have afflicted officials of the White Star Line when they heard on April 15, 1912 that their "unsinkable" steamer, *Titanic,* had gone to the bottom of the Atlantic Ocean with some 1,500 souls aboard or the panic that must have swept over bank executives and stock exchange officers on Tuesday, October 29, 1929, the date of the stock market crash that signaled the beginning of the Great Depression. The purpose of crisis communication is to respond appropriately in such situations to maintain public confidence and minimize the damage.

Egelhoff and Sen (1991) estimate from surveys that a typical, large organization confronts an average of ten crises per year. Certainly most crises do not rise to the level of public scrutiny and concern accorded to events such as the massive Alaskan oil spill that resulted from the grounding of the Exxon *Valdez* in 1989 or the frightening Tylenol cyanide tampering case of 1982 when seven people died and packaging for many foods and drugs changed forever. But all crises have the potential, as Englehart noted, to damage the value of an organization by damaging public perception of that organization. Major incidents such as the Tylenol tampering and *Valdez* grounding especially provide classic illustrations of effectiveness and ineffectiveness in crisis communication.

The case of the Exxon *Valdez* oil spill began when the *Valdez* struck Bligh Reef in Prince William Sound shortly after midnight on March 24, 1989, as the crew was trying to avoid heavy ice by going outside the normal ship lanes.

Alyeska Pipeline Company's contingency plan, approved by the Alaska Department of Environmental Conservation (ADEC), called for that company to be on the scene within five hours with equipment to begin containment of the spill. Instead, Alyeska, according to Keeble (1991), showed up in fifteen hours "with woefully insufficient gear" (p. 54).

Given Alyeska's inability to implement an effective response, Exxon itself wanted permission to spray the ever-worsening oil slick with chemical dispersants while it arranged for clean-up equipment and another tanker to pump all remaining oil off the *Valdez,* but opposition to the use of dispersants from members of the fishing industry and ADEC officials and an inadequate supply of dispersants delayed a decision until it was too late. On March 27, three days after the spill had begun, a major storm hit Alaska's Prince William Sound and pushed the oil over hundreds of miles of water, fouling shorelines and killing otters and birds.

According to Keeble, it was the spectacle of the dead–the oil-covered animals lying prostrate on the shores–that provided stark visual images for the media and riveted public attention as if the event were "a soap opera or science fiction thriller" (p. 168). The body was dead, the public sought the murderer, and the cold light of media attention focused on Joseph Hazelwood, the *Valdez* skipper, and on Exxon Corporation itself.

Exxon executive Frank Iarossi, who had come immediately to Alaska, began to hold two press conferences per day as the company issued statements from the corporate headquarters, but Williams and Treadaway characterized this effort as inadequate, saying that Exxon made a crucial mistake by assuming a reactive position. Assuming the spill could be contained, Exxon was slow to communicate, did not accept responsibility, and downplayed the potential for an environmental disaster. The March 27 storm made a shambles of that strategy.

Exxon also made a second major mistake, according to Williams and Treadaway, when the company tried to shift responsibility for the crisis by blaming other agencies, including Alyeska, ADEC, and the Coast Guard for delays and interference that rendered the clean up ineffective. These efforts were countered even by the governor of Alaska, who chastised Exxon publicly for this strategy. Exxon lost the public opinion battle on this issue, even though the company's complaints about other agencies may have been correct. After "repeated beatings from the press, local citizens, and fishermen" (Keeble, p. 62), Exxon refused to participate in press conferences. An Exxon Communications Group was soon assembled to manage the situation. Exxon responded to the media coverage with a public relations effort to direct attention away from what really had happened, "to keep the story thin and keep the public in it until the story faded . . . like a top forty tune on the radio" (Keeble, p. 169).

If Exxon PR people thought that the story would die like a top forty tune, they were wrong. In our own review, we found that *Newsweek, Time,* and *U.S. News & World Report* by themselves published sixteen major stories on the spill within eight weeks of its occurrence. By the end of 1989, these three news magazines along with several others had published at least eighty stories on the *Valdez* spill and its aftermath. There were also hundreds, perhaps even thousands, of newspaper stories and extensive network television coverage of the disaster.

Cases of failed crisis communication such as Exxon's often are contrasted against the Tylenol case as an example of an effective corporate response to a crisis, but even the Tylenol case has its critics. The Tylenol crisis began on September 29, 1982 with the first of seven deaths from Tylenol Extra Strength capsules that had been laced with cyanide. On October 1, Johnson and Johnson, owner of Tylenol manufacturer McNeil Consumer Products, recalled millions of bottles of the product and discontinued all advertising of the product. Moreover, the company cooperated with the media and used a public relations agency, Young and Rubicam, to monitor public reactions to the event, finding to its relief that 90 percent of the public knew the problem occurred only with capsules, not tablets, and believed that the manufacturer was not to blame.

Leonard Snyder (1983) said that Johnson and Johnson officials estimated that the crisis generated over 80,000 news stories. After the immediate crisis had past, that is, after it was apparent that no more deaths would occur, and the tampering was the work of a single psychopath, Johnson and Johnson faced the task of repositioning the product in the market. This was done with a "Thank you, America" sales promotion with coupons redeemable for $2.50 toward the purchase of any Tylenol product.

The entire incident, that is, the recall, the communication effort, and the repositioning, reportedly cost Johnson and Johnson $100 million, but the company was praised widely for its response in editorials by major newspapers and recognized with awards from the Public Relations Society of America. In spite of these accolades, Snyder, who was managing director of The 2nd Opinion Company in 1983, gave the Johnson and Johnson effort a rating of less than good. According to Synder, the company had no emergency plan for handling such a crisis (an oversight that company officials admitted) and actually put out some misleading information early in the crisis. One problem in particular concerned the use of cyanide as an agent in testing the product. The corporate public relations staffers, who were unaware of the use of cyanide in testing, had reported that cyanide was not used in manufacturing. This was true technically, but it became a problem when the media found out independently about the use of cyanide in testing. The confusion fueled speculation that the product may have been contaminated in manufacturing, although it soon became clear that the product tampering occurred in retail stores where Tylenol was sold and not during the production of the drug.

Johnson and Johnson saved the situation only because it was guided by the single principle of protecting its consumers, a principle which worked, but for which the company really had no operating plan. Put another way, we might say that Johnson and Johnson had some luck. And, of course, another major difference between this incident and the *Valdez* grounding was perceived responsibility. To the public, Johnson and Johnson, like the seven dead customers, fell victim to an anonymous killer, but the *Valdez* was owned and operated by Exxon. This point clearly was not lost on the Exxon executives who changed the ship's name when it went back into service.

Factors in Crisis Communication

Sturges (1994) says that discussion of crisis management usually focuses on three issues:

1. Planning and preparation for crisis events.
2. Behavior of the organization during the crisis.
3. Communication to important publics during the crisis.

We may think of these issues as elements to which organizations must attend in crisis management. Although communication is broken out as a separate element by Sturges, planning and preparation as well as organizational behavior during the crisis clearly are relevant to what is communicated and how it is communicated.

The idea of planning for a crisis may seem like a contradiction in terms, but such planning seems to be a central concern to most people who write about or have to engage in crisis communication and management. Williams and Treadaway noted that Exxon was fundamentally unprepared for the situation it confronted in Prince William Sound, so it failed to implement a communication strategy that would "help set the agenda for how the situation would be handled" (p. 63). Similarly, Synder complained that even Johnson and Johnson had no plan for handling a crisis situation "although the literature abounds with sound reasons and examples" (p. 33). Englehart recommends four basic steps in the planning process.

First, one should identify potential crises. What could potentially go wrong? Then one must evaluate the potential impact of a crisis, not only in terms of the physical event but also in terms of public response. One tool for accomplishing these first two steps is the "Worst Case Senario" technique (Barton, 1993). The label alone should provide you with a good idea of how this technique works. Third, one must assign specific responsibility for execution of the crisis management strategy. Who does what and when? According to Englehart, the number of actors should be limited: *"If you manage crisis by committee, you are doomed to failure. . . . There needs to be a chain of command and agreement on who's going to do the speaking"* (p. 28). Finally, the plan must be put in writing, although it is not a good idea to put too much in writing. How does one know when there is enough in writing? The answer to this question resides in a point that Englehart could have identified as a fifth critical step, namely, rehearsal. The plan should be tried out with drills.

Most of the advice about planning for crisis management is very useful, but it seems to carry with it an assumption that planning and preparation in and of themselves will take care of issues two and three, organizational behavior and communication with relevant publics during the crisis. The problem with this kind of thinking, according to Sturges, is that communication especially is "only alluded to in preparation discussions and rarely is the focus of specific conjecture or study" (p. 299). In other words, crisis management plans often lack a coherent and well-thought-out strategy of public communication. If a strategy exists at all, it may be based on assumptions that all crisis communication has the same objective and all relevant publics can be approached with the same strategy.

Sturges challenges the first of these two assumptions by arguing that the communication objective should depend on the stage of the crisis. Where communication programs can actually begin before a crisis occurs, messages should provide internalizing information to build positive public opinion toward the organization. When it appears that a crisis is imminent, the strategy should shift from internalizing messages to instructing messages that tell the public how to respond to the crisis. Instructing communication should increase greatly at the breakout stage of the crisis so that affected publics know what they are to do. As the crisis subsides, communication may shift to adjusting messages intended to help people cope with the effects of the crisis. Finally, as the crisis abates, the organization can return to an internalizing strategy.

The point of Sturges' analysis is that the wrong message at the wrong time may fail to effect the desired result and could even backfire by making an organization appear to be indifferent or out of touch. This was reflected in a tragic, but compelling way in events surrounding the assassination of Israeli Prime Minister Yitzhak Rabin. Rabin, a professional soldier who negotiated a peace with the Palestine Liberation Organization and shook hands with PLO leader Yasser Arafat, was murdered in November, 1995 by Yigal Amir, a young Israeli extremist who hoped that Rabin's death also would kill the peace process that Rabin had begun. During the weeks preceding the assassination, Israeli extremist organizations opposed to peace with the Palestinians held rallies and public demonstrations where Rabin was denounced variously as a traitor, a murderer, and a Nazi. Benjamin Netanyahu, the leader of Israel's Likud political party and a Rabin opponent, made a public appearance for at least one of these demonstrations.

Immediately after Rabin's murder, some Israeli extremists celebrated his death, defended Amir's actions, and began to make thinly veiled threats against Rabin's successor, Shimon Peres. Whatever their intention may have been with this kind of rhetoric, the extremists only succeeded in further alienating the majority of Israelis, who were shocked by the assassination and revulsed by extremist defenses of it. In contrast, Natanyahu and other Likud officials, understanding the danger that the situation posed for their country and looking for the right message for the situation, condemned the assassination, denounced violence in general, and called for unity among Israelis and democratic resolution of their disputes over the peace process. The message may have been right, but it also may have been too late. Pointing specifically to Netanyahu's appearance at anti-Rabin demonstrations, Leah Rabin, Yitzhak's widow, publicly blamed the Likud Party in general and Netanyahu in particular for "creating the climate that led to [her husband's] assassination" (Katz, 1995).

Even adapting messages to the stage of the crisis may be insufficient if the organization attempts to apply the same strategy to multiple publics. Ice (1991) pointed to this problem to explain the failure of Union Carbide's crisis communication effort when a gas leak from one of its chemical plants in Bhopal, India killed over 2,000 people and injured thousands more. The company, according to Ice, organized its messages almost entirely around the scientific and financial aspects of the tragedy. This may have been satisfactory for Union Carbide's stockholder public, but it certainly did not play well with other publics, including the victims, because the company seemed oblivious to the human dimensions of the accident. The lesson drawn by Ice from this case is that organizations must adapt message strategies to the needs and expectations of each relevant public.

Summary   Strategic communication in organizations is a complex process. Despite its linear appearance, it has the transactional characteristics of other communication contexts. Strategic communication emerges from the efforts of various individuals and organizational units, although much of the communication agenda is regulated by management through control over the resources that are required for communication programs.

Strategic communication programs should be concerned not only with transmission of messages in order to influence various publics but also with ways in which publics seek out and use information.

An organization's strategic communication efforts can be classified generally as internal or external. Internal communication, sometimes referred to as employee communication, usually involves management efforts to exert influence with organization members in general. Some of the most common uses of internal communication include orientation and indoctrination, safety and loss prevention, provision of information on compensation and benefits, explanation and facilitation of organizational change, and promotion of member morale.

External communication is a means through which organizations adapt to and influence relevant publics, including customers, voters, communities, regulators, and legislators. Traditionally, external communication has been dominated by public relations image-building strategists. Image building is a process of developing and publicizing specific organizational characteristics and behaviors that are consistent with the image being cultivated.

More recently, many organizations have turned their strategic resources toward public affairs and issues management activities that differ from traditional image building. Issues management involves a process of identifying and tracking public issues that may affect an organization. In some cases, organizations respond to issues by changing and communicating with relevant publics about the change. In other cases, organizations couple issues management with issues advocacy – a strategic attempt to shape public opinion on issues before political action on these issues results in legislation or regulation that affects the organization.

Crisis communication, especially where media have interests in pursuing a story about the crisis, is more complicated than most of the forms of public communication that we reviewed in this chapter. Exxon's public communication effort during the *Valdez* oil spill and Johnson and Johnson's during the Tylenol cyanide tampering case provide good examples. Generally, experts in crisis communication suggest that organizations must plan and rehearse plans for responding to crisis situations. In particular, they must understand that a crisis progresses through stages, and crisis communication requires different objectives and different kinds of messages at different stages. Messages in crisis communication also must be adapted to accommodate the expectations of multiple publics.

Discussion Questions/ Activities

1. Find some examples of internal communication. What kinds of topics and problems are addressed in these examples? What do you think the main purpose of internal communication seems to be?

2. Find some examples of external communication concerned with *organizational* (not product or service) image building. What are the organizations behind these messages trying to accomplish? How?

3. Watch some segments of television programs such as *Face the Nation* and *Meet the Press*. Can you identify some examples of issues advocacy in the advertisements on these programs?

4. Who controls the agenda for strategic communication? What are the ethical and philosophical issues involved in such control?

Additional Resources

Books

Arnold, W. E. (1980). *Crisis communication.* Dubuque, IA: Gorsuch, Scarisbrick.

Coates, J. F., et al. (1986). *Issues management: How you can plan, organize, and manage for the future.* Mt. Airy, MD: Lomond.

Dougherty, D. (1992). *Crisis communications: What every executive needs to know.* New York: Walker.

Fearn-Banks, K. (1995). *Crisis communication: A casebook approach.* Hillsdale, NJ: L. Erlbaum.

Renfro, W. L. (1993). *Issues management in strategic planning.* Westport, CT: Quorum Books.

Web Sites

http://www.custard.co.uk/links.html
    The Public Relations Jump Station. A list of public relations companies with Web sites.

References

Armstrong, R. A. (1981, Fall). Public affairs vs. public relations. *Public Relations Quarterly, 26.*

Arrington, C., Jr., & Sawaya, R. N. (1984). Managing public affairs: Issues management in an uncertain environment. *California Management Review, 26,* 148–160.

Barton, L. (1993). *Crisis in organizations: Managing and communicating in the heat of crisis.* Cincinnati, OH: South-Western.

Buchholz, R. (1982). Education for public issues management: Key insights from a survey of top practitioners. *Public Affairs Review, 3,* 65–76.

Chandler, R. C. (1988). *Causal attributions in organizational communication about positive and negative performance: An empirical investigation of corporate annual reports.* Paper presented at the annual meeting of the International Communication Association. New Orleans.

Cutlip, S. M., & Center, A. H. (1964). *Effective public relations* (3rd ed.). Englewood Cliffs, NJ: Prentice-Hall.

Egelhoff, W. G., & Sen, F. (1991). Six years and counting: Learning from crisis management at Bhopal. *Public Relations Review, 17,* 69–83.

Englehart, B. (1995). Crisis communication: Communicating under fire. *The Journal of Management Advocacy Communication, 1,* 23–28.

Ewing, R. P. (1979, Winter). The uses of futurist techniques in issues management. *Public Relations Quarterly,* 15–18.

Finn, D. (1962). Stop worrying about your image. *Harper's Magazine, 225.*

Gallup Public Opinion Index. June 1979.

Gardner, B. B., & Rainwater, L. (1955). The mass image of big business. *Harvard Business Review, 33.*

Goldhaber, G. M. (1993). *Organizational communication* (6th ed.). Dubuque, IA: Brown & Benchmark Publishers.

Heath, R. L., & Nelson, R. A. (1986). *Issues management: Corporate public policymaking in an information society.* Beverly Hills, CA: Sage.

Hill, J. W. (1977). Corporations: The sitting ducks. *Public Relations Quarterly, 22,* 8–10.

Hush, M. (1983). Corporate advertising: Stacking the odds. *Grey Matter: Tough Ideas on Advertising and Marketing, 54,* 1–12.

Industrial Communication Council. (1975). *Case studies in organizational communication.* New York, NY.

Ice, R. (1991). Corporate publics and rhetorical strategies: The case of Union Carbide's Bhopal crisis. *Management Communication Quarterly, 4,* 341–362.

Jones, B. L., & Chase, W. H. (1977). Managing public policy issues. *Public Relations Review, 5,* 3–23.

Katz, L. M. (1995). Rabin's widow firmly blames her husband's political foes. *USA Today, 8* November, 11A.

Keeble, J. (1991). *Out of the channel: The Exxon Valdez oil spill in Prince William Sound.* New York: Harper Collins.

Peterson, D. (1975). *The OSHA compliance manual.* New York: McGraw-Hill.

Post, James E. (1978). Corporate response models and public affairs management. *Public Relations Quarterly, 24,* 27–32.

Sethi, S. P. (1977). *Advocacy advertising and large corporations: Social conflict, big business image, the news media, and public policy.* Lexington, MA: D. C. Heath.

Sethi, S. P. (1982). *Up against the corporate wall: Modern corporations and social issues of the eighties* (4th ed.). Englewood Cliffs, NJ: Prentice-Hall.

Snyder, L. (1983). An anniversary review and critique: The Tylenol crisis. *Public Relations Review, 9,* 24–34.

Sturges, D. L. (1994). Communicating through crisis: A strategy for organizational survival. *Management Communication Quarterly, 7,* 297–316.

Williams, D. E., & Treadaway, G. (1992). Exxon and the Valdez accident: A failure in crisis communication. *Communication Studies, 43,* 56–64.

Williams, L. C., Jr. (1978). What 50 presidents and CEO's think about employee communications. *Public Relations Quarterly, 23,* 6–11.

Wiseman, G., & Barker, L. (1967). *Speech—Interpersonal communication.* Chicago: Chandler.

Part Four Case Studies

This part concludes with two cases on strategic communication and organizational change. The first focuses on an image-building program. The second concerns strategic communication of a corporate transformation plan.

Crafting an Image

For years the chemical industry has been battling a poor public image. In the last decade, a growing concern for environmental protection has created a new wave of legislation that has placed greater restrictions on the chemical industry and added to its decreasing credibility with the American public. In 1979, the North American Chemical Association (NACA) created a special task force to investigate the industry's image problems.

The task force was comprised of communications managers from various chemical companies throughout the U.S. and Canada. They began by compiling information on the public's concerns with the industry. When their research was complete, they had reached two conclusions: (1) the public was convinced that chemicals contributed to a high standard of living and (2) they were apprehensive about the potential dangers to human beings and to the environment. Specifically, data indicated that the public appreciated the benefits of chemicals and approved of them, but the public also felt that the chemical industry was jeopardizing the health of America through faulty operating practices. Overall, the public believed that the chemical industry was doing a poor job of managing waste disposal and of protecting against air and water pollution.

Based on this information, NACA decided to launch a public communication campaign to address the concern for health and safety and to highlight the industry's commitment and continuing efforts to protect the environment. The purpose of the campaign was to change the image of the industry, to make the public more aware of its current safety practices, and ultimately, to influence the government and financial community in order to reduce restrictive legislation.

Due to limited resources, NACA did not direct the campaign toward the entire public; rather, it targeted key groups within the country that would impact public opinion and public policy the most. These groups included politically active individuals, government representatives, educators, communicators, and "plant neighbors"–those individuals living in areas with a high concentration of chemical plants.

The advertising campaign was designed for the print media and included leading magazines and newspapers, such as *Time, Newsweek,* the *New York Times,* and the *Washington Post.* NACA conducted a two-phase advertising campaign with an advertising expenditure of $8 million to be spread over a three-year period. The first phase presented a chemical industry comprised of high technology and scientific innovation. One ad was titled "Improving Chemical Product Safety" and listed five steps the industry was taking to minimize risks to people and to the environment, such as improving detection methods and finding safer new chemicals and products.

Although persuasive, these ads contained little human interest, so they were replaced by a new wave of ads. The second advertising phase focused on the human side of the industry, namely, its employees. By featuring employees who were simultaneously chemical engineers and concerned parents as spokespersons for the industry, the chemical industry attempted to show that their employees were citizens first and engineers second. Essentially, the ad tried to convey the message that these employees would not be working for the chemical industry if they did not believe that the industry was concerned about the public's health and safety. For example, one ad quoted an employee who said, "I'm a chemical industry engineer but a concerned father first. I'm working to improve water quality for my kids and yours."

The NACA concluded its public advertising campaign in 1982 with mixed results. Although those exposed to the ads were viewing the chemical industry in more positive terms, the public as a whole still perceived the industry as making little effort toward controlling waste disposal and air/water pollution by comparison with other industries.

1. Does this case involve a "public relations" campaign, an "issues management" campaign, or elements of both? Explain why.
2. Evaluate NACA's strategy in planning and implementing the campaign. What steps were effective? What could have been improved?
3. Why do you think the results of the campaign were mixed?

Transformation 2000

Southwestern Energy Utility executives had hoped it would never happen. The company had operated for years as a monopoly in its market, and everyone (at least as far as SEU executives were concerned) had benefited. But now, like it or not, competition was coming. The National Energy Policy Act of 1992 had guaranteed it through deregulation. Nobody knew what the ultimate impact would be on SEU, but company executives had an uneasy feeling that the 6,000 employee company was not ready to compete in an environment where customers could "price-shop" and demand the highest quality service at the lowest possible cost.

In order to prepare for the transition, CEO Jake Pickens and President Sally Sixkiller decided to conduct a comprehensive study of the company and all of its operations. Dubbed "Performance Audit 2000," the study was intended to augment the corporation's strategic planning for positioning SEU to survive and succeed in the twenty-first century by answering two questions. What should SEU be in the future? How could SEU remain a high-performance, yet low-cost company in a competitive environment?

Pickens and Sixkiller understood from the outset the necessity that the study itself would have to be communicated to both internal and external stakeholders (customers, vendors, employees, stockholders, and the communities in which SEU operated). Moreover, provision would have to be made for input from these stakeholders into any plan for strategic transformation of the company, and the transformation plan itself would have to be "sold" to stakeholders. It wouldn't be easy, but Pickens and Sixkiller figured they had one advantage. The uncertainty about the new competitive environment would make people from company janitors to town mayors so nervous that everyone would want a strategic plan for SEU.

The first step, of course, was to involve all of top management to secure agreement on the concept of the study, then commission the services of a competent consulting firm to design it. Having accomplished this much, SEU then ran stories in the company magazine and newletters and put an announcement on the company's Web site to announce the purpose and timetable for the study. SEU also issued press releases to news organizations in its service areas. These methods were presumed to put the message out to all necessary groups, including employees, their family members, customers, and communities.

The study, which included surveys of employee opinions, focus group meetings with customers, careful analysis of the capabilities of potential competitors, and analysis of the economic environment in which SEU operated, went off without a hitch and produced many interesting findings, but the fundamental conclusion came down to this: Although the quality of SEU's service was excellent, SEU's prices were too high to fend off erosion of its customer base by competitors.

Prices are driven by profit and operating costs. SEU's Board of Directors realized that the company probably would no longer enjoy the profit potential that it had as a monopoly, and the board prepared accordingly for reductions. But less profit alone would not solve the problem. Operating costs had to be reduced dramatically, and this would mean "downsizing" the company and finding more efficient ways to do business.

Basically this meant that 600 (10 percent) of SEU's employees would lose their jobs, and those who remained would have to work harder and in different ways. For example, many middle management positions would disappear and more emphasis would be placed on self-managed work teams. SEU also would have to be much more "hard nosed" in negotiating contracts with vendors and property owners so it could be sure to get the best possible prices for goods, services, and land purchased by the company.

Some changes also would occur in the kinds of services that customers could get and in how they would get these services. For example, processing of payments on accounts would be centralized. Customers would no longer be able to pay their bills at the local utility office. Payments would have to be mailed to the corporate headquarters. Trouble reports also would have to be called in to a new, central 1–800 number. In short, everyone in SEU's service communities– employees, their families, local vendors who sold goods and services to SEU, and customers – would be affected by the change.

Once again, SEU contracted with a consulting firm to help it through this process. Beyond deciding to call this phase of the project "Transformation 2000," no decisions have been made about how to proceed.

1. You and a group of your classmates are the consultants with whom SEU has contracted to manage Transformation 2000. What are the issues that SEU executives should consider in designing and communicating the change program? What actions do you think they should take?
2. Compare the results of your discussion with those of other groups in the class.

NAME INDEX

SUBJECT INDEX

described, 30–31
implications of, 31–32
Hegemony
  and false consciousness, 257
  maintenance of, 254–256
Herzberg's two-factor theory, 161
Hierarchy
  in feminist theory, 262
  in systems theory, 45–46
  in traditional theory, 24, 26
Hispanic Americans, 237
Hopi Indian language, 94
Horizontal communication
  difficulties of, 119–120
  and Fayol's bridge, 118–119
  importance of, 118–119
Human relations movement
  criticisms of, 32
  at Harvard Business School, 32
  and the Hawthorne Studies, 30
Human resource development
  communication implications in, 35
  criticisms of, 36–37
  Likert's four systems, 34–35
  and Maslow's need hierarchy, 32–33
  participative management in, 34
  Theory X and Theory Y, 33–34
Hygiene factors, 161

IBM, 239, 259, 284
Identification, and concertive control, 64
Ideological manipulation, 257
Illustrators, in nonverbal communication, 100
Impoverished leader, 152
Individual behavior
  genetic influences on, 53, 57
  inadequacy of nature vs. nurture explanations,
    53–54
  variability and effects in organization, 29
Individualization, in assimilation, 141
Industrial Communication Research Center, 6
Industrial revolution, 20
Informal communication
  defined, 120
  features of, 121–122
  and the grapevine, 121–122
  problems in defining, 123
Informal space, 101
Information
  absolute vs. distributed, 104
  defined, 93
  diffusion of, 104
  equivocality in, 49
  and meaning, 93
Information adequacy
  concept of, 103–104
  relationship to other variables, 105–106
  and uncertainty reduction, 103
Information technology
  and communication skills, 190
  and computer-mediated communication,
    186–190
  effects on communication, 186–190
  effects on staffing and jobs, 184–186
  effects on structure, 181–184
  and international access, 177
  in the Internet and World Wide Web, 176–179
  in LANs and WANs, 173–176
  limitations and disadvantages of, 187–190

multimode capability in, 175
  and types of information systems, 171–173
Innovation function, in organizational
  communication, 103
Institute for Human Genetics, 57
Institute for Social Research, 153
Integrated data processing, 172
Integrated management information systems, 172
Integration, in Follett's theory, 28
Integrative bargaining, 282–283
Integrative thinking, in feminist theory, 76
Intergroup conflict, and coalitions, 279–282
Interlocked behavior cycles, in equivocality
  reduction, 50–51
Internal strategic communication, functions of,
  299–303
Internal system, in group processes, 136–137
International Communication Association, 6, 104
Internationalization, 15
Internet, 174, 176–179
Interorganizational conflict, 283–285
Interpersonal conflict
  competence-based approach, 276–278
  styles of, 273–274
Interpretive perspective
  as alternative to traditionalism, 11
  cultural metaphor in, 10
  defined, 10
  focus on symbols and meaning in, 11
  of organizational culture, 206
  research methods in, 210–222
Islam, 234
Isolate, in networks, 125
Issues advocacy, 309–310
Issues management, 309–313

Jacksonville Shipyards, 231
Japan, 38, 143
Japanese management
  and collectivistic culture, 38
  use of human resource development, 38
Japanese organizations
  compared to American, 38–39
  decision making in, 39, 119
  use of horizontal communication in, 119
Job satisfaction
  genetic influences on, 58
  in organizational communication studies, 7
Johnson and Johnson, 37, 315
Judaism, 234
Junior Achievement, Inc., 300

Kinesics, 100
Korea, 143

Laissez-faire leaders, 152
LAN, defined, 174
Language
  ambiguity of, 95–97
  and experience, 94–95
  features of, 93
  paradoxes in, 94
  use of group restricted codes, 97–98
Leader-member exchange theory,
  156–157

Leader-member relations
  and organizational objectives, 150
  quality of, 156–157
  and superior-subordinate communication,
    150–151
Leadership
  and gender, 155, 232–233
Leadership
  conditions rendering ineffective, 155
  and gender, 155, 232–233
  grid theory, 152–153
  and group effectiveness, 144–145, 150
  limits of in motivation, 159–161
  maintenance dimension, 154
  and mentor-protege relationships, 157–158
  styles of, 151–154
  task dimension, 154
  theories of, 151–157
  as a trait, 151
Legitimate power, 252
Legitimation, 253
Liaison, in networks, 125
Library of Congress, 240
Likud party of Israel, 317
Locus of control
  effects on communication, 163–165
  external vs. internal, 163

Maintenance function, in organizational
  communication, 102
Maintenance roles, 147
Majority rule, in group decision making, 143
Management information systems, 172
Management theory. *See* organization theory
Marxism, 253
Matrix organization, 45
McDonald's, 49–50
McNeil Consumer Products, 315
Meaning
  and ambiguity, 95–97
  defined, 93
  and information, 93
Mechanization, in information technology, 180
Mentor-protege relationships, 157–158
Metamorphosis, in assimilation, 140
Metaphor analysis, 215–217
Microemancipation, 79–80
Middle-of-the road leader, 152
Minority coalitions, in group decision making,
  142
Morale and satisfaction, as internal
  communication objective, 302–303
Motivation
  and control, 158–163
  Herzberg's two-factor theory of, 161–162
  importance in management theory, 7
  limits of leadership and supervision, 159–161
  Maslow's theory of, 32–33
Motivators, 161
Mountain Bell, 302
Multimode capability, 175, 176

Narrative analysis, 213–215
NASA, 6, 120
National Institute Against Prejudice and
  Violence, 238
National Science Foundation, 29